Blood & Circulatory Disorders Sourcebook

Basic Information about Disorders Such As Anemia, Hemorrhage, Shock, Embolism, and Thrombosis, along with Facts Concerning Rh Factor, Blood Banks, Blood Donation Programs, and Transfusions

Edited by Linda M. Ross. 600 pages. 1998. 0-7808-0203-9. $75.

Burns Sourcebook

Basic Information about Heat, Chemical, Electrical, and Sun Burns, along with Facts about Burn Treatment and Recovery, and Reports on Current Research Initiatives

Edited by Allan R. Cook. 600 pages. 1998. 0-7808-0204-7. $75.

Cancer Sourcebook

Basic Information on Cancer Types, Symptoms, Diagnostic Methods, and Treatments, Including Statistics on Cancer Occurrences Worldwide and the Risks Associated with Known Carcinogens and Activities

Edited by Frank E. Bair. 932 pages. 1990. 1-55888-888-8. $75.

"This publication's nontechnical nature and very comprehensive format make it useful for both the general public and undergraduate students."
— *Choice, Oct '90*

"This compact collection of reliable information, written in a positive, hopeful tone, is an invaluable tool for helping patients and patients' families and friends to take the first steps in coping with the many difficulties of cancer." — *Medical Reference Services Quarterly, Winter '91*

"An important resource for the general reader trying to understand the complexities of cancer."
— *American Reference Books Annual, '91*

Cancer Sourcebook for Women

Basic Information about Specific Forms of Cancer That Affect Women, Featuring Facts about Breast Cancer, Cervical Cancer, Ovarian Cancer, Cancer of the Uterus and Uterine Sarcoma, Cancer of the Vagina, and Cancer of the Vulva; Statistical and Demographic Data; Treatments, Self-Help Management Suggestions, and Current Research Initiatives

Edited by Allan R. Cook and Peter D. Dresser. 524 pages. 1996. 0-7808-0076-1. $75.

"This timely book is highly recommended for consumer health and patient education collections in all libraries." — *Library Journal, Apr '96*

"The availability under one cover of all these pertinent publications, grouped under cohesive headings, makes this certainly a most useful sourcebook."
— *Choice, Jun '96*

"Laudably, the book portrays the feelings of the cancer victim, as well as her mate . . . .both benefit from the gold mine of information nestled between the two covers of this book. It is hard to conceive of any library that would not want it as part of its collection. Recommended."
— *Academic Library Book Review, Summer '96*

". . . written in easily understandable, non-technical language. Recommended for public libraries or hospital and academic libraries that collect patient education or consumer health materials."
— *Medical Reference Services Quarterly, Spring '97*

New Cancer Sourcebook

Basic Information about Major Forms and Stages of Cancer, Featuring Facts about Primary and Secondary Tumors of the Respiratory, Nervous, Lymphatic, Circulatory, Skeletal, and Gastrointestinal Systems, and Specific Organs; Statistical and Demographic Data, Treatment Options, and Strategies for Coping

Edited by Allan R. Cook. 1,313 pages. 1996. 0-7808-0041-9. $75.

"This book is an excellent resource. The dialogue is simple, direct, and comprehensive."
— *Doody's Health Sciences Book Review, Nov '96*

"The amount of factual and useful information is extensive. The writing is very clear, geared to general readers. Recommended for all levels."
— *Choice, Jan '97*

Cardiovascular Diseases & Disorders Sourcebook

Basic Information about Cardiovascular Diseases and Disorders, Featuring Facts about the Cardiovascular System, Demographic and Statistical Data, Descriptions of Pharmacological and Surgical Interventions, Lifestyle Modifications, and a Special Section Focusing on Heart Disorders in Children

Edited by Karen Bellenir and Peter D. Dresser. 683 pages. 1995. 0-7808-0032-X. $75.

". . . comprehensive format provides an extensive overview on this subject." — *Choice, Jun '96*

"Easily understood, complete, up-to-date resource. This well executed public health tool will make valuable information available to those that need it most, patients and their families. The typeface, sturdy non-reflective paper, and library binding add a feel of quality found wanting in other publications. Highly recommended for academic and general libraries."
— *Academic Library Book Review, Summer '96*

Continues next page

Communication Disorders Sourcebook

Basic Information about Deafness and Hearing Loss, Speech and Language Disorders, Voice Disorders, Balance and Vestibular Disorders, and Disorders of Smell, Taste, and Touch

Edited by Linda M. Ross. 533 pages. 1996. 0-7808-0077-X. $75.

"This is skillfully edited and is a welcome resource for the layperson. It should be found in every public and medical library."
— *Doody's Health Sciences Book Review, May '96*

Congenital Disorders Sourcebook

Basic Information about Disorders Acquired during Gestation, Including Spina Bifida, Hydrocephalus, Cerebral Palsy, Heart Defects, Craniofacial Abnormalities, Fetal Alcohol Syndrome, and More, along with Current Treatment Options and Statistical Data

Edited by Karen Bellenir. 607 pages. 1997. 0-7808-0205-5. $75.

Consumer Issues in Health Care Sourcebook

Basic Information about Consumer Health Concerns, Including an Explanation of Physician Specialties, How to Choose a Doctor, How to Prepare for a Hospital Visit, Ways to Avoid Fraudulent "Miracle" Cures, How to Use Medications Safely, What to Look for when Choosing a Nursing Home, and End-of-Life Planning

Edited by Wendy Wilcox. 600 pages. 1998. 0-7808-0221-7. $75.

Contagious & Non-Contagious Infectious Diseases Sourcebook

Basic Information about Contagious Diseases like Measles, Polio, Hepatitis B, and Infectious Mononucleosis, and Non-Contagious Infectious Diseases like Tetanus and Toxic Shock Syndrome, and Diseases Occurring as Secondary Infections Such As Shingles and Reye Syndrome, along with Vaccination, Prevention, and Treatment Information, and a Section Describing Emerging Infectious Disease Threats

Edited by Karen Bellenir and Peter D. Dresser. 566 pages. 1996. 0-7808-0075-3. $75.

Diabetes Sourcebook

Basic Information about Insulin-Dependent and Noninsulin-Dependent Diabetes Mellitus, Gestational Diabetes, and Diabetic Complications, Symptoms, Treatment, and Research Results, Including Statistics on Prevalence, Morbidity, and Mortality, along with Source Listings for Further Help and Information

Edited by Karen Bellenir and Peter D. Dresser. 827 pages. 1994. 1-55888-751-2. $75.

"Very informative and understandable for the layperson without being simplistic. It provides a comprehensive overview for laypersons who want a general understanding of the disease or who want to focus on various aspects of the disease."
— *Bulletin of the MLA, Jan '96*

Diet & Nutrition Sourcebook

Basic Information about Nutrition, Including the Dietary Guidelines for Americans, the Food Guide Pyramid, and Their Applications in Daily Diet, Nutritional Advice for Specific Age Groups, Current Nutritional Issues and Controversies, the New Food Label and How to Use It to Promote Healthy Eating, and Recent Developments in Nutritional Research

Edited by Dan R. Harris. 662 pages. 1996. 0-7808-0084-2. $75.

"It is so refreshing to find a reliable and factual reference book. Recommended to aspiring professionals, librarians, and others seeking and giving reliable dietary advice. An excellent compilation."
— *Choice, Feb '97*

"Recommended for public and medical libraries that receive general information requests on nutrition. It is readable and will appeal to those interested in learning more about healthy dietary practices."
— *Medical Reference Services Quarterly, Fall '97*

Ear, Nose & Throat Disorders Sourcebook

Basic Information about Disorders of the Ears, Nose, Sinus Cavities, Tonsils, Adenoids, Pharynx, and Larynx, along with Statistical and Demographic Data and Reports on Current Research Initiatives

Edited by Linda M. Ross. 600 pages. 1998. 0-7808-0206-3. $75.

Endocrine & Metabolic Diseases & Disorders Sourcebook

Basic Information for the Layperson about Disorders Such As Graves' Disease, Goiter, Cushing's Syndrome, and Hormonal Imbalances, along with Reports on Current Research Initiatives

Edited by Linda M. Ross. 600 pages. 1998. 0-7808-0207-1. $75.

Continues on back end sheets

Consumer
Issues in
Health Care
SOURCEBOOK

Health Reference Series

Volume Thirty-five

Consumer Issues in Health Care SOURCEBOOK

*Basic Information about Health Care
Fundamentals and Related Consumer Issues
Including Exams and Screening Tests,
Physician Specialties, Choosing a Doctor,
Using Prescription and Over-the-Counter
Medications Safely, Avoiding Health Scams,
Managing Common Health Risks in the
Home, Care Options for Chronically or
Terminally Ill Patients, and a
List of Resources for Obtaining Help
and Further Information*

Edited by
Karen Bellenir

Omnigraphics, Inc.

Penobscot Building / Detroit, MI 48226

BIBLIOGRAPHIC NOTE

This volume contains documents and excerpts from publications issued by the following government agencies: Agency for Health Care Policy and Research (AHCPR), Environmental Protection Agency (EPA), Federal Trade Commission (FTC), National Cancer Institute (NCI), National Institute on Aging (NIA), National Institute of Mental Health (NIMH), U.S. Consumer Product Safety Commission (CPSC), U.S. Department of Health and Human Services (DHHS), U.S. Food and Drug Administration (FDA), U.S. Preventive Services Task Force (USPSTF), and the U.S. Public Health Service (PHS) Office of Disease Prevention and Health Promotion. This volume also contains copyrighted documents from the following organizations: American Association of Retired Persons, American Health Care Association, Consumers Union, National Council on Patient Information and Education, National Electrical Safety Foundation, National Funeral Directors Association, Nonprescription Drug Manufacturers Association, University of Minnesota, and the University of Washington (state). Copyrighted articles from the following periodical publications are also included: *Geriatrics*, and the *Washington Post*. All copyrighted material is reprinted with permission. Document numbers where applicable and specific source citations are provided on the first page of each chapter. Every effort has been made to secure all necessary rights to reprint the copyrighted material. If any omissions have been made, contact Omnigraphics to make corrections for future editions.

Edited by Karen Bellenir

Peter D. Dresser, Managing Editor, *Health Reference Series*

Omnigraphics, Inc.

Matthew P. Barbour, *Manager, Production and Fulfillment*
Laurie Lanzen Harris, *Vice President, Editorial Director*
Peter E. Ruffner, *Vice President, Administration*
James A. Sellgren, *Vice President, Operations and Finance*
Jane J. Steele, *Marketing Consultant*

Frederick G. Ruffner, Jr., Publisher

©1999, Omnigraphics, Inc.

Library of Congress Cataloging-in-Publication Data

Consumer issues in health care sourcebook : basic information about
  health care fundamentals and related consumer issues including
  exams and screening tests, physician specialties, choosing a doctor,
  using health scams, managing common health risks in the home, care
  options for chronically or terminally ill patients, and a list of
  resources for obtaining help and further information / edited by
  Karen Bellenir.
      p. cm. -- (Health reference series)
    Includes bibliographical references and index.
    ISBN 0-7808-0221-7 (lib. bdg.)
    1. Medical care. 2. Medical care -- United States. 3. Consumer
  education. 4. Patient education. I. Bellenir, Karen. II. Series.
  RA776.5.C655 1998   98-16643
    362.1--dc21   CIP

∞

This book is printed on acid-free paper meeting the ANSI Z39.48 Standard. The infinity symbol that appears above indicates that the paper in this book meets that standard.

Printed in the United States

Table of Contents

Part III: Medications

Part IV: Cautions for Health Care Consumers

Part V: Managing Common Health Risks in the Home

Part VI: Caring for Chronically or Terminally Ill Patients and Making End-of-Life Decisions

Part VII: Resources

Preface

About This Book

Today's health care consumer faces an ever-increasing number of complex choices. The traditional annual physical examination has been replaced with an array of screening tests, immunizations, prophylactic medications, and counseling interventions about lifestyle modification and safety awareness. Many medications previously available by prescription only can now be purchased over the counter. And, the proliferation of health care delivery options provides a wide assortment of alternatives unavailable a generation—or even a decade—ago.

Despite this complexity, however, more Americans are taking personal responsibility for their health care. This involves selecting and evaluating a primary care doctor, choosing from numerous physician specialties, actively participating in preventive measures, monitoring prescription drugs, making informed decisions about brand name medications and their generic counterparts, self-medicating with over-the-counter (OTC) drugs, and sorting out potentially fraudulent "cures" from legitimate new treatments.

This book is designed to provide the information health care consumers need as they evaluate the issues surrounding personal health maintenance. It offers current recommendations for preventive care, describes different types of physicians, offers help in understanding pharmacological choices, and includes a description of end-of-life medical care options. Health insurance, an important aspect of modern medical care, is touched upon only briefly; readers seeking information about insurance-related issues will find in-depth coverage in *Health Insurance Sourcebook*, Volume 25 of Omnigraphics' *Health Reference Series*.

How to Use This Book

This book is divided into parts and chapters. Parts focus on broad areas of interest. Chapters are devoted to single topics within a part.

Part I: Health Care Fundamentals provides general information about health care services. Individual chapters describe health care regimens for adults and children, offer immunization schedules, and describe recommended preventive services available from primary care physicians.

Part II: Physicians and Hospitals offers descriptions of physician specialties, gives information about evaluating a physician's level of competence, and offers tips on how to communicate effectively with health care providers. Advice is also included for surgical patients and others planning hospital visits. Patients seeking mental health care will find a guide to available services.

Part III: Medications provides important information about prescription and over-the-counter (OTC) medications. Answers to frequently asked questions about the efficacy of generic drugs or commonly used OTC products are provided. This section also includes cautions about the use of various medications in special circumstances and in special populations, such as among the very young or the elderly.

Part IV: Cautions for Health Care Consumers offers guidelines for choosing appropriate care and avoiding medical frauds.

Part V: Managing Common Health Risks in the Home looks at some common, but frequently overlooked, lifestyle modification and safety awareness issues that play an important role in health maintenance and preventive care.

Part VI: Caring for Chronically or Terminally Ill Patients and Making End-of-Life Decisions gives practical information for patients and caregivers facing difficult medical choices. It describes various types of medical care, offers information about assisted living and nursing home facilities, and provides facts for people who would like to make anatomical gifts. Patients and families with questions related to elder care and hospice options will find additional information in *Aging Sourcebook*, part of Omnigraphics' *Personal Concerns Series*.

Part VII: Resources lists organizational and on-line sources of further help and information.

Acknowledgements

Many people and organizations helped make this book a reality. Special thanks go to the American Association of Retired Persons, American Health Care Association, Consumers Union, National Council on Patient Information and Education, National Electrical Safety Foundation, National Funeral Directors Association, Nonprescription Drug Manufacturers Association, University of Minnesota, and the University of Washington (state) for granting permission to reprint their material. In addition, thanks go to Margaret Mary Missar for obtaining many of the documents included in this volume, Jenifer Swanson for searching the internet, and to Bruce—whose job description keeps expanding.

Note from the Editor

This book is part of Omnigraphics' *Health Reference Series*. The series provides basic information about a broad range of medical concerns. It is not intended to serve as a tool for diagnosing illness, in prescribing treatments, or as a substitute for the physician/patient relationship. All persons concerned about medical symptoms or the possibility of disease are encouraged to seek professional care from an appropriate health care provider.

Part One

Health Care Fundamentals

Chapter 1

Personal Health Guide

Introduction

Working with your clinician (doctor, nurse, nurse practitioner, physician assistant, or other care provider) to stay well is as important as getting treatment when you are sick. This *Personal Health Guide* will help you and your clinician make sure that you get the tests, immunizations (shots), and guidance you need to stay healthy.

How to Use the Personal Health Guide

Read the information in each section. Your answers to questions will help your clinician know what preventive care you need. If you don't understand something, be sure to ask your clinician about it.

Weight

Weighing too much or too little can lead to health problems. You should have your weight checked regularly by your clinician. He or she can tell you what is a healthy weight for you and how to get to and stay at that weight. See the sections on Physical Activity and Nutrition for more information on these two important topics.

Put Prevention Into Practice, U.S. Department of Health and Human Services, Public Health Service, June 1994.

Blood Pressure

Have your blood pressure checked at least every two years, and more often if it is high.

If you have high blood pressure, talk with your clinician about how to lower it by changing your diet, losing excess weight, exercising or (if necessary) taking medicine. If you need to take medicine, be sure to take it every day, as prescribed.

Getting your blood pressure under control will help protect you from heart disease, strokes and kidney problems.

Cholesterol

Have your cholesterol level checked at least every five years. Too much cholesterol can clog your blood vessels and cause heart disease and other serious problems. If your cholesterol is high, your clinician can tell you how to lower it by changing your diet, losing excess weight, exercising and (if necessary) taking medicine. Your clinician may also wish to check your levels of "bad" (LDL) and "good" (HDL) cholesterol.

Immunizations

Adults need immunizations ("shots") to prevent serious diseases. You should get a tetanus-diphtheria shot every ten years. At age 65 you should get a pneumococcal ("pneumonia") shot and begin having influenza ("flu") shots every year.

Tell your clinician if you are a public safety or health care worker, receive blood transfusions or other blood products, engage in male homosexual activity, or use illegal drugs. You may need immunizations against hepatitis.

Also tell your clinician if you have heart, lung, kidney or liver disease, diabetes, sickle cell anemia, immune system problems (including HIV infection), Hodgkin's disease, lymphoma, multiple myeloma or if you are a public safety or health worker. You may need influenza or pneumococcal shots before age 65.

For Parents

Immunizations are very important to protect your children from many types of disease. Be sure to get all of these immunizations for your children at the recommended ages. Don't be late! [For more information, see the immunization section in Chapter 2: Child Health Guide]

Oral Health Care

Good oral health care is important for your teeth and general health. With proper care, your teeth will last you for life.

- Visit your dentist regularly for checkups.
- Brush after meals with a soft or medium-bristled toothbrush, using a toothpaste with fluoride.
- Use dental floss daily.
- Limit the amount of sweets you eat, especially between meals.
- Do not smoke or chew tobacco products.

Breast Examination

For Women

You should have your breasts examined regularly by your clinician for lumps and other signs of cancer. You may want to check your own breasts for problems. Talk with your clinician about how often you need breast examinations and about doing breast self-exams.

Tell your clinician if you notice a lump in your breast, any liquid coming from the nipple or any change in the appearance of your breast.

Mammogram

For Women

You should begin having mammograms regularly by age 50. Some women may need mammograms earlier. A mammogram is an x-ray test that can detect a breast cancer when it is so small that it cannot be felt, and when it can be most easily cured. Talk with your clinician about when to begin and how often to have this important test.

Tell your clinician if your mother or a sister has had breast cancer. You may need to have mammograms earlier and more often than other women.

Pap Smear

For Women

You need to have Pap smears regularly. This simple test has saved the lives of many women by detecting cancer of the cervix early—when it is most easily cured. Talk with your clinician about how often you need this very important test.

Tell your clinician if you have had genital warts, sexually transmitted diseases (VD), multiple sexual partners or abnormal Pap smears. You may need Pap smears more often than other women.

Additional Preventive Care

Below is a list of additional types of preventive care that you may need, and the personal, family and medical characteristics that may make them important for you. Review this list with your clinician and decide what additional preventive care you need.

Rectal Examination, Stool Blood and Sigmoidoscopy Tests— If you are 50 years of age or older, particularly if you have had colon polyps, family members with colon cancer or have had breast, ovarian or uterine cancer yourself.

Prostate Examination—If you are a man 50 years of age or older.

Testicular Examination—If you are a man aged 15-35 years, particularly if you have had an atrophic or undescended testicle.

Mouth Examination—If, now or in the past, you have consumed a lot of alcohol or have smoked or chewed tobacco.

Thyroid Examination—If you have had radiation treatments of your upper body.

Skin Examination—If you have had skin cancer in your family or a lot of sun exposure.

AIDS (HIV) Test—If you had a blood transfusion between 1978 and 1985, have injected illegal drugs, have had multiple sexual partners or any male homosexual activity.

Syphilis, Gonorrhea or Chlamydia Tests—If you have had multiple sexual partners or any sexually transmitted diseases.

Tuberculosis Test—If you have injected illegal drugs, have been an alcoholic or a health care worker, have been exposed to someone with tuberculosis, have recently moved from Asia, Africa, Central or

South America, or the Pacific Islands, or if you have kidney failure or HIV infection.

Glucose Test—If you have had a family member with diabetes or have had diabetes during pregnancy.

Eye Examination—If you are over age 60, over age 40 and black, or have diabetes (at any age).

Estrogen Therapy—If you are a woman who has started menopause, particularly if you have a slender build or are white or Asian.

Aspirin Therapy—If you are a man 40 years of age or older, particularly if you have diabetes, high blood pressure, high cholesterol, early heart disease in your family, or if you smoke.

Smoking

Don't smoke. If you smoke, quit. It is the best thing you do to stay healthy. Ask your clinician to help you pick a date to quit and for advice on how to keep from starting again. If you fail the first time, don't give up. Keep trying and learn from your experience. You can succeed and live a healthier, longer life.

Physical Activity

All kinds of physical activity will help you feel better and maintain a healthy weight. Regular physical activity will also help you control your blood pressure and cholesterol, and strengthen your heart and muscles. Even daily activities such as housework, walking, or raking leaves will help. Pick activities that you enjoy, that fit into your daily routine, and that you can do with a friend. Try for a total of 30 minutes per day, 5 days per week.

Nutrition

Eating the right foods will help you live a longer, healthier life. Many illnesses such as diabetes, heart disease, and high blood pressure can be prevented or controlled through a healthy diet. It is never too late to start eating right. Follow the simple guidelines below.

Dietary Guidelines for Americans

- Eat a variety of foods.
- Maintain a healthy weight.
- Choose a diet low in fat, saturated fat and cholesterol.
- Choose a diet with plenty of vegetables, fruits and grain products.
- Use sugars only in moderation.
- Use salt and sodium only in moderation.
- If you drink alcoholic beverages, do so only in moderation (no more than 1 drink daily for women and 2 drinks daily for men).

Safety

Many serious injuries can be prevented by following basic safety rules.

- Always wear safety belts while in a car.
- Never drive after drinking alcohol.
- Always wear a safety helmet while riding on a motorcycle or bicycle.
- Use smoke detectors in your home. Change batteries every year and check to see that they work every month.
- Keeping a gun in your home can be dangerous. If you do. make sure that the gun and the ammunition are locked up separately.
- Keep the temperature of your hot water less than 120°F. This is especially important if there are children or older adults living in your home.
- Prevent falls by older adults. Repair slippery or uneven walking surfaces, improve poor lighting and install secure railings on all stairways.
- Be alert for hazards in your workplace and follow all safety rules.

AIDS

AIDS (Acquired Immunodeficiency Syndrome) is a fatal disease that breaks down the body's ability to fight infection and illness. AIDS is caused by a virus (HIV). By preventing HIV infection, you can prevent AIDS. Many different kinds of people have AIDS—male and female, married and single, rich and poor. There is currently no cure for AIDS and no vaccine to prevent HIV infection.

How Do You Get HIV?

Most people with HIV got infected by having sex with an infected partner. Many others got HIV when they shared needles to take drugs.

You cannot get infected with HIV from shaking hands with someone who has it, from working with someone who has it or from volunteering to help people with AIDS.

How To Reduce Your Risk Of Getting HIV

- You can reduce your risk of getting HIV by not having sex, by having sex with only one, mutually faithful, uninfected partner or by using a latex condom correctly every time you have sex.

- You can reduce your risk of getting HIV by not shooting drugs or sharing needles and syringes.

Family Planning

The birth of a child is a joyful event. However, it is best to have children when you are prepared to take care of them. If you are a sexually active man or woman and not ready to have a child, you should use a reliable method of contraception. Some of the different methods of contraception and their effectiveness in typical use over one year are listed below. Talk with your clinician about the best method of contraception for you.

Methods of Contraception

Reversible Methods

- **Medications**—birth control pills (97% effective), implants (over 99%), and shots (over 99%)
- **Intrauterine Devices (IUDs)**—(98%)
- **Barrier Methods**—condoms (88%), diaphragms (82%), cervical caps (64-82%), and vaginal sponges (64%-82%)
- **Natural Family Planning Methods**—(80%)
- **Spermicides** (alone)—foams and suppositories (79%)

Permanent Methods

- **Sterilization**—vasectomy (over 99%) and tubal ligation (over 99%)

Alcohol and Drug Abuse

Don't use illegal (street) drugs of any kind, at any time. Use prescription drugs only as directed by a clinician. Use non-prescription drugs only as instructed on the label. If you drink alcohol, do so only in moderation—no more than 1 drink daily for women and 2 drinks daily for men. Do not drink alcohol at all if you are pregnant or may be in the near future. Do not drink alcohol before or while driving a motor vehicle. If you have a problem with alcohol or drugs, see your clinician.

Do You Have a Drinking Problem?

Read the questions below. A "Yes" answer to any of these questions may be a warning sign that you have a drinking problem.

- Have you ever felt that you should cut down on your drinking?
- Have people annoyed you by criticizing your drinking?
- Have you ever felt bad or guilty about drinking?
- Have you ever had a drink first thing in the morning to steady your nerves or to get rid of a hangover?

Depression

We all feel "down" or "blue" at times. However, if these feelings are very strong or last for a long time, they may be due to a medical illness—depression. This illness can be treated, but it is often not recognized by patients and clinicians. Some of the warning signs of depression are listed below. If you have four or more of these warning signs, you should be sure to talk with your clinician about depression.

Warning Signs of Depression

- Feeling sad, hopeless or guilty
- Loss of interest and pleasure in daily activities
- Sleep problems (either too much or too little)
- Fatigue, low energy, or feeling "slowed down"
- Problems making decisions or thinking clearly
- Crying a lot
- Changes in appetite or weight (up or down)
- Thoughts of suicide or death

For More Information

If you would like to learn more about how to stay healthy and prevent disease, you should talk with your clinician or the local health department You may also obtain information by calling the telephone numbers listed below, most of which are toll-free.

Aging

- National Council on Aging: (202) 479-1200

AIDS

- CDC National AIDS Hotline: (800) 342-AIDS

Alcohol and Drug Abuse

- National Clearinghouse for Alcohol and Drug Information: (800) 729-6686

Cancer

- Cancer Information Service: (800) 4-CANCER

Child Abuse

- National Child Abuse Hotline: (800) 422-4453

Food and Drug Safety

- Food and Drug Administration, Office of Consumer Affairs: (301) 443-3170

Heart, Lung and Blood Diseases

- National Heart, Lung and Blood Institute, Information Center: (301) 251-1222

Maternal and Child Health

- National Maternal and Child Health Clearinghouse: (703) 821-8955 ext. 254

Mental Health

- National Mental Health Association: (800) 969-6642

Occupational Safety and Health

- National Institute for Occupational Safety and Health: (800) 356-4674

Physical Activity and Fitness

- Aerobic and Fitness Foundation: (800) BE FIT 86

Safety and Injury Prevention

- Consumer Product Safety Commission: (800) 638-CPSC
- National Highway Traffic Safety Administration, Auto Safety Hotline: (800) 424-9393

Sexually Transmitted Diseases

- CDC National STD Hotline: (800) 227-8922

Put Prevention Into Practice

"Put Prevention Into Practice" is a national initiative of the U.S. Department of Health and Human Services' Public Health Service in partnership with public and private health care organizations. (Neither the Public Health Service nor the U.S. Department of Health and Human Services endorses any particular product, service or organization.

The goal of "Put Prevention Into Practice" is to preserve the health of all Americans by improving the preventive care they receive. You can help to put prevention into practice by working with your health care providers to make sure you get all the preventive care you need. You can also do your part by following the health advice in this *Personal Health Guide*. Take charge of your health and live a longer and healthier life!

For more information about the "Put Prevention Into Practice" campaign, write: Put Prevention Into Practice, National Health Information Center, P.O. Box 1133, Washington, DC 20013-1133.

Chapter 2

Child Health Guide

A Message about Your Child's Health

Preventive care is as important for your child's health as treatment is when he or she is sick. This care includes immunizations, tests, and health guidance. Your child receives preventive care from the doctor or other health care provider at check-up visits and at other times. Proper preventive care helps keep your child healthy.

As a parent, you should know what preventive care your child needs. Work with your child's doctor or other health care provider to assure that he or she gets proper care.

The *Child Health Guide* has information on needed preventive care and on good health habits. Use it to help you keep track of your child's health and care through the years. This guide can help your child get a healthy start on life.

−M. Joycelyn Elders, M.D.
former Surgeon General,
U.S. Public Health Service

Check-Up Visits

Your child's doctor or other health care provider may want to see your child for check-up visits even when shots or test are not due. Some authorities recommend check-up visits at the following ages:

Produced by Put Prevention Into Practice, U.S. Department of Health and Human Services, Public Health Service, November 1994.

13

- 2-4 weeks;
- 2, 4, 6, 9, 12, 15 and 18 months; and
- 2, 3, 4, 5, 6, 8, 10, 12, 14, 16 and 18 years.

Your child's doctor or other health care provider will discuss with you increasing or decreasing the number of these visits to meet the individual needs of your child.

Immunizations

Your child needs immunizations. Immunizations (shots) protect your child from many serious diseases. Below is a list of immunizations and the ages when your child should receive them. Immunizations should be given at the recommended ages—even if your child has a cold or minor illness at the time. Ask your health care provider about when your child should receive these important shots. Ask also if your child needs additional immunizations.

- Polio (OPV): At 2 months, 4 months, 6 months, and 4-6 years.

- Diphtheria-Tetanus-Pertussis (DTP, DTP): At 2 months, 4 months, 6 months, 15 months, and 4-6 years. Tetanus-Diphtheria (Td) at 14-16 years.

- Measles-Mumps-Rubella (MMR): At 12-15 months and EITHER 4-6 years OR 11-12 years.

- *Haemophilus influenzae* type b (Hib): At 2 months, 4 months, 6 months, and 12-15 months; OR 2 months, 4 months, and 12-15 months, depending on the vaccine type.

- Hepatitis B (HBV): At birth, 1-2 months and 6-18 months; OR 1-2 months, 4 months, and 6-18 months.

- Chickenpox (VZV): At 12-18 months.

Growth Record

Your child's doctor or other health care provider will measure your child's height and weight regularly. Your child's head size will also be measured during the first 2 years of life. These measurements will help you and your health care provider know if your child is growing properly. Use growth charts to keep track of your child's growth. If you need help using these charts, ask your doctor or other health care provider.

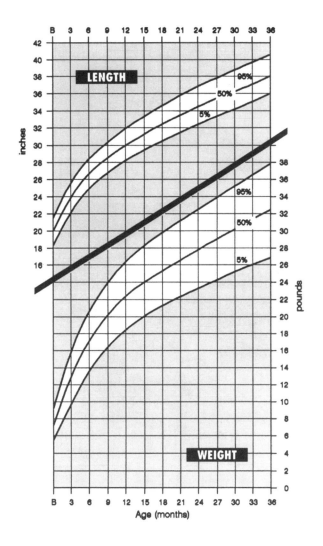

Figure 2.1. Growth Chart—Boys, birth to 3 years of age.

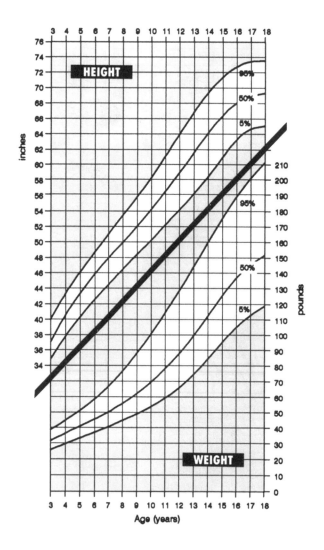

Figure 2.2. *Growth Chart—Boys, 3 to 18 years of age.*

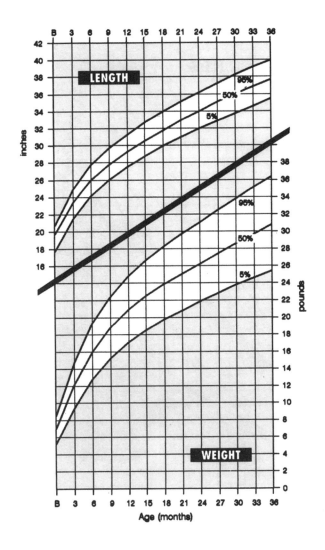

Figure 2.3*. Growth Chart—Girls, birth to 3 years of age.*

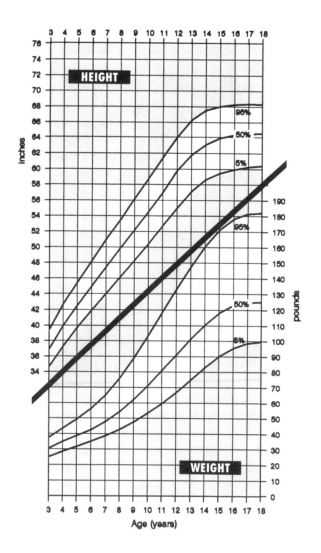

Figure 2.4. *Growth Chart—Girls, 3 to 18 years of age.*

High Blood Pressure

Your child should have blood pressure measurements regularly, starting at around 3 years of age. High blood pressure in children needs medical attention. It may be a sign of underlying disease and, if not treated, may lead to serious illness. Check with your child's doctor or health care provider about blood pressure measurements.

Anemia

Your child should be tested for anemia ("low blood") when he or she is still a baby (usually around the first birthday) and also may need anemia tests as he or she gets older. Anemia may cause your child to grow slowly, tire easily, and get infections more often. Anemia in children is usually caused by too little iron in the diet. Your child needs to eat iron-rich foods such as meats, green leafy, vegetables, and iron-fortified cereals. Check with your child's doctor or health care provider about anemia testing.

Lead

Lead can harm your child, slowing physical and mental growth and damaging many parts of the body. The most common way children get lead poisoning is by being around old house paint that is chipping or peeling. Some authorities recommend lead tests at 1 and 2 years of age. Any "yes" answers to the following questions may mean that your child needs lead tests earlier and more often than other children.

Has Your Child

- Lived in or regularly visited a house with peeling or chipped paint built before 1960? (This could include a day care center, preschool, the home of a babysitter, etc.)

- Lived in or regularly visited a house built before 1960 with recent, ongoing, or planned renovation or remodeling?

- Had a brother or sister, housemate, or playmate with lead poisoning?

- Lived with an adult whose job or hobby involves exposure to lead (such as refinishing furniture, making pottery or stained glass, or working in any of the industries listed in the next question)?

19

- Lived near a lead smelter, battery plant, car repair shop, glass or pipe factory, or other industry likely to release lead?

Vision and Hearing

Your child's vision should be tested before starting school, at about 3 or 4 years of age. Your child may also need vision tests as he or she grows. Some authorities recommend hearing testing beginning at 3 to 4 years of age. If at any age your child has any of the vision or hearing warning signs listed below, be sure to talk with your doctor or other health care provider.

Vision Warning Signs

- Eyes turning inward (crossing) or outward
- Squinting
- Headaches
- Not doing as well in school work as before
- Blurred or double vision

Hearing Warning Signs

- Poor response to noise or voice
- Slow language and speech development
- Abnormal sounding speech

SPECIAL WARNING: Listening to very loud music, especially with earphones, can permanently damage your child's hearing.

Additional Tests

Your child may need other tests to prevent health problems. Check this list with your child's doctor or other health care provider.

Newborn Screening (for PKU, thyroid and other inherited/ metabolic diseases)—If your child did not receive this blood test before coming home from the hospital, or received it before 24 hours of age. Some states require a repeat test during the first month of life.

Sickle Cell or Thalassemia Test—If your child has an African-American, Mediterranean, Asian, or Middle Eastern family background.

Tuberculosis (TB) Skin Test—If your child has had close contact with a person having TB, lives in an area where TB is more common than average (such as a Native American reservation, a homeless shelter, or an institution), or has recently moved from Asia, Africa, Central America, South America, the Caribbean, or the Pacific Islands.

Cholesterol Test—If your child has a parent with high cholesterol or a parent or grandparent with heart disease before age 55.

Urinalysis Test—If your child is less than 5 years of age, particularly if your child has had a bladder or kidney infection.

Development

Children grow and develop at different rates. The following list shows the ages by which most young children develop certain abilities. It is normal for a child to do some of these things later than the ages noted here. If your child fails to do many of these at the ages given, or you have questions about his or her development, talk with your child's doctor or other health care provider.

2 MONTHS
- Smiles, coos
- Watches a person, follows with eyes

4 MONTHS
- Laughs out loud
- Lifts head and chest when on stomach, grasps objects

6 MONTHS
- Babbles, turns to sound
- Rolls over, supports head well when sitting

9 MONTHS
- Responds to name, plays peek-a-boo
- Sits alone, crawls, pulls self up to standing

1 YEAR
- Waves bye-bye, says mama or dada
- Walks when holding on, picks up small objects with thumb and first finger

18 MONTHS
- Says 3 words other than mama or dada, scribbles
- Walks alone, feeds self using spoon

2 YEARS
- Puts 2 words together, refers to self by name
- Runs well, walks up stairs by self

3 YEARS
- Knows age, helps in buttoning clothing, washes and dries hands
- Throws ball overhand, rides tricycle

4 YEARS
- Knows first and last name, tells a story, counts 4 objects
- Balances on one foot, uses children's scissors

5 YEARS
- Names 4 colors, counts 10 objects
- Hops on one foot, dresses self

Nutrition

What your child eats is very important for his or her health. Follow the nutrition guidelines below.

Guidelines for a Healthy Diet

0-2 YEARS OLD:

- Breast milk is the best single food for infants from birth to 6 months of age. It provides good nutrition and protects against infection. Breast feeding should be continued for at least the first year, if possible.

- If breast feeding is not possible or not desired, iron-enriched formula (not cow's milk) should be used during the first 12 months of life. Whole cow's milk can be used to replace formula or breast milk after 12 months of age.

- Breast-fed babies, particularly if dark-skinned, who do not get regular exposure to sunlight may need to receive Vitamin D supplements.

- Begin suitable solid foods at 4-6 months of age. Most experts recommend iron-enriched infant rice cereal as the first food.

- Start new foods one at a time to make it easier to identify problem foods. For example, wait one week before adding each new cereal, vegetable, or other food.

- Use iron-rich foods, such as meats, iron-enriched cereals, and other grains.

- Do not give honey to infants during the first 6-12 months of life.

- Do not limit fat during the first 2 years of life.

2 YEARS AND OLDER:

- Provide a variety of foods, including plenty of fruits, vegetables, and whole grains.

- Use salt (sodium) and sugars in moderation.

- Encourage a diet low in fat, saturated fat, and cholesterol.

- Help your child maintain a healthy weight by providing proper foods and encouraging regular exercise.

Dental/Oral Health

Your child needs regular dental care starting at an early age. Talk with your dentist to schedule the first visit. Good oral health requires good daily care. Follow these guidelines.

FOR BABIES:

- If most of your child's nutrition comes from breast feeding, or if you live in an area with too little fluoride in the drinking water (less than .3 ppm for children less than 2 years old, less than .7 ppm for children over 2 years old), your child may need fluoride drops or tablets. Ask your health care provider or local water department about the amount of fluoride in your water.

- Don't use a baby bottle as a pacifier or put your child to sleep with a baby bottle. This can cause tooth decay and ear infections.

- Keep your infant's teeth and gums clean by wiping with a moist cloth after feeding.

- When multiple teeth appear, begin gently brushing your infant's teeth using a soft toothbrush and a very small (pea-sized) amount of toothpaste with fluoride.

FOR OLDER CHILDREN:

- Talk with your dentist about dental sealants. They can help prevent cavities in permanent teeth.

- Using dental floss can help prevent gum disease. Talk with your dentist about when to start.

- Do not permit your child to smoke or chew tobacco. Set a good example and don't smoke yourself.

- If a permanent tooth is knocked out, rinse it gently and put it back into the socket or into a glass of cold milk or water. See a dentist immediately.

Physical Activity

Your child needs regular physical activity through play and sports to stay fit. Good exercise habits learned early can help your child become an active and healthy adult. Adults who are physically active are less likely to be overweight or to have heart disease, high blood pressure, and other diseases. Set a good example for your child—get regular physical exercise yourself.

Physical Activity Tips for Children

- Encourage your child to walk or ride a bicycle to school and to visit friends.

- Plan physical activities with family or friends; exercise is more fun with others.

- Limit the time your child spends watching TV to less than 2 hours per day. Encourage going out to a playground, park, gym, or swimming pool instead.

- Encourage your child to be actively involved in sports, rather than only being an observer.

- Find out about exercise or sports programs at your child's school and in your community.

- Encourage children with disabilities to participate in physical activities as much as possible.

- Exercise should be fun. Don't make winning the only goal.

Smoking

Smoking is very harmful to your health (causing lung cancer, heart disease, and other serious illnesses) and to your child's health. If you smoke, your child is more likely to get infections of the ears, sinuses, and lungs. Smoking in the home may also cause lung cancer in family members who do not smoke.

Do not permit your child to smoke. Set a good example and don't smoke yourself. If you do smoke, talk with your doctor or other health care provider about getting help with quitting.

Safety

More children die from injuries than any other cause. The good news is that most injuries can be prevented by following simple safety guidelines. Talk with your doctor or other health care provider about ways to protect your child from injuries

Safety Guidelines Checklist

Read the list below and note each guideline that your family already follows. Work on those you don't.

FOR ALL AGES:

- Use smoke detectors in your home. Change the batteries every year and check to see that they work once a month.

- Keeping a gun in your home can be dangerous. If you do, make sure that the gun and ammunition are locked up separately and kept out of reach.

- Never drive after drinking alcohol.

- Teach your child traffic safety. Children under 9 years of age need supervision when crossing streets.

- Learn basic life-saving skills (CPR).

- Keep a bottle of ipecac at home to treat poisoning. Talk with a doctor or the local Poison Control Center before using it. Post the Poison Control Center number near your telephone.

INFANTS AND YOUNG CHILDREN:

- Use a car safety seat at all times until your child weighs at least 40 pounds. When possible, secure it in the center of the back seat.

- Keep medicines, cleaning solutions, and other dangerous substances in childproof containers, locked up and out of reach.

- Use safety gates across stairways (top and bottom) and guards on windows above the first floor.

- Keep hot water heater temperatures below 120° F.

- Keep unused electrical outlets covered with plastic guards.

- Baby walkers can be dangerous. Children using them should be closely supervised. Access should be blocked to stairways and to objects that can fall (such as lamps) or cause burns (such as stoves).

- Keep objects and foods that can cause choking away from your child, such as coins, balloons, small toy parts, hot dogs (unmashed), peanuts, and hard candies.

- Use fences that go all the way around pools and keep gates to pools locked.

A SPECIAL MESSAGE ABOUT SIDS

Sudden Infant Death Syndrome (SIDS) is the leading cause of death for infants. Some authorities believe that placing sleeping infants on the side or back, instead of the stomach, decreases the risk of SIDS.

FOR OLDER CHILDREN:

- Use car safety belts at all times. Use with a booster seat if your child weighs less than 70 lbs. The lap belt should be snug and low on the hips. The shoulder belt should cross the chest, not the face, neck, or stomach. If it does not fit properly, tuck it behind the shoulders instead.

- Make sure your child uses a safety helmet while riding on a bicycle or motorcycle.

- Make sure your child uses protective equipment (such as mouth guards, pads, sports goggles, and helmets) when playing contact sports, roller-skating, or skateboarding.

- Don't let your child use alcohol or illegal drugs. Many driving-, sports-, and violence-related injuries are caused by the use of alcohol or drugs.

- Read all instructions for safe handling of household tools, such as saws and lawn mowers. Teach your child to use these tools safely.

- Don't allow your child to ride on or drive heavy farm equipment, such as tractors, without special training.

- Teach your child to deal with anger and conflict without using violence. Set a good example for your child.

Child Abuse

Child abuse is a hidden, serious problem. It can happen in any family. The scars, both physical and emotional, can last for a lifetime. Because children can't protect themselves, we must protect them.

Ways to Prevent Child Abuse

- Teach your child not to let anyone touch his or her private parts.

- Tell your child to say "No" and run away from sexual touches.

- Take any reports by your child of physical or sexual abuse seriously. Report any abuse to your local or state child protection agency.

- If you feel angry and out of control, leave the room, take a walk, take deep breaths, or count to 100. Don't drink alcohol or take drugs. These can make your anger harder to control.

- If you are afraid you might harm your child, get help now! Call someone and ask for help. Talk with a friend or relative, other parents, or your health care professional. Take time for yourself. Share child care between parents, trade baby-sitting with friends, or use day care.

As Your Child Grows Up

As your child grows up, he or she will have to begin dealing with many important health issues not included in this *Child Health Guide*. Some examples of these issues are:

- Alcohol
- Drugs
- Tobacco
- Sexuality
- AIDS
- Birth Control

Talk to your child's doctor or other health care provider about these important issues even while your child is still young. You may also get assistance from authorities listed in the following section.

Start early to teach your child to make responsible choices—not mistakes that can have a lifelong effect. Take the time to "be there" for your child—listening, advising, and supporting. The rewards will be well worth the effort.

For More Information

If you would like more information about how to help your child stay healthy, talk with your child's doctor or other heath care provider. You can also get information by calling your local health department (look in the phone book) or the authorities listed below, many of which have toll-free numbers.

AIDS

- CDC National AIDS Hotline: (800) 342-AIDS

Alcohol and Drugs

- National Clearinghouse for Alcohol and Drug Information: (800) 729-6686

Child Abuse

- National Child Abuse Hotline: (800) 422-4453

Counseling/Crisis Intervention

- National Youth Crisis Hotline: (800) HIT-HOME

Food and Drug Safety

- Food and Drug Administration, Office of Consumer Affairs: (301) 443-3170

General Child Health Information

- American Academy of Family Physicians: (800) 274-2237
- American Academy of Pediatrics: (800) 433-9016

Immunizations

- General Information—Centers for Disease Control and Prevention: (404) 332-4553
- Vaccine Adverse Event Reporting System: (800) 822-7967

Maternal and Child Health

- National Maternal and Child Health Clearinghouse: (703) 821-8955 ext. 254

Safety and Injury Prevention

- Consumer Product Safety Commission: (800) 638-CPSC
- National Highway Traffic Safety Administration Auto Safety Hotline: (800) 424-9393
- The Children's Safety Network: (703) 524-7802

Sexually Transmitted Diseases

- CDC National STD Hotline: (800) 227-8922

Put Prevention Into Practice

"Put Prevention Into Practice" is a national initiative of the U.S. Department of Health and Human Services' Public Health Service in partnership with public and private health care organizations. (Neither the Public Health Service nor the U.S. Department of Health and Human Services endorses any particular product, service or organization.) The goal of "Put Prevention Into Practice" is to preserve the health of all Americans by improving the preventive care they receive. You can help to put prevention into practice by working with your health care providers to make sure you get all the preventive care you need. You can also do your part by following the health advice in this Personal Health Guide. Take charge of your health and live a longer and healthier life!

For more information about the "Put Prevention Into Practice" campaign, write: Put Prevention Into Practice, National Health Information Center, P.O. Box 1133, Washington, DC 20013-1133.

Chapter 3

Choosing and Using a Health Plan

Changes and Choices

Health care in America is changing rapidly. Twenty-five years ago, most people in the United States had indemnity insurance coverage. A person with indemnity insurance could go to any doctor, hospital, or other provider (which would bill for each service given), and the insurance and the patient would each pay part of the bill.

But today, more than half of all Americans who have health insurance are enrolled in some kind of managed care plan, an organized way of both providing services and paying for them. Different types of managed care plans work differently and include preferred provider organizations (PPOs), health maintenance organizations (HMOs), and point-of-service (POS) plans.

You've probably heard these terms before. But what do they mean, and what are the differences between them? And what do these differences mean to you?

Overview

This chapter can help you make sense of your choices for getting health care insurance:

- See the questions and answers on important things you should know when "Choosing a Plan."

Agency for Health Care Policy and Research (AHCPR) and Health Insurance Association of America (HIAA), AHCPR Pub. No. 97-0011, March 1997.

- To get the most out of the plan you choose, see the tips in the section "Using Care."
- For more help, see "Sources of Additional Information" at the end of the chapter.

Even if you don't get to choose the health plan yourself (for example, your employer may select the plan for your company), you still need to understand what kind of protection your health plan provides and what you will need to do to get the health care that you and your family need.

The more you learn, the more easily you'll be able to decide what fits your personal needs and budget.

Choosing a Plan

What are my health plan choices?

Choosing between health plans is not as easy as it once was. Although there is no one "best" plan, there are some plans that will be better than others for you and your family's health needs. Plans differ, both in how much you have to pay and how easy it is to get the services you need. Although no plan will pay for all the costs associated with your medical care, some plans will cover more than others.

Almost all plans today have ways to reduce unnecessary use of health care-and keep down the costs of health care, too. This may affect how easily you get the care you *want*, but should not affect how easily you get the care you *need*.

Plans change from year to year, so you should carefully consider each plan, using the questions outlined in this chapter. If you get health insurance where you work, you should start with your employee benefits office. Its staff should be able to tell you what is covered under the plans available. You can also call plans directly to ask questions.

Health insurance plans are usually described as either indemnity (fee-for-service) or managed care. These types of plans differ in important ways that are described below. With any health plan, however, there is a basic premium, which is how much you or your employer pay, usually monthly, to buy health insurance coverage. In addition, there are often other payments you must make, which will vary by plan. In considering any plan, you should try to figure out its total cost to you and your family, especially if someone in the family has a chronic or serious health condition.

Indemnity and managed care plans differ in their basic approach. Put broadly, the major differences concern choice of providers, out-of-pocket costs for covered services, and how bills are paid. Usually, indemnity plans offer more choice of doctors (including specialists, such as cardiologists and surgeons), hospitals, and other health care providers than managed care plans. Indemnity plans pay their share of the costs of a service only after they receive a bill. Managed care plans have agreements with certain doctors, hospitals, and health care providers to give a range of services to plan members at reduced cost. In general, you will have less paperwork and lower out-of-pocket costs if you select a managed care type plan and a broader choice of health care providers if you select an indemnity-type plan.

Over time, the distinctions between these kinds of plans have begun to blur as health plans compete for your business. Some indemnity plans offer managed care-type options, and some managed care plans offer members the opportunity to use providers who are "outside" the plan. This makes it even more important for you to understand how your health plan works.

Besides indemnity plans, there are basically three types of managed care plans: PPOs, HMOs, and POS plans.

Indemnity Plan

With an indemnity plan (sometimes called fee-for-service), you can use any medical provider (such as a doctor and hospital). You or they send the bill to the insurance company, which pays part of it. Usually, you have a deductible—such as $200—to pay each year before the insurer starts paying.

Once you meet the deductible, most indemnity plans pay a percentage of what they consider the "Usual and Customary" charge for covered services. The insurer generally pays 80 percent of the Usual and Customary costs and you pay the other 20 percent, which is known as coinsurance. If the provider charges more than the Usual and Customary rates, you will have to pay both the coinsurance and the difference.

The plan will pay for charges for medical tests and prescriptions as well as from doctors and hospitals. It may not pay for some preventive care, like checkups.

Managed Care

- *Preferred Provider Organization (PPO).* A PPO is a form of managed care closest to an indemnity plan. A PPO has arrangements with doctors, hospitals, and other providers of care who have agreed to accept lower fees from the insurer for their services. As a result, your cost sharing should be lower than if you go outside the network. In addition to the PPO doctors making referrals, plan members can refer themselves to other doctors, including ones outside the plan.

If you go to a doctor within the PPO network, you will pay a copayment (a set amount you pay for certain services—say $10 for a doctor or $5 for a prescription). Your coinsurance will be based on lower charges for PPO members.

If you choose to go outside the network, you will have to meet the deductible and pay coinsurance based on higher charges. In addition, you may have to pay the difference between what the provider charges and what the plan will pay.

- *Health Maintenance Organization (HMO).* HMOs are the oldest form of managed care plan. HMOs offer members a range of health benefits, including preventive care, for a set monthly fee. There are many kinds of HMOs. If doctors are employees of the health plan and you visit them at central medical offices or clinics, it is a staff or group model HMO. Other HMOs contract with physician groups or individual doctors who have private offices. These are called individual practice associations (IPAs) or networks.

  HMOs will give you a list of doctors from which to choose a primary care doctor. This doctor coordinates your care, which means that generally you must contact him or her to be referred to a specialist.

  With some HMOs, you will pay nothing when you visit doctors. With other HMOs there may be a copayment, like $5 or $10, for various services.

  If you belong to an HMO, the plan only covers the cost of charges for doctors in that HMO. If you go outside the HMO, you will pay the bill. This is not the case with point-of-service plans.

Point-of-Service (POS) Plan

Many HMOs offer an indemnity-type option known as a POS plan. The primary care doctors in a POS plan usually make referrals to other providers in the plan. But in a POS plan, members can refer themselves outside the plan and still get some coverage.

If the doctor makes a referral out of the network, the plan pays all or most of the bill. If you refer yourself to a provider outside the network and the service is covered by the plan, you will have to pay coinsurance.

Your Primary Care Doctor

Your primary care doctor will serve as your regular doctor, managing your care and working with you to make most of the medical decisions about your care as a patient. In many plans care by specialists is only paid for if you are referred by your primary care doctor.

An HMO or a POS plan will provide you with a list of doctors from which you will choose your primary care doctor (usually a family physician, internist, obstetrician-gynecologist, or pediatrician). This could mean you might have to choose a new primary care doctor if your current one does not belong to the plan.

PPOs allow members to use primary care doctors outside the PPO network (at a higher cost). Indemnity plans allow any doctor to be used.

Where do I get these health plans?

Group Policies

You may be able to get group health coverage—either indemnity or managed care—through your job or the job of a family member.

Many employers allow you to join or change health plans once a year during open enrollment. But once you choose a plan, you must keep it for a year. Discuss choices and limits with your employee benefits office.

Individual Policies

If you are self-employed or if your company does not offer group policies, you may need to buy individual health insurance. Individual policies cost more than group policies.

Some organizations—such as unions, professional associations, or social or civic groups—offer health plans for members. You may want to talk to an insurance broker, who can tell you more about the indemnity and managed care plans that are available for individuals. Some States also provide insurance for very small groups or the self-employed.

Medicare

Americans age 65 or older and people with certain disabilities can be covered under Medicare, a Federal health insurance program.

In many parts of the country, people covered under Medicare now have a choice between managed care and indemnity plans. They also can switch their plans for any reason. However, they must officially tell the plan or the local Social Security office, and the change may not take effect for up to 30 days. Call your local Social Security office or the State office on aging to find out what is available in your area.

Medicaid

Medicaid covers some low-income people (especially children and pregnant women), and disabled people. Medicaid is a joint Federal-State health insurance program that is run by the States.

In some cases, States require people covered under Medicaid to join managed care plans. Insurance plans and State regulations differ, so check with your State Medicaid office to learn more.

Pre-Existing Conditions

A pre-existing condition is a medical condition diagnosed or treated before joining a new plan. In the past, health care given for a pre-existing condition often has not been covered for someone who joins a new plan until after a waiting period. However, a new law—called the Health Insurance Portability and Accountability Act—changes the rules.

Under the law, most of which goes into effect on July 1, 1997, a pre-existing condition will be covered without a waiting period when you join a new group plan if you have been insured the previous 12 months. This means that if you remain insured for 12 months or more, you will be able to go from one job to another, and your pre-existing condition will be covered—without additional waiting periods—even if you have a chronic illness.

If you have a pre-existing condition and have not been insured the previous 12 months before joining a new plan, the longest you will have to wait before you are covered for that condition is 12 months.

To find out how this new law affects you, check with either your employer benefits office or your health plan.

What plan benefits are offered?

Most plans provide basic medical coverage, but the details are what counts. The best plan for someone else may not be the best plan for you. For each plan you are considering, find out how it handles:

- Physical exams and health screenings.
- Care by specialists.
- Hospitalization and emergency care.
- Prescription drugs.
- Vision care.
- Dental services.

Also ask about:

- Care and counseling for mental health.
- Services for drug and alcohol abuse.
- Obstetrical-gynecological care and family planning services.
- Ongoing care for chronic (long-term) diseases, conditions, or disabilities.
- Physical therapy and other rehabilitative care.
- Home health, nursing home, and hospice care.
- Chiropractic or alternative health care, such as acupuncture.
- Experimental treatments.

Some plans offer members health education and preventive care, but services differ. Ask questions such as:

- What preventive care is offered, such as shots for children?
- What health screenings are given, such as breast exams and Pap smears for women?
- Does the plan help people who want to quit smoking?

What is most important to me in a plan?

In choosing a plan, you have to decide what is most important to you. All plans have tradeoffs. Ask yourself these questions:

- How comprehensive do I want coverage of health care services to be?
- How do I feel about limits on my choice of doctors or hospitals?
- How do I feel about a primary care doctor referring me to specialists for additional care?
- How convenient does my care need to be?
- How important is the cost of services?
- How much am I willing to spend on premiums and other health care costs?
- How do I feel about keeping receipts and filing claims?

You might also want to think about whether the services a plan offers meet your needs. Call the plan for details about coverage if you have questions. Consider:

- Life changes you may be thinking about, such as starting a family or retiring.
- Chronic health conditions or disabilities that you or family members have.
- If you or anyone in your family will need care for the elderly.
- Care for family members who travel a lot, attend college, or spend time at two homes.

How do I compare health plans?

After you review what benefits are available and decide what is important to you, you can compare plans. Many things should be considered. These include services offered, choice of providers, location, and costs. The quality of care is also a factor to think about (see the next section).

Services

Look at the services offered by each plan. What services are limited or not covered? Is there a good match between what is provided and what you think you will need? For example, if you have a chronic disease, is there a special program for that illness? Will the plan provide the medicines and equipment you may need?

Find out what types of care or services the plan won't pay for. These usually are called exclusions.

Few indemnity and managed care plans cover treatments that are experimental. Ask how the plan decides what is or is not experimental. Find out what you can do if you disagree with a plan's decision on medical care or coverage.

Choice

What doctors, hospitals, and other medical providers are part of the plan? Are there enough of the kinds of doctors you want to see? Do you need to choose a primary care doctor? If you want to see a specialist, can you refer yourself or must your primary care doctor refer you? Do you need approval from the plan before going into the hospital or getting specialty care?

Location

Where will you go for care? Are these places near where you work or live? How does the plan handle care when you are away from home?

Costs

No health insurance plan will cover every expense. To get a true idea of what your costs will be under each plan, you need to look at how much you will pay for your premium and other costs.

- Are there deductibles you must pay before the insurance begins to help cover your costs?

- After you have met your deductible, what part of your costs are paid by the plan? Does this amount vary by the type of service, doctor, or health facility used?

- Are there copayments you must pay for certain services, such as doctor visits? If you use doctors outside a plan's network, how much more will you pay to get care?

- If a plan does not cover certain services or care that you think you will need, how much will you have to pay?

- Are there any limits to how much you must pay in case of major illness?

- Is there a limit on how much the plan will pay for your care in a year or over a lifetime? A single hospital stay for a serious condition could cost hundreds of thousands of dollars.

You can't know in advance what your health care needs for the coming year will be. But you can guess what services you and your family might need. Figure out what the total costs to your family would be for these services under each plan.

How do I find out about quality?

Quality is hard to measure, but more and more information is becoming available. There are certain things you can look for and questions you can ask. Whatever kind of plan you are considering, you can check out individual doctors and hospitals. For doctors, see "Tips on Choosing a Doctor" in this chapter.

Many managed care plans are regulated by Federal and State agencies. Indemnity plans are regulated by State insurance commissions.

Your State department of health or insurance commission should be able to tell you about any plan you are interested in.

You can also find out if the managed care plan you are interested in has been "accredited," meaning that it meets certain standards of independent organizations. Some States require accreditation if plans serve special groups, such as people in Medicaid. Some employers will only contract with plans that are accredited.

Several national organizations review and accredit plans and institutions (see "Sources of Additional Information"). You can contact these organizations to see if a plan you are considering, or an institution in the plan, is accredited.

Another approach is to ask the plan how it ensures good medical care. Does the plan review the qualifications of doctors before they are added to the plan? Plans are supposed to review the care that is given by their doctors and hospitals. How does the plan review its own services, and has it made changes to correct problems? How does the plan resolve member complaints?

Some managed care plans survey members about their health care experiences. Ask the plan for a report of the survey results.

Some plans and independent organizations are also beginning to produce "report cards." These reports often include satisfaction survey results and other information on quality, such as if a plan provides preventive care (for example shots for children and Pap smears for women) or if the plan follows up on test results. Report cards may also include information on how many members stay in or leave the plan, how many of the plan's doctors are board certified, or how long you may have to wait for an appointment.

Report cards can only give you an idea of how a plan works and may not give a full picture of a plan's quality. Ask plans if their activities have been reported in report cards developed by outside groups (business or consumer organizations).

Also keep any eye out for magazine articles that rate health plans.

Finally, you can talk to current members of the plan. Ask how they feel about their experiences, such as waiting times for appointments, the helpfulness of medical staff, the services offered, and the care received. If there are programs for your particular condition, how are the patients in it doing?

Tips on Choosing a Doctor

Your doctor will be your partner in care, so it is important to choose carefully from the doctors available to you. In some managed care plans, you will generally be limited to choosing from only certain doctors; in other plans, some doctors may be "preferred," which means they are part of a network and you will pay less if you use them. Ask your plan for a list or directory of providers. The plan may also offer other help in choosing.

You can ask doctors you know, medical societies, friends, family, and coworkers to recommend doctors. You may also contact hospitals and referral services about doctors in your area.

Once you have the names of doctors who interest you, make sure they are accepting new patients. Here's how to check doctors out:

- Ask plans and medical offices for information on their doctors' training and experience.

- Look up basic information about doctors in the Directory of Medical Specialists, available at your local library. This reference has up-to-date professional and biographic information on about 400,000 practicing physicians.

- Use "AMA Physician Select," which is the American Medical Association's free service on the Internet for information about physicians (http://www.amaassn.org).

You may also want to find out:

- Is the doctor board certified? Although all doctors must be licensed to practice medicine some also are board certified. This means the doctor has completed several years of training in a specialty and passed an exam. Call the American Board of Medical Specialties at (800) 776-2378 for more information.

- Have complaints been registered or disciplinary actions taken against the doctor? To find out, call your State Medical Licensing Board. Ask Directory Assistance for the phone number.

- Have complaints been registered with your State department of insurance? (Not all departments of insurance accept complaints.) Ask Directory Assistance for the phone number.

Once you have narrowed your search to a few doctors, you may want to set up "get acquainted" appointments with them. Ask what charge there might be for these visits, if any. Such appointments give you a chance to interview the doctors—for example, to find out if they have much experience with any health conditions you may have.

Using Care

How can I get the most from my plan?

You will get the best care if you:

Stay Informed

- Read your health insurance policy and member handbook. Make sure you understand them, especially the information on benefits, coverage, and limits. Sales materials or plan summaries cannot give you the full picture.

- See if your plan has a magazine or newsletter. It can be a good source of information on how the plan works and on important policies that affect your care.

- Talk to your health benefits officer at work to learn more about your policy.

- Ask how the plan will notify you of changes in the network of providers or covered services while you are part of the plan.

Take Charge

- Ask your doctor about regular screenings to check your health. Discuss your risk of getting certain conditions. What lifestyle choices and changes might you need to make to lower your risks or prevent illness?

- Ask questions and insist on clear answers. Ask about the risks and benefits of tests and treatments. Tell your doctor what you like and dislike about your choices for care.

- Make sure you understand and can follow the doctor's instructions. You may want to bring another person along or take notes to help you remember things.

Keep Track

- Write down your concerns. Start a health log of symptoms to help you better explain any health problems when you meet with your doctor.

- Set up health files for family members at home. This will help you to monitor care. Include health histories of shots, illnesses, treatments, and hospital visits. Ask for copies of lab results. Keep a list of your medicines, noting side effects and other problems (such as other drugs and foods that should not be taken at the same time).

How do I obtain care?

Learning what you can expect from your health plan and how it works are key steps to getting the care you need.

Ask these questions:

- When are the offices open? What if I need care after hours?

- How do I make appointments? How quickly can I expect to be seen for illness or for routine care?

- If I need lab tests, are they done in the doctor's office or will I be sent to a laboratory?

- Will most of my appointments be with the primary care doctor? Will nurse practitioners or physicians' assistants sometimes give care as well?

- Is there an advice hotline? Some plans have toll-free phone services that help members decide how to handle a problem that may not require a doctor's visit.

Find out how your plan provides care outside the service area and what you must do to get care. This is especially important if you travel often, are away from home for long periods, or have family members away at school.

What if I have to go to the hospital?

The time to find out what rules your plan has on hospital care is before you need it.

Planned Hospitalizations

Unless it is a medical emergency, your health plan or primary care doctor will probably have to give advance approval (preadmission certification) for you to go to the hospital. Otherwise, the cost of your hospital care may not be covered. Ask these questions:

- What hospitals are part of the plan network?

- Is there a limit on how long I can stay in the hospital?
- Who decides when I am to be discharged?
- Will needed followup care, such as nursing home or home health care, be covered by the plan?
- If I have a serious medical problem, will the plan provide someone to oversee care and make sure my needs are met?

Ask how your plan handles getting a second doctor's opinion on whether surgery or another treatment is needed. Are second opinions encouraged or required? Who pays?

Emergency or Urgent Care

If you have a true medical emergency, you should go to the nearest hospital as fast as possible. It is important for you to know what kind of medical problems are defined as emergencies and how to arrange for ambulance service, if needed. Most plans must be told within a certain time after emergency admission to a hospital. If the hospital is not part of the plan network, you may be transferred to a network hospital when your condition is stable. Ask these questions:

- How does the plan define "emergency care?" What conditions or injuries are considered emergencies?

- How does the plan handle "urgent care" after normal business hours? Urgent care is for problems that are not true emergencies but still need quick medical attention. Check with your plan to find out what it considers to be urgent care. Examples may include sore throats with fever, ear infections, and serious sprains. Call your primary care doctor or the plan's hotline for advice about what to do. The plan may also have urgent care centers for members.

- How do I get urgent care or hospital care if I am out of the area? How must I tell the plan and how soon after I get the care?

What if I am not satisfied with my care?

Getting the best care and services means understanding how your health plan works, what your rights are, and how to complain if you need to.

You have the right to get copies of test results as well as medical information about yourself. If you are in a managed care plan, you can ask to change your primary care doctor if you are unhappy with the relationship. You may also be able to switch plans during open enrollment.

Most plans have an appeals process that both you and your doctor may use if you disagree with the plan's decisions. If your plan refuses to provide or pay for services, you can complain or file a grievance about any decision you feel is unfair—or you can appeal it.

You can contact the member services division of your plan for more information or to complain. Use your plan's complaint process fully before taking other action.

Be sure to keep written records of:

- All correspondence with the plan.
- Claims forms and copies of bills.
- Phone conversations—the date and time, the people you speak with, and the nature of each call.

If the plan does not satisfy you, you may decide to bring the matter to the attention of your employee benefits manager, your State insurance commissioner, your State department of health, or the legal system. If you are a Medicare or Medicaid beneficiary, you have additional ways through those programs to file a grievance about the care received from a plan or provider. For information, contact your State's medical Peer Review Organization or State Medicaid Program.

Sources of Additional Information

Many organizations have information that can help you understand your health care choices. Some helpful materials and contacts are listed.

General Information

"Checkup on Health Insurance Choices"
"Questions To Ask Your Doctor Before You Have Surgery"
Agency for Health Care Policy and Research
Publications Clearinghouse
P.O. Box 8547
Silver Spring, MD 20907
(800) 358-9295

"The Consumers Guide to Health Insurance"
Health Insurance Association of America
555 13th St., N.W., 600 East
Washington, DC 20004-1109
(202) 824-1600

"Guide to Health Insurance for People with Medicare"
"Your Medicare Handbook"
"Managed Care Plans"
Health Care Financing Administration
7500 Security Blvd.
Baltimore, MD 21244-1850
(800) 638-6833

"Putting Patients First"
National Health Council
1730 M St., NW, Suite 500
Washington, DC 20036-4505
(202) 785-3910

"Managed Care: An AARP Guide"
American Association of Retired Persons
611 E St., N.W.
Washington, DC 20049
(202) 434-2277

"Choosing Quality: Finding the Health Plan That's Right for You"
National Committee for Quality Assurance
2000 L St., N.W., Suite 500
Washington, DC 20036
(800) 839-6487

"Consumers' Guide to Health Plans"
"Consumers' Checkbook"
Center for the Study of Services
733 15th St., N.W., Suite 820
Washington, DC 20005
(202) 347-7283

Accreditation and Quality

Accreditation Association for Ambulatory Health Care
9933 Lawler Ave.
Skokie, IL 60077-3708
(847) 676-9610

Accredits outpatient health care settings such as ambulatory surgery centers, radiation oncology centers, and student health centers. Call for a list of accredited organizations.

Community Health Accreditation Program
350 Hudson St.
New York, NY 10014
(800) 669-1656, extension 242

Accredits community, home health, and hospice programs; public health departments; and nursing centers. Call for a list of accredited organizations.

Consumer Coalition for Quality Health Care
1275 K Street, N.W.
Suite 602
Washington, DC 20005
(202) 789-3606

A national, nonprofit organization of consumer groups advocating for consumer protections and quality assurance programs and policies. Call with general questions about quality issues or for consumer materials on managed care and activities at the State level.

Joint Commission on Accreditation of Healthcare Organizations
One Renaissance Blvd.
Oakbrook Terrace, IL 60181
(630) 792-5000

Accredits hospitals and organizations that provide home care, long-term care, behavioral health care, and laboratory and ambulatory care services. Call for the status of accredited organizations or for general information about quality.

The Medical Quality Commission
310 Old Ranch Pkwy., Suite 205
Seal Beach, CA 90740-2750
(310) 936-1100

Accredits medical groups and IPAs (not individual physicians). Call for a list of accredited groups.

National Committee for Quality Assurance
2000 L St., N.W., Suite 500
Washington, DC 20036
(800) 839-6487
Web Site: http://www.ncqa.org

Accredits HMOs and other managed care organizations. Call for the NCQA Accreditation Status List, Accreditation Summary Report, publications list, or for general information about quality.

Utilization Review Accreditation Commission
1130 Connecticut Ave. N.W., Suite 450
Washington, DC 20036
(202) 296-0120

Accredits PPOs and other managed care networks. Call for a list of accredited organizations.

Chapter 4

Immunizations for Children and Adults

Kids' Vaccinations

Before vaccines became widely available, diseases like measles, mumps and whooping cough were common in childhood, and thousands died or were left blind, deaf or brain-damaged by them. Today, vaccines have totally or nearly eradicated several diseases such as smallpox, polio, diphtheria, and Hib infections, according to the national Centers for Disease Control and Prevention (CDC).

Yet other diseases persist, mostly in unvaccinated babies and toddlers—the children who are most vulnerable to the effects of disease. An estimated 37 to 56 percent of American children are not fully immunized by age 2, according to CDC. In some inner city areas, only 10 percent of children have been properly immunized.

Some people blame the low rates on inconvenience. There are 10 diseases to vaccinate against, with as many as 16 doses in about five visits to the doctor before a child's second birthday.

Others point out that parents are required to have children vaccinated only before enrolling them in school or day care. Ninety-six

This chapter contains text from "Kids' Vaccinations," *FDA Consumer*, March 1994, reprinted as Pub. No. (FDA) 969011; "Immunization... Not Just Kids' Stuff," *Prevention Report*, Volume 12: Issue 2, 1997; "Adults Need Tetanus Shots, Too," by Evelyn Zamula, *FDA Consumer*, July-August 1996, reprinted as Pub. No. (FDA) 96-9017; and "How FDA Works to Ensure Vaccine Safety," by Isadora B. Stehlin, *FDA Consumer*, March 1996, reprinted as Pub. No. (FDA) 96-9015.

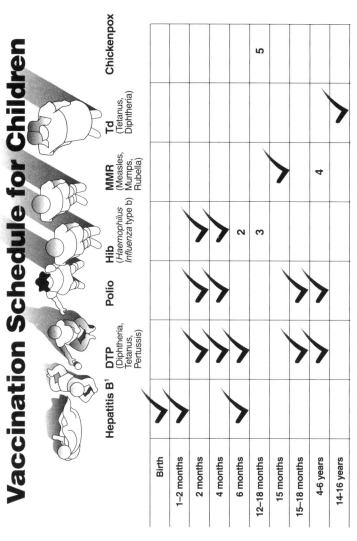

Vaccination Schedule for Children

	Hepatitis B[1]	DTP (Diphtheria, Tetanus, Pertussis)	Polio	Hib (Haemophilus Influenza type b)	MMR (Measles, Mumps, Rubella)	Td (Tetanus, Diphtheria)	Chickenpox
Birth	✓						
1–2 months	✓						
2 months		✓	✓	✓			
4 months		✓	✓	✓			
6 months		✓		2			
12–18 months			3		✓		
15 months		✓			✓		
15–18 months		✓	✓				
4-6 years					4		
14-16 years						✓	5

1 — This schedule is for high-risk infants (those whose mothers have tested positive for hepatitis B). These infants should receive hepatitis B immune globulin at or shortly after the first vaccine dose. Infants not at high risk also should be vaccinated against hepatitis B. Check with your doctor for the appropriate schedule.
2 — May not be required, depending on type of vaccine used. Check with your doctor.
3 — Given at 12, 15, or 18 months, depending on type of vaccine. Check with your doctor.
4 — Where required by public health authorities for school entry. Otherwise: 11–12 years. Check with your doctor.
5 — Can be given along with MMR or anytime between 12 to 18 months. Older children who have not had chickenpox and have not been vaccinated previously should get the vaccine by their 13th birthday.

(Source: U.S. Food and Drug Administration)

percent of children have their shots before entering school, according to CDC. But babies and toddlers not in structured day care are most likely to miss their shots.

The cost of vaccines may be another factor in low immunization rates. According to CDC, vaccines for one child in 1993 cost about $89 in the public sector and $213 in the private sector, in addition to administrative fees usually charged. Only half of health insurance plans cover childhood vaccines, though many public health departments offer them free or at a reduced fee based on income. Congress allocated $500 million for fiscal year 1994 to provide free vaccinations to all uninsured children and to educate parents about the need for childhood immunizations.

Education is necessary, physicians say, because many parents do not understand how dangerous childhood illnesses are.

"They're not real in people's minds," says Gromisch. "Years before the whooping cough vaccine, many children died of whooping cough. In inner cities a few years ago where vaccination rates are dismal, people continued to die [of whooping cough]."

In fact, diseases that are uncommon in most parts of the United States today are nearly epidemic in American communities where children are not properly vaccinated.

Measles, for instance, had dropped to a record low of fewer than 1,500 cases in 1983, according to CDC. A resurgence of measles between 1989 and 1991, however, resulted in 55,000 cases and 132 deaths, mostly among unvaccinated babies and toddlers. In urban areas, minority children are four to nine times as likely to get measles as white children.

The resurgence of childhood illnesses costs money as well as lives. According to the National Academy of Sciences' Institute of Medicine, every $1 in vaccinations saves $10 in later healthcare costs.

Required Vaccines

Whether a child receives vaccinations at a pediatrician's office or health department, the healthcare provider is expected to keep careful records of when each shot was given and what brand it was. Some brands have slightly different schedules than others. Parents should ask for copies of the shot record to keep at home as a reminder for the next round.

Even if a child misses an appointment, it's possible to catch up. Says Gromisch of the AAP, "Usually it's not too late. In general, if you miss a vaccine, you can get it the next time around."

Immunization schedules have changed in recent years. Several new vaccines have been added, and old ones have been reformulated to be safer than ever. Here is a list of vaccinations recommended for children.

Hib. Before the vaccine to protect against *Haemophilus influenzae* type b, this bacterial infection struck 1 child in 200 before the fifth birthday. Of those, 12,000 children a year developed meningitis, which killed 1 in 20 and caused brain damage for 1 in 4. Hib can also infect blood, joints, bones, soft tissues, the throat, and the membrane surrounding the heart.

Hib vaccines are the latest development among childhood immunizations, and their benefits have been far-reaching. The first Hib vaccine was available in 1987 for children 15 to 18 months old. But in 1990, FDA licensed the first vaccine effective in babies under a year old, the age group in which Hib infections are most damaging.

Hib vaccines are "conjugate" vaccines, made up of small pieces of bacterial polysaccharides, or sugars, linked to proteins. They have nearly eradicated Hib infections among vaccinated children in the United States, according to CDC.

FDA has licensed four Hib vaccines, in addition to the combination Tetramune vaccine. The most recently approved vaccine is distributed in the United States under two brand names, OmniHib and ActHIB.

Depending on the brand of vaccine, Hib is given in either three or four doses by the time the child is 12 to 18 months old. Side effects are very minor, consisting mostly of low-grade fever and soreness at the site of the shot.

DTP. The DTP shot is a combination inoculation against diphtheria, tetanus, and pertussis. It is given at 2, 4, 6, and 15 to 18 months of age, with a booster between 4 and 6 years.

Diphtheria is an infection of the throat, mouth and nose. It's extremely rare today, but highly contagious. The infection causes a sore throat and cough. Sometimes a fine web of gray membrane forms over the tonsils, blocking the windpipe and suffocating the child. If not promptly treated, diphtheria can also lead to pneumonia, heart failure, and paralysis.

Pertussis, or whooping cough, is life-threatening, especially in children under 1 year. It's caused by a bacterium that clogs the airways with mucus, causing a severe cough that sounds like a "whoop." The coughing can last two months, inviting other infections such as pneumonia or bronchitis.

The pertussis component of DTP causes more adverse reactions than any other vaccine. Most common are fever, soreness at the site of the shot, and irritability. In rare cases, the vaccine causes very high fever and convulsions.

FDA licensed in 1992 a version of the pertussis vaccine with potential for fewer local and febrile reactions. Unlike the old version, which is made from whole cells of pertussis bacteria that have been killed, the new vaccine is "acellular," made from portions of the cells. It has fewer side effects and has been approved for the fourth dose, given between 15 and 18 months, and the last dose, given before school entry. Scientists have not determined yet whether the acellular vaccine is safe and effective for infants.

Tetanus is a rare infection caused by bacteria found in dirt, gravel, and rusty metal. It enters the body through a cut, creating a toxin, or poison, that causes the muscles to spasm. The toxin attacks jaw muscles first, often resulting in lockjaw. Tetanus can also cause the breathing muscles to spasm, resulting in death for 3 out of 10 people who get it.

The primary series of tetanus shots is given as part of the DTP shot during infancy. After that, the tetanus vaccine should be given as a booster every 10 years throughout life.

Hepatitis B. Hepatitis B is a viral disease transmitted through blood and body fluids. In its acute phase it can cause liver failure and death. It can also become chronic, causing liver damage over a number of years.

Except for infants born to mothers with this infection, children are not at great risk of developing hepatitis B, but health-care workers, homosexuals, intravenous drug users, and some ethnic groups and nationalities are. Attempts to vaccinate adults have been largely unsuccessful, however. It's easier to reach children because school enrollment requires immunization.

Therefore, for lifelong protection, CDC has recommended that all infants be vaccinated before 15 months of age in three doses. There are no serious reactions to the vaccine.

Polio. Polio is remembered by many older Americans as a frightening disease that was epidemic during the 1950s. In 1952, more than 20,000 people—mostly children—were afflicted, according to CDC. Polio's first symptoms are fever, sore throat, headache, and stiff neck. The potentially fatal disease can soon progress to paralysis of the lower limbs and chest, making walking and breathing difficult or impossible. There is no cure for the disease.

There are two polio vaccines. One is an inactivated polio vaccine (IPV) in which the polio virus has been killed. Licensed in 1955, this vaccine is injected into the patient. The second vaccine is made from live polio viruses. This oral polio vaccine (OPV) was licensed in 1963 and is taken as drops in the mouth.

Since the development of the oral vaccine, the incidence of polio has dropped to fewer than 10 cases per year. In fact, the oral vaccine has entirely prevented polio caused by the wild virus (not vaccine related) in North and South America since 1991, according to the PanAmerican Health Organization.

However, in the last two decades the oral vaccine itself has caused paralytic polio in a very few children who received the vaccine, and in a few adults who came in close contact with recently vaccinated children. The risk of contracting polio this way is no more than 1 in 1.5 million. It is greatest for people who have immune deficiencies such as AIDS, cancer, or other diseases that make it hard for the body to fight infection. Because of this risk, CDC recommends that IPV be given to children who have immune deficiencies or who live with adults who do. Parents who have not been vaccinated for polio should consider getting vaccinated with IPV before the child receives the oral vaccine.

A number of lawsuits have been filed against Lederle Laboratories, Inc., manufacturer of the oral vaccine. While the government was found negligent in its applications of some regulations on vaccine approval and vaccine lot release, the court has nevertheless affirmed the safety and importance of the vaccine.

The district court judge in Maryland wrote in April 1991, ". . . the scientists who established and implemented the OPV program were (and are) extraordinarily able professionals who consistently acted in the public interest as they reasonably perceived it to be. They made judgments on extremely difficult questions which, strictly from the standpoint of public health, appear to have been entirely proper."

Although the modern IPV does not appear to cause adverse reactions, at this time public health authorities, including CDC, recommend the oral polio vaccine because it is more effective. It doesn't require continual booster shots, it is easier to administer, and it also helps spread immunity to the population at large. The oral vaccine is given at 2, 4, and 15 to 18 months, and again between 4 and 6 years.

MMR. The MMR vaccine protects against measles, mumps and rubella (German measles).

Measles is a highly contagious disease that causes high fever, cough, and a spotty rash. Possible complications include ear infections and pneumonia as well. More rarely, measles can infect the brain, causing convulsions, hearing loss, mental retardation, and even death. Babies under 2 and adults get much sicker with measles than do elementary school children.

The MMR vaccine is given in two doses, at 15 months and again between 4 and 6 years or before junior high or middle school. Most children have no side effects from the MMR vaccine, but about 5 to 15 percent develop a fever. A few develop a measles-like rash, swelling of the lymph glands, and mild pain in the joints.

Mumps is known for causing painful, swollen salivary glands under the jaw, as well as fever and headache. Mumps can be a very serious disease, causing meningitis or hearing loss. Teenage and adult males who get mumps may have painful swelling of the testicles for several days, although no infertility problems later. They get much sicker and suffer longer than children do with the disease.

Rubella is also called German measles. It's a mild disease in children, but rubella endangers the fetus when a pregnant woman catches it. As many as half of the women who contract rubella while pregnant, especially during the first three months, miscarry or deliver babies with heart disease, blindness, hearing loss, or learning problems. Before the rubella vaccine was approved in 1969, some 20,000 babies were born with severe birth defects because their mothers were exposed to the disease while pregnant.

Women with no proof of rubella immunity can be tested for it and should receive the vaccine before getting pregnant. Pregnant women not should receive the rubella vaccine, nor should a woman get pregnant within three months after getting the vaccine because it will endanger the fetus.

Chickenpox. An estimated 3.7 million Americans get chickenpox each year, with more than 90 percent of cases in people younger than 15.

Although chickenpox is generally mild and not normally life-threatening, CDC estimates that there are 9,300 chickenpox-related hospitalizations and 50 to 100 deaths annually, mainly among young children.

On March 17, 1995, FDA licensed a new vaccine, Varivax (varicella virus vaccine live). Commonly known as the chickenpox vaccine, it will prevent the typical cases of itchy, uncomfortable, weeklong rashes and mild fevers, and the rarer cases of serious illness caused by the virus.

Before receiving approval from FDA, researchers tested Varivax in about 11,000 children and adults. Scientists predict that it will be

70 to 90 percent effective in preventing the disease. Of those who did get chickenpox after vaccination, almost all had a mild form of the disease.

Adverse reactions to the vaccine were generally mild and included pain, rash, hardness and swelling at the injection site, fever, and generalized rashes.

On April 10, 1995, the American Academy of Pediatrics recommended the vaccine for all healthy children between 12 months and 13 years who have not had chickenpox. For children between 12 and 18 months, the academy recommends giving the vaccine at the same time as the first measles, mumps and rubella shot. Older children should be vaccinated at the earliest convenient time.

A single injection of the vaccine is recommended for children ages 12 months to 12 years, while two injections four to eight weeks apart are recommended for adolescents and adults who have never had chickenpox.

"We're not really sure why teens and adults don't get immunity with one shot," says Krause. "The immune response to a single shot if you're 13 or older is not nearly as good as it is if you're younger. But two shots provide immune responses comparable to what younger people get."

For children, the vaccine has been shown to be safe and effective and can be administered at the same time as the measles, mumps and rubella vaccine. (The MMR vaccine is given at 15 months and again between 4 and 6 years or before junior high or middle school.) Public health officials hope that being able to give the chickenpox vaccine along with an already scheduled vaccine will encourage vaccination.

Benefits of Vaccination

Despite occasional serious reactions from vaccines, for the vast majority of children, benefits of immunity greatly outweigh the risks.

Before any vaccine is licensed by FDA, it has been tested and evaluated thoroughly both in the laboratory and in clinical trials. Besides reviewing scientific studies on vaccines before licensing them, the agency is involved in basic research leading to the development of new and safer products. The acellular pertussis vaccine, for example, was developed in part based on research by FDA scientists.

Agency scientists have developed methods to test vaccines in the laboratory before using them on children. They have also developed accurate methods for testing those children to see if they have appropriate immune responses to new vaccines.

FDA continues to encourage the timely inoculation of all children in this country against childhood diseases, and to make sure those vaccines are as safe and effective as possible.

Vaccines and the Law

In 1986, Congress passed the National Childhood Vaccine Injury Act to help ensure vaccine safety and availability, and to compensate people injured by vaccination. The act established the National Vaccine Injury Compensation Program to compensate those who suffer certain vaccine-related injuries or death. The act also required health-care providers and manufacturers of specified vaccines to report certain serious adverse reactions they encounter. FDA and CDC keep track of these reports through the Vaccine Adverse Event Reporting System, or VAERS.

VAERS tracks serious vaccine reactions, not common fevers and soreness from shots. Serious reactions include death, life-threatening illness, hospitalization, and disability resulting from a vaccine. Patient identity is kept confidential.

Monthly reports from VAERS are sent to FDA's Center for Biologics Evaluation and Research, which evaluates possible safety issues. Anyone may file a report. To receive a VAERS reporting form, call (1-800) 822-7967.

From its beginning to September 1993, VAERS received more than 20,000 reports. Though it helps in assessing the number of adverse reactions to vaccines nationwide, VAERS is a "passive" system that relies on reporting from health-care professionals and others. For instance, VAERS does not directly compare the incidence of disease among recently vaccinated people with disease among people who have not been vaccinated.

The National Vaccine Injury Compensation Program protects doctors and manufacturers from lawsuits while providing compensation for those injured from vaccines. It's designed to be easier and faster than traditional legal remedies for medical injuries.

Individuals claiming more than $1,000 in expenses from vaccine injury may be eligible for as much as $250,000 compensation. Any death from a vaccine is awarded the highest amount in compensation.

Some injuries may be compensated without proof that the vaccine was at fault. These are spelled out in a vaccine injury table. Most injuries must occur within hours or days of a vaccine to be considered a result of the shot. For more information about what injuries may be compensated, call (1-800) 338-2382.

Immunization ... Not Just Kids' Stuff

As the U.S. population ages, increasing levels of adult immunization—particularly against influenza and pneumococcal disease—is taking on critical importance. Influenza and pneumonia combined remain the fifth leading cause of death among elderly persons. Both influenza and *Streptococcus pneumoniae*, the most common cause of pneumonia leading to hospitalization, may be preventable by vaccination. Indeed, the National Institute on Aging promotes the vaccine to prevent pneumococcal disease with this simple message: "It's Worth a Shot." The same can be said for other adult immunizations.

In its 1994 report on the status of adult immunization, the National Vaccine Advisory Committee (NVAC) cited the fewer than 500 deaths annually from vaccine-preventable diseases of childhood. By comparison, as many as 50,000 to 70,000 adults die each year of complications of influenza, pneumococcal infections, and hepatitis B.

According to the draft Adult Immunization Action Plan of the Department of Health and Human Services (HHS), the annual cost of complications due to influenza, pneumococcal infections, hepatitis B, and other vaccine-preventable diseases of adults tops $10 billion, not including the value of years of life lost. In sum, shots save lives. They can help avoid needless suffering and unnecessary costs caused by complications from various infectious diseases, and, as many family members and health-care workers know, they can prevent infection of others. However, despite the availability of safe and effective vaccines, a substantial portion of susceptible adults are not being immunized.

For shots to work, however, people have to roll up their sleeves and get them. The Adult Immunization Action Plan, which follows the NVAC 1994 report cited above, will be coordinated by the HHS National Vaccine Program Office. The plan identifies five goals and specific action steps for HHS agencies to address the high mortality from vaccine-preventable diseases and the low immunization coverage levels among adults in the United States. The goals are to increase the demand for adult vaccination by improving provider and public awareness; increase the capacity of the health care delivery system to deliver vaccines effectively to adults; expand financing mechanisms to support the increased delivery of vaccines to adults; monitor and improve the performance of the Nation's immunization program; and enhance the capability and capacity to conduct research on vaccine-preventable diseases of adults, adult vaccines, adult immunization practices, new and improved vaccines, and international programs for adult immunization. HHS also emphasizes continued vigilance in childhood immunization.

Who Should Get Shots?

Unlike childhood immunization, adult immunization has no statutory requirements. Different vaccines have different target groups among adults. From the annual flu shot to the once-in-a-lifetime pneumoccocal vaccine, shots for adults vary in terms of when they are given and how often (for the Adult Immunization Schedule, see http://www.cdc.gov/nip/adult.htm). The *Guide to Clinical Preventive Services, 2nd edition*, a report of the U.S. Preventive Services Task Force, provides recommendations covering adult immunizations against influenza, pneumococcal disease, tetanus, and diphtheria; measles, mumps, and rubella; hepatitis B; hepatitis A; and varicella. Other government and professional organizations have issued adult immunization guidelines. The Advisory Committee on Immunization Practices sets Federal vaccine policy, which differs very little from guidelines published by the American College of Physicians/Infectious Disease Society of America, the American Academy of Pediatrics, and the American Academy of Family Physicians. The American College of Obstetricians and Gynecologists has issued detailed guidelines on the use of vaccines during pregnancy.

Everyone aged 65 and older should get the pneumococcal vaccine once; some experts say anytime after age 50. Anyone over the age of 2 years with a chronic disease or a weak immune system also should get the vaccine. One shot lasts most people a lifetime although some people may need revaccination upon their physician's advice. The shot does not protect against viral pneumonia or other pneumonia-causing bacteria.

Influenza vaccine, unlike the pneumococcal vaccine, must be given every year: each season's vaccine is especially tailored to that season's viruses. Recommendations are essentially the same as the pneumococcal vaccination—everyone aged 65 and older and anyone over the age of 2 years with a chronic disease or weakened immune system. CDC also recommends the influenza vaccination for pregnant women and for residents of nursing homes, health-care workers, nursing home staff, and volunteers who provide home care to people in the above groups; plus other at-risk groups.

Flu shots are free for beneficiaries who receive them from Medicare-participating physicians. Medicare also covers a vaccination against pneumococcal disease. Public and private groups urge all health insurance plans to include adult coverage for flu, pneumococcal, and hepatitis B shots.

Progress in Flu Immunization

The rates for adult flu immunization are improving: The 1994 National Health Interview Survey, which reports the most recent data, indicates a 55 percent immunization rate, which is approaching the year 2000 target. Medicare reimbursement for flu vaccination, which began in 1993, has helped boost the immunization rate, putting the Nation close to the Healthy People 2000 objective of a 60 percent annual immunization rate for those 65 and older. Preliminary results from HCFA's Horizons Pilot Project, designed specifically to increase the flu vaccination rate among African Americans, indicate an increase in flu immunizations in such target areas as Mississippi. Horizon partners, including Historically Black Colleges and Universities, are using lessons learned from the 1996 flu shot season in their 1997 efforts.

In 1995, the Medicare reimbursement program paid for 11 million shots, resulting in an estimated 5,000 fewer hospitalizations and $25 million in savings to the Medicare program. Still, only half of the Medicare beneficiaries were immunized, with much lower rates among African Americans. HCFA has intensified efforts to reach under-served populations.

Information Is Prevention

Programs for childhood immunization have lowered health care costs and improved the well-being of the Nation's children. The same results can be realized for adults. Vaccine-preventable diseases are significant adult health problems, and vaccines for adults are available, safe, and effective.

As the HHS Adult Immunization Action Plan indicates, disseminating information in print, on the air, and electronically is not the only strategy to be pursued. Changes in clinical practice, increased financial support, improved surveillance, and support for research are needed. Certainly, the programs under way prove, "It's Never Too Late To Immunize."

It's Never Too Late ... To Immunize for Chickenpox

Adults who get chickenpox (varicella) are at much greater risk of complications and death than children. According to the Centers for Disease Control and Prevention (CDC), three women have died this year [1997] of chickenpox after being infected by young children. Although more than 95 percent of adult Americans have had this highly contagious disease, adults who are not sure should be tested and vaccinated.

CDC's Advisory Committee on Immunization Practices recommends that all children be vaccinated at 12 to 18 months of age. Vaccination also is approved for children under 13 who have not had chickenpox and for people over 13 who come in close contact with persons at high risk for serious complications (health-care workers and family contacts of people whose immune systems are suppressed, such as AIDS and cancer patients).

For more information about vaccine-preventable diseases, contact CDC's National Immunization Hotline at (800) 232-2522 (English) or (800) 232-0233 (Spanish).

Adults Need Tetanus Shots, Too

Kathleen Bedford had her 15 minutes of fame in a hospital lecture room full of medical students when she was 65. Because there are only about two cases of tetanus a year in the eastern part of England where she lives, the hospital held a special session for the students. For most of them, it was their first—and maybe their last—opportunity to observe someone with the infection. With her injured leg suspended in a protective frame, Bedford was the center of attention. She would have preferred celebrity in some other way.

Bedford pierced the calf of her leg with a pitchfork crusted with dirt in a freak gardening accident. She was rushed to the emergency room. Her leg was bandaged from ankle to thigh, but she received no further treatment.

When she returned to the emergency room 24 hours later, feeling quite ill, the leg was highly inflamed. After the surgeon on duty took one horrified look at her leg, he rushed her to the operating room and cut her calf open deeply across the puncture site to expose the wound to air. During the next six weeks, the wound had to remain open; hence the frame. Bedford recalls she was treated with "all kinds of pills and shots" and escaped any secondary infection, such as pneumonia.

She experienced only one tetanus symptom—transitory stiffness. But the disease could have been avoided had she been properly immunized. Like many other older adults, Bedford had neglected to keep up her immunity to tetanus with periodic booster doses of tetanus vaccine.

'Lockjaw' Symptoms

Tetanus is an acute, often fatal disease that occurs worldwide. It affects the central nervous system, producing both the stiffness or muscular rigidity that Bedford experienced and convulsive muscle spasm. Tetanus can be localized, with muscle contractions in the part of the body where the infection began, or it can be generalized, affecting the whole body. About 80 percent of reported tetanus cases are generalized. The incubation period ranges from 2 to 50 days, but symptoms usually occur 5 to 10 days after infection. The shorter the incubation period, the greater the chance of death. The most frequent symptom is a stiff jaw, caused by spasm of the muscle that closes the mouth—accounting for the disease's familiar name "lockjaw." Muscle stiffness all over the body may follow. An infected person may also have other symptoms: difficulty swallowing, restlessness and irritability, stiff neck, arms or legs, fever, headache, and sore throat. As the disease progresses, the victim may develop a fixed smile and raised eyebrows due to facial muscle spasms. Spasms of the diaphragm and the muscles between the ribs may interfere with breathing, often requiring mechanical ventilation. The abdominal or back muscles may become rigid. In severe cases, patients may become so sensitive to any kind of disturbance that they suffer painful spasms all over their bodies with profuse sweating if the bed is jarred or if they feel a draft or hear a noise. Convulsions can be severe enough to break bones.

Hyperactivity of the autonomic (involuntary) nervous system may raise blood pressure dangerously or cause heart arrhythmias (irregular beats). Although tetanus victims can usually think clearly when conscious, coma may follow repeated spasms. Aspiration pneumonia is a common late complication and is found in 50 to 70 percent of autopsied cases. The mortality rate is about 25 percent in the United States and 50 percent worldwide.

Bacterial Cause

The bacteria that cause tetanus belong to the Clostridium family, also responsible for some other serious diseases, such as botulism and the type of gangrene suffered in war wounds. Clostridia bacteria are what scientists call "obligate anaerobic"—that is, they thrive only in the absence of oxygen. They also form spores, reproductive cells with thick walls that enable them to withstand unfavorable environmental conditions. Spores are tough to kill and highly resistant to heat and the usual antiseptics that treat wounds.

Tetanus bacteria may enter the body through a puncture wound or scratch. In the presence of dead tissue, tetanus spores reproduce and manufacture a poison (exotoxin) that travels through the body and causes tetanus symptoms. Though tetanus bacteria are found everywhere in the environment—in soil, street dust, and in animal intestines and feces—natural immunity to the disease is rare. This is why immunization is so important.

Vaccination with tetanus toxoid (tetanus vaccine) causes the body to respond to an inactivated form of the tetanus toxin by developing antibodies to tetanus. Tetanus toxoid is virtually 100 percent effective in preventing tetanus. It is prepared by growing tetanus bacteria (*Clostridium tetani*) in a special medium, and then detoxifying the resulting tetanus toxin with formaldehyde. The Food and Drug Administration reviews the manufacturer's testing records for each lot of vaccine to ensure that the product is safe and effective for its intended use. FDA also sometimes tests random lots to ensure that the manufacturer's testing records are accurate.

Side effects of vaccination are few. As with the DTP shot received by children (to immunize against diphtheria, tetanus, and pertussis), redness or formation of a small hard lump at the vaccination site are possible. Some individuals may have allergic reactions, such as hives, skin rash, or itching. More serious adverse reactions include the rare cases of anaphylaxis (an allergic reaction involving difficulty in breathing or swallowing and facial swelling that can be fatal) and possibly Guillain-Barré syndrome, a nerve inflammation. People who have had a severe reaction to the vaccine should not receive further doses.

Adult Immunizations

Some individuals may be protected for life against tetanus after a properly administered primary series of vaccinations, but in most people antitoxin levels fall with time. Adults should receive booster doses every 10 years, along with diphtheria immunization. "We are now recommending an adult immunization visit at age 50 years," says CDC's Roland Sutter, M.D., "when people can check their records to see if they are actually up-to-date with vaccinations, particularly for Td. Quite a number of older persons haven't received the primary series. If they haven't been immunized, this visit serves as an opportunity to initiate the series."

When given to adults, the first two primary doses of Td are administered at least four weeks apart, and the third dose is administered 6 to 12 months after the second. In some individuals, antibody levels may fall too low to provide protection before 10 years have passed. That's why people who sustain a deep or contaminated wound should receive a booster dose if it has been more than five years since the last dose. Immunization is especially recommended for:

- adults, especially those 50 years and older, because most of the tetanus cases in recent years have occurred in this age group

- persons who are not sure whether they have received the initial series of tetanus shots or boosters

- travelers, especially to countries with hot, damp climates and soil rich in organic matter

- agricultural workers and others who work with dirt or manure

- persons whose jobs or recreational activities expose them to cuts and scrapes

- those who are recovering from tetanus, because having a case of tetanus does not confer lasting immunity, as is true for some other diseases

- injured persons who may require emergency tetanus treatment depending on their immunization status (primary immunization, boosters) and the type of wound received

- pregnant women who have not been immunized or may be inadequately immunized or who may deliver their infants in unhygienic circumstances. After immunization, antibodies to the disease are passed from the mother to the fetus through the placenta.

Beyond Rusty Nails

The connection between a wound caused by a rusty/dirty nail and the necessity for a tetanus shot is fixed so firmly in the public mind that even the television cartoon character Homer Simpson knew he had to get a tetanus shot after stepping on a nail. But people don't realize that tetanus can be contracted in other ways. Any puncture wound, especially one that is deep, can be infected with tetanus. Some seamstresses have contracted tetanus from sewing needles. Animal scratches and bites, and other wounds contaminated by both human and animal feces and saliva, are potential breeding grounds for tetanus bacteria. Infection can develop in wounds in which the flesh is torn or burned, or in wounds resulting from projectiles, such as arrows, bullets or shrapnel, or in those caused by crushing or frostbite. The disease may follow trivial wounds caused by thorns or splinters, as well as highly contaminated wounds, if oxygen is unable to reach the injured tissues. Tetanus can also develop after surgery, dental infections, and abortion. Cephalic tetanus, a rare form of the disease, is associated with chronic ear infections, in which tetanus bacteria are present in the inner ear. Tetanus has also been reported in people with no known acute injury, chronic wound, or other medical condition.

In developing countries, tetanus is a major health problem. Childbirth may take place under unsanitary conditions, causing infection in the uterus afterwards. Tetanus in newborns has emerged worldwide as the predominant form of tetanus, as the baby's umbilical stump is often sealed with mud or clay or other contaminated substances. CDC's *Morbidity and Mortality Weekly Report* of May 6, 1994, discusses two cases of tetanus that occurred in Kansas in 1993—the first cases reported in that state since 1987—that show the importance of immunization.

The first case involved an 82-year-old man, hospitalized because of shortness of breath and weakness and difficulty chewing and swallowing. When doctors examined him, they found he had difficulty opening his jaw and noted an abrasion on his right elbow resulting from a fall two days earlier. He had never been vaccinated. Doctors administered both tetanus toxoid and tetanus immune globulin (TIG). (An injection of tetanus toxoid after the injury does not give immediate full immunity. TIG confers temporary immunity to those people who have low or no immunity to tetanus toxin by providing antitoxin directly to the body, ensuring that protective levels of antitoxin are reached quickly rather than waiting for the body's immune response.) In the next few weeks, his body was racked by spasms, followed by respiratory failure and pneumonia, which necessitated the use of a breathing machine. After treatment with antibiotics, diuretics, and neuromuscular blocking agents, he recovered and was discharged a few weeks later.

The second case involved a diabetic 57-year-old man who had stepped on a rusty nail and sought emergency treatment for tetanus that same day. Hospital personnel cleaned the wound and administered tetanus toxoid. Four days later, he returned to the emergency department complaining of severe pain in the foot, as well as chills, fever and vomiting. When he developed pain and a stiff neck, he was hospitalized immediately with a diagnosis of tetanus and received TIG. After a number of life-threatening heart and lung problems, he died following an episode of cardiac arrest. His relatives reported that he had not been previously vaccinated with tetanus toxoid.

The surviving and the deceased tetanus victims each spent about a month in the hospital and ran up medical bills of about $150,000 apiece. At that time, public health clients could have received a tetanus shot for $3.30, while vaccination with a private physician would have cost just a few dollars more.

Tetanus has become a rare disease in the United States as well as in England, with only 36 reported U.S. cases in 1994, though there may be more unreported cases. The disease has become uncommon not because tetanus bacteria have been eliminated from the environment—they're still all around us—but because immunization has provided protection.

Since adults 50 years or older account for 70 percent of tetanus infections, mature people should make certain they have received boosters within the last 10 years. If they don't know whether they were immunized as children, the primary series of shots should be completed.

How FDA Works to Ensure Vaccine Safety

The gasping for breath and desperate hacking of whooping cough. The iron lungs and braces of polio. Birth defects from rubella. For many people today, those signs of terrible diseases are the stuff of history books, thanks to vaccines. But the rare case of vaccine-associated polio or the death of an infant soon after receiving a dose of pertussis vaccine may make people wonder—are vaccines safe enough, or could they be safer?

For the Food and Drug Administration's Center for Biologics Evaluation and Research (CBER), vaccine safety, along with effectiveness, is central to regulation of these preparations.

Clinical Trials

The first step to licensing a new vaccine is safety testing in animals. If the laboratory animals immunized with the vaccine don't have serious reactions, FDA consults with the vaccine manufacturer or sponsor on further refining of the manufacturing process.

Because the weakened viruses used for vaccines are grown in animal or human cells, "we spend a tremendous amount of time studying the safety of those cells," says M. Carolyn Hardegree, M.D., director of CBER'S office of vaccine research and review.

For example, the manufacturer of the recently licensed Varicella (chickenpox) vaccine had to prove the human cell line used to grow the virus was not contaminated with any other viruses, such as hepatitis.

Only after those studies have been done does testing in people begin. FDA requires new vaccines to undergo several phases of clinical trials—testing in people—for safety and effectiveness.

Phase 1 trials evaluate basic safety and identify only very serious or very common adverse events. These trials are small—between 20 and 100 patients—and last just several months.

Phase 2 trials include several hundred patients and last anywhere from several months to two years. This allows for more information on safety and preliminary information on effectiveness to be collected.

Unless severe reactions or a lack of effectiveness surfaces during the first two phases, the trials are expanded in Phase 3 to include several hundred to several thousand people. These trials continue to measure effectiveness and safety.

If, towards or at the end of the Phase 3 trials, the manufacturer believes there are adequate data to show that the vaccine is safe and effective for its intended use, the manufacturer applies to FDA for two licenses—one for the vaccine (product license) and one for the manufacturing plant (establishment license).

An internal FDA committee then reviews the clinical data, proposed labeling, and manufacturing protocols that ensure a consistent product, and the results of the agency's own confirmatory tests of the vaccine's components and the final product. The review process includes an inspection of the manufacturing facility.

Advisory Committees

FDA advisory committees are groups of experts outside government that review data and issues associated with products and recommend what action the agency should take.

"Advisory committees may be brought in at any stage in the review process," says Hardegree. "For example, before we went into Phase 1 trials of some of the first AIDS vaccines, we showed the [proposed studies] to the Vaccines and Related Biological Products Advisory Committee. As we move into determining what might be appropriate efficacy studies, we might let them see that early on." Involving the committees throughout the process is a good idea, she says, because these expert advisors bring a wealth of scientific background to address vaccine issues confronting FDA.

"Through the years, we've been very fortunate to have an outstanding advisory group," says Hardegree. "We've had members who have been willing to serve as consultants for many years after their four-year term, and they provide a continuity on some of the issues that were discussed years ago and are still being studied today." Committee recommendations are not binding on FDA, but the agency considers them carefully when deciding whether to license a vaccine for marketing.

Green Light

Licensing of a vaccine is only the beginning of FDA's oversight. Manufacturers must submit samples of each vaccine lot and results of their own tests for potency, safety, and purity to the agency before release.

Each lot must be tested because vaccines are derived from living organisms that are sensitive to environmental factors and are susceptible to contamination.

"Tests generally applicable to all products include those for bacterial and fungal sterility, general safety, purity, identity, suitability of constituent materials, and potency," explains Hardegree. "Sterility testing is performed on both bulk- and final-container material. In addition, cell-culture-derived vaccines must be tested for [disease-causing organisms]. All ingredients such as diluents, preservatives or adjuvants must meet generally accepted standards of purity."

The importance of these tests was established years ago. In 1955, the virus-inactivated Salk polio vaccine first went on the market. Unfortunately, virus in some batches of the vaccine produced by one manufacturer was not totally inactivated, and some of the children who got that vaccine developed polio.

Inadequate tests were the culprit, explains Hardegree.

The tests manufacturers must perform on each lot are spelled out in the *Code of Federal Regulations* or in the product license application. When the manufacturer sends the lot samples, along with the results of testing, to FDA, "we either test the lot sample ourselves or go with the manufacturer's documentation," says Jerome A. Donlon, M.D., Ph.D., director of CBER's office of establishment licensing and product surveillance. With vaccines for diseases that attack the nervous system, such as the live polio vaccine, "we test every lot because of the tremendous potential for harm," he explains. Over the last 10 years, there have been only three vaccine recalls. One lot was recalled after FDA detected particulates; another was mislabeled. The third lot was recalled because of potential problems after an FDA inspection found violations of good manufacturing practices at the production plant.

Assessing Risks with Polio Vaccines

In 1955, the year the polio vaccine was licensed, an individual lot of that vaccine infected 60 people directly and 89 who came in contact with them because the manufacturer had failed to totally inactivate the virus. But, as awful as that was, parents of other children weren't deterred from having their children vaccinated.

"When a disease is rampant, the public will accept high-risk products," says Jerome A. Donlon, M.D., Ph.D., director of CBER's office of establishment licensing and product surveillance.

There have been no reported cases of paralysis caused by naturally occurring polio virus in the United States since 1979. However, according to the national Centers for Disease Control and Prevention's Advisory Committee on Immunization Practices, about six to eight people get polio from the live vaccine each year.

Unlike the vaccine-associated cases in 1955, these modern cases are not caused by manufacturing failures. Instead, most of the cases are in people with previously undetected immune deficiencies.

The problem is that the virus, though weakened, is still active. The committee has recommended a new polio vaccination policy that will include a greatly enhanced role for inactivated (killed) polio vaccine.

Continuing Studies

Although clinical trials are carefully designed to uncover potential adverse reactions before FDA licenses a vaccine, "we obviously can't get all the information premarketing," says Susan Ellenberg, Ph.D., director of CBER's division of biostatistics and epidemiology. "You're never going to be able to do studies big enough to detect risks that might happen at a level of one in 100,000 or one in 1 million. We'd never get vaccines on the market. Still, such risks are important to detect because of the large population exposed. So we have to develop postmarketing surveillance programs."

For some vaccines, there are formal Phase 4 studies under way. At FDA's request, the manufacturer of the new chickenpox vaccine, licensed by FDA March 17, 1995, will monitor several thousand vaccinated children for 15 years to determine the long-term effects of the vaccine and possible need for a booster immunization.

For most vaccines, the government relies on the Vaccine Adverse Event Reporting System (VAERS) to identify problems after marketing begins.

FDA and the national Centers for Disease Control and Prevention manage VAERS, a system the two agencies developed in response to the National Childhood Vaccine Injury Act of 1986. Anyone—physicians, vaccine manufacturers, patients, or the parents of a patient—can report to VAERS an adverse event that may be associated with any vaccine.

"What we're most interested in with VAERS is identifying any new problem, particularly serious problems, that might be so rare that it wasn't noticed or detected during the clinical trials," says Ellenberg.

However, many events that might be associated with vaccines go unreported. "We don't have to have 100 percent reporting," says Donlon. Ellenberg agrees. Still, she adds, "We need enough reports to permit detection of rare events and to allow us to make reliable comparisons of reporting rates among vaccine lots. Our ability to do this improves if doctors make more reports and make them more timely."

Donlon points out that the report of an adverse event to VAERS is not documentation that a vaccine caused the event. He says doctors shouldn't make that judgment.

"Just report it," he says, "even if you've never seen it before. Maybe many others around the country are seeing the same thing."

For example, a mother recently called FDA because her child's hair had fallen out each time the child received a dose of the hepatitis B vaccine. The mother said she asked the pediatrician whether the vaccine could have caused the hair loss, but the pediatrician was sure that couldn't be the case. In fact, after the second dose of the vaccine and subsequent hair loss, the doctor was preparing to do a scalp biopsy to determine the cause.

A search of the VAERS database found 45 cases of hair loss after hepatitis B vaccination. Of those, 15 cases were like this one, in which hair loss happened after each of two doses of the vaccine.

"That's called 'positive rechallenge,'" says Ellenberg, "and it gives you a much stronger belief that the event was actually due to the product. Now, hair falling out is not a life-threatening event. But if people are aware it could happen, then they won't be imagining the worst, and invasive, unnecessary tests may not have to be performed."

Besides identifying previously unknown adverse events, VAERS is an important tool for monitoring individual lots of vaccines. "We don't expect there to be problems with vaccine lots," says Ellenberg, "because the regulations are very stringent. But even though we don't expect to find anything, we look [at the reports to VAERS] every week, and if there really was a problem with a lot, we could move very rapidly to get that lot off the market.

"One of the first things we do if we see a lot that has an elevated number of adverse events is look at its "sister" lots, the other lots that came from the same larger bulk lot. If those lots also have high rates of adverse events, it would raise our level of suspicion that there might be a problem. If, however, the other lots had average or even low rates we would feel that this is just more likely chance variation."

Another key factor to assess the significance of the number of adverse events is the size of the lot.

"A lot with hundreds of thousands of doses is going to be associated with more events than a lot with tens of thousands of doses," says Ellenberg.

VAERS is designed to detect signals or warnings that there might be a problem rather than to answer questions about what caused the adverse event, according to "Research Strategies for Assessing Adverse Events Associated with Vaccines," a 1994 report by the Institute of Medicine. These signals can lead to hypotheses about causality, which can then be tested by other methods, such as epidemiologic or laboratory studies.

Developing New Pertussis Vaccines

Recent results of pertussis (whooping cough) vaccine clinical trials show that three experimental vaccines are highly effective in infants.

The trials were sponsored by the National Institute of Allergy and Infectious Disease (NIAID), part of the National Institutes of Health, in Bethesda, Md., and conducted in Italy and Sweden. The results also showed that the experimental vaccines caused fewer side effects than a vaccine currently used in the United States.

Scientists in FDA's Center for Biologics Evaluation and Research have been instrumental in developing and evaluating acellular vaccines, such as those tested in Italy and Sweden, and have collaborated with NIAID and the vaccine manufacturers to design the European trials.

Acellular vaccines contain only the parts of the pertussis bacterium thought to be important for immunity. U.S. vaccines licensed for use in infants are called whole-cell vaccines, because they contain the whole, inactivated pertussis organism.

Seizures were reported rarely in the trials, but no more frequently in any of the pertussis vaccine groups than in the control group. Side effects, such as redness, pain and swelling at the site of the injection, fever, and protracted crying, were reported less commonly with the acellular vaccines than with the whole-cell one.

FDA has made special efforts to encourage manufacturers to submit applications for the use of acellular pertussis vaccines in infants. The agency will target such applications for complete review within six months of receiving them. However, actual times to any licensing can vary, depending on the quality and completeness of the data submitted.

FDA recommends that parents continue to have their children vaccinated against pertussis with available vaccines.

All vaccines pose some risks of side effects, but for both whole-cell and acellular pertussis vaccines, serious, long-lasting problems are extremely rare. Pertussis itself can be fatal.

Background Rates Cause Confusion

"The problem with any vaccine that's given to very young children is that there are a lot of background adverse events occurring in the first year of life," says Ellenberg. A reaction thought to be due to a vaccine may actually have been from something else, such as an ear infection, explains Hardegree.

Children less than a year old are at greatest risk for high fevers, seizures, and sudden infant death syndrome (SIDS). These events are seen both in the presence and absence of vaccination. The SIDS death rate is approximately 1.3 per 1,000 live births during the first year of life, according to Ellenberg. During that same period, babies receive the DPT vaccine three times—at 2, 4 and 6 months.

"You don't have to be a mathematician to appreciate the fact that, by chance, SIDS will sometimes occur shortly after the vaccine was administered," says Ellenberg. "The calculations that we have been able to do suggest that the numbers of SIDS following vaccination that have been reported to VAERS are not beyond what would be expected by chance. And there have been some well-conducted, focused studies that demonstrate that SIDS is not associated with DPT vaccination. But, on the basis of VAERS data alone, we don't have proof that vaccines are *not* contributing to these problems and we certainly don't have proof that they *are* contributing."

Adding to the confusion is the fact that DPT is only one of many infant vaccines. The recommended childhood immunization schedule includes vaccines for hepatitis B, Haemophilus b, measles, mumps, rubella, and polio, all during the first 12 months.

At the other end of the age spectrum, deaths are also reported after administration of the influenza vaccine. "Often these vaccines are given to people in nursing homes," explains Ellenberg. Unfortunately, this population has a relatively high death rate anyway, so it's almost impossible to say whether a given death is associated with the vaccine, she says.

As inevitable as some of those deaths, as well as other adverse events, may be, FDA remains vigilant in its efforts to improve vaccine safety. The agency will continue to be aggressive, says Hardegree, in its efforts, along with manufacturers and other government agencies, to get safer vaccines on the market.

Select Immunization Resources

Adult Immunization Schedule
(800) 232-2522
http://www.cdc.gov/nip/adult.htm

All Kids Count
(404) 371-0466; (404) 371-1087 (Fax)
http://www.allkidscount.org

American Academy of Pediatrics
(800) 433-9016
National Headquarters:
(847) 228-5005; (847) 228-5097 (Fax)
Email: kidsdocs@aap.org
http://www.aap.org

Every Child by Two
(202) 651-7226; (202) 651-7001 (Fax)
Email: ECBT@ana.org
http://www.ecbt.org

Immunization Action Coalition
(612) 647-9009; (612) 647-9131 (Fax)
Email: editor@immunize.org
http://www.immunize.org/

Manual for the Surveillance of Vaccine-Preventable Diseases
Go to http://www.dynares.com/nip/manual. htm for links to the first four
(of five) sections of the Manual for the *Surveillance of Vaccine-Preventable Diseases* and for access to other materials. The manual can be used
by nurses, physicians, sanitarians, infection control practitioners,
laboratorians, epidemiologists, disease reporters, and others involved in
surveillance and reporting. A fifth section of the manual, not on the web
site, contains appendixes, including worksheets, reporting forms, *MMWR*
documents, immunization program manager and epidemiology program
office phone lists, and other reference documents. A print copy (including appendixes) may be ordered from the:

National Immunization Program,
Information and Distribution Center,
fax: (404) 639-8828;
Email: nipinfo@cdc.gov.

Medicare Billing Made Easy for Influenza and Pneumococcal Pneumonia Vaccinations Informational Kit
Health Care Financing Administration
(703) 920-1234

Morbidity and Mortality Weekly Report
http://www.cdc.gov/epo.mmwr/mmwr.html

National Child Care Information Center
(800) 616-2242
Email: Anne Goldstein, Director, at agoldstein@acf.dhhs.gov
http://ericps.ed.uiuc.edu/nccic/abtnccic.html

National Council of La Raza
(202) 785-1670
http://www.hispanic.org/nclr.htm

National Immunization Program
Centers for Disease Control and Prevention
(800) CDC-SHOT
http://www.cdc.gov/nip/default2.htm

National Institute on Aging
http://www.nih.gov/nia/

National Institute on Aging Information Center
(800) 222-2225
Email: niainfo@access.digex.net

To receive a free copy of the *1997 Resource Guide for Adult Immunization* or a free brochure on the *1997 Campaign Kit* (kit is $10.95), contact:

National Coalition for Adult Immunization
4733 Bethesda Avenue, Suite 750
Bethesda, MD 20814-5228
(301) 907-0878 (Fax)
Email: adultimm@aol.com
http://www.medscape.com/Affiliates/NCAI/

Vacunas desde la cuna (National Hispanic Immunization Hotline)
(800) 232-0233

Chapter 5

Recommended Preventive Services: Screening Tests and Clinician Counseling

Implementing Preventive Care

Never has preventive health care been more important than today. Many of the most serious disorders encountered in clinical practice can be prevented or postponed by immunizations, chemoprophylaxis, and healthier life-styles, or detected early with screening and treated effectively. To an unprecedented extent, clinicians now have the opportunities, skills, and resources to prevent disease and promote health as well as to cure disease.

However, preventive care has also never been more complex. The yearly physical examination, a reassuringly simple but relatively ineffective ritual, has been supplanted by a shifting array of tests, immunizations, prophylactic medications, and counseling interventions— many of which have not been a part of traditional training curricula. In addition, differing sets of preventive services are recommended by

Selected excerpts from *Clinician's Handbook of Preventive Services*, Put Prevention Into Practice, U.S. Department of Health and Human Services, Public Health Service, 1994. Screening tests and counseling considerations selected for inclusion in this chapter were chosen on the basis of their recommendation by the U.S. Preventive Services Task Force (excluding recommendations for pregnant women and newborns) as reported in the *Guide to Clinical Preventive Services, Second Edition*, U.S. Department of Health and Human Services, Office of Public Health and Science, Office of Disease Prevention and Health Promotion, 1996. Neither the Public Health Service nor the U.S. Department of Health and Human Services endorses any particular organization or its activities, products, or service.

government agencies, professional organizations, voluntary associations, and academic experts, which may lead to confusion on the part of clinicians.

In the face of these perceived contradictions, it is important to emphasize that there is basic agreement among authorities about recommendations for most types of preventive care. This is illustrated in Figure 5.1 and Figure 5.2, in which the preventive care recommendations of major U.S. authorities are summarized in a timeline format. The dark bars in these timelines denote agreement among all major U.S. authorities; the light bars denote agreement among some, but not all, major U.S. authorities.

The delivery of preventive care, even for services on which all authorities agree, is far from satisfactory. For example, the vaccination rate of adults 65 and older against pneumococcal infections is only about 20%. Delivery rates are also low for other basic types of preventive care—often less than 50%. There are multiple reasons for these poor rates, including: lack of clinician time, often related to inadequate reimbursement; lack of clinician interest and knowledge; lack of patient involvement and knowledge; and lack of office or clinic systems to promote preventive care. Some of these factors are beyond the control of the practicing clinician, but many are not. There is much that clinicians can do to help ensure that their patients receive the preventive care they need.

[In the text that follows] every effort has been made to ensure that the listings in the "Recommendations of Major Authorities" sections accurately represent the current positions of these authorities. Recommendations are listed alphabetically by organization. Similar recommendations are often grouped together to facilitate comparisons by the reader. Appearance in the *Clinician's Handbook* does not necessarily imply endorsement of a specific authority or its recommendations by either the U.S. Department of Health and Human Services or the Public Health Service; readers are encouraged to evaluate the scientific basis for individual recommendations. Similarly, the citation of a group's recommendations does not imply that the group has endorsed the *Clinician's Handbook* or its contents. A complete listing of authorities cited may be found at the end of this chapter.

The sections on the "Basics of..." how to perform each type of preventive service have been prepared using a numerical, stepwise format that generally reflects the temporal sequence of decision-making in patient care, not order of importance. Thus, issues regarding whether a preventive service should be performed are addressed initially, the specifics of how to perform the service follow, and a discussion of the

76

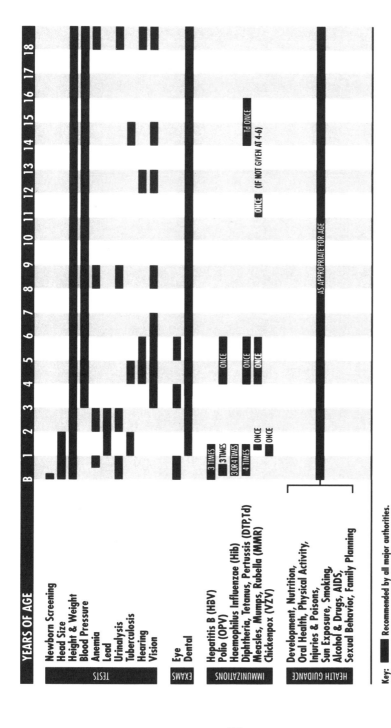

Figure 5.1. Child Preventive Care Timeline: Recommendations of Major Authorities.

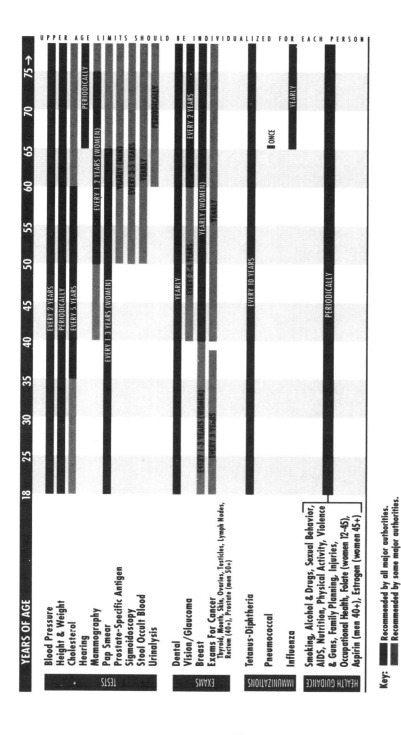

Figure 5.2. Adult Preventive Care Timeline: Recommendations of Major Authorities.

follow-up care and potential adverse effects conclude each section. Steps for the work-up of abnormalities detected by screening tests are generally not included.

In some cases, the data supporting the optimal method of performing a particular preventive procedure are scant or absent. This is especially true for some physical examination and counseling procedures. Often, expert opinion has been relied on for guidance. In these situations, conditional language is generally used, such as "some authorities believe...". The reader is urged to consider information of this type provisional in nature and subject to revision as research progresses.

The items listed in the "Patient (or Family) Resources" sections have been selected after an extensive review of materials solicited from government agencies and professional and voluntary organizations. However, there are undoubtedly other, equally useful publications that have not been included. The materials listed here are provided as a starting point for clinicians in building a library of high-quality literature and resources for patients. The availability of these materials and correctness of ordering instructions have been verified. Appropriateness in any specific case must be determined by the individual clinician.

Alcohol and Other Drug Abuse

Substance abuse is the harmful or hazardous use of alcohol, tobacco, or other (legal and illegal) drugs. It is a leading cause of premature and preventable illness, disability, and death in the United States. Alcohol abuse is related to more than half of all traffic fatalities, 67% of drownings and murders, 70% to 80% of deaths in fires, and 35% of suicides. The abuse of alcohol costs society nearly twice as much as all other drugs combined—approximately $85.8 billion annually. This figure includes medical treatment and indirect economic losses, such as reduced worker productivity, early death, and property damage. The emotional costs to alcohol abusers, victims of alcohol-related crimes, and family members are also very high.

The abuse of other drugs costs society approximately $47 billion per year. In 1991, 12.7% of individuals reported currently using illicit drugs, and 37% reported use in the past. Marijuana is used more than once per week by an estimated 4.6 million adults, and nearly 580,000 adults use cocaine one or more times per week. Drug abuse is an increasingly important risk factor for HIV infection. Approximately 27% of HIV-infected patients have injection drug use as a risk factor, either alone or in combination with homosexual activity. In addition to providing a route of entry into the body for the HIV virus, some types of drug use may lower resistance to the HIV virus by impairing cell-mediated immunity.

Primary care providers often fail to recognize alcohol and drug abuse problems in their patients. Some studies report detection rates as low as 30%. Minimal interventions by primary care clinicians, such as advice to modify current use patterns and warnings about adverse health consequences, can have beneficial effects, especially for patients in the early stages of addiction. More intensive interventions, such as referral to outpatient or inpatient treatment facilities, can be life-saving for patients in more advanced stages of alcohol and other drug dependence problems.

Recommendations of Major Authorities

American Academy of Family Physicians and U.S. Preventive Services Task Force—All adults should be asked to describe their use of alcohol and other drugs. Routine measurement of biochemical markers and drug testing is not recommended as the primary method of detecting alcohol and other drug abuse in asymptomatic individuals. Individuals in whom alcohol or drug abuse or dependence is confirmed should receive appropriate counseling, treatment, and referrals. All people who use intoxicating drugs should be counseled about the hazards of operating a motor vehicle or performing other potentially dangerous activities while intoxicated. Injection drug users should be counseled to avoid sharing or using unsterilized needles and syringes.

American College of Obstetricians and Gynecologists—Women should be asked about their use of alcohol and other drugs.

American College of Physicians—The physician's role in recognizing and treating chemical dependence requires knowledge of the symptoms of chronic and excessive drug use and increased sensitivity to and awareness of behavior associated with such problem use. The physician's role in preventing chemical dependency includes patient education and counseling about the appropriate use of substances upon which dependence is likely. Thoughtful and knowledgeable prescribing practices that minimize the likelihood of producing or maintaining iatrogenic chemical dependence are essential.

American Medical Association—All physicians with clinical responsibility for diagnosis of and referral for alcoholism and drug abuse problems should be able to recognize alcohol- or drug-caused dysfunction and should be aware of the medical complications, symptoms, and syndromes with which alcoholism or drug abuse commonly presents. All complete health examinations should include an in-depth history of alcohol and other drug use. The physician should evaluate patient requirements and community resources so that an adequate level of care may be prescribed, with patients' needs matched to appropriate resources and with referrals made to a resource that provides appropriate medical care.

Canadian Task Force on the Periodic Health Examination— Although no single screening instrument has shown optimal accuracy in detecting problem drinking, there is good evidence that case-finding, counseling, and follow-up are effective in managing the problem. Research has indicated that specific questions and approaches may be incorporated into the periodic health examination to raise clinical suspicion and prompt further inquiry; approaches may be combined sequentially to increase either sensitivity or specificity.

Basics of Counseling for Abuse of Alcohol and Other Drugs

Identification

1. *Conducting an alcohol/drug history:* Identifying the patient with substance abuse problems is the necessary first step toward providing help. History-taking should begin with questions about relatively nonthreatening subjects—such as the number of cups of caffeinated beverages the patient drinks per day—before moving on to questions about the types, amounts, duration, and patterns of use of legal and illegal substances. Questions about frequency and quantity are of limited utility in detecting substance abuse because of the tendency of patients to underreport use. However, such questions may be helpful in identifying individuals who drink large quantities (e.g. binge drinkers, who consume 9 or more drinks per occasion). Corroboration of information by family and others who know the patient well may be helpful. Questions about the negative consequences of abuse can also be helpful in assessing the magnitude of the problem. Areas that may be addressed include: driving history, employment history, educational progress, legal problems, family life, social activities, and enrollment in treatment programs. Asking

81

about family history of substance abuse will help the clinician assess the patient's genetic vulnerability. If the patient has made previous attempts to stop or moderate alcohol or drug use, he or she should be asked about the methods, barriers encountered, and degree of success.

2. *Use of brief screening questionnaires:* The use of brief, self-administered screening questionnaires can help identify patients in need of more detailed evaluation. The CAGE questionnaire for alcohol abuse screening [a four-question instrument described in the *Journal of the American Medical Association*, 1984;252:1905-1907] is the shortest of such instruments and has relatively good sensitivity (approximately 85%) and specificity (approximately 89%). The CAGE questions have been recently adapted to include other drugs and evaluated as the CAGEAID questionnaire [see Brown, RL. Identification and office management of alcohol and drug disorders. In: Fleming MF, Barry KL, eds. *Addictive Disorders*. St. Louis, MO: Mosby Year Book; 1992]. A World Health Organization 6-country collaborative project recently developed the 10-item Alcohol Use Disorders Identification Test (AUDIT). In initial testing, this questionnaire has been found to have sensitivity and specificity values of greater than 90%. Some authorities recommend the use of a brief trauma questionnaire, to screen for the frequent injuries that alcoholics sustain. Also available are several excellent but more lengthy screening questionnaires, some self-administered, that may be more appropriate for research and special applications than for routine use in primary care.

3. *Asking about physical symptoms:* The clinician should ask the patient about physical symptoms of substance abuse. Examples include frequent headaches or other chronic tension states, absence from work based on vague physical complaints, insomnia, unexplained mood changes, gastrointestinal disorders, uncontrolled hypertension, impotence and other sexual disorders, and neuropathies.

4. *Physical examination:* The physical examination is a relatively insensitive and nonspecific method of detecting alcohol or drug abuse. Some signs of alcohol abuse include weight gain or loss, labile or refractory hypertension, abnormal skin vascularization, conjunctival injection, tongue or hand tremor,

epigastric tenderness, and hepatomegaly. Damaged nasal mucosa and weight loss may be present with cocaine use. Hypodermic marks may be present with injection drug use. Signs of previous or current trauma are other clues to substance abuse problems.

5. *Laboratory tests:* The use of laboratory tests, such as liver enzymes and erythrocyte mean corpuscular volume, are helpful in evaluating physiological damage, but are not good screening tools for detecting alcohol abuse. Gamma-glutamyl transferase level is the most sensitive biochemic test for alcohol abuse, but even this has a sensitivity of only 25% to 36%. Urine drug screens can help confirm drug use but give no information about the quantity or frequency of the use. An estimated 5% to 30% of positive drug screens are false positives, depending on the drug, the method of analysis, and the population being tested. In general, these tests should not be used as screening tools in the primary care setting, and certainly they should not be used without patient consent.

6. *Screening protocols:* Some authorities recommend combining a variety of different screening approaches into a protocol. An example of such a protocol, adapted from one developed by the National Institute on Alcohol Abuse and Alcoholism, is shown in Figure 5.3.

Counseling

1. *Establishing a therapeutic relationship:* The provider should express genuine concern and maintain an honest, nonjudgmental approach with substance abuse patients. Arguing with, confronting, or labeling the patient should be avoided. An attempt should be made to maintain a partnership with the patient, in which the clinician functions as an expert consultant. Trust is essential; the patient should be assured that information disclosed will be kept confidential to the maximum extent possible.

2. *Making the medical office or clinic off-limits for substance abuse:* This should be true for tobacco, alcohol, and other drugs. Counseling a patient who is under the influence of alcohol or other drugs is not productive and may be counterproductive because of the indirect encouragement it gives to the patient for abuse.

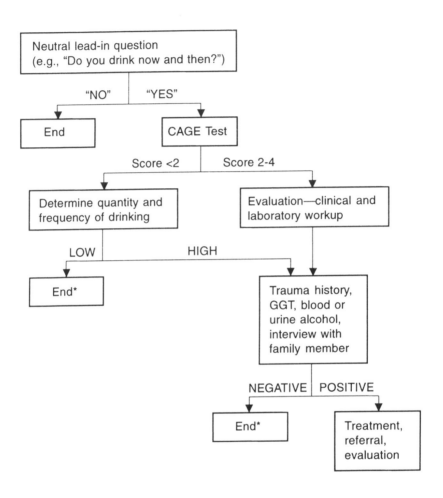

Figure 5.3. *Alcoholism Screening Protocol. *However, follow-up visits may be appropriate. Adapted from: National Institute on Alcohol Abuse and Alcoholism. Seventh Special Report to the U.S. Congress on alcohol and Health. Rockville, MD: U.S. Department of Health and Human Services; 1990. USDHHS Publication ADM 90-1656.*

Such patients should be scheduled for return appointments to occur when they are not under the influence.

3. *Presenting information about negative health consequences:* This should be done in a straightforward, nonjudgmental manner. For example, "Your trouble sleeping, the difficulty in controlling your blood pressure, and the recent problems at home with your family make me concerned that alcohol may be the main problem. I would like to discuss this possibility with you more."

   Injection drug users should be warned about the risk of HIV, hepatitis B, and other disorders from using contaminated or shared needles. Information about cleaning needles with bleach should be provided.

4. *Emphasizing personal responsibility and self-efficacy:* The clinician should convey to the patient a sense of optimism and confidence that he or she can control his or her substance use.

5. *Conveying a clear message and setting goals:* The clinician should communicate clearly, and firmly to the patient a recommendation to stop substance abuse. It may be helpful to assist the patient in setting a date for abstinence or goals for step-wise moderation of substance use. The patient should be helped to anticipate physiologic and psychologic withdrawal symptoms and plan for potential relapses or "slips."

6. *Involving family and other supports:* The assistance and patience of family members can be critical for the success of the patient's efforts at abstinence or moderation. Involving others must be done only with patient consent.

7. *Establish a working relationship with community treatment resources:* Many patients may benefit from the structure provided by peer counseling, support groups, inpatient treatment, and other modalities. The clinician should become familiar with the support and treatment resources available in the community so that appropriate referrals, if needed, can be made.

8. *Providing follow-up:* Monitoring and supporting patient success is essential and desirable, even for patients referred for treatment. Return appointments should be scheduled at regular intervals, particularly during the first weeks of each patient's efforts to stop or moderate use.

Patient Resources

Alcohol: What to Do If It's a Problem for You. American Academy of Family Physicians, 8880 Ward Parkway, Kansas City, MO 64114-2797; (800) 944-0000.

Alcohol and Women. American College of Obstetricians and Gynecologists, 409 12th Street SW, Washington, DC 20024; (800) 762-2264.

Let's Talk Facts about Substance Abuse. American Psychiatric Association, 1400 K Street NW, Washington, DC 20005; (800) 368-5777.

Numerous publications are available from National Clearinghouse for Alcohol and Drug Information; (800) 729-6686.

Breast Cancer Screening and Mammography

Breast Examination

Breast cancer is the most common type of cancer among women in the United States, accounting for an estimated 182,000 new cases in 1994. It is the second leading cause of cancer death in women (after lung cancer), and will cause an estimated 46,000 deaths in 1994. The average woman has one chance in nine of developing breast cancer during her lifetime. Major risk factors for breast cancer are age over 50 and personal or family (first degree relative) history of breast cancer. Other factors associated with very modest increases risk include first pregnancy after 30 years of age, nulliparity, menarche before 12 years of age, menopause after 50 years of age, postmenopausal obesity, some types of benign breast disease, high socioeconomic status, and a personal history of ovarian or endometrial cancer. Women with localized disease have a 5-year survival rate of approximately 93%. If distant metastasis has occurred, the 5-year survival rate is 18%. When performed by a clinician, breast examination has a sensitivity of approximately 45%.

Recommendations of Major Authorities

Women Under 40 Years of Age

American Academy of Family Physicians—Clinical breast examination should be performed every 1 to 3 years on women aged 30 to 39.

American Cancer Society—Women should have clinical breast examinations every 3 years from age 20 to 39 years.

American College of Obstetricians and Gynecologists—Women over age 18 years should have clinical breast examination during the periodic evaluation, yearly, or as appropriate.

Canadian Task Force on the Periodic Health Examination and **U.S. Preventive Services Task Force**—Physicians may elect to perform clinical breast examination on women under age 40 who are at high risk, especially those whose first-degree relatives have had breast cancer diagnose before menopause.

Women 40 Years of Age and Over

American Academy of Family Physicians, American Cancer Society, American College Obstetricians and Gynecologists, and **American College of Physicians**—Annual clinical breast examination should be performed on women 40 years of age and older.

Canadian Task Force on the Periodic Health Examination and **U.S. Preventive Services Task Force**— Clinical breast examination should be performed on women aged 50 and over every 1 to 2 years. Physicians may elect to perform clinical breast examination on women under age 50 who are at high risk, especially those whose first-degree relatives have had breast cancer diagnosed before menopause. These recommendations are under review.

Basics of Breast Examination

1. *General Considerations:* Breast examination involves bilateral inspection and palpation of the breasts (and areolae) and the axillary and supraclavicular areas. Examination should be performed in both the upright and supine positions.

2. *Inspection:* The breasts should be visually examined under good lighting with the patient sitting or standing with her hands on her hips. Focus should be on symmetry and contour of the breasts; position of the nipples; skin changes such as puckering, dimpling, or scaling of the skin; scars; nipple discharge; nipple retraction; and appearance of a mass. Any bulging, discoloration, or edema of the lymphatic drainage areas (i.e., the supraclavicular and axillary regions) should be noted.

3. *Screening for Retraction:* The breast tissue should be observed
    for signs of retraction while the patient lifts her arms slowly
    over her head. Both breasts should move symmetrically. With
    the patient's arms lowered and palms pressed together at waist
    level, signs of retraction should again be observed for. The pa-
    tient with large breasts should be asked to lean forward and
    the symmetric forward movement of the breasts should be noted.
    There should be no evidence of fixation to the chest wall.

4. *Breast Palpation:* It is very important that palpation be sys-
    tematic. Two commonly used patterns of palpation are to start
    with the nipple and move out radially to the periphery—much
    like spokes on a wheel—or to move outward from the nipple
    and around the breast in a spiral, or corkscrew, pattern. Re-
    gardless of the pattern used, the clinician should be thorough
    and not miss any areas. One of the best predictors of examina-
    tion accuracy is the length of time spent by the examiner.
    Care should be taken to palpate the tail of Spence, which ex-
    tends from the upper outer quadrant to the axilla. The first
    three fingers should be used to press firmly in a small circular
    motion. The amount of pressure should vary from firm, to de-
    tect deep masses, to light, to detect superficial ones. All of the
    breast tissue should be palpated with the patient both upright
    and supine. First, with the woman in an upright position, the
    breast should be palpated using a bimanual technique. The
    inferior aspect of the breast should be supported with one
    hand while the other hand palpates the breast. Each breast
    should next be palpated with the patient in a supine position
    with the arm on the side to be examined raised over her head.

5. *Axillary and Supraclavicular Node Palpation:* The axillary
    and supraclavicular areas should be palpated for adenopathy
    while the patient is sitting. While lifting and supporting the
    woman's arm, the clinician's fingers should be placed high
    into the axilla [an area that includes the upper side of the
    chest and armpit] and moved down firmly to palpate in four
    directions: along the chest wall, along the anterior border of
    the axilla, along the posterior border of the axilla, and along
    the inner aspect of the upper arm. It may be helpful to move
    the patient's arm through the full range of motion to increase
    the surface area that can be reached. The supraclavicular
    nodes should be palpated while the patient is sitting and re-
    laxed, with neck flexed slightly forward. It may help to have

the patient's head turned slightly toward the side being examined. The supraclavicular nodes may be felt in the angle
formed by the clavicle and sternocleidomastoid muscle.

6. *Areolae:* The examiner should check for nipple discharge by
   gently squeezing the nipple. Discharge is easier to elicit when
   the patient is in an upright position. Nipple inversion may be
   normal. However, changes in nipple inversion should not occur after puberty and inverted nipples should not be fixed
   (i.e., it should be possible to pull the nipple out).

7. *Breast Self-Examination:* The American Academy of Family
   Physicians, the American Cancer Society, the American Col-
   lege of Obstetricians and Gynecologists, and the National
   Cancer Institute recommend that clinicians encourage women
   to examine their breasts every month. Clinicians may wish to
   instruct their female patients in breast self-examination.
   Pamphlets on breast self-examination are listed in Patient
   Resources at the end of this section.

Mammography

Mortality from breast cancer is strongly influenced by stage at
detection. The 5-year survival rate is 93% for women found to have
localized disease. The 5-year survival rate for with women distant
spread is only 18%. African-American women have somewhat lower
survival rates than white women at every stage of diagnosis. Mammography is the most effective means of early detection for breast
cancer, with sensitivity estimates of 70% to 90% and specificity estimates of 90% to 95%. Although mammography can detect small tumors in younger women, there has been controversy about whether
mammography screening actually reduces mortality in women less
than 50 years of age.

Well-maintained, modern mammography equipment is very safe,
using very low levels of radiation. Screening does, however, carry the
added risk of morbidity from unnecessary biopsies performed to follow up false-positive mammograms.

Recommendations of Major Authorities

For women 50 and older:

All major authorities, including **American Academy of Family
Physicians, American Cancer Society, American College of**

Obstetricians and Gynecologists, American College of Physicians, Canadian Task Force on the Periodic Health Examination, and **U.S. Preventive Services Task Force (USPSTF)**—Routine mammography screening is recommended. Yearly screening is recommended by all these authorities, with the exception of USPSTF, which recommends a frequency of 1 to 2 years. **American Geriatrics Society** recommends that women over 65 years of age receive mammograms at least every two or three years until at least 85 years of age. **National Cancer Institute** states that experts agree that routine mammography and clinical breast examination screening every 1 to 2 years can reduce breast cancer mortality by about one-third in women aged 50 and over.

For women under 50:

American Cancer Society and **American College of Obstetricians and Gynecologists**—Women 40-49 years of age should receive screening mammograms every 1 to 2 years. **National Cancer Institute** states that experts do not agree on the role of routine screening mammography for women aged 40 to 49.

High-Risk Women

American Academy of Family Physicians and **American College of Obstetricians and Gynecologists**—Women with a family history of premenopausally diagnosed breast cancer in a first-degree relative should have mammography regularly beginning at 35 years of age.

American College of Physicians—Women 40 years of age and older who have a family history of breast cancer or who are otherwise at increased risk should have annual mammography.

Canadian Task Force on the Periodic Health Examination and U.S. Preventive Services Task Force—Physicians may elect to recommend mammography starting at age 35 for women at high risk, especially those whose first-degree relatives have had breast cancer diagnosed before menopause.

Basics of Mammography Screening

1. Clinicians should clearly communicate the importance of mammograms. Patients often report as a major reason for not

getting a mammogram the fact that they simply did not know they needed one. It is important that women understand the need for regular mammograms, not just one.

2. Pamphlets, videotapes, and other media should be used to educate and motivate patients to obtain mammography.

3. Because cost can be a significant barrier for patients in obtaining mammography, the clinician should be knowledgeable about low-cost, high-quality mammography facilities available in the community and should make referrals to these facilities as needed.

4. The patient should wear pants or a skirt, since she will have to undress from the waist up. She should be instructed not to use deodorants, powders, or other topical applications on the breasts or in underarm areas as these may cause artifacts on the mammogram.

5. Because of potential perimenstrual breast tenderness, it is preferable to schedule mammography at other times in the patient's menstrual cycle.

6. Mild discomfort is common during the performance of a mammogram. The patient should be instructed to tell the technician if discomfort becomes unacceptable.

7. Clinicians should verify that mammography facilities use only dedicated mammography equipment that meets minimum safety and image-quality standards. Facilities that receive, Medicare reimbursement must use equipment that complies with minimum standards for patient safety. The American College of Radiology provides certification for compliance with minimum standards for image quality. As of October 1, 1994, all U.S. mammography facilities will have to be certified by the Food and Drug Administration (FDA) as providing quality mammography. Certification requirements will cover personnel, equipment, radiation exposure, quality assurance programs, and record keeping and reporting. Further information on this program is available from FDA Center for Devices and Radiological Health, Office of Training and Assistance, Division of Mammography Quality and Radiation Programs, HFZ-240, 5600 Fishers Lane, Rockville, MD 20857.

8. Clinicians should establish a tracking system to make sure that mammograms that are ordered are actually performed,

that results return in a timely fashion, and that patients who are not seen frequently can be called or contacted by letter about the importance of getting mammograms and other needed preventive care. Patients should be encouraged to keep track of and prompt their own mammograms through use of a patient-held record form or card.

9. Any palpable breast lump, even with a normal mammogram, requires a careful evaluation, including possible biopsy.

Patient Resources

Breast Cancer: Steps to Finding Breast Lumps Early. American Academy of Family Physicians, 8880 Ward Parkway, Kansas City, MO 64114-2797; (800) 944-0000.

Detecting and Treating Breast Problems; Mammography. American College of Obstetricians and Gynecologists, 409 12th Street, SW, Washington, DC 20024-2188; (202) 638-5577 or (800) 762-2264.

How to Do Breast Self Examination. American Cancer Society, 1559 Clifton Rd. NE, Atlanta, GA 30329-4251; (800) ACS-2345.

Breast Exams: What You Should Know; Questions and Answers about Breast Lumps; Smart Advice for Women 40 and Over; What You Need to Know About Breast Cancer; A Mammogram Once a Year for Life. Office of Cancer Communications, National Cancer Institute, Bldg. 31, Rm. 10A24, Bethesda, MD 20892; (800) 4-CANCER.

Cervical Cancer Screening

Approximately 15,000 cases of invasive cervical cancer will be diagnosed and 4600 women will die of cervical cancer in the United States in 1994. Risk factors for cervical cancer include early age at first intercourse, having multiple sexual partners, and smoking. Rates for carcinoma in situ reach a peak for both black and white women between 20 and 30 years of age. After the age of 25, however, the incidence of invasive cancer in black women increases dramatically with age while in white women the incidence rises more slowly. Over 25% of invasive cervical cancers occur in women older than 65, and 40% to 50% of all women who die from cervical cancer are over 65 years of age.

The effectiveness of early detection through Papanicolaou (Pap) smear testing and early treatment has been impressive, resulting in a marked decrease in mortality from cervical cancer. The incidence of invasive cervical cancer has been estimated to have been decreased 70% by screening. However, a large proportion of women, particularly elderly black women and middle-aged poor women, have not had regular Pap smears. In some areas, as many as 75% of women over 65 have not had a Pap smear within the previous five years.

Depending on the technique used, Pap testing has a sensitivity of 50% to 90% and a specificity of 90% to 99%. A large proportion of false-negative pap smears are thought to be due to poor technique in performance (as many as half of all false negatives) and inadequate laboratory interpretation. Because of the long lead time from development of precancerous changes to invasive carcinoma (8 to 9 years by some estimates), almost all precancerous or early stage malignancies initially missed can still be detected by repeat testing.

Recommendations of Major Authorities

American Academy of Family Physicians—Women who are sexually active or (if the sexual history is thought to be unreliable) are 18 years of age or older should have annual Pap tests. After a woman has had three or more consecutive satisfactory normal annual examinations, the Pap test may be performed at the discretion of the physician and the patient, but not less frequently than every 3 years.

American Cancer Society, American College of Obstetricians and Gynecologists, and **National Cancer Institute**—All women should begin having annual Pap tests at the onset of sexual activity or at 18 years of age, whichever occurs first. After a woman has had three or more consecutive satisfactory normal annual examinations, the Pap test may be performed less frequently at the discretion of the patient and clinician.

American College of Physicians—Sexually active women between 25 and 65 years of age should be screened with a Pap smear every 3 years. Women 66 to 75 years of age who have not been screened within the 10 years prior to age 66 should be screened every 3 years. Women at increased risk for cervical cancer should be screened every 2 years. Initial screening tests may be done as frequently as annually for two or three examinations to ensure diagnostic accuracy.

Canadian Task Force on the Periodic Health Examination—There is fair justification for including a Pap smear as part of the periodic health examination. The optimum age and frequency at which these smears should be taken is not known, but since the incidence of cervical cancer is positively associated with early age of sexual activity and multiplicity of sexual partners, smears should probably be taken at least annually in women in these high-risk groups. For those not in high-risk groups, an initial smear should be taken soon after a woman begins sexual activity, then another 1 year later, then every 3 years until about 15 years after first intercourse, then every 5 years until age 60.

U.S. Preventive Services Task Force—All women who are or have been sexually active should have regular Pap tests. Testing should begin at the age when the woman first engages in sexual intercourse. Adolescents whose sexual history is thought to be unreliable should be presumed to be sexually active at age 18. Pap tests are appropriately performed at an interval of 1 to 3 years, to be recommended by the clinician based on the presence of risk factors (e.g., early onset of sexual intercourse, history of multiple sexual partners, low socioeconomic status). Pap smears may be discontinued at age 65, but only if the provider can document previous Pap screening in which smears have been consistently normal.

Basics of Pap Smear Screening

1. It is important that the performance of a Pap smear not be an unpleasant or painful experience for the patient. Clinicians should be sure to clearly explain the importance of the procedure and the steps in carrying it out.

2. Patients should be instructed not to douche on the day of the examination. A Pap smear should not be performed if the patient has significant menstrual flow or obvious inflammation.

3. The Pap smear should be performed before the bimanual examination and before obtaining culture specimens. In general, the speculum should not be lubricated with anything except water, as contamination of Pap smear specimens with lubrication jelly tends to obscure cellular detail. Use of a small amount of lubricating jelly may be necessary for speculum insertion in some older patients.

4. The cervix and vagina should be completely visualized before collection of the specimen. Excess cervical mucus should be gently removed with a swab.

5. The gold standard for the adequacy of a Pap smear has traditionally been the presence of endocervical cells in the sample. This is because 90% of cervical cancers develop at the junction of the squamous epithelium of the vagina and the columnar epithelium of the endocervix (located at the external os in young women and inside the endocervical canal in older women). Studies differ on whether the presence of endocervical cells actually improves detection rates of abnormalities, but the presence of endocervical cells remains widely accepted as a standard of adequacy for Pap smears.

6. A variety of implements have been used to obtain Pap smear samples, including simple cotton swabs, wooden and plastic spatulas, and endocervical and combined endocervical-exacervical brushes. The best sensitivity (defined as presence of endocervical cells) is obtained by using both a spatula (preferably Ayer's type) and an endocervical brush. The spatula should be used first because of the bleeding commonly caused by the endocervical brush and the susceptibility of endocervical cells to drying effects.

7. The spatula should be firmly, yet gently rotated circumferentially around the os at least one complete turn, to obtain a 360° sample. The specimen should be promptly transferred to a slide. Patients who have been exposed to DES should also have smears taken circumferentially with a spatula from the upper two thirds of the vagina. In obtaining the endocervical sample, the brush should be inserted into the os no deeper than the length of the bristled section. It should be rotated 360° (avoiding excessive rotation), and then the specimen transferred by rolling on a slide.

8. Specimens should be uniformly applied to the slides without clumping. Fixation should be performed promptly, and care must be taken to minimize air drying of the specimens. If one slide is used for both specimens, it is important to collect, transfer, and fix the endocervical sample as quickly as possible. The use of two separate slides can help avoid prolonged air exposure of the spatula specimen while the endocervical specimen is being collected. This does, however, double the amount of work for the cytotechnologist. The use of a combined endocervical-exacervical brush requires the collection and fixation of only a single specimen (thus decreasing the

risk of air drying), but it has been shown to be somewhat less sensitive than using a spatula and an endocervical brush.

9. Providers should inquire about the quality control of laboratories to which specimens are sent. Laboratories should be certified by the American Society of Cytologists or the College of American Pathologists, or both. Many authorities recommend that laboratories use the new Bethesda System developed by a National Cancer Institute consensus conference for reporting results. The Bethesda System standardizes classification categories and provides for reporting on aspects of the sample not addressed in traditional Pap smear reports, such as adequacy and hormonal effects. In the Bethesda System, human papillomavirus (HPV) infection is classified as a low-grade squamous intraepithelial lesion; both moderate and severe dysplasia are classified as high-grade squamous intraepithelial lesions. There is some concern, not substantiated by research, that these classifications may lead to excess colposcopic exams for HPV infection and moderate dysplasia. The National Workshop on Screening for Cancer of the Cervix has issued guidelines for Pap smear reporting and follow-up in Canada.

10. Only about 60% of women with abnormal Pap smears return for follow-up. Clinicians should establish a tracking system to make sure that Pap smears are performed regularly, that results return in a timely fashion, that patients with abnormal results are contacted, and that women who are not seen frequently are called or contacted by letter about the importance of getting Pap smears and other needed preventive care. Patients should be encouraged to keep track of and prompt their own Pap smears through use of a patient-held record form or card.

Patient Resources

The Pap Test. American College of Obstetricians and Gynecologists, 409 12th St. SW, Washington DC 20024; (800) 762-2264.

Cholesterol Screening

High blood cholesterol is a major modifiable risk factor for coronary heart disease (CHD)—the leading cause of death for both men and women in the United States. Approximately 1.25 million myocardial infarctions and 500,000 deaths from CHD occur each year. In large population-based studies, total cholesterol levels are directly related to CHD incidence. In the Multiple Risk Factor Intervention Trial (MRFIT), the 6-year risk of death from CHD in normotensive, nonsmoking, middle-aged men with blood cholesterol levels less than 182 mg/dL was one fourth that of men with blood cholesterol levels greater than or equal to 245 mg/dL. Epidemiologic studies have shown that cholesterol lipoprotein subfractions play an important role in CHD. LDL-cholesterol is directly and HDL-cholesterol is inversely associated with CHD incidence.

A meta-analysis of cholesterol-lowering trials performed mainly in middle-aged men has shown that lowering blood cholesterol through diet or drug therapy significantly reduces the risk of CHD death and nonfatal myocardial infarction. In secondary prevention trials among those who have had a myocardial infarction, the reduction in CHD mortality is associated with a reduction in total mortality. In primary prevention trials, however, reduced total mortality has not been shown, and there have been variable increases in different causes of noncardiac mortality offsetting the decline in CHD deaths. It is unclear whether this is a chance finding reflecting the limited statistical power of the primary prevention studies for observations on total mortality or whether it reflects effects of cholesterol lowering.

Recommendations of Major Authorities

American Academy of Family Physicians—Adults (19 years of age and older) should have measurement of nonfasting or fasting total blood cholesterol performed at least every 5 years.

American College of Obstetricians and Gynecologists—Adults (19 years of age and older) should have cholesterol measured every 5 years until 64 years of age, and then every 3 to 5 years thereafter.

American College of Physicians—Total cholesterol measurement is recommended at least once in early adulthood and at intervals of 5 or more years up to age 70. The LDL and HDL cholesterol and serum triglyceride levels should be measured in individuals with an elevated total serum cholesterol level. The decision to perform these additional tests should be individualized. Factors to be taken into account include age, gender, number of other cardiovascular risk factors, and the patients' willingness to comply with drug and dietary treatment of hypercholesterolemia.

Table 5.4. NCEP Coronary Heart Disease Risk Factors Other Than LDL-Cholesterol*

Postive Risk Factors

Age
>   Male 45 years or older
>   Female 55 years or older or premature menopause without estrogen
>   replacement therapy

Family history of premature CHD
(definite myocardial infarction or sudden death)
>   father/first degree male relative less than 55 years
>   mother/first degree female relative less than 65 years

Cigarette smoking

Hypertension
>   140/90 mmHg** or higher, or on anti-hypertensive medication

Low HDL-cholesterol (<35 mg/dL)

Diabetes mellitus

Negative Risk Factors***

HDL Cholesterol 60 mg/dL or greater

*High risk, defined as two or more CHD risk factors (after positive and negative factors have been summed), leads to more vigorous intervention. Age (defined differently for men and for women) is treated as a risk factor because rates of CHD are higher in the elderly than in the young, and in men than in women of the same age. Obesity is not listed as a risk factor because it operates through other risk factors that are included (hypertension, hyperlipidemia, decreased HDL-cholesterol, and diabetes mellitus), but it should be considered a target for intervention. Physical inactivity is similarly not listed as a risk factor, but it too should be considered a target for intervention, and physical activity is recommended as desirable for everyone. High risk due to coronary or peripheral atherosclerosis [also should be considered in implementing an intervention strategy].

**Confirmed by measurements on several occasions

***If the HDL-cholesterol level is 60 mg/dL or greater subtract one risk factor (because high HDL-cholesterol levels decrease CHD risk)

Adapted from: National Cholesterol Education Program. Second Report of the National Cholesterol Education Program Expert Panel on Detection, Evaluation, and Treatment of High Blood Cholesterol in Adults (Adult Treatment Panel II). Bethesda, MD: National Institutes of Health, National Heart, Lung, and Blood Institute. USDHHS Pub. No. NIH 93-3095, 1993.

Canadian Task Force on the Periodic Health Examination— There is insufficient evidence for the inclusion or exclusion of universal screening for hypercholesterolemia in a periodic health examination. Nonetheless, case-finding through repeated measurements of the nonfasting total blood cholesterol level should be considered in men 30 to 59 years of age. Individual clinical judgment on whether testing is appropriate should be exercised in all other circumstances.

National Cholesterol Education Program (NCEP) of the National Heart, Lung, and Blood Institute—Adults (20 years of age and older) should have a measurement of total blood cholesterol at least once every 5 years; HDL-cholesterol should be measured at the same time if accurate results are available. Lipoprotein analysis should be performed for all patients with CHD. In patients without CHD, lipoprotein analysis should be performed in any of the following circumstances: 1) if the total cholesterol is 240 mg/dL or above; 2) if the total cholesterol is 200 to 239 mg/dL and the patient also has two or more CHD risk factors; 3) if the patient has an HDL-cholesterol less than 35 mg/dL. See Table 5.4 for NCEP recommendations on CHD risk factors and patient classification and identification.

U.S. Preventive Services Task Force—Periodic measurement of total serum cholesterol (nonfasting) is most important for middle-aged men, and it may also be clinically prudent in young men, women, and the elderly. The optimal frequency for cholesterol measurement in asymptomatic individuals has not been determined on the basis of scientific evidence and is left to clinical discretion. This recommendation is currently under review.

Basics of Cholesterol Screening

1. Patients who are acutely ill, losing weight, pregnant, or nursing should not be screened, as their cholesterol levels may not be representative of usual levels. Because cholesterol levels in patients who have had myocardial infarction within the last 3 months are likely to be lower than usual, results obtained during this period should be rechecked.

2. Patients need not vary their usual eating habits before undergoing screening for total blood cholesterol or HDL-cholesterol. Patients undergoing lipoprotein analysis should fast (water and black coffee are acceptable) for 12 hours before testing.

3. If possible, cholesterol tests should be performed on venous blood samples, as cholesterol concentrations measured from finger-stick blood samples may be unreliable. The NCEP cut points for diagnostic and therapeutic actions refer to venous serum samples.

4. To prevent an effect of posture or stasis on the cholesterol value, venipuncture should be carried out only after the patient has been in the sitting position for at least 5 minutes, and the tourniquet should be applied for as brief a period as possible.

5. In interpreting results, clinicians should be familiar with the effects of medications on cholesterol levels. Anabolic steroids, progestins, bile salts, and chlorpromazine increase blood cholesterol. Clinicians should also be knowledgeable about conditions that may cause increased cholesterol levels, such as hypothyroidism, nephrotic syndrome, diabetes mellitus, and obstructive liver disease.

6. Cholesterol tests should be analyzed by an accredited laboratory that meets current standards for precision and accuracy. The Laboratory Standardization Panel of the National Cholesterol Education Program has set a goal that laboratories have systematic and precision errors of less than 3% in processing total cholesterol samples. Clinicians should inquire about a laboratory's performance history and quality-control methods before using it for screening.

7. Cholesterol values in plasma samples tend to be lower than serum samples because of the effects of EDTA in plasma samples. NCEP has determined cholesterol level cut points based on serum samples and has designated that cholesterol levels obtained from plasma samples be multiplied by 1.03 to arrive at a serum equivalent.

8. Cholesterol values in mg/dL can be converted to mmol/L by multiplying by 0.02586. Triglyceride levels can be similarly converted by multiplying by 0.01129.

9. NCEP's Step I and Step II Diet for treatment for patients with elevated cholesterol levels includes the following examples of foods to choose or decrease (careful selection of processed foods is necessary to stay within the sodium guideline: less than 2400 mg):

Lean meat, poultry, and fish: 5 to 6 ounces per day or less

- *Choose:* beef, pork lamb—lean cuts well trimmed before cooking; poultry without skin; fish, shellfish; processed meat—prepared from lean meat, e.g., lean ham, lean frankfurters, lean meat with soy protein or carrageen

- *Decrease:* beef, pork, lamb—regular ground beef, fatty cuts, spare ribs, organ meats; poultry with skin, fried chicken; fried fish, fried shellfish; regular luncheon meat, e.g., bologna, salami, sausage, frankfurters

Eggs: 4 or fewer yolks per week (Step 1); two or fewer yolks per week (Step II)

- *Choose:* Egg whites (two whites can be substituted for one whole egg in recipes), cholesterol-free egg substitute

- *Decrease:* Egg yolks (if more than 4 per week on Step I or if more than 2 per week on step II); includes eggs used in cooking and baking

Low-Fat Dairy Products: 2-3 servings per day

- *Choose:* Milk—skim, 1/2%, or 1% fat (fluid, powdered, evaporated), buttermilk; Yogurt—nonfat or low-fat yogurt or yogurt beverages

- *Decrease:* Whole milk (fluid, evaporated, condensed), 2% fat milk (lowfat milk), imitation milk; Whole milk yogurt, whole milk yogurt beverages

Dairy Products

- *Choose:* Cheese—low-fat natural or processed cheese; Low-fat or nonfat varieties, e.g., cottage cheese—low-fat, non-fat, or dry curd (0% to 2%); Frozen dairy dessert—ice milk, frozen yogurt (low-fat or nonfat); Low-fat coffee creamer; Low-fat or nonfat sour cream

- *Decrease:* Regular cheeses (American, blue, Brie, cheddar, Colby, Edam, Monterey Jack, whole-milk mozzarella, Parmesan, Swiss), cream cheese, Neufchatel cheese; cottage cheese (4% fat); ice cream; cream, half & half, whipping cream; nondairy creamer, whipped topping, sour cream

Fats and Oils: 6-8 or fewer teaspoons per day

- *Choose:* unsaturated oils—safflower, sunflower, corn, soybean, cottonseed, canola, olive, peanut; margarine—made from unsaturated oils listed above, light or diet margarine, especially soft or liquid forms; salad dressings—made with unsaturated oils listed above, or low-fat or fat-free; seeds and nuts—peanut butter, other nut butters; cocoa powder

- *Decrease:* coconut oil, palm kernel oil, palm oil; butter, lard, shortening, bacon fat, hard margarine; dressings—made with egg yolk, cheese, sour cream, whole milk; coconut; milk chocolate

Breads and Cereals: 6 or more servings per day

- *Choose:* breads—whole-grain bread, English muffins, bagels, buns, corn or flour tortilla; cereals—oat, wheat, corn, multigrain; pasta; rice; dry beans and peas; crackers, low-fat—animal-type, graham, soda crackers, breadsticks, melba toast; homemade baked goods using unsaturated oil, skim or 1% milk, and egg substitute—quick breads, biscuits, cornbread muffins, bran muffins, pancakes, waffles

- *Decrease:* bread in which eggs, fat, and/or butter are a major ingredient; croissants; most granolas; high-fat crackers; commercial baked pastries, muffins, biscuits

Soups

- *Choose:* reduced- or low-fat and reduced-sodium varieties, e.g., chicken or beef noodle, minestrone, tomato, vegetable, potato, reduced-fat soups made with skim milk

- *Decrease:* soup containing whole milk, cream, meat fat, poultry fat, or poultry skin

Vegetables: 3-5 servings per day

- *Choose:* fresh, frozen, or canned, without added fat or sauce

- *Decrease:* vegetables fried or prepared with butter, cheese, or cream sauce

Fruits: 2-4 servings per day

- *Choose:* fruit—fresh, frozen, canned, or dried; fruit juice—fresh, frozen, or canned

- *Decrease:* fried fruit or fruit served with butter or cream sauce

Sweets and Modified-Fat Desserts

- *Choose:* beverages—fruit-flavored drinks, lemonade, fruit punch; sweets—sugar, syrup, honey, jam, preserves, candy made without fat (candy corn, gumdrops, hard candy), fruit-flavored gelatin; frozen dessert—low-fat and nonfat yogurt, ice milk, sherbet, sorbet, fruit ice, popsicles; cookies, cake, pie, pudding—prepared with egg whites, egg substitutes, skim milk or 1% milk, and unsaturated oil or margarine; ginger snaps, fig and other fruit bar cookies, fat-free cookies, angel food cake

- *Decrease:* candy made with milk chocolate, coconut oil, palm kernel oil, palm oil; ice cream and frozen treats made with ice cream; commercial baked pies, cakes, doughnuts, high-fat cookies, cream pies

Examples of foods to choose or decrease for the NCEP Step I and Step II diets is taken from: *National Cholesterol Education Program. Second Report of the National Cholesterol Education Program Expert Panel on Detection, Evaluation, and Treatment of High Blood Cholesterol in Adults (Adult Treatment Panel II).* Bethesda, MD: National Institutes of Health, National Heart, Lung, and Blood Institute. NIH Pub. No. 93-3095, 1993.

10. All patients who are obese, regardless of cholesterol level, should receive dietary and weight reduction counseling. All patients who are physically inactive, regardless of cholesterol level, should receive counseling on increasing physical activity.

Patient Resources

Cholesterol: What You Can Do to Lower Your Level. American Academy of Family Physicians, 8880 Ward Parkway, Kansas City, MO 64114-2797; (800) 944-0000.

Cholesterol and Your Health. American College of Obstetricians and Gynecologists, 409 12t St. SW, Washington, DC 20024-2188; (800) 762-2264.

Cholesterol and Your Heart; Dietary Treatment of Hypercholesterolemia: A Manual for Patients; Eat Less Fat and High Cholesterol Foods; and many other materials. American Heart Association, 7320 Greenville Ave., Dallas, TX 75231; (800) 242-8721.

Eating to Lower Your High Blood Cholesterol; So You Have High Blood Cholesterol. National Heart, Lung, and Blood Institute Information Center, PO Box 30105, Bethesda, MD 20824-0105; (301) 251-1222.

Dietary Guidelines and Your Diet; The Food Guide Pyramid; Nutrition and Your Health; Dietary Guidelines for Americans (3rd ed); *Nutritive Value of Foods;* and other materials. Superintendent of Documents, U.S. Government Printing Office, Washington, DC 20405; (202) 783-3238.

Colorectal Cancer Screening

There will be approximately 149,000 new cases of colorectal cancer and 56,000 deaths caused by it in 1994. On average, clinically diagnosed colorectal cancer deprives its victims of 6 to 7 years of life. Principal risk factors for colorectal cancer include a history of one of the familial polyposis syndromes, familial cancer syndromes, colorectal cancer in first-degree relatives, or a personal history of ulcerative colitis, adenomatous polyps, or endometrial, ovarian, or breast cancer. If detected at an early stage, colorectal cancer can be successfully treated with surgery.

Fecal Occult Blood Testing

Malignancies and, to a lesser extent, polyps bleed intermittently. This bleeding can be detected by tests that identify occult blood or breakdown products of blood in fecal material. Recent evidence indicates that the sensitivity of commonly used fecal occult blood tests for detecting colorectal cancer in low-risk, asymptomatic patients may be as low as 25%. (Rehydration of dried samples before testing can increase sensitivity, at the cost of producing more positive results.) The predictive value of a positive fecal occult blood test for colorectal cancer in general populations is only 5% to 10%. Thus, up to 75% of cancers will be missed and up to 20 patients will undergo workups that will be negative for every case of colorectal cancer detected by fecal occult blood testing.

Until recently, no studies had shown decreased mortality as a result of fecal occult blood testing. In 1993, however, Mandel et al found that yearly fecal occult blood testing using rehydrated stool specimens decreased mortality from colorectal cancer by about one third. In that study, guaiac-impregnated paper slides were used to test for fecal blood. [Mandel JS, Bond JH, Church TR, et al. Reducing mortality from colorectal cancer by screening for fecal occult blood. *New England Journal of Medicine.* 1993;328:1365-71).

Recommendations of Major Authorities

American Academy of Family Physicians (AAFP), Canadian Task Force on the Periodic Health Examination, and **U.S. Preventive Services Task Force (USPSTF)**—There is insufficient evidence to recommend either initiating or terminating the routine provision of fecal occult blood testing in low-risk, asymptomatic individuals (see above). These recommendations are currently under review. AAFP and USPSTF recommend that it may be clinically prudent to offer screening, including fecal occult blood testing, to individuals 50 years of age or older who are at increased risk for disease. [USPSTF's *Guide to Clinical Preventive Services, Second Edition* states "Screening for colorectal cancer is recommended for all persons aged 50 and older with annual fecal occult blood testing (FOBT), or sigmoidoscopy (periodicity unspecified), or both. There is insufficient evidence to determine which of these screening methods is preferable or whether the combination of FOBT and sigmoidoscopy produced greater benefits than does either test alone" p. 89.]

American Cancer Society (ACS), American College of Physicians (ACP), American Gastroenterological Association, American Society for Gastrointestinal Endoscopy, and **National Cancer Institute (NCI)**—Annual fecal occult blood testing should be done for all asymptomatic individuals without known risk factors beginning at 50 years of age. ACP recommends annual fecal occult blood testing beginning at 40 years of age for individuals at high risk for disease. ACS and NCI recommend that special surveillance be considered for individuals at high risk for disease, without specifically designating fecal occult blood testing.

American College of Obstetricians and Gynecologists—Fecal occult blood testing should be done for all women 40 years of age and older as part of their periodic health examination.

Basics of Fecal Occult Blood Screening

1. Many tests are available for detecting fecal occult blood. These are of three basic types: guaiac-impregnated cards and other carriers that detect the peroxidase-like activity of hemoglobin (Hemoccult®); quantitative tests based on the conversion of heme to fluorescent porphyrins (HemoQuant®); and immunoassay tests for human hemoglobin. Currently only the first two types are routinely used in practice. Guaiac-based tests have the disadvantage of giving false-negative and false-positive results because of a number of dietary factors, and thus are more accurate in patients on a special diet. Guaiac-based tests have the advantages of being relatively easy for patients and clinicians to use, and they are relatively specific for lower gastrointestinal tract bleeding. The quantitative porphyrin tests are not affected by dietary factors and are potentially more sensitive, depending on the cut point designated for a positive result. Recent evidence indicates, however, that at matched levels of specificity, the quantitative porphyrin tests are not significantly more sensitive than guaiac-based tests. Quantitative porphyrin tests have the potential disadvantages of not being specific for lower gastrointestinal bleeding and of requiring interpretation by a laboratory.

2. Stool samples should not be collected if hematuria or obvious rectal bleeding, such as from hemorrhoids, is present. Women should be instructed to avoid collecting stool samples during and just after a menstrual period.

3. If possible, medications that cause gastric irritation and bleeding should be avoided for at least 48 hours prior to and during the testing period. These include: aspirin, nonsteroidal anti-inflammatory drugs, corticosteroids, anticoagulants, reserpine, antimetabolites, chemotherapeutic agents, and alcohol in excess. Avoidance of aspirin and nonsteroidal anti-inflammatory drugs for 7 days is recommended by the manufacturer of Hemoccult®. When using guaiac-based tests, patient adherence to the dietary guidelines for at least 48 hours prior to and during the testing period can help avoid

false-positive and false-negative results. Despite reports in earlier years, dietary iron does not cause false-positive tests. Application of antiseptic preparations containing iodine to the anal area should be avoided immediately before and during the testing period to prevent false-positive results.

4. When guaiac-impregnated cards are used, two separate samples from different sections of three consecutive bowel movements should be collected using the supplied applicator and applied as thin smears to the cards. Patients should be instructed to return samples as soon as possible for processing. Optimally, processing of the cards should occur within 6 days, but definitely not after 14 days. Rehydration of the samples with a drop of water before application of the developer increases sensitivity by approximately 30% to 40%, but it also decreases specificity by 2% to 3%, leading to significantly more false-positive results. For this reason, authorities disagree about the use of rehydration. A positive result on even one sample qualifies the entire test as positive. Cards and developer should be stored at room temperature and protected from heat and light.

5. If patients are asked to return samples through the mail, special U.S. Postal Service-approved envelopes should be used, not standard paper envelopes.

6. Because of the intermittent nature of bleeding by colorectal cancer, malignancy cannot be conclusively ruled out by repeat fecal occult blood testing. Follow-up of positive fecal occult blood screening requires diagnostic procedures (e.g., sigmoidoscopy, colonoscopy, barium enema).

Digital Rectal Examination

Invasive colorectal cancer is the most preventable visceral cancer. Most cases arise from adenomatous polyps that take approximately 10 years to progress to an invasive stage. Patients presenting with regional disease have a 5-year survival rate of approximately 50%, whereas those presenting with localized disease have a 5-year survival rate of 85% for rectal cancer and 91% for colon cancer. It is estimated that fewer than 10% of colorectal cancers can be palpated by digital rectal examination.

Prostate cancer is the most common type of cancer in men, after skin cancer. It is estimated that 1 of every 10 men in the United States will develop prostate cancer. There will be approximately 200,000 new cases in 1994 in the United States, with approximately 38,000 deaths in that period. Risk factors include advanced age and African-American race. Dietary fat may also be associated with prostate cancer. Digital rectal examination has a sensitivity of 33% to 69% and a specificity of 49% to 97% for detecting prostate cancer. There is little evidence that screening by digital rectal examination decreases mortality from prostate cancer. Some authorities believe this may be due to either its inability to detect tumors at an early, treatable stage or to the fact that some tumors grow so rapidly that yearly screening cannot detect most of them at an early, treatable stage, or both.

Recommendations of Major Authorities

American Academy of Family Physicians—Digital rectal examination should be included in the periodic health examination of individuals 40 years of age and older.

American Cancer Society—Annual digital rectal examination should be performed for all patients starting at 40 years of age.

American College of Obstetricians and Gynecologists—Digital rectal examination should be included in the periodic health examination of women 40 years of age and older as part of the pelvic exam.

American Society of Colon and Rectal Surgeons—Annual digital rectal examination should be performed for asymptomatic, low-risk individuals 40 years of age and older and for asymptomatic individuals over 35 years of age with either a family history of colorectal adenomatous polyps or cancer in one or more first-degree relatives.

American Urological Association—Digital rectal examination should be performed annually for men 40 to 49 years of age who have a family history of prostate cancer, and for all men over 50.

Canadian Task Force on the Periodic Health Examination—Digital rectal examination is feasible, relatively cost-effective, and acceptable for detecting prostate cancer and can be adapted to case-finding in the primary care setting. However, the use of digital rectal examination is not recommended for screening for colorectal cancer.

National Cancer Institute—A rectal examination should be included as a part of the periodic health examination. The clinician should identify high-risk patients for special surveillance, including those with a strong family history of colon cancer or a personal history of adenomas or inflammatory bowel disease.

U.S. Preventive Services Task Force—There is insufficient evidence to recommend for or against routine digital rectal examination as an effective screening test for prostate cancer in asymptomatic men. No recommendation has been made regarding the use of the examination for colorectal cancer screening. [USPSTF's *Guide to Clinical Preventive Services, Second Edition* states "Screening for colorectal cancer is recommended for all persons aged 50 and older with annual fecal occult blood testing (FOBT), or sigmoidoscopy (periodicity unspecified), or both.... There is ... insufficient evidence to recommend for or against routine screening with digital rectal examination, barium enema, or colonoscopy, although recommendations against such screening in average-risk persons may be made on other grounds. Persons with a family history of hereditary syndromes associated with a high risk of colon cancer should be referred for diagnosis and management" p. 89.]

Basics of Rectum and Prostate Examination

1. *General Considerations:* Male and female patients may be examined in the left lateral decubitus position or standing, bent over the examination table. Female patients may also be examined in the lithotomy position during a pelvic examination. The post-examination testing of fecal matter on the gloved finger for occult blood is of unknown value because trauma caused by the examination potentially may produce false-positive results.

2. *Inspection:* The anal opening should be visually inspected, with note made of any skin breakdown, fissures, and protrusions from the anal opening.

3. *Palpation:* The exam is performed by inserting the lubricated, gloved index finger into the anal opening. The gloved finger should be inserted just past the rectal sphincter and not advanced until the sphincter relaxes. When this procedure is followed, rectal exams may be uncomfortable, but most are not painful. All sides of the rectum should be palpated for polyps,

109

which may be sessile (attached by a base) or pedunculated (attached by a stalk). Intraperitoneal metastases may be felt anterior to the rectum as hard, shelf-like projections into the rectum. In men, the posterior and lateral lobes of the prostate gland should be thoroughly palpated. The normal prostate gland is approximately 2.5 cm x 4 cm and does not protrude into the rectum by more than 1 cm. It should feel smooth and rubbery throughout and have a palpable central groove. Asymmetry of the prostate gland or the presence of a hard, irregular nodule, or both, are typical presentations of prostate cancer.

Sigmoidoscopy

Of the three widely used methods of screening for colorectal cancer (digital rectal examination and fecal occult blood testing being the other two), examination using a sigmoidoscope is the most specific and sensitive. Because it enables the examiner to perform a biopsy during the procedure, the specificity of sigmoidoscopy approaches 100%. Sensitivity is largely determined by the skill of the examiner and the length of the instrument. Approximately 30% of colorectal cancers are within reach of the 25-cm rigid sigmoidoscope. The 35-cm flexible sigmoidoscope can reach 45% to 50% of cancers, and the 60-cm flexible sigmoidoscope can reach 50% to 60%. Screening with sigmoidoscopy has been limited by costs, patient and provider noncompliance, and controversy about effectiveness. Patient compliance problems have been somewhat diminished by the advent of the more comfortable flexible instruments. The 35-cm sigmoidoscope is particularly well-accepted by patients, and the 60-cm sigmoidoscope is relatively well-accepted. The controversy about effectiveness has revolved around a lack of evidence that screening with sigmoidoscopy decreases mortality from colorectal cancer. Two recently published case-control studies [Selby JV, Friedman GD, Quesenberry CG, Weiss NS. A case-control study of screening sigmoidoscopy and mortality from colorectal cancer. *New England Journal of Medicine.* 1992; 84:1572-1575; and, Newcomb PA, Norfleet RG, Storer B, Surawicz, Marcus PM. Screening sigmoidoscopy and colorectal cancer mortality. *JNCI.* 1992; 84:1572-1575] have demonstrated significant decreases in risk (59% and 79%, respectively) of death from colorectal cancer for screened patients. In the Selby study, significant benefit was suggested from rigid sigmoidoscopy screening performed as infrequently as every 10 years.

Recommendations of Major Authorities

Normal Risk

American Academy of Family Physicians, Canadian Task Force on the Periodic Health Examination, and **U.S. Preventive Services Task Force (USPSTF)**—There is insufficient evidence to recommend either initiating or terminating the provision of sigmoidoscopy screening for low-risk, asymptomatic individuals. This recommendation is currently under review by USPSTF. [USPSTF's *Guide to Clinical Preventive Services, Second Edition* states "Screening for colorectal cancer is recommended for all persons aged 50 and older with annual fecal occult blood testing (FOBT), or sigmoidoscopy (periodicity unspecified), or both. There is insufficient evidence to determine which of these screening methods is preferable or whether the combination of FOBT and sigmoidoscopy produced greater benefits than does either test alone" p. 89.]

American Cancer Society, American College of Obstetricians and Gynecologists, American College of Physicians (ACP), American Gastroenterological Association, American Society for Gastrointestinal Endoscopy, and **National Cancer Institute**—Patients at normal risk should be screened with sigmoidoscopy every 3 to 5 years beginning at 50 years of age. ACP has stated that performance of an air-contrast barium enema every 5 years is an acceptable alternative to sigmoidoscopy.

Increased Risk

All major authorities—Patients at increased risk of colorectal cancer should receive more frequent screening. What constitutes increased risk and the nature and frequency of recommended screening differs slightly among the authorities.

American Academy of Family Physicians and U.S. Preventive Services Task Force—It may be clinically prudent to offer screening to individuals aged 50 and older who have a first-degree relative with colorectal cancer; a personal history of endometrial, ovarian, or breast cancer; or a previous diagnosis of inflammatory bowel disease, adenomatous polyps, or colorectal cancer. Periodic colonoscopy is recommended for all people with a family history of familial polyposis or cancer family syndrome. [USPSTF's *Guide to Clinical Preventive Services, Second Edition* states "Screening for colorectal cancer is recommended for all persons aged 50 and older with annual fecal occult blood testing (FOBT), or sigmoidoscopy (periodicity unspecified), or both.... There is insufficient evidence to recommend for or against routine screening with ...colonoscopy... Persons with a family history of hereditary syndromes associated with a high risk of colon cancer should be referred for diagnosis and management" p. 89.]

American Cancer Society—For patients having a first-degree relative with a history of colorectal cancer at 55 years of age or younger, the entire colon and rectum should be examined with colonoscopy or air-contrast barium enema every 5 years beginning at 35 to 40 years of age. Members of families with a history of familial adenomatous polyposis should receive earlier screening utilizing flexible sigmoidoscopy. Members of families with a history of hereditary nonpolyposis colorectal cancer require earlier and more intense surveillance utilizing colonoscopy. Individuals with inflammatory bowel disease are at exceptionally high risk and require individualized treatment. Patients under the age of 55 years with a first-degree family member with a history of colorectal cancer are at increased risk and may need earlier and more frequent examinations. People with a history of breast, ovarian, or endometrial cancer are at some increased risk but should follow screening recommendations for normal-risk patients.

American College of Obstetricians and Gynecologists—Colonoscopy should be a part of primary preventive care for individuals with a personal history of inflammatory bowel disease or colonic polyps, or a family history of familial polyposis coli, colorectal cancer, or cancer family syndrome.

American College of Physicians—Individuals 40 years and older who have familial polyposis, inflammatory bowel disease, or a history of colon cancer in a first-degree relative should be screened with air-contrast barium enema or colonoscopy every 3 to 5 years.

American Gastroenterological Association and **American Society for Gastrointestinal Endoscopy**—Individuals with a first-degree relative with a history of colon cancer should have colonoscopy performed every 5 years beginning at age 40 years, especially if the relative developed cancer before age 60 years. Women undergoing irradiation for gynecologic cancer should have flexible sigmoidoscopy every 3 years after diagnosis and beginning radiation therapy. Women with previous gynecologic or breast cancer should have flexible sigmoidoscopy every 3 to 5 years after diagnosis. Patients with left-sided ulcerative colitis for over 15 years and patients with universal colitis for over 8 years should have colonoscopy with multiple biopsies every 1 to 2 years. Patients with a family history of familial polyposis and associated syndromes should have flexible sigmoidoscopy annually from age 10 to 12 years to age 40 years, and every 3 years thereafter. Patients with a family history of hereditary nonpolyposis colorectal cancer should have colonoscopy every 2 years beginning at age 25 years, or at an age 5 years younger than the age of the earliest colon cancer diagnosis in the family.

Canadian Task Force on the Periodic Health Examination—Periodic colonoscopy should be included in the clinical management of patients with a history of colorectal cancer, adenomatous polyps, or ulcerative colitis of 10 years duration. Periodic sigmoidoscopy among family members of patients with familial polyposis, who are at highest risk for colonic cancer, should begin at an early age and should be followed by periodic colonoscopy after 30 years of age.

National Cancer Institute—The physician should identify for special surveillance high-risk patients, including those with a strong family history of colon cancer or with a personal history of adenomas, colon cancer, or inflammatory bowel disease.

Basics of Sigmoidoscopy Screening

1. Sigmoidoscopy is a rather complex procedure that requires considerable technical training and practice. It is beyond the scope of this book to fully explain the performance of this procedure; only very basic aspects will be addressed.

2. *Sigmoidoscope type:* Most authorities recommend use of a flexible sigmoidoscope (preferably 60 cm in length) rather than a rigid sigmoidoscope, because of better patient acceptance and ability to visualize lesions higher in the sigmoid colon.

3. *Training:* Sigmoidoscopy should be performed only by or under the supervision of a trained examiner. Training should be obtained from an experienced endoscopist. Training may consist of diagnostic instruction with audiovisual materials, endoscopic models, and photo atlases, followed by patient demonstrations and successful completion of a number of supervised examinations.

4. *Patient preparation:* Proper bowel preparation is essential for performance of an adequate screening examination. Recommendations for bowel preparation differ somewhat. The minimum preparation consists of two enemas a few hours before examination.

5. *Instrument cleaning:* Proper instrument cleaning is essential for patient safety and maintenance of equipment. The instrument should be promptly cleaned and inspected after use to remove organic materials. A 2% aqueous glutaraldehyde-based disinfectant should be used to clean instruments between procedures. Exposure times of 20 to 30 minutes are recommended to achieve high-level disinfection. Other agents, such as povidone-iodine solution, alcohol, surgical scrubs, phenolics, quaternary ammonium compounds, and water, have not been found to be acceptable for disinfecting sigmoidoscopes. The safety and efficacy of automatic endoscope washers have not been established. The same individual(s) in the office should consistently perform the decontamination to ensure quality. Endoscopes should be air-dried and stored in a hanging position to diminish bacterial contamination.

6. *Maintenance of Competence:* Clinicians should perform sigmoidoscopy routinely in order to maintain their competence. Performance of only occasional procedures may lead to missed or inappropriate diagnoses or a high rate of complications, or both.

7. *Follow-up of Abnormal Results:* All authorities agree that patients found to have adenomatous polyps of 1 cm or larger need colonoscopic examination of the entire colon. Approximately 10% of individuals screened will have small tubular adenomas less than 1 cm in diameter. Controversy exists about whether patients with these lesions need colonoscopic follow-up in view of their low potential for malignancy.

Patient Resources

Cancer of the Colon and Rectum — Research Report; What You Need to Know About Cancer of the Colon and Rectum. Office of Cancer Communications, National Cancer Institute, Bldg. 31, Rm. 10A24, Bethesda, MD 20892; (800) 4-CANCER.

Colonoscopy: Questions and Answers; Polyps of the Colon and Rectum: Questions and Answers. American Society of Colon and Rectal Surgeons, 800 E Northwest Highway, Suite 1080, Palatine, IL 60067; (708) 359-9184

Hearing Loss Screening

Hearing loss increases in prevalence with age and is very common in older adults. Approximately one fourth of adults aged 65 to 74 years and one half of adults 85 years and older report some degree of hearing loss. Hearing loss, particularly when it develops late in life and is progressive in nature, can compromise the ability to perform many important activities, such as using the telephone, driving, and shopping. It also may lead to social withdrawal, depression, and exacerbation of coexisting psychiatric problems. Some older people with hearing loss also have cognitive impairment, and there is evidence that improvement of hearing may contribute to improvement in cognitive ability. Many types of hearing loss can be improved with the use of hearing aids; however, only 10% to 15% of patients who could benefit from a hearing aid actually use one.

Recommendations of Major Authorities

American Academy of Family Physicians and **U.S. Preventive Services Task Force**—Hearing screening is not necessary for asymptomatic adults under 65, except for those who are exposed regularly to excessive noise (e.g., in recreational or occupational settings). Screening of workers for noise-induced hearing loss should be performed in the context of existing worksite programs and occupational medicine guidelines. Elderly patients should be periodically evaluated regarding their hearing, counseled regarding the availability of hearing aids, and referred appropriately for any abnormalities. The optimal frequency of hearing assessment should be determined by clinical discretion. It is unclear that benefits are sufficient to justify the substantial cost of audiometric screening of the nearly 30 million Americans over age 65. A more practical but unproven strategy might include a careful historical evaluation of hearing in older individuals, a simple otoscopic examination for cerumen and other findings, and patient education regarding the availability of efficacious hearing aid devices.

American College of Obstetricians and Gynecologists—Women 65 years and older should be evaluated for hearing loss.

American Speech-Language-Hearing Association—Considerable debate concerning the efficacy of selected screening protocols for older adults has taken place in recent years, and it remains to be seen whether the choice of protocol actually influences compliance with the follow-up recommendations. The clinician may choose to use a hearing handicap questionnaire, pure-tone audiometry, or both. The rationale for using a questionnaire and pure-tone audiometry in combination is that compliance with audiologic recommendations is often greater when individuals perceive their hearing loss to be a handicap. Selection of the protocol should take into consideration cost, compliance data for the particular population, and the specificity, sensitivity, and predictive values of screening. Equipment used should be appropriately calibrated, and self-assessment scales must be reliable. Compliance-improving strategies (e.g., educational materials) should be an integral part of any screening program and appropriate follow-up services should be available.

Canadian Task Force on the Periodic Health Examination— There is fair justification for looking for hearing loss in a periodic health examination of adults. Further study is warranted if adults report being hard of hearing or fail to respond to the normal spoken voice; have a medical or family history placing them at high risk for hearing loss (e.g., family history of hearing loss, occupational history of exposure to noise, pursuit of noisy leisure activities, or history of recurring ear problems).

Basics of Hearing Screening

1. All older adult patients should be questioned about signs of hearing loss. Because patients may not be fully aware of impairment, family members also should be questioned, if possible.

2. A screening questionnaire may be used to screen for communication problems and social and emotional handicaps stemming from hearing loss. Questionnaires may be filled out by the patient or administered by staff. Screening questionnaires have the advantage of identifying patients who perceive hearing loss to be a problem and who, therefore, may be particularly motivated to use a hearing aid. Some authorities recommend using both a questionnaire and pure-tone testing for screening. This may modestly improve sensitivity and specificity.

3. Pure-tone screening can be administered using either a standard pure-tone audiometer or a hand-held audioscope (an otoscope that emits tones of calibrated frequencies and intensities). With either method, the environment in which screening is administered should be as quiet as possible. Frequencies used should be within the speech range. There is disagreement about the sound intensity that should be used in screening. Following are two examples of suggested screening protocols:

   • Pure tones are presented at 25 dB at 1000, 2000, and 4000 Hz. Failure to respond to any one frequency in either ear at 25 dB constitutes a "fail." For adults under 65, this may be the preferred protocol. The majority of those over 65 years of age screened with this protocol, however, may fail. Because of this, some authorities recommend using a 40 dB tone at 4000 Hz.

   • Pure tones are presented at 25 and 40 dB at 1000, 2000, and 4000 Hz (optional). Failure to respond to the 40 dB signal at any one frequency in either ear constitutes a "fail." Inability to hear any one frequency at 25 dB places an individual "at risk" for hearing loss. A referral for audiologic assessment may be appropriate if the person reports being handicapped by their hearing loss. Persons who fail the screening should be monitored annually to determine whether their hearing loss is progressive.

4. Simple physical examination procedures for hearing screening, such as the whispered voice and finger rub tests, are not recommended by major authorities. Although they are fairly accurate crude hearing tests, they are insensitive to disorders of central auditory processing and speech understanding.

5. Patients found to have evidence of hearing loss by screening should be considered for referral to a specialist for comprehensive audiologic evaluation, especially if they feel handicapped by the hearing loss. Because approximately 10% of individuals with hearing loss are amenable to medical or surgical treatment, and some patients are incorrectly identified as having hearing loss by screening, patients should not be referred directly to a hearing aid dealer.

6. The primary care clinician should make sure that appropriate follow-up management is provided to all patients referred for audiologic evaluation. Patients may need considerable support and training to use their hearing aids effectively.

Patient Resources

Age Page: Hearing and the Elderly. National Institute on Aging, Bldg. 31, Rm. SC27, Bethesda, MD 20892; (301) 496-1752.

Answers to Questions about Noise and Hearing Loss and *How To Buy a Hearing Aid.* American Speech-Language-Hearing Association, 10801 Rockville Pike, Rockville, MD 20852; (800) 638-TALK (voice or TTY), (301) 897-8682 (in Maryland).

Hypertension (High Blood Pressure) Screening

Approximately 50 million Americans have elevated blood pressure warranting monitoring or drug therapy. These persons are at increased risk for coronary artery disease, peripheral vascular disease, stroke, renal disease, and retinopathy. Treatment for hypertension is very effective. Antihypertensive therapy has contributed to a 57% reduction in stroke mortality and a 50% reduction in mortality from coronary artery disease since 1972. The benefits of antihypertensive therapy are greatest in those with the most marked elevations in blood pressure; however, even patients with Stage 1, or mild, hypertension benefit from treatment. Recent research has demonstrated the importance of treating "isolated" systolic hypertension, especially in older adult patients.

Recommendations of Major Authorities

American Academy of Family Physicians—Blood pressure should be measured at every visit, with a minimum frequency of every 2 years.

American College of Obstetricians and Gynecologists—Blood pressure should be measured as part of periodic evaluation visits, which should occur yearly or as appropriate.

American College of Physicians—Blood pressure should be measured in adults every 1 to 2 years. Normotensive patients should have blood pressure measurements at least yearly if any of the following pertains: 1) diastolic blood pressure between 85 and 89 mm Hg; 2) African-American heritage; 3) moderate or extreme obesity; 4) a first-degree relative with hypertension; 5) a personal history of hypertension.

National High Blood Pressure Education Program (NHBPEP) of the National Heart, Lung, and Blood Institute— Blood pressure measurements should be performed on adults at least every 2 years, and at each patient visit if possible. Patients with diastolic blood pressures of 85 to 89 mm Hg should have their blood pressure rechecked within 1 year.

U.S. Preventive Services Task Force—Adults should have blood pressure measured regularly, with the optimal interval left to clinical discretion. For those whose diastolic blood pressure is 85 to 89 mm Hg, measurement should be performed at least yearly.

Basics of Blood Pressure Screening

1. The patient should be advised to avoid using tobacco and caffeine for 30 minutes prior to the measurement.

2. The patient should be seated in a quiet environment free from temperature extremes for at least 5 minutes before the measurement is performed.

3. The measurement should be performed with a mercury sphygmomanometer, if available. An aneroid manometer may be used if it is periodically calibrated according to manufacturer's recommendations. A validated electronic device meeting the requirements of the American National Standard for Electronic or Automated Sphygmomanometers set forth by the Association for the Advancement of Medical Instruments may also be used.

4. The manometer should be positioned at the clinician's eye level, if possible, to assure accuracy in reading.

5. An appropriate sized cuff should be used. The bladder of the cuff should encircle 80% to 100% of the arm. The cuff width should be 40% of the circumference of the upper arm. Narrow cuffs lead to falsely elevated readings; wide cuffs may falsely lower the reading.

6. The patient's arm should be bare. Constriction of the upper arm by a rolled shirt sleeve should be avoided. The arm should be supported horizontally so the cuff is positioned at heart level (the fourth intercostal space). If the arm cannot be positioned appropriately, a correction factor should be utilized: For each 1 cm above or below heart level, 0.8 mm Hg should be added or subtracted, respectively.

7. The stethoscope must be lightly applied to the antecubital fossa. Excess pressure results in falsely low diastolic blood pressure readings.

8. The cuff pressure should be rapidly increased to about 30 mm Hg beyond the point at which the radial pulse is no longer palpable. The pressure indicator's rate of descent should be no greater than 2 to 3 mm Hg per second.

9. In adults, the systolic (SBP) and diastolic (DBP) pressure readings should be identified by the pressures corresponding to the first of two consecutive sounds and the disappearance of sound (not muffling), respectively. Disappearance should be confirmed by listening for 10 to 20 mm Hg below the last sound heard.

10. The average of at least two readings should be used unless the first two differ by more than 5 mm Hg, in which case additional readings should be obtained. To allow blood to be released from arm veins, there should be an interval of 1 to 2 minutes before pressure measurements are repeated in the same arm.

11. Blood pressure should be measured in both arms initially and remeasured at subsequent visits using the arm with the highest initial pressures.

12. Diagnosis of hypertension requires confirmation during at least two subsequent visits (unless SBP is 210 mm Hg or greater, or DBP is 120 mm Hg or greater, or both).

13. Because blood pressure readings obtained in a medical setting may not be typical of a patient's usual blood pressure, monitoring at home or work by the patient, family, or friends may be valuable. If this is done, measurement devices must be calibrated initially and rechecked at least yearly. The person taking the blood pressure should be instructed in proper technique and

the technique rechecked periodically. In certain clinical situations, continuous ambulatory blood pressure monitoring may provide a useful adjunct to episodic blood pressure monitoring performed by the provider or patient.

14. Life-style modifications can help prevent the development of hypertension and should be the initial treatment modality for the first 3-4 months for patients with Stage I (mild) or Stage 2 (moderate) hypertension.

Table 5.5. Categories for Blood Pressure Levels in Adults: Age 18 Years and Older

Category	Blood Pressure Level (mm Hg)	
	Systolic	*Diastolic*
Normal	<130	<85
High normal	130-139	85-89
Hypertension*		
Stage 1	140-159	90-99
Stage 2	160-179	100-109
Stage 3	180-209	110-119
Stage 4	≥210	≥120

Note: "Hypertension" is the medical term for high blood pressure. These categories are from the National High Blood Pressure Education Program, JNCV Report. (< = less than; ≥ = greater than or equal to). Table taken from NIH Pub. No. 94-3281.

Patient Resources

Blacks and High Blood Pressure; Eating Right to Lower Your Blood Pressure; High Blood Pressure and What You Can Do About It; Six Good Reasons to Control Your High Blood Pressure. National Heart, Lung, and Blood Institute Information Center, P.O. Box 30105, Bethesda, MD 20824-0105; (301) 251-1222.

Lead Poisoning Screening

Lead poisoning is one of the most common and preventable childhood environmental health problems in the United States. Although low-income, inner-city children have higher rates of lead poisoning, no socioeconomic group, geographic area, or racial or ethnic population is spared. In 1990, up to 3 million children under 6 years of age, 15% of all children in this age group, had blood lead levels greater than 10 μg/dL. Studies have shown associations between diminished intelligence, impaired neurobehavioral development, decreased hearing acuity, and growth inhibition and lead levels as low as 10 to 15 μg/dL. A recent study [Ruff HA, Bijur PE, Markowitz M, Yeou-Cheng M, Rosen JR. Declining blood lead levels and cognitive changes in moderately lead-poisoned children. *JAMA.* 1993;269:1641-1654] demonstrated in a cohort of children with moderate lead poisoning (25 to 55 μg/dL), most of whom received residential lead abatement, that decreases in blood lead levels were associated with improvements in cognitive functioning. Higher levels can cause severe damage to the central nervous, renal, and hematopoietic systems and can be fatal.

Recommendations of Major Authorities

American Academy of Family Physicians—Until 6 years of age, children should be assessed for risk of lead exposure, using a structured questionnaire (see Table 5.6). Children with an increased risk for lead exposure should have whole blood lead level testing.

American Academy of Pediatrics—Pediatric-care providers should increase their efforts to screen children for lead exposure. Blood lead screening should be a part of routine health supervision for children and can best be addressed by increasing children's access to health care. Because lead is ubiquitous in the U.S. environment, this screening should occur at about 9 to 12 months of age and, if possible, again at about 24 months of age. The Centers for Disease Control and Prevention has raised the possibility that there may be low-risk communities that do not require screening, but no explicit guidance has been developed for determining a community's risk. As more data are collected, it may become evident that there are locales where selective screening of children is more appropriate than routine screening. Currently no adequate laboratory capacity exists nationwide to screen each child, but the requirement to phase in screening should generate those resources.

Centers for Disease Control and Prevention (CDC)—All children should have routine blood lead-level testing, except in communities where large numbers or percentages of children have been screened and found not to have elevated levels. A structured question-naire (see Table 5.6) should be used to assess risk. A child for whom an answer to any of the questions is "yes" should be considered at high risk. Infants at low risk of lead poisoning should be screened at 12 months of age and, if the initial test result is <10 µg/dL and resources allow, at 24 months of age. Infants at high risk should be screened initially at 6 months of age and, if the initial test result is <10 µg/dL, every 6 months. After two consecutive measurements are <10 µg/dL, or three are <15 µg/dL, the child should be retested in one year. High-risk children ≥36 and <72 months of age without previous test-ing should have blood lead testing. Re-screening should occur any time history suggests exposure has increased. In general, screening may stop at 6 years of age, unless indicated (for example, in a developmen-tally delayed child with pica).

U.S. Preventive Services Task Force (USPSTF)—Recommen-dation currently under review. [USPSTF's *Guide to Clinical Preven-tive Services, Second Edition* states, "Screening for elevated lead levels by measuring blood lead at least once at age 12 months is rec-ommended for all children at increased risk of lead exposure. All chil-dren with identifiable risk factors should be screened, as should all children living in communities in which the prevalence of blood lead levels requiring individual intervention, including residential lead hazard control or chelation therapy, is high or is undefined. Evidence is currently insufficient to recommend an exact community prevalence below which targeted screening can be substituted for universal screening" p. 247.]

Basics of Lead Screening

1. Risk assessment and counseling should begin during prenatal visits and continue after birth during regular office visits un-til at least the age of 6 years.

2. Each child's risk of lead toxicity should be evaluated. For this purpose a structured set of questions such as that developed by CDC (Table 5.6) can be very helpful. If the answer to any of these questions is positive, the child is considered at high risk for exposure.

3. Screening by measurement of the blood lead level is more sen-sitive and specific than measurement of the erythrocyte proto-porphyrin (EP) level. Blood lead levels <25µg/dL cannot be

reliably detected by EP testing. elevated EP levels (≥35µg/dL) require confirmation with blood lead testing.

4. Because of possible contamination of capillary specimens from environmental sources, venous blood samples are preferable to capillary sampling for blood lead levels. Elevated blood lead results (≥15 µg/dL) obtained on capillary specimens must be confirmed using venous blood. A child with a capillary lead level ≥70 µg/dL should be considered a medical emergency and retested with a venous sample immediately.

5. Blood lead test results can be interpreted and managed according to the CDC recommendations.

6. Laboratories where blood is tested for lead levels should participate in a blood-lead proficiency testing program, such as the collaborative program between the Health Resources and Services Administration and CDC. Information on this program is available by calling (404) 488-7330.

Table 5.6. Recommended Questions for Assessing Exposure Risk

Does your child live in or regularly visit a house with peeling or chipping paint built before 1960? (This includes day care centers, preschools, homes of baby-sitters or relatives, etc.)

Does your child live in or regularly visit a house built before 1960 with recent, ongoing, or planned renovation or remodeling?

Does your child have a brother or sister, housemate or playmate being followed or treated for lead poisoning (blood lead level ≥15 µg/dL)?

Does your child live with an adult whose job or hobby involves exposure to lead? (Such hobbies include ceramics, furniture refinishing, and stained glass work.)

Does your child live near an active lead smelter, battery recycling plant, or other industry likely to release lead?

Adapted from: Centers for Disease Control. Preventing Lead Poisoning in Young Children: A Statement by the Centers for Disease Control. *Atlanta, GA: Centers for Disease Control; 1991.*

7. Because iron deficiency can enhance lead absorption and toxicity, all children with blood levels ≥20 μg/dL should be tested for iron deficiency.

8. In addition to screening, it is important to provide guidance to parents about creating an environment safe from lead exposure for their children. Counseling should include advice on eliminating peeling or chipping paint, decreasing the lead content or water, preventing contact via hobbies or contaminated work clothing, remaining alert for pica behavior, and assuring good hygiene.

Family Resources

Getting the Lead Out. Food and Drug Administration. Superintendent of Documents, Consumer Information Center-3C, PO Box 100, Pueblo, CO 81002.

Home Buyer's Guide to Environmental Hazards. Environmental Protection Agency, Superintendent of Documents, Consumer Information Center-3C, PO Box 100, Pueblo, CO 81002.

Important Facts about Childhood Lead Poisoning Prevention. Centers for Disease Control and Prevention, Lead Poisoning Prevention Program, 1600 Clifton Rd., Atlanta, GA 30333; (404) 488-4880.

What Everyone Should Know about Lead Poisoning. Alliance to End Childhood Lead Poisoning, 600 Pennsylvania Ave. SE, Suite 100, Washington, DC 20003 (individual copies); Channing L. Bete Co., Inc., 200 State Rd., South Deerfield, MA 01373; (800) 628-7733 (bulk copies).

What You Should Know about Lead-Based Paint in Your Home. U.S. Consumer Product Safety Commission, Washington, DC 20207; (800) 638-2666.

Obesity Screening

Approximately 32 million American adults (24% of men and 27% of women) are overweight. Mortality rates are increased for individuals with weights only 10% above desirable weight. Most authorities recognize weights 20% or more above desirable weight to constitute obesity and to be associated with multiple attendant health risks.

Hypertension and noninsulin dependent diabetes mellitus (Type II) are three times more prevalent in the obese. The risks of hypercholesterolemia and coronary artery disease are also increased, as are the risks of several types of cancer including colon, rectal, prostate, gallbladder, biliary tract, breast, cervical, endometrial, and ovarian cancers. Abdominal adiposity, measured by waist-to-hip circumference ratio (WHR), is associated with increased risk of diabetes, hypertension, coronary heart disease, stroke, and death from all causes. Recent research indicates that WHR may be a stronger predictor of mortality than measures of general body adiposity.

Weight loss, through changes in diet, increased physical activity, and other interventions, can decrease the risk of most forms of morbidity associated with obesity. In order for weight loss to be beneficial it must be sustained. Recent research indicates that fluctuations in weight may be an independent risk factor for increased total mortality and mortality from coronary artery disease.

Recommendations of Major Authorities

American Academy of Family Physicians and **U.S. Preventive Services Task Force**—All adults should receive periodic measurement of height and weight. The optimal frequency for measuring height and weight in adults is a matter of clinical discretion. Those individuals who are 20% or more above desirable weight should receive appropriate nutritional and exercise counseling.

Canadian Task Force on the Periodic Health Examination—Height and weight measurements should be made at the discretion of the clinician.

U.S. Department of Agriculture, U. S. Department of Health and Human Services—Calculation of the ratio of waist circumference to hip circumference should be used, in addition to height and weight measurements, to determine if a person's weight is "healthy."

Basics of Body Measurement Screening

1. Height is most accurately measured with the patient barefoot or in socks or stockings only. Care should be taken to make sure that the patient is standing as erect as possible with feet flat on the floor. If a height-measuring rod attached to a scale is used, its accuracy should be checked regularly, as such rods tend to become inaccurate with use.

2. Weight is most accurately measured with the patient wearing minimal or no clothing. A balance beam or electronic scale (not a spring-type scale) should be used for measurement.

3. There is currently considerable debate about the definition of a "healthy" weight. Two basic methods are used for evaluating weight: 1) reference to standardized height-weight tables and 2) calculation of body mass index (BMI).

    *   Clinicians have been most accustomed to using height-weight tables adapted from those that were developed by the Metropolitan Life Insurance Company in 1959 from mortality data of its insured population. These have been the most widely used height-weight tables, but they have certain limitations. In practice, body frame cannot be easily measured and must be estimated visually. Also, these tables are based on an insured population, which may not be totally representative of the general population.

    *   In recent years, some authorities have endorsed using BMI to evaluate healthy weight. BMI values are believed to correlate more accurately with total body fat content. The formula for calculation of BMI is:

$$\frac{\text{Weight (kg)}}{\text{Height}^2 \text{ (m)}}$$

    Values above 26.4 for men and 25.8 for women correspond to the 20% over desirable weight limits derived from the Metropolitan Life Insurance tables, and are commonly cited by some other experts as constituting overweight.

    *   Some authorities believe that the normal ranges of BMI and weight increase with age. The National Academy of Sciences (1989) published a table of desirable BMI values in relation to age. Other authorities have questioned the validity of age adjustments.

4. The determination of WHR is also useful for assessing patients, particularly those with borderline high weight who have personal or family medical histories placing them at increased health risk. WHR is determined by measuring the abdominal (waist) circumference and the hip circumference. The abdominal circumference is measured at the level of the umbilicus (or

127

the level of greatest anterior extension of the abdomen) with the patient standing. The hip circumference is determined by measuring the greatest circumference at the level of the buttocks. Both measurements should be performed at the end of a normal expiration and without indenting the skin. The formula for calculating WHR is:

$$\frac{\text{Abdominal Circumference}}{\text{Hip Circumference}}$$

WHR values above 1.0 for men and above 0.8 for women are associated with increased risk of diabetes, hypertension, heart disease, and stroke.

Patient Resources

Nutrition and Your Health: Dietary Guidelines for Americans (3rd ed, 1990). U.S. Dept. of Agriculture and U.S. Dept. of Health and Human Services. Available from: Consumer Information Center—3C, Dept. 514-X, Pueblo, CO 81009.

Check Your Weight and Heart Disease I.Q. National Heart, Lung, and Blood Institute Information Center, P.O. Box 30105, Bethesda, MD 20824-0105; (301) 251-1222.

Weight Control: Losing Weight and Keeping It Off. American Academy of Family Physicians, 8880 Ward Parkway, Kansas City, MO 64114-2797; (800) 944-0000.

Rubella Immunity Screening

Rubella is a generally mild illness that when contracted by pregnant women, particularly in the first trimester, can lead to miscarriage, stillbirth, and congenital rubella syndrome (CRS)—the common features of which are hearing loss, developmental delay, growth retardation, and cardiac and ocular defects. The incidence of rubella and CRS decreased markedly after introduction of rubella vaccine in 1969. In 1988, there were only 225 cases of rubella and 6 cases of CRS reported in the United States. Between 1988 and 1991, however, the number of reported cases of rubella increased 6-fold and the incidence of CRS increased 15-fold. The majority of new cases of rubella occur in young adults who are unvaccinated, particularly in settings of mass congregation, such as colleges, prisons, and religious communities.

Rubella vaccine is approximately 95% effective at conferring immunity. This immunity is probably lifelong. Screening and subsequent immunization of susceptible women of childbearing age has been shown to decrease the incidence of CRS. Evidence that screening and immunization of susceptible men and older women decreases incidence of CRS is weak. For this reason, most authorities recommend concentrating screening and immunization efforts on women of childbearing age.

Recommendations of Major Authorities

All major authorities, including **Advisory Committee on Immunization Practices (ACIP), American Academy of Family Physicians, American Academy of Pediatrics (AAP), American College of Obstetricians and Gynecologists, American College of Physicians (ACP), Canadian Task Force on the Periodic Health Examination,** and **U.S. Preventive Services Task Force**—Women of childbearing age who lack documented evidence of immunity or prior immunization should be immunized. All of these authorities emphasize the importance of immunizing women, and some (ACIP, AAP, ACP) recommend immunization of susceptible males as well.

Basics of Rubella Immunization

1. *Indications:* All women of childbearing age should be screened for immunity to rubella. Those who have neither documentation of prior immunization after 12 months of age nor documented immunity by antibody testing should be immunized. Reported history of infection should not be taken as evidence of immunity. Antibody testing may be offered to those suspected of lacking immunity, but authorities agree that immunization may be provided without this testing. Screening and vaccination of other adults may be considered, especially in high-risk settings (e.g., colleges, military bases).

2. *Vaccine Types:* Rubella vaccine is made from a live virus. The currently available vaccine is designated RA 27/3 and is available in either a monovalent form (rubella only) or in combinations: measles-rubella (MR), rubella-mumps, and measles-mumps-rubella (MMR). Any of these vaccines may be used in adults, but authorities recommend using MMR, unless contraindicated.

3. *Dosage and Administration:* A dose of 0.5 mL of reconstituted vaccine (of any type) should be administered subcutaneously, using a 5/8- to 3/4-inch 23-25 gauge needle.

4. *Precautions:* Although limited studies have shown no evidence of vaccine-induced CRS, pregnant women should not be given rubella vaccine, and all women receiving vaccine should be advised not to become pregnant for 3 months after vaccination. Women who do become pregnant within 3 months of vaccination should be counseled about concern for the fetus, but they generally should not be advised that interruption of the pregnancy is necessary. Patients who are immunocompromised (except for HIV-positive patients) should not be immunized.

   Immune globulin-containing preparations, such as IG, HBIG, VZIG, packed red blood cell, whole blood, or plasma, may interfere with immune response to MMR vaccination. MMR should not be given from 2 weeks before to 3-11 months (depending on the immune globulin content of the preparation) after such preparations are given. Vaccination should be repeated after the window of immune globulin interference has expired, or antibody testing should be performed to determine immunity status. See Advisory Committee on Immunization Practices (*MMWR*, in press) for more detailed information regarding this issue.

   The postpartum vaccination of rubella-susceptible women with rubella or MMR vaccine should not be delayed because of the receipt of anti-$Rh_0(D)Ig$ (human) or any other blood product containing IG. Women given a postpartum rubella immunization who have received anti-$Rh_0(D)Ig$ (human) during the last trimester or at delivery should have immunity confirmed by antibody level testing 3 months after the immunization.

   Immunization should be delayed for adults with febrile illnesses. Caution should be taken in administering rubella vaccine in the form of MMR to adults with a history of allergy to eggs. Adults who have experienced anaphylactic reactions to topically or systemically administered neomycin should not be given rubella vaccine.

5. *Adverse Reactions:* Approximately 25% of adults immunized with rubella vaccine develop arthralgia, and 13% to 15% report arthritis-like symptoms. These symptoms generally develop 1 to 3 weeks after vaccination, persist for 1 day to 3

weeks, and rarely recur. Rarely, recurrent arthralgia and sometimes arthritis persist for an extended length of time. Paresthesias and pain in the arms and legs may also rarely develop and follow the same course as arthralgias. These adverse reactions seem to occur more often in non-immune patients after vaccination. Other adverse reactions include low-grade fever, rash, and lymphadenopathy. Providers are encouraged to report adverse reactions of all kinds particularly if serious or unusual, to the Vaccine Adverse Event Reporting System (VAERS). VAERS forms and instructions are available in the *FDA Drug Bulletin* (Food and Drug Administration) and the *Physician's Drug Reference*, or by calling the 24-hour VAERS information recording at (800) 822-7967.

6. *Vaccine Storage and Handling:* Reconstituted vaccine should be discarded if not used within 8 hours. Unreconstituted vaccine should be stored at 2° to 8°C (36° to 46°F) or colder and should be protected from light. Handle all vaccine preparations according to manufacturers' instructions.

Smoking Cessation Counseling

Smoking is the leading cause of preventable death in the United States. Approximately 430,000 people die of tobacco-related causes annually. Smoking cessation is the single most important patient counseling topic because of its potential for patient benefit. Figure 5.7 shows the benefits of smoking cessation for different parts of the smoker's body. There is also evidence that exposure of nonsmokers to environmental tobacco smoke leads to lung cancer and possibly coronary heart disease. The exposure of children to environmental tobacco smoke leads to increased rates of chronic middle ear effusions, pneumonia, and other respiratory tract infections.

Primary care clinicians can play a key role in helping patients quit smoking. Even very simple interventions by primary care clinicians can lead to 5% to 10% long-term quit rates. More extensive interventions, including the use of nicotine gum and patches, can lead to rates that are significantly higher. If all primary care providers made even simple interventions with smoking patients, the national smoking cessation rate could be doubled. Recent studies indicate, however, that fewer than half of smoking patients receive any assistance in quitting from their health care providers.

131

Key
"CS" refers to continuing smokers,
"NS" refers to never smokers.

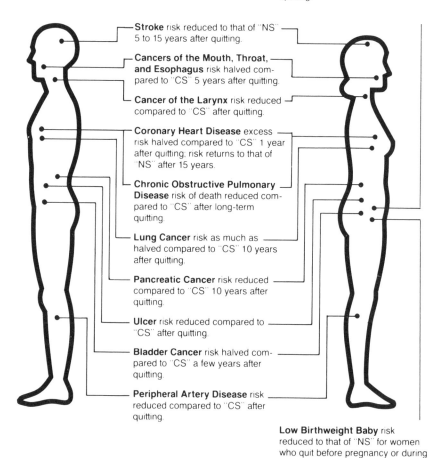

Cervical Cancer risk reduced compared to "CS" a few years after quitting.

Stroke risk reduced to that of "NS" 5 to 15 years after quitting.

Cancers of the Mouth, Throat, and Esophagus risk halved compared to "CS" 5 years after quitting.

Cancer of the Larynx risk reduced compared to "CS" after quitting.

Coronary Heart Disease excess risk halved compared to "CS" 1 year after quitting; risk returns to that of "NS" after 15 years.

Chronic Obstructive Pulmonary Disease risk of death reduced compared to "CS" after long-term quitting.

Lung Cancer risk as much as halved compared to "CS" 10 years after quitting.

Pancreatic Cancer risk reduced compared to "CS" 10 years after quitting.

Ulcer risk reduced compared to "CS" after quitting.

Bladder Cancer risk halved compared to "CS" a few years after quitting.

Peripheral Artery Disease risk reduced compared to "CS" after quitting.

Low Birthweight Baby risk reduced to that of "NS" for women who quit before pregnancy or during first trimester.

From: Centers for Disease Control, Office on Smoking and Health. *The Health Benefits of Smoking Cessation: A Report of the Surgeon General, 1990 at a Glance.* Rockville, MD: Centers for Disease Control; 1990. USDHHS publication CDC 90-8419.

Figure 5.7. *Benefits of Smoking Cessation*

Recommendations of Major Authorities

All major authorities, including **American Academy of Family Physicians, American Cancer Society, American College of Obstetricians and Gynecologists, American College of Physicians, Canadian Task Force on the Periodic Health Examination, National Heart, Lung, and Blood Institute, National Cancer Institute, National Institute of Dental Research,** and **U.S. Preventive Services Task Force**—Clinicians should provide smoking cessation counseling, treatment, and referral to patients who smoke.

Several major authorities, including **Joint Commission on Accreditation of Healthcare Organizations**—Smoking should be prohibited in health-care facilities.

Basics of Smoking Cessation Counseling

Adapted from: Glynn TJ, Manley MW. *How to Help Your Patients Stop Smoking: A National Cancer Institute Manual for Physicians.* Bethesda, MD: National Institutes of Health, 1989. USDHHS publication NIH 89-3064.

1. Health-care providers should create a smoke-free office, as follows:

   - Select a date for the office to become smoke-free.
   - Advise all staff and patients of this plan.
   - Post no-smoking signs in all office areas.
   - Remove ashtrays.
   - Display nonsmoking materials and cessation information prominently.
   - Do not use waiting room magazines that contain tobacco advertising. A list of such magazines is available [Goldsmith MS. Magazines without tobacco advertising (Medical News and Perspectives). *JAMA.*, 1991;266: 3099-3102].

2. Consideration should be given to designating an office smoking cessation coordinator who will be responsible for seeing that the smoking cessation program is carried out.

3. Clinicians should ask about smoking at every opportunity:
    - "Do you smoke?"
    - "How much?"
    - "How soon after waking do you have your first cigarette?"
    - "Are you interested in stopping smoking?"
    - "Have you ever tried to stop before? If so, what happened?"

4. Assessment of patient smoking status can be facilitated by using a brief, self-administered questionnaire (see Table 5.8). Staff can help patients fill out the questionnaire or ask the questions verbally.

Table 5.8. Smoking Assessment

1. Do you now smoke cigarettes?

2. Does the person closest to you smoke cigarettes?

3. How many cigarettes do you smoke a day?

4. How soon after you wake up do you smoke your first cigarette?
    Within 30 minutes
    More than 30 minutes

5. How interested are you in stopping smoking?
    Not at all
    A little
    Some
    A lot
    Very

6. If you decided to quite smoking completely during the next 2 weeks, how confident are you that you would succeed?
    Not at all
    A little
    Some
    A lot
    Very

From: Glynn TJ, Manley MW. How To Help Your Patients Stop Smoking: A National Cancer Institute Manual for Physicians. *Bethesda, MD: National Institutes of Health; 1989. USDHHS publication NIH 89-3064.*

5. A sticker or other visual cue should be placed on the charts of patients who smoke as a reminder of the need to address the issue of smoking at every visit. Similar stickers may be placed on the charts of children of smokers to serve as cues to talk to parents about the ways their smoking endangers their children. It may also be helpful to use a flow chart in patient records to keep track of smoking cessation interventions.

6. All smokers should be advised to stop.

   • Clinicians should state this clearly, for example: "As your physician (or other healthcare provider), I must advise you to stop smoking now."

   • The message to quit should be personalized. Reference should be made to the patient's clinical condition, smoking history, family history, personal interests, and social roles. During illnesses, especially if smoking-related, patients may be more receptive to smoking cessation interventions.

7. Providers should assist patients in stopping.

   • Setting a quit date: Patients should be helped to pick a date within the next 4 weeks, acknowledging that no time is ideal. Stopping at high-stress times is not advisable; suggesting a significant date (e.g., the patient's or a spouse's birthday or the first day of the month) may be helpful.

   • Providing self-help materials (see Patient Resources): The smoking cessation coordinator or a support staff member can review the materials with patients, if desired.

   • Consideration should be given to prescribing nicotine gum or patch, especially for highly addicted patients (those who smoke one pack a day or more or who smoke their first cigarette within 30 minutes of waking). Tables 5.9 and 5.10 present basic information about nicotine gum and patch use, respectively.

   • Consideration should be given to signing a stop-smoking contract with patients.

   • For patients who are not willing to quit now, motivational literature should be provided and the patients asked again at the next and subsequent visits.

Table 5.9. Information about Nicotine Gum Use

Preparation

Patients should stop smoking before beginning nicotine gum use and be involved in a smoking cessation program under the care of a physician or other health-care provider.

Dosage

Patients should use one piece of gum whenever they have the urge to smoke. Patients should be instructed not to exceed 30 pieces of 2 mg gum per day. For patients who have trouble with an as-needed approach, a fixed dosage schedule (e.g., one piece every 60-90 minutes) may be more appropriate. At least two boxes (192 pieces), of the 2 mg gum should be prescribed at the initial visit. A common problem is that patients use the gum too sparingly in the first few days after quitting and relapse because of lack of nicotine.

Administration

Each piece of nicotine gum should be chewed slowly and intermittently for about 30 minutes. Chewing quickly can release the nicotine too rapidly and reduce the effect of the gum. Each piece of gum should be chewed enough to soften it or until the taste or "tingling" from the nicotine is felt. Then it should be "parked" in contact with the oral mucosa so that the nicotine can be absorbed. The gum should be rechewed gently every few minutes to release more nicotine.

Duration of therapy

The need for refills should be assessed at follow-up visits. The dose of nicotine gum should be tapered after about 3 months. Use of the gum for more than 6 months is not recommended.

Adverse reactions

Potential side effects of nicotine gum use are sore jaw, mouth irritation, heartburn, nausea, sore throat, and palpitations.

Contraindications

Nicotine gum is contraindicated for patients who have had a recent myocardial infarction, severe or worsening angina, or life-threatening arrhythmias. It is also contraindicated for patients who are pregnant, nursing, or are unable to chew.

Adapted from: Glynn TJ, Manley MW. How To Help Your Patients Stop Smoking: A National Cancer Institute Manual for Physicians. Bethesda, MD: National Institutes of Health; 1989. USDHHS publication NIH 89-3064.

Table 5.10. Information about Nicotine Patch Use

Preparation

Patients should stop smoking before beginning to use the nicotine patch and be involved in a smoking cessation program under the care of a physician or other health-care provider. Although the patches have proven to be beneficial even in the absence of supportive care, they are much more effective when used in conjunction with a smoking cessation program.

Dosage

All patch manufacturers recommend an initial treatment dose followed by one or two weaning doses. Most manufacturers advise starting at the highest dose patch available, except with small patients (less than 100 lb.) and those with a history of cardiovascular disease.

Administration

The patch should be applied only once a day to a clean, dry and non-hairy site on the trunk or upper arm. The patch should be applied promptly on removal from its protective pouch to prevent evaporative loss of nicotine from the system. Application sites should not be reused for at least a week to prevent skin irritation. For all-day systems, the used patch should be removed after 24 hours and a new one applied to another site. For the 16-hour system, the patch should be applied on waking and removed at bedtime.

Duration of therapy

Depending on the type of patch, the recommended duration of therapy ranges from 10 to 16 weeks.

Adverse reactions

The most common side effect of the nicotine patch is a mild, transient (15 to 60 minutes) itching or burning at the site after application. Erythema, sometimes accompanied by edema, also occurs frequently at the patch site. Other common side effects include contact sensitization (rare), headache, vertigo, insomnia, somnolence, abnormal dreams, myalgia, arthralgia, abdominal pain, nausea, dyspepsia, diarrhea, and nervousness. Anxiety, irritability, and depression may also occur, but are more often symptoms of nicotine withdrawal than patch toxicity.

Contraindications

Contraindications to nicotine patch use include serious cardiac arrhythmias, severe or worsening angina, recent myocardial infarction, hypersensitivity or allergy to nicotine, and pregnancy. The patch should be used with caution in patients with psoriasis, dermatitis (atopic or eczematous), active peptic ulcers, severe renal impairment, accelerated hypertension, hyperthyroidism, pheochromocytoma, or insulin-dependent diabetes mellitus.

Adapted from: Glynn TJ, Manley MW. How To Help Your Patients Stop Smoking: A National Cancer Institute Manual for Physicians. Bethesda, MD: National Institutes of Health. In press.

- Consideration should be given to referring patients to a group clinic or intensive smoking cessation program. This option should be discussed with patients to determine if they have had experience, and are comfortable with, a group discussion format. Information on reputable programs can be obtained by calling the National Cancer Institute Information Service: (800) 4-CANCER.

8. Follow-up is an important part of the process.

   - A member of the office staff should call or write patients within 7 days after the initial visit, reinforcing the decision to stop and reminding patients of their quit date.

   - A follow-up visit should be scheduled within 1-2 weeks after the patient's quit date.

   - At the first follow-up visit, patients should be asked about their smoking status to provide support and help prevent relapse. Relapse is common; if it happens, patients should be encouraged to try again immediately.

   - A second follow-up visit should be scheduled in 1 to 2 months. For patients who have relapsed, the circumstances of the relapse and other special concerns should be discussed.

Patient Resources

Clearing the Air; Guia para Dejar de Fumar; Why Do You Smoke?; and other materials. Office of Cancer Communications, National Cancer Institute, Bldg. 31, Rm. l0A24, Bethesda, MD 20892; (800) 4-CANCER.

Check Your Smoking I.Q.: An Important Quiz for Older Smokers; and other materials. National Heart, Lung, and Blood Institute Smoking Education Program, PO Box 30105, Bethesda, Maryland 20824-0105; (301) 251-1222.

How to Quit Cigarettes; The Fifty Most Often Asked Questions about Smoking and Health and the Answers; and other materials. American Cancer Society, 1559 Clifton Rd. NE, Atlanta, GA 30329-4251; (800) ACS-2345.

Smoking in Women. American College of Obstetricians and Gynecologists, 409 12th St. SW, Washington, DC 20024; (800) 762-2264.

Smoking: Steps to Help You Break the Habit. American Academy of Family Physicians, 8880 Ward Parkway, Kansas City, MO 64114-2797; (800) 944-0000.

Vision Impairment Screening—In Children

Refractive errors are the most common vision disorders of children, occurring in 20% by 16 years of age. Amblyopia ("lazy eye") develops in 2% to 4% of children. The risk of developing amblyopia is greatest during the first 2 to 3 years of life, but the potential for its development exists until visual development is complete at 9 years of age. Left untreated, amblyopia may lead to irreversible visual deficits. Strabismus occurs in 2% of children and is one of the primary causes of amblyopia. Other eye diseases occurring during infancy and childhood include cataracts (1 per 1000 live births), congenital glaucoma (1 per 10,000 live births), retinoblastoma (1 per 20,000 live births), and retinopathy of prematurity. More than 100,000 eye injuries occur annually in the general population, an estimated 90% of which are preventable.

Through careful history, examination, vision testing, and appropriate referral, amblyopia and other ophthalmologic disorders can be detected and visual impairment lessened or averted. Early detection and prompt intervention are essential.

Recommendations of Major Authorities

Normal-Risk Children

American Academy of Family Physicians and **U.S. Preventive Services Task Force**—All children should have testing for amblyopia and strabismus once before entering school, preferably at 3 to 4 years of age. Stereotesting is more effective than visual acuity testing for this purpose. Routine visual acuity testing is not recommended for asymptomatic school-age children. Clinicians should be alert for signs of ocular misalignment in examining all infants and children.

American Academy of Ophthalmology (AAO), American Academy of Pediatrics (AAP), American Association for Pediatric Ophthalmology and Strabismus (AAPOS), and **American Optometric Association (AOA)**—Eye and vision screening should be performed at birth and at approximately 6 months, 3 years, and 5 years of age. AAO has published recommendations regarding screening

139

methods and indications for referral to be used by primary care clinicians in screening preschool children. AAP recommends that clinicians perform objective vision screening on school-aged children at 3, 4, 5, 6, 8, 12, and 18 years of age. AAO and AAPOS recommend that screening after 5 years of age be carried out at routine school checks or after the appearance of symptoms. AOA recommends that color vision screening be included in the routine screening of boys prior to school entry.

Canadian Task Force on the Periodic Health Examination— Eye examination and the cover/uncover test should be performed on children during the first week of life and at 2 to 4 weeks, 2 months, and 2 to 3 and 5 to 6 years of age. Visual acuity testing with a wall chart should be performed at 2 to 3 and 5 to 6 years of age. Visual acuity testing is discretionary for children at 10 to 11 years of age.

High-Risk Children

American Academy of Ophthalmology—Asymptomatic children should have a comprehensive examination by an ophthalmologist if they are at high risk due to: health and developmental problems that make screening by the primary care clinician difficult or inaccurate (e.g., retinopathy of prematurity or diagnostic evaluation of a complex disease with ophthalmic manifestations); a family history of conditions that cause or are associated with eye or vision problems (e.g., retinoblastoma, significant hyperopia, strabismus [particularly accommodative esotropia], amblyopia, congenital cataract, or glaucoma); multiple health problems, systemic disease, or use of medications that are known to be associated with eye disease and vision abnormalities (e.g., neurodegenerative disease, juvenile rheumatoid arthritis, systemic steroid therapy, systemic syndromes with ocular manifestations, or developmental delay with visual system manifestations).

American Optometric Association—The primary care clinician should remain alert for visual/ocular abnormalities associated with the following high-risk groups: babies who are premature, have been on oxygen therapy, or are of low birth weight; infants with a family history of retinoblastoma, congenital cataracts, or metabolic or genetic disease; infants whose mothers have had rubella, venereal disease, or AIDS-related infections during pregnancy. All infants weighing less than 1500 grams or less than 34 weeks gestation should be screened for retinopathy of prematurity with an ophthalmoscopic fundus evaluation through dilated pupils before the 6th week of life and at least every 6 months for the first 2 years of life.

Basics of Vision Screening

1. *History:* Gathering information in the following areas is important in screening for present or potential visual disorders:

   - Family history of vision or eye problems.

   - History of maternal, intrapartum, or neonatal conditions that may place the child at high risk for visual disorders (see Recommendations for High-Risk Children).

   - Parental concerns about a child's visual functioning—It is important to listen carefully to parents who note that their child has a problem with his or her eyes or vision. Parental observations are often correct.

   - School performance—Worsening grades and other school difficulties may be signs of vision problems.

2. *Physical Examination:* A comprehensive examination of the eye includes the lids, lashes, tear ducts, orbit, conjunctive, sclera, cornea, iris, pupillary responsiveness, range of motion, anterior chamber, lens, vitreous, retina, and optic nerve and vessels. It can be difficult to gain cooperation of young children with an ophthalmoscopic examination. It may be helpful to demonstrate the examination procedure on the parent beforehand and to have the child sit on the parent's lap.

3. *Testing Procedures:*

   - *Red Reflex:* The red reflex exam may be performed with an ophthalmoscope or other light source. In a darkened room, the light source should be held at arm's length from the infant and the infant's attention drawn to look directly at the light. Both retinal reflexes should be red or red-orange and of equal intensity.

   - *Corneal Light Reflex:* The corneal light reflex test, for detection of strabismus, is also performed with an ophthalmoscope or other light source. Corneal light reflections should fall symmetrically on corresponding points of the patient's eyes. Improper alignment will appear as asymmetry of reflections.

141

- *Differential Occlusion:* The test for differential occlusion is performed by gently covering the infant's eyes, one at a time. Aversion to the occlusion is normal. However, this test may give a false-positive result and is generally less accurate than the corneal light reflex test for detecting strabismus.

- *Fixation:* In examining for fixation, a light or a small object is held in front of the infant. In a normal exam, the infant's eyes will be aligned in the same direction, without deviation.

- *Cover/Uncover:* The cover/uncover test is performed by having the child focus on a stationary target. While placing a hand or cover in front of one eye, the examiner observes the other eye. Movement of the observed eye is abnormal and demonstrates the presence of strabismus. As the covered eye is uncovered, the examiner observes it for movement. Movement is abnormal and indicates the presence of heterophoria.

- *Stereotesting:* Stereopsis (binocular depth perception) can be tested using a stereotesting technique, such as the Random Dot E stereogram. While wearing polarized glasses, the child views test cards that contain fields of random dots. If stereopsis is present, the child will see a form stand out from the background of the cards.

- *Visual Acuity:* Several eye charts are available to test visual acuity in children. In order of decreasing cognitive difficulty, these are: Snellen Letters, Snellen Numbers, Tumbling E, HOTV, Allen Figures, and LH (Leah Hyvarinen) Test. The test with the highest level of difficulty that the child is capable of performing should be used. In general, the Snellen tests are too advanced for use by preschool children. Visual acuity may be tested at 10, 15, or 20 feet (using the appropriate chart). For young children, a distance of 10 feet may result in better compliance due to closer interaction with the examiner. Care should be taken to make sure the child does not "peek" with the eye not being tested. This may require that the examiner hold the occluder or that an adhesive occluder be used. A passing score should be given for a line on which the child gives more than 50% correct responses. Recommended criteria for referral to an ophthalmologist or optometrist vary slightly. In general, referral should be made for any child with a difference in scores of two or more lines between eyes; children younger than 5 years of age scoring 20/40 or worse in either eye; and children 5 years of age or older scoring 20/30 or worse in either eye.

4. *Safety Counseling:* Parents and children should be counseled about eye safety and the appropriate use of protective equipment. Children who participate in school shop or science labs or in certain sports (i.e., racquetball, squash) should wear safety lenses and safety frames approved by the American National Standards Institute. Children with good vision in only one eye should wear safety lenses and safety frames to protect the good eye, even if they do not otherwise need to wear glasses.

Family Resources

Amblyopia: Is It Affecting Your Child's Sight?; Cataracts in Children: Eye Safety and Children; Eyeglasses for Infants and Children; Home Eye Test for Children and Adults; Strabismus. American Academy of Ophthalmology, PO Box 7424, San Francisco, CA 94120; (415) 561-8500.

Answers to Your Questions About: Lazy Eye, Nearsightedness, Astigmatism, Eye Coordination, Color Deficiency, Crossed-Eyes; Signs of a Child's Vision Problems; Toys, Games and Your Child's Vision; Your Child's Eyes; Your Preschool Child's Eyes; Your School-Aged Child's Eyes. American Optometric Association, 243 N. Lindbergh Blvd., MO 63141; (314) 991-4100.

Vision Impairment Screening—In Adults

Vision loss is common in adults and increases in prevalence with advancing age. Approximately 13% of individuals 65 years of age or older and 28% of those over 85 years of age report some degree of visual impairment. More than 90% of older people require the use of corrective lenses at some time. Common visual disorders affecting adults include cataracts, macular degeneration, glaucoma, and diabetic retinopathy. Visual disorders in older adults frequently lead to trauma from falls, automobile crashes, and other types of unintentional injuries. A substantial number (18% in one study) of hip fractures are attributable to impaired vision. Many older adults are unaware of decreases in their visual acuity, and up to 25% may have incorrect corrective lens prescriptions.

Surgical treatment for cataracts can lead to improved vision and quality of life. Medical and surgical treatment may help prevent visual loss due to glaucoma. Early laser surgical treatment can help prevent visual loss due to diabetic retinopathy and (in some cases) macular degeneration. Visual acuity testing is easily and accurately performed by primary care clinicians. However, glaucoma screening, as usually practiced by primary care clinicians using a Schiotz tonometer, is relatively insensitive and nonspecific. The predictive value of a positive Schiotz test is only about 5%.

Recommendations of Major Authorities

American Academy of Family Physicians and **U.S. Preventive Services Task Force (USPSTF)**—Vision screening may be appropriate in asymptomatic older individuals. The frequency of this screening should be left to the discretion of the clinician. USPSTF recommends examination by an eye specialist beginning at 65 years of age for glaucoma, but does not recommend an optimal frequency.

American Academy of Ophthalmology—A comprehensive eye examination, including screening for visual acuity and glaucoma by an ophthalmologist, should be performed every 3 to 5 years in African Americans aged 20 to 39 years, and regardless of race, every 2 to 4 years in individuals aged 40 to 64 years, and every 1 to 2 years beginning at 65. Diabetic patients, at any age, should have exams at least yearly.

American College of Obstetricians and Gynecologists—Women 65 years of age and older should be evaluated for visual acuity yearly or as appropriate.

American Optometric Association—A comprehensive eye and vision examination is recommended for all adults as follows: ages 20-64, every 1-2 years; ages 65 and over, yearly. Persons at increased risk for eye disease (e.g., with diabetes, hypertension, or any eye disease) should have examinations as recommended by their eye-care professional.

Canadian Task Force on the Periodic Health Examination—Visual acuity testing for asymptomatic adults should be optional.

There is poor justification on scientific grounds for inclusion of primary open-angle glaucoma screening in a periodic health examination.

National Eye Institute—A comprehensive eye examination, including screening for visual acuity and glaucoma, should be performed by an eye care professional every 2 years beginning at age 40 years in African Americans and age 60 years in all other individuals. Diabetic patients, at any age, should have yearly exams.

Basics of Vision Screening

1. Older adults and individuals at high risk should be referred to eye-care professionals for periodic examinations. See Recommendations of Major Authorities.

2. Visual acuity screening should be performed with a standard Snellen wall chart at a distance of 20 feet. A tumbling "E" chart may be used for patients who are not familiar with the Western alphabet. A passing score should be given for each line with a majority of correct responses. Each eye should be tested separately. Corrective lenses should be worn during screening. Patients with significant changes in visual acuity or visual acuity of 20/40 or less using corrective lenses should be referred to an eye-care specialist for further examination.

3. Risk factors for glaucoma include increasing age, family history of glaucoma, African-American race, diabetes mellitus, and myopia. Primary care clinicians should evaluate each patient's risk factors for glaucoma and other ocular problems and refer appropriate patients to eye-care professionals for screening.

4. Loss of vision can begin slowly and go unnoticed for some time, particularly in older adults. Primary care clinicians should encourage patients to seek evaluation at the first sign of vision problems. The use of a standardized, self-administered questionnaire can help identify individuals needing evaluation of their vision. More extensive questionnaires have been developed [Mangione CM, Phillips RS, Seddon MJ, et al. Development of the activities of daily vision scale: a measure of visual functional status. *Med Care.* 1992;30:1111-1126].

145

Patient Resources

Age-Related Macular Degeneration; Cataracts; Diabetic Retinopathy; Don't Lose Sight of Diabetic Eye Disease; Don't Lose Sight of Glaucoma; Glaucoma. National Eye Health Education Program, National Institutes of Health, Box 20/20, Bethesda, MD 20892; (301) 496-5248.

Age Page—Aging and Your Eyes. National Institute on Aging, Bldg. 31, Rm. 5C27, Bethesda, MD 20892; (301) 496-1752.

Your Vision, the Second Fifty Years; Do Adult Vision Problems Cause Reading Problems? and other publications. American Optometric Association, 243 N. Lindbergh Blvd., St. Louis, MO 63141; (314) 991-4100.

Major Authorities Cited

[For the reader's convenience, this list includes contact information for all major authorities cited in the *Clinician's Handbook of Preventive Services* irrespective of their inclusion in the excerpts provided in this chapter. Authorities are listed in alphabetical order.]

American Academy of Dermatology, 930 N. Meacham Road, Schaumberg, IL 60618; (708) 330-0230; (708) 330-0050 fax.

American Academy of Family Physicians, 8880 Ward Parkway, Kansas City, MO 64114-2797; (800) 944-0000; (816) 822-0580 fax

American Academy of Ophthalmology, P.O. Box 7424, San Francisco, CA 94120; (415) 561-8500; (415) 561-8533 fax

American Academy of Otolaryngology-Head and Neck Surgery, 1 Prince Street, Alexandria, VA 22314; (703) 836-4444; (703) 683-5100 fax

American Academy of Pediatric Dentistry, 211 E. Chicago Avenue, Suite 700, Chicago, IL 60611; (312) 337-2169; (312) 337-6329 fax

American Association of Pediatric Ophthalmology and Strabismus, P.O. Box 193832 San Francisco, CA 94119; (415) 561-8505; (415) 561-8575 fax

American Academy of Pediatrics, 141 Northwest Point Boulevard, P.O. Box 927, Elk Grove, IL 60009-0927; (800) 433-9016; (708) 228 5097 fax

American Cancer Society, 1559 Clifton Road NE, Atlanta, GA 30329-4251; (800) ACS-2345

American College of Obstetricians and Gynecologists, 409 12th Street SW, Washington, DC 20024; (202) 863-2502; (202) 488-3985 fax

American College of Physicians, Independence Mall West, Sixth Street at Race, Philadelphia, PA 19104; (215) 351-2400; (215) 351-2829 fax

American College of Sports Medicine, P.O. Box 1440, Indianapolis, IN 46202-1440; (317) 637-9200; (317) 634-7817 fax

American Dental Association, 211 E. Chicago Avenue, Chicago, IL 60611; (800) 947-4746; (312) 440-3542 fax

American Diabetes Association, 1660 Duke Street, Alexandria, VA 22314; (703) 549-1500, (800) ADA-DISC

American Dietetic Association, 216 W. Jackson Boulevard, Suite 800, Chicago, IL 60606-6995; (312) 899-0040; (312) 899-1979 fax

American Gastroenterological Association, 6900 Grove Road, Thoroughfare, NJ 08086; (609) 848-1000; (609) 848-5274 fax

American Geriatrics Society, 770 Lexington Avenue #300, New York, NY 10021; (212) 308-1414; (212) 832-8646 fax

American Heart Association, 7320 Greenville Avenue, Dallas, TX 75231; (800) 242-1793; (214) 706-1341 fax

American Medical Association, 515 N. State Street, Chicago, IL 60610; (312) 464-4804; (312) 464-4184 fax

American Nurses Association, 600 Maryland Avenue SW #100W, Washington, DC 20024-2571; (202) 554-4444; (202) 554-2262 fax

American Optometric Association, 243 N. Lindbergh Boulevard, St. Louis, MO 63141; (314) 991-4100; (314) 991-4101 fax.

American Society of Colon and Rectal Surgeons, 800 E. Northwest Highway, Suite 1080, Palatine, IL 60067; (708) 290-9184

American Society of Dentistry for Children, 211 E. Chicago Avenue, Suite 1430, Chicago, IL 60611; (312) 943-1244; (312) 943-5341 fax

American Society for Gastrointestinal Endoscopy, 13 Elm Street, Manchester, MA 01944; (508) 526-8330; (508) 526-4018 fax

American Speech-Language-Hearing Association, 10801 Rockville Pike, Rockville, MD 20852; (800) 638-8255, (301) 897-5700; (301) 571-0457 fax

American Thoracic Society, 1740 Broadway, 14th Floor, New York, NY 10019; (212) 315-8700; (212) 315-6498 fax

American Thyroid Association, Montefiore Medical Center, 111 E. 210th Street, Bronx, NY 10467; (718) 882-6047; (718) 882-6085 fax

American Urological Association, 1120 N. Charles Street, Baltimore, MD 21201-5559; (410) 727-1100; (410) 625-2390 fax

Canadian Task Force on Periodic Health Examination, Department of Pediatrics, Faculty of Medicine, Dalhousie University, Halifax, Nova Scotia B3H 1V7, Canada; (902) 428-8115; (902) 422-9229 fax

Council for Education of the Deaf, Gallaudet University, 800 Florida Avenue NE, Washington, DC 20002; (202) 651-5020; (202) 651-5708 fax

National Medical Association, 1012 10th Street NW, Washington, DC 20001; (202) 347-1895; (202) 842-3293 fax

Skin Cancer Foundation, P.O. Box 561, New York, NY 10156; (212) 725-5176; (212) 725-5751 fax

Society of General Internal Medicine, 700 13th Street NW, Suite 250, Washington, DC 20005; (202) 393-1662; (202) 783-1347 fax

U.S. Federal Agencies

Agency for Health Care Policy and Research, Publications Clearinghouse, P.O. Box 8547, Silver Spring, MD 20907; (800) 358-9295

Advisory Committee on Immunization Practices, Centers for Disease Control and Prevention, Mailstop A-20, Atlanta, GA 30333; (404) 639-3851

Centers for Disease Control and Prevention, Division of Immunization, Mailstop E-52, Atlanta, GA 30333; (404) 639-8226; (404) 639-8626 fax

Centers for Disease Control and Prevention, Division of Tuberculosis Elimination, Mailstop E-10 Atlanta, GA 30333; (404) 639-8125; (404) 639-8254 fax

National Cancer Institute, Building 31, Room 10A24, Bethesda, MD 20892; (800) 4-CANCER

National Eye Institute, Box 20/20, Bethesda, MD 20892; (301) 496-5248

National Heart, Lung, and Blood Institute, P.O. Box 30105, Bethesda, MD 20824-0105; (301) 251-1222

National Institute of Dental Research, 9000 Rockville Pike, Bethesda, MD 20892; (301) 496-4261; (301) 496-9988 fax

National Institutes of Health Consensus Development Conferences, NIH Consensus Program Clearing House, P.O. Box 2577, Kensington, MD 20891; (800) 644-6627; (301) 816-2494 fax

National Transportation Safety Board, 490 L'Enfant Plaza East, Washington, DC 20594; (202) 382-0660

U.S. Preventive Services Task Force, c/o Office of Disease Prevention and Health Promotion, Switzer 2132, 330 C Street SW, Washington, DC 20201; (202) 205-8660; (202) 205-9478 fax

Chapter 6

Medic Alert:
Emergency Medical
Identification

What Is Medic Alert?

Medic Alert, a nonprofit membership organization with 2.2 million members, is the nation's leading emergency medical information service. It was established by Dr. Marion Collins and his wife, Chrissie Collins, in 1956. Dedicated to helping save lives in emergencies, Medic Alert, through its 24-hour Emergency Response Center, speeds vital medical facts to emergency responders: paramedics, police, firemen, nurses, EMTs, and physicians. These professionals save lives.

How Can Emergency Medical Information Help You

In a serious accident or medical emergency, you may be disoriented, unconscious, or unable to speak. When that happens, your body-worn Medic Alert emblem identifies you as someone who needs special treatment. Emergency responders around the world recognize this. When they see the Medic Alert emblem, they call the Emergency Response Center. This Center is staffed 24 hours a day by trained personnel ready to dispatch your vital medical facts anywhere in the world. The information they provide (about such conditions as diabetes, asthma, and drug allergies) enables medical personnel to diagnose you correctly and avoid mistakes. Correct treatment can spell the difference between life and death.

Adapted from "Tapping Volunteer Potential," an undated publication produced by Medic Alert and "May I Tell You More about Medic Alert?" ©1996 Medic Alert®; reprinted with permission of the Medic Alert Foundation, 2323 Colorado Avenue, Turlock, CA 95382.

Other Situations Where Medical Identification Is Helpful

In addition to providing information about people with specific medical conditions, Medic Alert can provide identification in other situations as well. These include: business travelers who need a permanent location for their medical files; joggers who do not carry wallets or purses; young children who often do not carry personal identification; and senior citizens with Alzheimer's disease or other types of dementia who are subject to becoming lost or wandering.

How Does the Emergency Response Center Work?

The Medic Alert emblem—worn on a bracelet or necklace—is engraved with your most critical medical conditions and personal ID number, along with the phone number of the Emergency Response Center. When emergency medical personnel see your emblem and call the Emergency Response Center collect from anyplace in the world, Medic Alert's staff sends them your vital medical facts in seconds, either by phone or by fax.

Who Responds to Medic Alert?

The Medic Alert emblem is recognized by emergency responders around the world. Medic Alert's endorsers include: American College of Emergency Physicians; Emergency Nurses Association; American Hospital Association; National Association of Emergency Medical Technicians; International Association of Chiefs of Police; National Sheriff's Association; American Academy of Family Physicians; American Academy of Medical Assistants; American Academy of Physician Assistants; American Academy of Orthopedic Surgeons; and the National Associations of Pharmacists (APhA, NARD, NACDS, and ASHP)

For More Information

You can reach Medic Alert by calling 1-800-432-5378 in the U.S. (or 209-668-3333 outside the U.S.). Applications for membership can be made by phone or mail. First year membership costs $35. After that, an annual renewal fee of $15 keeps your membership current and allows you to update your records as often as necessary, without additional charge.

Medic Alert on the Internet

Medic Alert's website at www.medicalert.org was under construction at press time. E-mail may be sent to postmaster@medicalert.org.

Part Two

Physicians and Hospitals

Chapter 7

Who's Who in Health Care

In many cases, the family doctor is no longer the sole provider of medical care and advice for older Americans. Older people are treated not only by doctors and nurses, but by technicians, medical assistants, and therapists. With this variety of health providers, it is important to understand which professionals can offer the best and least costly care for a specific problem and which services normally will be paid by Medicare.

The following definitions cover some, but not all, of the medical practitioners frequently seen by older people.

Doctors of medicine (M.D.) use all accepted methods of medical care. They treat diseases and injuries, provide preventive care, do routine checkups, prescribe drugs, and do some surgery. M.D.s complete medical school plus 3 to 7 years of graduate medical education. They must be licensed by the state in which they practice.

Doctors of osteopathic medicine (D.O.) provide general health care to individuals and families. The training osteopaths receive is similar to that of an M.D. In addition to treating patients with drugs, surgery, and other treatments, a D.O. may emphasize movement in treating problems of muscles, bones, and joints.

Family practitioners are M.D.s or D.O.s who specialize in providing comprehensive, continuous health care for all family members, regardless of age or sex.

National Institute on Aging (NIA), *Age Page*, 1991.

155

Geriatricians are physicians with special training in the diagnosis, treatment, and prevention of disorders in older people. Geriatric medicine recognizes aging as a normal process, not a disease state.

Internists (M.D. or D.O.) specialize in the diagnosis and medical treatment of diseases in adults. Internists do not deliver babies.

Surgeons treat diseases, injuries, and deformities by operating on the body. A general surgeon is qualified to perform many common operations, but many specialize in one area of the body. For example, neurosurgeons treat disorders relating to the nervous system, spinal cord, and brain; orthopedic surgeons treat disorders of the bones, joints, muscles, ligaments, and tendons; and thoracic surgeons treat disorders to the chest.

The above physicians may refer patients to the following specialists:

- **Cardiologist**—a heart specialist
- **Dermatologist**—a skin specialist
- **Endocrinologist**—a specialist in disorders of the glands of internal secretion, such as diabetes
- **Gastroenterologist**—a specialist in diseases of the digestive tract
- **Gynecologist**—a specialist in the female reproductive system
- **Hematologist**—a specialist in disorders of the blood
- **Nephrologist**—a specialist in the function and diseases of the kidneys
- **Neurologist**—a specialist in disorders of the nervous system
- **Oncologist**—a specialist in cancer
- **Ophthalmologist**—an eye specialist
- **Otolaryngologist**—a specialist in diseases of the ear, nose, and throat
- **Physiatrist**—a specialist in physical medicine and rehabilitation
- **Psychiatrist**—a specialist in mental, emotional, and behavioral disorders
- **Pulmonary Specialist**—a physician who treats disorders of the lungs and chest
- **Rheumatologist**—a specialist in arthritis and rheumatism
- **Urologist**—a specialist in the urinary system in both sexes and the male reproductive system.

Most of the services of M.D.s and D.O.s are covered by Medicare.

Dental Care

Dentists (D.D.S. or D.M.D.) treat oral conditions such as gum disease and tooth decay. They give regular checkups and routine dental and preventive care, fill cavities, remove teeth, provide dentures, and check for cancers in the mouth. Dentists can prescribe medication and perform oral surgery. A general dentist might refer patients to a specialist such as an **oral surgeon**, who does difficult tooth removals and surgery on the jaw; an **endodontist**, who is an expert on root canals; a **periodontist**, who is knowledgeable about gum diseases; or a dentist who specializes in geriatrics. Medicare will not pay for any dental care except for surgery on the jaw or facial bones.

Eye Care

Ophthalmologists (M.D. or D.O.) specialize in the diagnosis and treatment of eye diseases. They also prescribe eyeglasses and contact lenses. Ophthalmologists can prescribe drugs and perform surgery. They often treat older people who have glaucoma and cataracts. Medicare helps pay for all medically necessary surgery or treatment of eye diseases and for exams and eyeglasses to correct vision after cataract surgery. But it will not pay for a routine exam, eyeglasses, or contact lenses.

Optometrists (O.D.) generally have a bachelor's degree plus 4 years of graduate training in a school of optometry. They are trained to diagnose eye abnormalities and prescribe, supply, and adjust eyeglasses and contact lenses. In most states optometrists can use drugs to diagnose eye disorders. An optometrist may refer patients to an ophthalmologist or other medical specialist in cases requiring medication or surgery. Medicare pays for only a limited number of optometric services.

Opticians fit, supply, and adjust eyeglasses and contact lenses which have been prescribed by an ophthalmologist or optometrist. They cannot examine or test the eyes, or prescribe glasses or drugs. Opticians are licensed in 22 states and may have formal training. Traditionally, most opticians are trained on the job.

Mental Health Care

Psychiatrists (M.D. or D.O.) treat people with mental and emotional difficulties. They can prescribe medication and counsel patients, as well as perform diagnostic tests to determine if there are physical problems. Medicare will pay for a portion of both inpatient and outpatient psychiatric costs.

157

Psychologists (Ph.D., Psy.D., Ed.D., or M.A.) are health care professionals trained and licensed to assess, diagnose, and treat people with mental, emotional, or behavioral disorders. Psychologists counsel people through individual, group, or family therapy. Medicare will pay for a portion of psychologists' counseling services when performed in connection with the services of a psychiatrist or other physician.

Nursing Care

Registered nurses (R.N.) may have 2, 3, or 4 years of education in a nursing school. In addition to giving medicine, administering treatments, and educating patients, R.N.s also work in doctors' offices, clinics, and community health agencies. Medicare does not cover private duty nursing. It helps pay for general nursing services by reimbursing hospitals, skilled nursing facilities, and home health agencies for part of the nurses' salaries.

Nurse practitioners (R.N. or N.P.) are registered nurses with training beyond basic nursing education. They perform physical examinations and diagnostic tests, counsel patients, and develop treatment programs. Nurse practitioners may work independently, such as in rural clinics, or may be staff members at hospitals and other health facilities. They are educated in a number of specialties, including gerontological nursing. Medicare will help pay for services performed under the supervision of a doctor.

Licensed practical nurses (L.P.N.) have from 12 to 18 months of training and are most frequently found in hospitals and long-term care facilities where they provide much of the routine patient care. They also assist physicians and registered nurses.

Rehabilitative Care

Occupational therapists (O.T.) assist those whose ability to function has been impaired by accident, illness, or other disability. They increase or restore independence in feeding, bathing, dressing, homemaking, and social experiences through specialized activities designed to improve function. Occupational therapy services are paid by Medicare if the patient is in a hospital or a skilled nursing facility or is receiving home health care. Coverage is also available for services provided in physicians' offices or to hospital outpatients, O.T.s have either a bachelor's or master's degree with special training in occupational therapy.

Physical therapists (P.T.) help people whose strength, ability to move, or sensation is impaired. They may use exercise, heat, cold, or water therapy or other treatments to control pain, strengthen muscles, and improve coordination. All P.T.s complete a bachelor's degree and some receive further postgraduate training. Patients are usually referred to a physical therapist by a doctor, and Medicare pays some of the costs of outpatient treatments. Physical therapy performed in a hospital or skilled nursing facility is covered by Medicare.

Speech-language pathologists are concerned with speech and language problems. **Audiologists** are concerned with hearing disorders. Both specialists test and evaluate patients and provide treatment to restore as much normal function as possible. Many speech-language pathologists work with stroke victims, people who have had their vocal cords removed, or those who have developmental speech and language disorders. Audiologists work with people who have difficulty hearing. They recommend and sometimes dispense hearing aids. Speech language pathologists and audiologists have at least a master's degree. Most are licensed by the state in which they practice. Medicare generally will cover the diagnostic services of speech language pathologists and audiologists; it will not cover routine hearing evaluations or hearing aid services.

General Care

Pharmacists are knowledgeable about the chemical makeup and correct use of medicines—the names, ingredients, side effects, and uses in the treatment of medical problems. Pharmacists have legal authority to dispense drugs according to formal instructions issued by physicians, dentists, or podiatrists. They also can provide information on non-prescription products sold in pharmacies. Pharmacists must complete 5 or 6 years of college, fulfill a practical experience requirement, and pass a state licensing examination to practice.

Physician Assistants (P.A.) usually work in hospitals or doctor's offices and do some of the tasks traditionally performed by doctors, such as taking medical histories and doing physical examinations. Education for a P.A. includes 2 to 4 years of college followed by a 2-year period of specialized training. P.A.s must always be under the supervision of a doctor. Medicare will pay for the services provided by a P.A. only if they are performed in a hospital or doctor's office under the supervision of a physician.

Podiatrists (D.P.M.) diagnose, treat, and prevent diseases and injuries of the foot. They may do surgery, make devices to correct or prevent foot problems, provide toenail care, and prescribe certain drugs. A podiatrist completes 4 years of professional school and is licensed. Medicare will cover the cost of their services except routine foot care. (However, routine foot care is covered if it is necessary because of diabetic complications.)

Registered Dieticians (R.D.) provide nutrition care services and dietary counseling in health and disease. Most work in hospitals, public health agencies, or doctors' offices, but some are in private practice. R.D.s complete a bachelor's or a graduate degree with a program in dietetics/nutrition and complete an approved program in dietetic practice such as an internship. Medicare generally will not pay for dietitian services; however, it does reimburse hospitals and skilled nursing facilities for a portion of dietitian's salaries.

"Nutritionist" is a broad term. Currently, practitioners who wish to call themselves nutritionists need not fulfill a licensing or certification requirement. The title may be used by a wide range of people, including R.D.s, those who take a correspondence or other short-term course in nutrition, or even people who are self-taught. Before seeking the advice of a health practitioner in nutrition, it is a good idea to ask what kind of training and practical experience the person has received.

Social workers in health care settings go after community services for patients, provide counseling when necessary, and help patients and their families handle problems related to physical and mental illness and disability. They frequently coordinate the multiple aspects of care related to illness, including discharge planning from hospitals. A social worker's education ranges from a bachelor's degree to a doctorate. Most have a master's degree (M.S.W.). Medicare covers services provided by social workers if they work in such settings as hospitals, home health care agencies, hospices, and health maintenance organizations.

Summary

These and other health professionals are especially important to older adults, some of whom require a great deal of medical attention. Ideally, all health professionals will work together to provide older people with care that is comprehensive, cost-effective, and compassionate.

For additional resources on health and aging, write to the National Institute on Aging Information Center, P.O. Box 8057, Gaithersburg, MD 20898-8057.

Chapter 8

Checking Up On Your Doctor

If you're shopping for a good doctor you can trust, the Information Age has spawned several new services that promise to help you learn more about a physician's history and training, or even to identify the incompetent and dishonest ones. A new company sells "comprehensive background information on every medical doctor." The American Medical Association (AMA) offers "information on virtually every licensed physician in the United States...verified for accuracy and authenticity." A consumer group offers a book listing your state's "questionable doctors." A Massachusetts legislator says the new law he sponsored will generate "comprehensive physician report cards."

In fact, it's not all that easy to tell good doctors from bad. Sources like these can help, but the information you might want is scattered and incomplete. The more negative the information, the harder, and more expensive, it is to find. And the most thorough catalog of problem doctors, compiled by a government agency, is off-limits to the public. Still, various sources of public information on doctors are worth considering if you understand what they can, and cannot, tell you.

Credentials

Confirming a physician's background is the first place to start. In one study, a managed-care plan found that 5% of physicians applying to work for it had made up phony credentials, including false residency training, board certification, and clinical experience. In another study, 12% of all "specialists" advertising in a Connecticut phone book did not have the standard board certification for their claimed specialty.

Confirming this sort of information is relatively simple now. The American Medical Association has put its file of 650,000 U.S. physicians, both members and non-members, onto the World Wide Web. Access is free at http://www.ama-assn.org. (Once there, follow the links to "Physician Select.") The information is quite basic, including medical school, residency training and specialties. It also tells whether the doctor has been certified by a specialty board, though it doesn't name the specialty. Much the same sort of information can be found in the AMA's Medical Directory, available in some libraries. Or often you can obtain the information from the physician's local medical society.

If you are seeing a specialist, the doctor's certification by a specialty board can be verified by phone. For medical doctors, call (800) 776-2378. For osteopathic doctors, call (800) 621-1773, ext. 7445.

Disciplinary Actions

For negative information about a doctor, you'll have to look elsewhere. The primary sources are the state medical boards, which investigate patients' complaints and may discipline doctors by suspending or revoking their licenses. You can learn whether a doctor had problems with licensing and disciplinary actions by calling or writing your state's medical board. If you call, be prepared to wait on hold for several minutes or more. Some states also charge for copies of files.

You may be able to skip the effort if your library has a copy of *13,012 Questionable Doctors*, a three-volume compendium published earlier this year by the Public Citizen Health Research Group. It compiles discipline reports from medical boards in all 50 states. The nationwide report costs $250, but individual states' reports, which include cross-references to a doctor's disciplinary actions in other states, cost $15 each. The book's major drawback: Information in the most recent edition is now nearly two years old. To order a book, call (800) 410-8478.

You can check both your doctor's AMA listing and state disciplinary records at one time by purchasing a report from Medi-Net, a new California company that promises information on every licensed U.S. doctor. Medi-Net has licensed the AMA database and supplements it with disciplinary records from all the states as well as several Federal agencies. The company's service costs $15 for the first doctor, $5 for each additional doctor. Call (888) 275-6334.

But Medi-Net's assistance falls short, in part because, like the other information providers, it can't avoid one major gap in relying on state records: You generally won't be told if the medical board has filed charges against a doctor unless the case has resulted in some sort of disciplinary action. That can take some time.

For instance, Medi-Net's press release cites, as an example of "medical malpractice and negligence," the well-publicized case of a Boston medical reporter's death from an overdose of an anti-cancer drug. In fact, we discovered, the Massachusetts medical board won't say whether it is investigating charges against the two doctors who were reported to be implicated in that death. So Medi-Net's own reports on the two doctors, which we requested, mentioned nothing about the case and said that there were no disciplinary actions against them. Even worse, Medi-Net also failed to report a fact that is public: The license of one of the doctors expired a year ago.

Malpractice History

Toughest of all to discover is whether a previous patient has sued your doctor for malpractice, and more important, how that case turned out. In theory, you could find part of this information by visiting your local courthouse (usually at the county level) and asking the court clerks for the index of defendants in civil cases. But that's a major chore. Moreover, the files might not reveal the worthiness of the accusation, and the records won't tell you anything about your doctor's history elsewhere.

Nationwide malpractice information is collected by the federal government (insurance companies are required to report any payments they make to malpractice plaintiffs), but the data are not public. In addition to malpractice payments, this database, called the National Practitioner Data Bank, contains state disciplinary actions and names of doctors who have lost their admitting privileges at hospitals. Now six years old, it has reports of such marks against 86,000 medical doctors, osteopaths, dentists, podiatrists, and chiropractors. The information is released to hospitals and health maintenance organizations to help them screen the doctors they hire, although, as we reported in August, HMOs may not screen their physicians very rigorously.

Proposals to open the data bank to the public have gone nowhere. One strong opponent is the AMA, which fears that consumers won't be able to distinguish innocent doctors whose insurers decide to settle rather than challenge lawsuits from those doctors truly guilty of malpractice.

To deal with this concern, one bill, filed in the Senate in July, would let the public see only the records of the 6,500 medical practitioners who have at least three separate disciplinary actions or malpractice payments listed.

Last summer, Massachusetts took a promising move toward public access: a new law that requires the state medical board to issue "report cards" on all physicians. These would list, in one place, education, certifications, affiliations that might lead to conflict of interest, disciplinary actions, and malpractice history.

Consumer Reports Recommendations

While most physicians, like most other people, are trustworthy, some are not. And even many honest doctors are not as skilled as you might want. So it's worth learning what you can about the background of a doctor you're considering. Just don't rely too heavily on the new information sources. They can be useful, but they're far from definitive. They would be much more useful if more information were available. Either Congress needs to open the National Practitioner Data Bank or other states should keep an eye on Massachusetts' new system to see if it's worth emulating. For more advice, Consumer Reports Books offers *Examining Your Doctor*. To order, call (800) 500-9760.

Chapter 9

Talking with Your Doctor

Opening Thoughts

How well you and your doctor talk to each other is one of the most important parts of getting good health care. Unfortunately, this isn't always easy. It takes time and effort on your part as well as your doctor's.

In the past, the doctor typically took the lead and the patient followed. Today, a good patient-doctor relationship is more of a partnership, with both patient and doctor working together to solve medical problems and maintain the patient's good health.

This means asking questions if the doctor's explanations or instructions are unclear, bringing up problems even if the doctor doesn't ask, and letting the doctor know when a treatment isn't working. Taking an active role in your health care puts the responsibility for good communication on both you and your doctor.

Things to Consider When Selecting a Doctor

- Is the location of the doctor's office important? How far can I travel to see the doctor?
- Is the hospital the doctor admits patients to important to me?
- Is the age, sex, race, or religion of the doctor important?
- Do I prefer a single doctor or a group practice?

National Institutes of Health (NIH), National Institute on Aging, NIH Pub. No. 94-3452, December 1994.

165

- Do I have to choose a doctor who is covered by my insurance plan?
- Does the doctor accept Medicare?
- Is the doctor board certified? In what field?

Choosing a Doctor You Can Talk To

The first step in good communication is finding a doctor with whom you can talk. Having a main doctor (often called your primary doctor) is one of the best ways to ensure your good health. This doctor knows you and what your health normally is like. He or she can help you make medical decisions that suit your values and daily habits and can keep in touch with other medical specialists and health care providers you may need.

If you don't have a primary doctor or are not at ease with the doctor you currently see, now may be the time to find a new doctor. The suggestions below can help you find a doctor who meets your needs.

1. **Decide what you are looking for in a doctor.** A good first step is to make a list of qualities that are important to you. Then, go back over the list and decide which are most important and which are nice, but not essential.

2. **Identify several possible doctors.** After you have a general sense of what you are looking for, ask friends and relatives, medical specialists, and other health professionals for the names of doctors with whom they have had good experiences. A doctor whose name comes up often may be a strong possibility. Rather than just getting a name, ask about the person's experiences. For example, say "What do you like about Dr. Smith?" It may be helpful to come up with a few names to choose from, in case the doctor you select is not currently taking new patients.

3. **Consult reference sources.** The *Directory of Physicians in the United States* and the *Official American Board of Medical Specialties Directory of Board Certified Medical Specialists* are available at many libraries. These references won't recommend individual doctors, but they will provide a list to choose from. Doctors who are "board certified" have had training after regular medical school and have passed an exam certifying them as specialists in certain fields of medicine. This includes the primary care fields of general internal medicine, family medicine, and geriatrics. Board certification is one way to tell

about a doctor's expertise, but it doesn't address doctor's communication skills.

4. **Learn more about the doctors you are considering.**
    Once you have selected two or three doctors, call their offices. The office staff can be a good source of information about the doctor's education and qualifications, office policies, and payment procedures. Pay attention to the office staff—you will have to deal with them often! You may want to set up an appointment to talk with a doctor. He or she is likely to charge you for such a visit.

5. **Make a choice.** After choosing a doctor, make the first appointment. This visit may include a medical history and a physical examination. Be sure to bring your medical records and a list of your current medicines with you. If you haven't interviewed the doctor, take time during this visit to ask any questions you have about the doctor and his or her practice. After the appointment, ask yourself whether this doctor is a person with whom you could work well. If you are not satisfied, schedule a visit with one of your other candidates.

What Are the Doctor's Office Policies?

- Is the doctor taking new patients?
- What days/hours does the doctor see patients?
- Does the doctor ever make house calls?
- How far in advance do I have to make appointments?
- What is the length of an average visit?
- In case of an emergency, how fast can I see the doctor?
- Who takes care of patients after hours or when the doctor is away?

Questions to Ask the Doctor

- Do you have many older patients?
- What are your views on health and aging?
- How do you feel about involving the patient's family in care decisions?
- Will you honor living wills, durable powers of attorney for health care, and other advance directives?
- Do you still work with your patients when they move to a nursing home?

167

What Can I Do? Tips for Good Communication

A basic plan can help you communicate better with your doctor, whether you are starting with a new doctor or continuing with the doctor you've been visiting. The following tips can help you and your doctor build a partnership.

Getting Ready for Your Appointment

Be prepared—make a list of your concerns. Before going to the doctor, make a list of what you want to discuss. For example, are you having a new symptom you want to tell the doctor about? Did you want to get a flu shot or pneumonia vaccine? If you have more than a few items to discuss, put them in order so you are sure to ask about the most important ones first. Take along any information the doctor or staff may need such as insurance cards, names of your other doctors, or your medical records. Some doctors suggest you put all your medicines in a bag and bring them with you, others recommend bringing a list of medications you take.

Make sure you can see and hear as well as possible. Many older people use glasses or need aids for hearing. Remember to take your eyeglasses to the doctor's visit. If you have a hearing aid, make sure that it is working well, and wear it. Let the doctor and staff know if you have a hard time seeing or hearing. For example, you may want to say, "My hearing makes it hard to understand everything you're saying. It helps a lot when you speak slowly."

Consider bringing a family member or friend. Sometimes it is helpful to bring a family member or close friend with you. Let your family member or friend know in advance what you want from your visit. The person can remind you what you planned to discuss with the doctor if you forget, and can help you remember what the doctor said.

Plan to update the doctor. Think of any important information you need to share with your doctor about things that have happened since your last visit. If you have been treated in the emergency room, tell the doctor right away. Mention any changes you have noticed in your appetite, weight, sleep, or energy level. Also tell the doctor about any recent changes in the medication you take or the effect it has had on you.

Your doctor may ask you how your life is going. This isn't just polite talk or an attempt to be nosy. Information about what's happening in your life may be useful medically. Let the doctor know about any major changes or stresses in your life, such as a divorce or the death of a loved one. You don't have to go into detail; you may just want to say something like, "I thought it might be helpful for you to know that my sister passed away since my last visit with you," or "I had to sell my home and move in with my daughter."

Sharing Information with Your Doctor

Be honest. It is tempting to say what you think the doctor wants to hear; for example, that you smoke less or eat a more balanced diet than you really do. While this is natural, it's not in your best interest. Your doctor can give you the best treatment only if you say what is really going on.

Stick to the point. Although your doctor might like to talk with you at length, each patient is given a limited amount of time. To make the best use of your time, stick to the point. Give the doctor a brief description of the symptom, when it started, how often it happens, and if it is getting worse or better.

Ask questions. Asking questions is key to getting what you want from the visit. If you don't ask questions, your doctor may think that you understand why he or she is sending you for a test or that you don't want more information. Ask questions when you don't know the meaning of a word (like aneurysm, hypertension, or infarct) or when instructions aren't clear (e.g., does taking medicine with food mean before, during, or after a meal?). You might say, "I want to make sure I understand. Could you explain that a little further?" It may help to repeat what you think the doctor means back in your own words and ask, "Is this correct?" If you are worried about cost, say so.

Share your point of view. Your doctor needs to know what's working and what's not. He or she can't read your mind so it is important for you to share your point of view. Say if you feel rushed, worried, or uncomfortable. Try to voice your feelings in a positive way. For example, "I know you have many patients to see, but I'm really worried about this. I'd feel much better if we could talk about it a little more." If necessary, you can offer to return for a second visit to discuss your concerns.

Getting Information from Your Doctor and Other Health Professionals

Take notes. It can be difficult to remember what the doctor says, so take along a note pad and pencil and write down the main points, or ask the doctor to write them down for you. If you can't write while the doctor is talking to you, make notes in the waiting room after the visit. Or, bring a tape recorder along, and (with the doctor's permission) record what is said. Recording is especially helpful if you want to share the details of the visit with others.

Get written or recorded information. Whenever possible, have the doctor or staff provide written advice and instructions. Ask if your doctor has any brochures, cassette tapes, or videotapes about your health conditions or treatments. For example, if your doctor says that your blood pressure is high, he or she may give you brochures explaining what causes high blood pressure and what you can do about it. Some doctors have videocassette recorders for viewing tapes in their offices. Ask the doctor to recommend other sources, such as public libraries, nonprofit organizations, and government agencies, which may have written or recorded materials you can use.

Remember that doctors don't know everything. Even the best doctor may be unable to answer some questions. There still is much we don't know about the human body, the aging process, and disease. Most doctors will tell you when they don't have answers. They also may help you find the information you need or refer you to a specialist. If a doctor regularly brushes off your questions or symptoms as simply part of aging, think about looking for another doctor.

Talk to other members of the health care team. Today, health care is a team effort. Other professionals, including nurses, physician assistants, pharmacists, and occupational or physical therapists, play an active role in your health care. These professionals may be able to take more time with you.

Where Do I Begin? Getting Started with a New Doctor

Your first meeting is the best time to begin communicating positively with your new doctor. When you see the doctor and office staff, introduce yourself and let them know how you like to be addressed. The first few appointments with your new doctor also are the best times to:

- **Learn the basics of the office.** Ask the office staff how the office runs. Learn what days are busiest and what times are best to call. Ask what to do if there is an emergency, or when the office is closed.

- **Share your medical history.** Tell the doctor about your illnesses or operations, medical conditions that run in your family, and other doctors you see. You may want to ask for a copy of the medical history form before your visit so you have all the time and information you need to complete it. Your new doctor may ask you to sign a medical release form to get copies of your medical records from doctors you have had before. Be prepared to give the new doctor your former doctors' names and addresses, especially if they are in a different city.

- **Give information about your medications.** Many people take several medicines. It is possible for medicines to interact, causing unpleasant and sometimes dangerous side effects. Your doctor needs to know about *all* of the medicines you take, including over-the-counter (non-prescription) drugs, so bring everything with you to your first visit, including eye drops, vitamins, and laxatives. Tell the doctor how often you take each and describe any drug allergies or reactions you have had and which medications work best for you. Be sure your doctor has the phone number of your regular drug store.

- **Tell the doctor about your habits.** To provide the best care, your doctor must understand you as a person and know what your life is like. The doctor may ask about where you live, what you eat, how you sleep, what you do each day, what activities you enjoy, your sex life, and if you smoke or drink. Be open and honest with your doctor. It will help him or her to understand your medical conditions fully and recommend the best treatment choices for you.

Is the Doctor's Office Convenient?

- Where is the doctor's office located?
- Is parking available nearby? What is the cost?
- Is the office on a bus or subway line?
- Does the building have an elevator? Ramps for a wheelchair? Adequate lighting?

Questions to Ask Your Doctor about Prevention

- Should I get a flu shot, pneumonia shot, and/or other immunizations?
- How often should I have a breast or prostate examination?

171

- Would changing my diet or exercise habits help me avoid specific diseases?

A symptom is evidence of a disease or disorder in the body. Examples of symptoms include pain, fever, unexplained weight loss or gain, or disrupted sleep.

What Should I Say? Talking about Your Health

Talking about your health means sharing information about how you feel both physically and emotionally. Knowing how to describe your symptoms, discuss treatments, and talk with specialists will help you become a partner in your health care. Here are some issues that may be important to you when you talk with your doctor.

Preventing Disease and Disability

Until recently, preventing disease in older people received little attention. But things are changing. It's never too late to stop smoking, improve your diet, or start exercising. Getting regular checkups and seeing other health professionals such as dentists and eye specialists help promote good health. Even people who have chronic diseases, like arthritis or diabetes, can prevent further disability and in some cases, control the progress of the disease.

If a certain disease or health condition runs in your family, ask your doctor if there are steps you can take to help prevent it. If you have a chronic condition, ask how you can manage it and if there are things you can do to prevent it from getting worse. If you want to discuss health and disease prevention with your doctor, say so when you make your next appointment. This lets the doctor plan to spend more time with you as well as to prepare for the discussion.

Sharing Any Symptoms

It is very important for you to be clear and concise when describing your symptoms. Your description helps the doctor identify the problem. A physical exam and medical tests provide valuable information, but it is your symptoms that point the doctor in the right direction.

Tell the doctor when your symptoms started, what time of day they happen, how long they last (seconds? days?), how often they occur, if they seem to be getting worse or better, and if they keep you from going out or doing your usual activities. Take the time to make some notes about your symptoms before you call or visit the doctor. Concern about your symptoms is not a sign of weakness. It is not necessarily complaining to be honest about what you are experiencing.

Questions to Ask Yourself about Your Symptoms

- What exactly are my symptoms?
- Are the symptoms constant? If not, when do I experience them?
- Do the symptoms affect my daily activities? Which ones? How?

Learning More about Medical Tests

Sometimes doctors need to do blood tests, x-rays, or other procedures to find out what is wrong or to learn more about your medical condition. Some tests, such as Pap smears, mammograms, glaucoma tests, and screenings for prostate and colorectal cancer, are done on a regular basis to check for hidden medical problems.

Before having a medical test, ask your doctor to explain why it is important and what it will cost, and, if possible, to give you something to read about it. Ask how long the results of the test will take to come in.

When the results are ready, make sure the doctor tells you what they are and explains what they mean. You may want to ask your doctor for a written copy of the test results. If the test is done by a specialist, ask to have the results sent to your primary doctor.

Questions to Ask Your Doctor about Medical Tests

- What will we know after the test?
- How will I find out the results? How long will it take to get the results?
- What steps does the test involve? How should I get ready?
- Are there any dangers or side effects?

A diagnosis is the identification of a disease or physical problem. The doctor makes a diagnosis based on the symptoms the patient is experiencing and on the results of his or her examination, laboratory work, and other tests.

Questions to Ask Your Doctor about the Diagnosis

- What may have caused this condition? Will it be permanent?
- How is this condition treated or managed? What will be the long-term effects on my life?
- How can I learn more about it?

173

Discussing Your Diagnosis and What You Can Expect

If you understand your medical condition, you can help make better decisions about treatment. If you know what to expect, it may be easier for you to deal with the condition.

Ask the doctor to tell you the name of the condition and why he or she thinks you have it. Ask how it may affect your body, and how long it might last. Some medical problems never go away completely. They can't be cured, but they can be treated or managed. You may want to write down what the doctor says to help you remember.

It is not unusual to be surprised or upset by hearing you have a new medical problem. Questions may occur to you later. When they do, make a note of them for your next appointment.

Sometimes the doctor may want you to talk with other health professionals who can help you understand how to manage your condition. If you have the chance to work with other health professionals, take advantage of it. Also, find out how you can reach them if you have questions later.

Talking about Treatments

Although some medical conditions do not require treatment, most can be helped by medicine, surgery, changes in daily habits, or a combination of these. You will benefit most from treatment when you know what is happening and are involved in making decisions. If your doctor suggests a treatment, be sure you understand what it will and won't do and what it involves. Have the doctor give you directions in writing, and feel free to ask questions.

If your doctor suggests a treatment that makes you uncomfortable, ask if there are other treatments to consider. For example, if the doctor recommends medicine for your blood pressure, you may want to ask if you can try lowering it through diet and exercise first. If cost is a concern, ask the doctor if less expensive choices are available. The doctor can work with you to develop a treatment plan that meets your needs.

Making the Most of Medications

Your doctor may prescribe a drug for your condition. Make sure you know the name of the drug and understand why it has been prescribed for you. Ask the doctor to write down how often and how long you should take it. Make notes about any other special instructions such as foods or drinks you should avoid. If you are taking other medications, make sure your doctor knows, so he or she can prevent harmful drug interactions.

Sometimes medicines affect older people differently than younger people. Let the doctor know if your medicine doesn't seem to be working or if it is causing problems. Don't stop taking it on your own. If another doctor (for example, a specialist) prescribes a medication for you, call your primary doctor to let him or her know. Also call to check with your doctor before taking any over-the-counter medications. You may find it helpful to keep a chart of all the medicines you take and when you take them.

Questions to Ask Your Doctor about Treatment

- How soon should treatment start? How long will it last?
- Are there other treatments available?
- How much will the treatment cost? Will my insurance cover it?
- Are there any risks associated with the treatment?

Questions to Ask Your Doctor and Pharmacist about Medications

- What are the common side effects? What should I pay attention to?
- What should I do if I miss a dose?
- Are there foods, drugs, or activities I should avoid while taking this medicine?

The pharmacist also is a good source of information about your medicines. In addition to answering questions, the pharmacist keeps records of all the prescriptions you get filled at that drug store. Because your pharmacist keeps these records, it is helpful to use a regular drug store.

A pharmacist also can help you select over-the-counter medicines that are best for you. At your request, the pharmacist can fill your prescriptions in easy-to-open containers and may be able to provide large print prescription labels.

Changing Your Daily Habits

Doctors and other health professionals may suggest you change your diet, activity level, or other aspects of your life to help you deal with medical conditions. Sometimes the doctor's suggestions may not be acceptable to you. For example, the doctor might recommend a diet that includes foods you cannot eat or do not like. Tell your doctor if

175

you don't feel a plan will work for you and explain why. There may be other choices. Keep talking with your doctor to come up with a plan that works.

Questions to Ask Your Doctor about Changing Your Habits

- How will this change help me?
- Do you have any reading material or videotapes on this topic?
- Are there support groups or community services that might help me?

Seeing Specialists

Your doctor may send you to a specialist for further evaluation. You also may request to see one yourself, although your insurance company may require that you have a referral from your primary doctor.

When you see a specialist, ask that he or she send information about further diagnosis or treatment to your primary doctor. This allows your primary doctor to keep track of your medical care. You also should let your primary doctor know at your next visit about any treatments or medications the specialist recommended.

A visit to the specialist may be short. Often, the specialist already has seen your medical records or test results and is familiar with your case. If you are unclear about what the specialist tells you, ask him or her questions. For example, if the specialist says that you have a medical condition that you aren't familiar with, you may want to say, "I don't know very much about that condition. Could you explain what it is and how it might affect me?" or, "I've heard it's painful. What can be done to prevent or manage the pain?" You also may ask for written materials to read or call your primary doctor to clarify anything you haven't understood.

Questions to Ask Your Specialist

- What is your diagnosis?
- What treatment do you recommend? How soon do I need to begin the new treatment?
- Will you discuss my care with my primary doctor?

Surgery

In some cases, surgery may be the best treatment for your condition. If so, your doctor will refer you to a surgeon. Knowing more about the operation will help you make an informed decision. It also will help you get ready for the surgery, which, in turn, makes for a better recovery. Ask the surgeon to explain what will be done during the operation and what reading material or videotapes you can look at before the operation. Find out if you will have to stay overnight in the hospital to have the surgery, or if it can be done on an outpatient basis. Minor surgeries that don't require an overnight stay can sometimes be done at medical centers called "ambulatory surgical centers."

When surgery is recommended, it is common for the patient to seek a second opinion. In fact, your insurance company may require it. Doctors are used to this practice, and most will not be insulted by your request for a second opinion. Your doctor may even be able to suggest other doctors who can review your case. Hearing the views of two different doctors can help you decide what's best for you.

Questions to Ask Your Surgeon about Surgery

- What is the success rate of the operation? How many of these operations have you done successfully?

- What problems occur with this surgery? What kind of pain and discomfort can I expect?

- Will I have to stay in the hospital overnight? How long is recovery expected to take? What does it involve?

If You Are Hospitalized

If you have to go to the hospital, some extra guidelines may help you. First, most hospitals have a daily schedule. Knowing the hospital routine can make your stay more comfortable. Find out how much choice you have about your daily routine, and express any preferences you have about your schedule. Doctors generally visit patients during specific times each day. Find out when the doctor is likely to visit so you can have your questions ready.

In the hospital, you may meet with your primary doctor and various medical specialists, as well as nurses and other health professionals. If you are in a teaching hospital, doctors-in-training, known as medical students, interns, residents, and fellows, also may examine you. Many of these doctors-in-training already have a lot of knowledge. They may be able to take more time to talk with you than other staff. Nurses also can be an important source of information, especially since you will see them on a regular basis.

Questions to Ask Medical Staff in the Hospital

- How long can I expect to be in the hospital?
- When will I see my doctor? What other doctors and health professionals will I see?
- What is the daily routine in this part of the hospital?

If You Have to go to the Emergency Room

A visit to the emergency room is always stressful. If possible, take along the following items: your health insurance card or policy number, a list of your medications, a list of your medical problems, and the names and phone numbers of your doctor and one or two family members or close friends. Some people find it helpful to keep this information on a card in their wallets or purses.

While in the emergency room, ask questions if you don't understand tests or procedures that are being done. Before leaving, make sure you understand what the doctor told you. For example, if you have bandages that need to be changed, be sure you understand how and when it is to be done. Tell your primary doctor as soon as possible about your emergency room care.

Questions to Ask Medical Staff in the Emergency Room

- Will you talk to my primary doctor about my care?
- Do I need to arrange any further care?
- May I get instructions for further care in writing?

Can I Really Talk About That? Discussing Sensitive Subjects

Much of the communication between doctor and patient is personal. To have a good partnership with your doctor, it is important to talk about sensitive subjects, like sex or memory problems, even if you are embarrassed or uncomfortable. Doctors are used to talking about personal matters and will try to ease your discomfort. Keep in mind that these topics concern many older people. For more information on the topics discussed below, see the resource list at the end of this chapter.

It is important to understand that problems with memory, depression, sexual function, and incontinence are not normal parts of aging. If your doctor doesn't take your concerns about these topics seriously or brushes them off as being part of normal aging, you may want to consider looking for a new doctor.

Sexuality

Most health professionals now understand that sexuality remains important in later life. If you are not satisfied with your sex life, don't automatically assume it's due to your age. In addition to talking about age-related changes, you can ask your doctor about the effects of an illness or a disability on sexual function. Also, ask your doctor what influence medications or surgery may have on your sexual life. If you aren't sure how to bring the topic up, try saying, "I have a personal question I would like to ask you..." or, "I understand that this condition can affect my body in many ways. Will it affect my sex life at all?"

Incontinence

About 15 to 30 percent of older people living at home have problems controlling their bladder—this is called urinary incontinence. Often, certain exercises or other measures are helpful in correcting or improving the problem. If you have trouble with control of your bladder or bowels, it is important to let the doctor know. In many cases, incontinence is the result of a treatable medical condition. When discussing incontinence with your doctor, you may want to say something like, "Since my last visit there have been several times that I couldn't control my bladder. I'm concerned, because this has never happened to me before."

Grief, Mourning, and Depression

As people grow older, they experience losses of significant people in their lives, including spouses and cherished friends. A doctor who knows about your losses is better able to understand how you are feeling. He or she can make suggestions that may be helpful to you.

Although it is normal to feel grief and mourning when you have a loss, later life does not have to be a time of ongoing sadness. If you feel down all the time or for more than a few weeks, let your doctor know. Also tell your doctor about symptoms such as lack of energy, poor appetite, trouble sleeping, or lack of interest in life. These could be signs of medical depression. If you feel sad and withdrawn and are having trouble sleeping, give your doctor a call. Depression can be a side effect of medications or a sign of a medical condition that needs attention. It often can be treated successfully—but only if your doctor knows about it.

179

Memory Problems

One of the greatest fears of older people is problems with their ability to think and remember. For most older people, thinking and memory remain good throughout the later years. If you seem to have problems remembering recent events or thinking clearly, let your doctor know. Try to be specific about the changes you have noticed, for example, "I've always been able to balance my checkbook without any problems, but lately I'm finding that I get very confused." The doctor will probably want you to undergo a thorough checkup to see what might be causing your symptoms.

In many cases, these symptoms are caused by a passing, treatable condition such as depression, infection, or a side effect of medication. In other cases, the problem may be Alzheimer's disease or a related condition that causes ongoing loss of skills such as learning, thinking, and remembering. While there currently is no way to determine for sure if a person has Alzheimer's disease, a careful history, physical evaluation, and mental status examination are still important. They help the doctor rule out any other, perhaps treatable, causes of your symptoms and determine the best plan of care for you.

Care in the Event of a Serious Illness

You may have some concerns or wishes about your care if you become seriously ill. If you have questions about what choices you have, ask your doctor. You can specify your desires through documents called advance directives such as a living will or durable power of attorney for health care. Advance directives allow you to say what you'd prefer if you were too ill to make your wishes known. In an advance directive you can name a family member or other person to make decisions about your care if you aren't able.

In general, the best time to talk with your doctor about these issues is when you are still relatively healthy. If you are admitted to the hospital or a nursing home, you will be asked if you have any advance directives. If the doctor doesn't raise the topic, do so yourself. To make sure that your wishes are carried out, write them down. You also should talk with family members so that they understand your wishes.

Problems with Family

Even strong and loving families can have problems, especially under the stress of illness. Although family problems can be painful to discuss, talking about them can help your doctor help you. Your doctor may be able to suggest steps to improve the situation for you and other family members.

If you feel you are being mistreated in some way, let your doctor know. Some older people are subjected to abuse by family members or others. Abuse can be physical, verbal, psychological, or even financial in nature. Your doctor may be able to provide resources or referrals to other services that can help you if you are being mistreated.

Feeling Unhappy with Your Doctor

Misunderstandings can come up in any relationship, including between a patient and his or her doctor. If you feel uncomfortable with something your doctor or the doctor's staff has said or done, be direct. For example, if the doctor does not return your telephone calls, you may want to say something like, "I realize that you care for a lot of patients and are very busy, but I feel frustrated when I have to wait for days for you to return my call. Is there a way we can work together to improve this?" Being honest is much better for your health than avoiding the doctor. If you have a long-standing relationship with your doctor, working out the problem may be more useful than looking for a new doctor.

Who Else Will Help? Involving Your Family and Friends

It can be helpful to take a family member or friend with you when you go to the doctor's office. You may feel more confident if someone else is with you. Also, a friend or relative can help you remember what you planned to tell or ask the doctor. He or she also can help you remember what the doctor says. But don't let your companion take too strong a role. The visit is between you and the doctor. You may want some time alone with the doctor to discuss personal matters. For best results, let your companion know in advance how he or she can be most helpful.

If a relative or friend helps with your care at home, having that person along when you visit the doctor may be useful. In addition to the questions you have, your caregiver may have concerns he or she wants to discuss with the doctor. Some things caregivers may find especially helpful to discuss are: what to expect in the future, sources of information and support, community services, and ways they can maintain their own well-being.

Even if a family member or friend can't go with you to your appointment, he or she can still help. For example, the person can serve as your sounding board, helping you to practice what you want to say to the doctor before the visit. And after the visit, talking about what the doctor said can remind you about the important points and help you come up with questions to ask next time.

What's Next? Some Closing Thoughts

Good health care always depends on good communication with your doctor and other health professionals. We hope the information in this text will help you take an active role in your health care.

Getting More Information

You can make the best use of your time with your doctor by being informed. This often includes drawing on other sources of health information such as home medical guides, books and articles available at libraries, organizations such as the American Heart Association and the Arthritis Foundation, other institutes within the National Institutes of Health, and self-help groups.

The National Institute on Aging (NIA) has information about a variety of issues related to aging, including menopause, incontinence, and pneumonia. Large-print Age Pages are available on topics such as depression, stroke, safe use of medications, and types of doctors you may see.

To order publications or to request a publications list, call the NIA Information Center at 1-800-222-2225; TTY 1-800-222-4225. You also may want to encourage your doctor to order these publications for his or her office.

For a fact sheet and other publications about Alzheimer's disease, contact the NIA Alzheimer's Disease Education and Referral (ADEAR) Center at 1-800-438-4380.

Additional Resources

Sexuality

Sexuality Information and Education Council of the United States
Suite 2500
130 West 42nd Street
New York, NY 10036
1-212-819-9770

Incontinence

Help for Incontinent People (HIP)
P.O. Box 544
Union, SC 29379
1-800-BLADDER

The Simon Foundation
P.O. Box 835
Wilmette, IL 60091
1-800-237-4666

Grief, Mourning, and Depression

NIMH Depression Awareness, Recognition and Treatment Program
Room 10-85
5600 Fishers Lane
Rockville, MD 20857
1-800-421-4211

Memory Problems

Alzheimer's Association
Suite 1000
919 North Michigan Avenue
Chicago, IL 60611
1-800-272-3900

Alzheimer's Disease Education and Referral (ADEAR) Center
P.O. Box 8250
Silver Spring, MD 20907-8250
1-800-438-4380

National Stroke Association
Suite 1000
8480 East Orchard Road
Englewood, CO 80111-5015
1-800-367-1990

Care in the Event of a Terminal Illness

National Hospice Organization

Suite 901
1901 North Moore Street
Arlington, VA 22209
1-800-658-8898

Problems With Family

Children of Aging Parents

Suite 302-A
1609 Woodbourne Road
Levittown, PA 19057-1511
1-215-945-6900

Eldercare Locator Service

Suite 100
1112 16th Street NW
Washington, DC 20036
1-800-677-1116

National Center on Elder Abuse

Suite 500
810 First Street NE
Washington, DC 20002
1-202-682-2470

Chapter 10

Questions to Ask Your Doctor Before You Have Surgery

Are you facing surgery? You are not alone. Millions of Americans have surgery each year. Most operations are not emergencies. This means you have time to ask your surgeon questions about the operation and time to decide whether to have it, and if so, when and where. This text does **not** apply to emergency surgery.

The most important questions to ask about elective surgery are why the procedure is necessary for you and what alternatives there are to surgery. If you do not need to have the operation, then you can avoid any risks that might result. All surgeries and alternative treatments have risks and benefits. They are only worth doing if the benefits are greater than the risks.

Your primary care doctor—that is, your regular doctor—may be the one who suggests that you have surgery and may recommend a surgeon. You may want to identify another independent surgeon to get a second opinion. Check to see if your health insurance will pay for the operation and the second opinion. If you are eligible for Medicare, it will pay for a second opinion. You should discuss your insurance questions with your health insurance company or your employee benefits office.

Overview

This chapter provides 12 questions to ask your primary care doctor and surgeon before you have surgery—and the reasons for asking them.

Agency for Health Care Policy and Research (AHCPR) Pub. No. 95-0027, January 1995.

The answers to these questions will help you be informed and help you make the best decision. Sources are listed at the end of this booklet to help you get more information from other places.

Your doctors should welcome questions. If you do not understand the answers, ask the doctors to explain them clearly. Patients who are well informed about their treatment tend to be more satisfied with the outcome or results of their treatment.

What Operation Are You Recommending?

Ask your surgeon to explain the surgical procedure. For example, if something is going to be repaired or removed, find out why it is necessary to do so. Your surgeon can draw a picture or a diagram and explain to you the steps involved in the procedure.

Are there different ways of doing the operation? One way may require more extensive surgery than another. Ask why your surgeon wants to do the operation one way over another.

Why Do I Need the Operation?

There are many reasons to have surgery. Some operations can relieve or prevent pain. Others can reduce a symptom of a problem or improve some body function. Some surgeries are performed to diagnose a problem. Surgery also can save your life. Your surgeon will tell you the purpose of the procedure. Make sure you understand how the proposed operation fits in with the diagnosis of your medical condition.

Are There Alternatives to Surgery?

Sometimes, surgery is not the only answer to a medical problem. Medicines or other non-surgical treatments, such as a change in diet or special exercises, might help you just as well—or more. Ask your surgeon or primary care doctor about the benefits and risks of these other choices. You need to know as much as possible about these benefits and risks to make the best decision.

One alternative may be "watchful waiting," in which your doctor and you check to see if your problem gets better or worse. If it gets worse, you may need surgery right away. If it gets better, you may be able to postpone surgery, perhaps indefinitely.

What Are the Benefits of Having the Operation?

Ask your surgeon what you will gain by having the operation. For example, a hip replacement may mean that you can walk again with ease.

Ask how long the benefits are likely to last. For some procedures, it is not unusual for the benefits to last for a short time only. There might be a need for a second operation at a later date. For other procedures, the benefits may last a lifetime.

When finding out about the benefits of the operation, be realistic. Sometimes patients expect too much and are disappointed with the outcome, or results. Ask your doctor if there is any published information about the outcomes of the procedure.

What Are the Risks of Having the Operation?

All operations carry some risk. This is why you need to weigh the benefits of the operation against the risks of complications or side effects.

Complications can occur around the time of the operation. Complications are unplanned events, such as infection, too much bleeding, reaction to anesthesia, or accidental injury. Some people have an increased risk of complications because of other medical conditions.

In addition, there may be **side effects** after the operation. For the most part, side effects can be anticipated. For example, your surgeon knows that there will be swelling and some soreness at the site of the operation.

Ask your surgeon about the possible complications and side effects of the operation. There is almost always some pain with surgery. Ask how much there will be and what the doctors and nurses will do to reduce the pain. Controlling the pain will help you be more comfortable while you heal, get well faster, and improve the results of your operation.

What If I Don't Have This Operation?

Based on what you learn about the benefits and risks of the operation you might decide not to have it. Ask your surgeon what you will gain—or lose—by not having the operation now. Could you be in more pain? Could your condition get worse? Could the problem go away?

Where Can I Get a Second Opinion?

Getting a second opinion from another doctor is a very good way to make sure having the operation is the best alternative for you. Many health insurance plans require patients to get a second opinion before they have certain non-emergency operations. If your plan does not require a second opinion, you may still ask to have one. Check with your insurance company to see if it will pay for a second opinion. If you get one, make sure to get your records from the first doctor so that the second one does not have to repeat tests. (For more information on second opinions, see the section titled *For More Information* near the end of this chapter.)

What Has Been Your Experience in Doing the Operation?

One way to reduce the risks of surgery is to choose a surgeon who has been thoroughly trained to do the procedure and has plenty of experience doing it. You can ask your surgeon about his or her recent record of successes and complications with this procedure. If it is more comfortable for you, you can discuss the topic of surgeons' qualifications with your regular or primary care doctor. (For more information about surgeons' qualifications, see the section titled *Surgeons' Qualifications* near the end of this chapter.)

Where Will the Operation Be Done?

Most surgeons practice at one or two local hospitals. Find out where your operation will be performed. Have many of the operations you are thinking about having been done in this hospital? Some operations have higher success rates if they are done in hospitals that do many of those procedures. Ask your doctor about the success rate at this hospital. If the hospital has a low success rate for the operation in question, you should ask to have it at another hospital.

Until recently, most surgery was performed on an inpatient basis—patients stayed in the hospital for one or more days. Today, a lot of surgery is done on an outpatient basis in a doctor's office, a special surgical center, or a day surgery unit of a hospital. Outpatient surgery is less expensive because you do not have to pay for staying in a hospital room.

Ask whether your operation will be done in the hospital or in an outpatient setting. If your doctor recommends inpatient surgery for a procedure that is usually done as outpatient surgery—or just the opposite, recommends outpatient surgery that is usually done as inpatient surgery—ask why. You want to be in the right place for your operation.

What Kind of Anesthesia Will I Need?

Anesthesia is used so that surgery can be performed without unnecessary pain. Your surgeon can tell you whether the operation calls

for local, regional, or general anesthesia, and why this form of anesthesia is recommended for your procedure.

Local anesthesia numbs only a part of your body for a short period of time—for example, a tooth and the surrounding gum. Not all
procedures done with local anesthesia are painless. *Regional anesthesia* numbs a larger portion of your body—for example, the lower part
of your body—for a few hours. In most cases, you will be awake with
regional anesthesia. *General anesthesia* numbs your entire body for
the entire time of the surgery. You will be unconscious if you have
general anesthesia.

Anesthesia is quite safe for most patients and is usually administered by a specialized physician (anesthesiologist) or nurse anesthe-
tist. Both are highly skilled and have been specially trained to give
anesthesia.

If you decide to have an operation, ask to meet with the person
who will give you anesthesia. Find out what his or her qualifications
are. Ask what the side effects and risks of having anesthesia are in
your case. Be sure to tell him or her what medical problems you have—
including allergies—and any medications you have been taking, since
they may affect your response to the anesthesia.

How Long Will It Take Me to Recover?

Your surgeon can tell you how you might feel and what you will be
able to do—or not do—the first few days, weeks, or months after surgery. Ask how long you will be in the hospital. Find out what kind of supplies, equipment, and any other help you will need when you go home.
Knowing what to expect can help you cope better with recovery.

Ask when you can start regular exercise again and go back to work.
You do not want to do anything that will slow down the recovery process. Lifting a 10-pound bag of potatoes may not seem to be "too much"
a week after your operation, but it could be. You should follow your
surgeon's advice to make sure you recover fully as soon as possible.

How Much Will the Operation Cost?

Health insurance coverage for surgery can vary, and there may be
some costs you will have to pay. Before you have the operation, call
your insurance company to find out how much of these costs it will
pay and how much you will have to pay yourself.

Ask what your surgeon's fee is and what it covers. Surgical fees
often also include several visits after the operation. You also will be

billed by the hospital for inpatient or outpatient care and by the anesthesiologist and others providing care related to your operation.

Surgeons' Qualifications

You will want to know that your surgeon is experienced and qualified to perform the operation. Many surgeons have taken special training and passed exams given by a national board of surgeons. Ask if your surgeon is "board certified" in surgery. Some surgeons also have the letters F.A.C.S. after their name. This means they are Fellows of the American College of Surgeons and have passed another review by surgeons of their surgical practices.

For More Information

Surgery

The American College of Surgeons (ACS) has a free series of pamphlets on "When You Need an Operation." For copies, write to the ACS, Office of Public Information, 55 E. Erie Street, Chicago, IL 60611, or call 312-664-4050. Pamphlets in this series range from those providing general information about surgery to those explaining specific surgical procedures.

Second Opinion

For a free brochure on "Medicare Coverage for Second Surgical Opinions: Your Choice Facing Elective Surgery," write to Health Care Financing Administration, Room 555, East High Rise Building, 6325 Security Boulevard, Baltimore, MD 21207. Ask for Publication No. HCFA 02173.

To get the name of a specialist in your area who can give you a second opinion, ask your primary doctor or surgeon, the local medical society, or your health insurance company. Medicare beneficiaries may also obtain information from the U.S. Department of Health and Human Services' Medicare hotline: call toll-free 800-638-6833.

Anesthesia

Free booklets on what you should know about anesthesia are available from the American Society of Anesthesiologists (ASA) or the American Association of Nurse Anesthetists (AANA). For copies, write to ASA at 520 North Northwest Highway, Park Ridge, IL 60068, or call 708-825-5586; or AANA at 222 S. Prospect Avenue, Park Ridge, IL 60068-4001, or call 708-692-7050.

Pain Control

"Pain Control After Surgery: A Patient's Guide" is available free from the Agency for Health Care Policy and Research (AHCPR). For a copy of this consumer version of the AHCPR-supported clinical practice guideline and for information on other patient guides, write to the AHCPR Publications Clearinghouse, P.O. Box 8547, Silver Spring, MD 20907, or call toll-free 800-358-9295.

General

For almost every disease, there is a national or local association or society that publishes consumer information. Check your local telephone directory. There are also organized groups of patients with certain illnesses that can often provide information about a condition, alternative treatments, and experience with local doctors and hospitals. Ask your hospital or doctors if they know of any patient groups related to your condition. Also, your local public library has medical reference materials about health care treatments.

Chapter 11

A Little Advance Planning Helps Same-Day Surgery Go Smoothly

The next time you have surgery, you may be part of the fastest-growing trend in health care: same-day surgery. You arrive at the hospital in the morning, have surgery, and return home later in the day. While same-day surgery saves time and money, it also means patients must take greater charge of their recuperation.

"Some of the surgeries we did as inpatient procedures just a few months ago are now being handled in same-day surgery," says Heidi Keyes, assistant nurse manager in charge of Surgery Center Recovery at University of Washington Medical Center.

Much of this change can be attributed to new surgical techniques and faster anesthetic agents. People awaken more quickly from surgery, and are able to go home sooner.

Keyes cautions against underestimating a surgical procedure simply because you're released soon after. "Any time you receive anesthesia, there are risks involved," she explains "It may leave you groggy for a good 24 hours after surgery—longer if you're taking pain medications—and you won't be functioning at full effectiveness."

It's important not to underestimate your recovery period. "Just because you go home just a few hours after surgery doesn't mean you're ready to resume your normal activities," Keyes cautions. "Think about what you would be doing if you had stayed in the hospital following surgery. You wouldn't be cooking dinner, or strolling the supermarket aisles.

From *Health Beat*, University of Washington, Health Sciences Center, updated August 14, 1997. *Health Beat* may be accessed on line at http://www.hslib.washington.edu/your_health/hbeat/

You'd be in bed, resting, with people taking care of you. That's exactly what you should do at home."

Although pre- and post-operative preparation varies depending on the procedure, here are some steps everyone can take to prepare for same-day surgery:

- Recruit someone to spend at least the first 24 hours with you. The anesthesia may make you groggy for at least that long, and you'll need someone to make sure you get ample liquids and nourishment, take your medication on schedule, and help you get to the bathroom. Your caregiver will be better able to notice any postoperative problems that you might miss in your groggy state.

- Stock the pantry. You can generally eat whatever you can tolerate as long as your doctor does not restrict your diet, although it's best to steer clear of greasy or spicy foods. Good choices are foods high in fiber, such as grains, fruits and vegetables. Drink plenty of water or juice; fluids are necessary to flush the anesthetic from your body and help in healing and recovery.

- Decide where you'll be resting, and set up a table or tray where you can keep food, juices and other supplies handy.

- If your doctor recommends that you keep the surgery site above the level of your heart to reduce swelling, round up enough pillows to help with the elevation.

- Pick up some books to read while you recuperate, or stop by the neighborhood video store and rent some movies.

- If you have children or others whom you normally care for, find someone to pitch in while you recuperate. Not only will you be physically tired, you'll also be mentally "fuzzy."

- If you'll be unable to walk unassisted after surgery, practice with crutches beforehand. Or, if the surgery will be on your dominant hand, you may want to practice writing with your other hand.

- Do a safety check around your house. Make sure you have a clear path from your bed to the bathroom. Use a night light or leave a light on to help you find your way.

- Plan for some restrictions in your activities. You won't be able to drive for at least 24 hours, or longer if you're affected by pain medication. You may not be able to lift anything heavier than 10 pounds, and you may not be able to bathe or shower for a few days, depending on the site of the surgery.

Keyes warns that well-meaning family and friends can do more harm than good, especially if their constant calls and visits keep you from getting the rest you need. If friends really want to help, Keyes suggests asking them to bring you dinner, or rent a movie for you. They'll feel good having helped and you'll be getting the help you really need.

Chapter 12

Hospital Hints

Going to the hospital is somewhat like traveling to a foreign country—the sights are not familiar, the language sounds strange, and the people are all new. No matter what the reason for the trip—whether it's an overnight visit for a few tests or a longer stay for medical treatment or major surgery—nearly everyone worries about entering the hospital. Learning more about hospitals and the people who work there may help make the trip less stressful.

The following hints are meant for people who plan to enter the hospital by choice rather than for those who go to the hospital because of an emergency. Relatives and friends of patients who enter the hospital because of an emergency also may find this information useful.

What to Bring

It's best to pack as little as you can. However be sure to bring the following items:

- a few nightclothes, a bathrobe, and sturdy slippers (put your name on all personal items);
- comfortable clothes to wear home;
- a toothbrush, toothpaste, shampoo, comb and brush, deodorant, and razor;
- a list of all the medicines you take, including prescription and non-prescription drugs;

National Institute on Aging (NIA), *Age Page*, February 1990.

- details of past illnesses, surgeries, and any allergies;
- your health insurance card;
- a list of the names and telephone numbers (home and business) of family members to contact in case of an emergency; and
- $10 or less for newspapers, magazines, or any other items you may wish to buy in the hospital gift shop.

What Not to Bring

Leave cash, jewelry (including wedding rings, earrings, and watches), credit cards, and checkbooks at home or have a family member or friend keep them. If you must bring valuables, ask if they can be kept in the hospital safe during your stay. In addition, leave electric razors, hair dryers, and curling irons at home since they may not be grounded properly and could be unsafe.

Admission

The first stop in the hospital is the admitting office. Here, the patient or a family member signs forms allowing the hospital staff to provide treatment and to release medical information to the insurance company. Those who don't have private health insurance can talk with an admissions counselor about other payment methods and sources of financial aid such as Medicaid and Medicare.

Hospital Staff

After getting settled in your room, you will begin to meet the members of your health care team.

Doctors. Each patient has an attending physician, who is in charge of that person's overall care while in the hospital. The attending physician may be the patient's regular doctor, a member of the hospital staff to whom the patient has been referred, or a specialist. In a teaching hospital (where doctors train), a number of physicians care for each patient. The attending physician directs the house staff, which includes medical students, residents (doctors who have just graduated from medical school), and fellows (doctors who receive training in a special area of medicine after their residency training). Together, these doctors "round," or see patients, about once a day. Patients gain from the knowledge of senior staff members but may undergo many exams by doctors who are in training. In a non-teaching hospital, patients are treated by attending physicians only.

Nurses. Registered nurses, nurse practitioners, licensed practical nurses, nurse's aides, and nursing students provide many patient-care services. For example, nurses give medicines, check vital signs (blood pressure, temperature, and pulse), provide treatments, and teach patients to care for themselves. The head nurse coordinates nursing care for each patient on the unit (the floor or section of the hospital where your room is located).

Physical therapists. Physical therapists teach patients to build muscles and improve coordination. They may use exercise, heat, cold, or water therapy to help patients whose ability to move is limited.

Occupational therapists. Occupational therapists work with patients to restore, maintain, or increase their ability to perform daily tasks such as cooking, eating, bathing, and dressing.

Respiratory therapists. Respiratory therapists prevent and treat breathing problems. For example, they teach patients exercises to prevent lung infections after surgery.

Technicians. Technicians conduct a variety of laboratory tests such as blood and urine tests and x-rays.

Dietitians. Dietitians teach patients how to plan a well-balanced diet.

Pharmacists. Pharmacists know the chemical makeup and correct use of drugs. They prepare the medicines used in the hospital.

Social workers. Social workers offer support to patients and their families. They can provide details about how to obtain health care and social services after leaving the hospital; for example, they know about financial aid programs, support groups, and home-care services.

More detailed information about some members of the hospital staff is found in the chapter titled "Who's Who in Health Care."

Geriatric Assessment

Some older people have many complex problems which may threaten their ability to live independently after they go home from the hospital. In some hospitals, a team that includes a doctor, nurse, and social worker looks at the special needs of older patients. This team also may include other specialists and therapists. The team performs a thorough exam, called a geriatric assessment, to learn about the patient's physical and mental health, family life, income, living arrangements, access to community services, and ability to perform daily tasks. The team diagnoses health problems and develops a plan to help older patients get the health care and social services they need.

Hospital Geography

Hospitals have many patient-care areas. For example, patients may be in a private (one bed) or semi-private (two bed) room. The intensive care unit (also called the ICU) has special equipment and staff to care for very ill patients. Coronary care units (CCU's) give intensive medical care to patients with severe heart disease. In both the ICU and CCU, visiting hours are strictly limited and only family members are allowed to see patients. Surgery is done in the operating room (OR). After an operation, patients spend time in the recovery room before going back to their own room.

In the emergency room (ER), trained staff treat life-threatening injuries or illnesses. Patients who are badly hurt or very sick are seen first. Because the ER is so busy, some patients may have to wait before they are seen by an emergency medical technician (paramedic), nurse, or doctor.

Safety Tips

Because medical equipment is not familiar and medications can make you feel tired or weak, it's good to take a few extra safety steps while in the hospital:

- Use the call bell when you need help.
- Use the controls to lower the bed before getting in or out.
- Be careful not to trip over the many wires and tubes that may be around the bed.
- Try to keep the things you need within easy reach.
- Take only prescribed medicines.
- If you brought your own medicines with you, tell your nurse or doctor, and take them only with your doctor's permission.
- Be careful getting in and out of the bathtub or shower. Hold on to grab bars for support.
- Use handrails on stairways and in hallways.
- If you must smoke, do so only where allowed, and never smoke around oxygen.

Questions

During your hospital stay, you may have many questions about your care. Always feel free to ask your doctor these questions. Your doctor is there to provide the care you need and to discuss your concerns. Your nurse or social worker also may be able to answer many of your questions or help you get the information you need.

You may find it useful to write down your questions as you think of them. For example, you may want to ask your doctor or nurse some or all of the following questions:

- What will this test tell you? Why is it needed, and when will you know the results?
- What treatment is needed, and how long will it last?
- What are the benefits and risks of treatment?
- When can I go home?
- When I go home, will I have to change my regular activities?
- How often will I need checkups?
- Is any other follow-up care needed?

Discharge

Before going home, you must have discharge orders from your doctor and a release form from the hospital's business office. Discharge planning before leaving the hospital can help you prepare for your health and home-care needs after you go home. This service is often provided by a registered nurse, social worker, or the hospital's discharge planner. Discharge planning is offered in the hospital so that, if needed, a visiting nurse, hospital equipment, meals-on-wheels, or other services will be there when you get home. The discharge planner also knows about senior centers, nursing homes, and other long-term care services. If you, your family, or a close friend have questions about your follow-up care or living arrangements after you leave the hospital, the discharge planner may be able to help.

In Case of Emergency

In the event of a serious illness or accident, it's vital to seek medical help right away. In many areas, you can reach emergency help by calling 911 or the telephone operator. Be sure to tell the operator the type of emergency and your location.

If you have a minor injury or your symptoms aren't severe, call your family doctor or a nearby clinic before going to the emergency room (ER) of a hospital. Sometimes a visit to the ER isn't needed.

If your doctor thinks you should go to the ER, he or she can make things easier for you by calling the hospital to let them know you are coming. Your doctor also may arrange to meet you there.

If there is time, try to take the following items with you to the ER:

- your health insurance card or policy number;
- your doctor's name and telephone number;
- a list of the medicines you take, including prescription and non-prescription drugs;
- details of other medical problems; and
- the names and telephone numbers of close family members.

You may want to write all of this information on a note card that you can carry in your wallet or purse. Persons with some medical problems (such as diabetes, epilepsy, and allergies) should wear or carry identification (for example, an ID bracelet or ID card) to let rescue workers and hospital personnel know about these hidden conditions.

If possible, ask a relative or friend to go to the hospital with you for support.

For More Information

Hill-Burton hospitals give free hospital care to qualified people who cannot afford to pay. For a list of these hospitals in your area, call the Hill-Burton Program hotline at 1-800-638-0742 (toll free) or 1-800-492-0359 (toll free to residents of Maryland).

The American Hospital Association provides information about hospitals and patients' rights. Their address is 840 North Lake Shore Drive, Chicago, Illinois 60611; telephone 312-280-6000.

Chapter 13

A Guide to Mental Health Services

A Message from the Center for Mental Health Services

The Center for Mental Health Services was created to help states improve treatment and support services for people with mental illness, their families, and their communities. The Center works with a wide range of partners—from other Federal agencies and state and local mental health systems to mental health professionals, consumers, and family members—to achieve the highest quality and most accessible mental health services possible.

Who needs mental health services? Hundreds of thousands of people. Among them are people with serious and persistent mental illness; America's children and adolescents who have a variety of mental, emotional, and behavioral problems; homeless persons with mental illness; the growing numbers of people with or at risk of HIV/AIDS; underserved residents of rural areas; and survivors of natural disasters such as floods and hurricanes. The center hopes to respond to their mental health needs through treatment demonstration programs, outreach and case management programs, and support of consumer-run and self-help alternative program. It also provides information about recognizing mental illness, seeking appropriate care, and locating treatment and support services.

—Bernard S. Arons, M.D., Director

National Institutes of Health, National Institute of Mental Health, Substance Abuse and Mental Health Services Administration, NIH Pub. No. 94-3585, 1994.

A Message from the National Institute of Mental Health

Research conducted and supported by the National Institute of Mental Health (NIMH) brings hope to millions of people who suffer from mental illness and to their families and friends. In many years of work with animals as well as human subjects, researchers have advanced our understanding of the brain and vastly expanded the capability of mental health professionals to diagnose, treat, and prevent mental and brain disorders.

Today we stand at the threshold of a new era in brain and behavioral sciences. Through research, we are continually learning more about the structure and function of the brain. As our knowledge increases, we ill understand more about mental disorders such as depression, bipolar disorder, schizophrenia, panic disorder, and obsessive-compulsive disorder and how they can be effectively treated. We will reach out to individuals in need—to those affected by violence and abuse, to the aged, children, women, minorities, the homeless, and the severely mentally ill.

To achieve the goal of serving those in need, the Institute will work with the Center for Mental Health Services and other professional and advocacy groups to integrate the knowledge gained through clinical research with those of service systems research.

—Rex William Cowdry, M.D., Acting Director

Introduction

Twenty percent of adult Americans—or one in five—will have a mental illness during their lifetime that is severe enough to require treatment, and many more have problems that prevent them from enjoying their lives. Often these people live in silence, rather than admit they need help.

Asking for help is not an easy thing for many people to do, but it is a wise more when a person feels that something is wrong. The text in this chapter offers a guide to finding mental health services.

Many individuals who are looking for help for themselves or a loved one ask the same questions. Following are some of the most commonly asked questions and their answers.

Q. *When I need help, where can I go?*
A. For information about resources available in your community, contact your local mental health center or one of the local affiliates of

national organizations listed at the end of this chapter. These agencies can provide you with information on services designed to meet the needs of people with mental disorders such as depression, schizophrenia, panic disorder, and other anxiety conditions. In addition, they will have information regarding services designed for specific cultural groups, children, the elderly, HIV-infected individuals, and refugees.

Q. *I don't have adequate personal finances, medical insurance, or hospitalization coverage—where would I get the money to pay for the services I may need?*

A. In publicly funded mental health centers, such as those funded by State, city or county governments, the cost of many services is calculated according to what you can afford to pay. So, if you have no money, or very little, services are still provided. This is called a sliding-scale or sliding-fee basis of payment.

Many employers make assistance programs available to their employees, often without charge. These programs—usually called Employee Assistance Programs—are designed to provide mental health services, including individual psychotherapy, family counseling, and assistance with problems of drug and alcohol abuse.

Q. *Are there other places to go for help?*

A. Yes, there are alternatives. Many mental health programs operate independently. These include local clinics, family service agencies, mental health self-help groups, private psychiatric hospitals, private clinics, and private practitioners. If you go to a private clinic or practitioner, you will pay the full cost of the services, less the amount paid by your insurer or some other payment source.

There are also many self-help organizations that operate drop-in centers and sponsor gatherings for group discussions to deal with problems associated with bereavement, suicide, depression, anxiety, phobias, panic disorder, obsessive-compulsive disorder, schizophrenia, drugs, alcohol, eating disorders (bulimia, anorexia nervosa, obesity), spouse and child abuse, sexual abuse, rape, and coping with the problems of aging parents—to name a few. In addition, there are private practitioners who specialize in treating one or more of these problems. You may contact local chapters of organizations listed at the end of this chapter to learn about various services available in your community.

Q. *I don't like to bother other people with my problems. Wouldn't it be better just to wait and work things out by myself?*

A. That's like having a toothache and not going to the dentist. The results are the same—you keep on hurting and the problem will probably get worse.

Q. *Suppose I decide to go ahead and visit a mental health center. What goes on in one of those places?*

A. A specially trained staff member will talk with you about the things that are worrying you.

Q. *Talk? I can talk to a friend for free—why pay someone?*

A. You're quite right. If you have a wise and understanding friend who is willing to listen to your problems, you may not need professional help at all. But often that's not enough. You may need a professionally trained person to help you uncover what's really bothering you. Your friend probably does not have the skills to do this.

Q. *How can just talking make problems disappear?*

A. When you're talking to someone who has a professional training and has helped many others with problems similar to yours, that person is able to see the patterns in your life that have led to your unhappiness. In therapy, the job is to help you recognize those patterns—and you may try to change them. There may be times, however, when you will need a combination of "talk" therapy and medication.

Q. *Are psychiatrists the only ones who can help?*

A. No. A therapist does not have to be a psychiatrist. Many psychologists, social workers, nurses, mental health counselors, and others have been specially trained and licensed to work effectively with people's mental and emotional difficulties. Psychiatrists are medical doctors and can prescribe medication.

Q. *Since I work all day, it would be hard to go to a center during regular working hours. Are centers open at night or on weekends?*

A. Often centers offer night or weekend appointments. Just contact the center for an appointment, which may be set up for a time that is convenient for both you and the center.

Q. *And how about therapists in private practice-do they sometimes see their patients after working hours?*

A. Many therapists have evening hours to accommodate their patients. Some even see patients very early in the morning.

Q. *I feel that I would be helped by going to a mental health center. Actually, I think my spouse could be helped too. But the idea of going to a "mental health center" would seem threatening to my spouse. Could I just pretend that it's something else?*

A. No indeed. It's better to talk your spouse into it than to lie. Don't jeopardize trust by being deceptive. However, you may want to discuss it first with the center. Marital or family therapy is available when a problem exists that involves more than one family member.

Q. *If I go to a mental health center, what kind of treatment will I get?*

A. There are many kinds of treatment. A professional at the center will work with you in determining the best form for your needs. Depending on the nature of the illness being treated, psychotherapy and/or treatment with medication may be recommended. Sometimes, joining a group of people who have similar problems is best; at other times, talking individually to a therapist is the answer.

Q. *Does talking therapy for mental and emotional problems always work?*

A. Sometimes it does, and sometimes it doesn't. It primarily depends on you and the therapist. It is important to share your concerns in a serious, sincere, and open manner. Only if you are completely honest and open can you expect to receive the best support and advice.

Q. *What if I really try, but I still can't feel comfortable with the therapist?*

A. There should be a "fit" between your personality and that of the therapist. Someone else—or some other method—may be more suitable for you. You can ask your therapist for a referral to another mental health professional, or, if you prefer, you can call one of the associations listed at the end of this chapter for the names of other therapists in your area.

Q. *What if I am receiving medication and don't think it is helping?*

A. If there is little or no change in your symptoms after 5 to 6 weeks, a different medication may be tried. Some people respond better to one medication than another. Some people also are helped by combining treatment with medications and another form of therapy.

Q. *Does a mental health center provide services for children?*

A. Yes. Children's services are an important part of any center's program. Children usually respond very well to short-term help if they are not suffering from a severe disorder. Families often are asked to participate and are consulted if the child is found to have a serious disorder—such as autism, childhood depression, obsessive-compulsive disorder, attention deficit hyperactivity disorder, or anorexia nervosa or bulimia—and long-term treatment is needed.

Q. *I have an elderly parent who has trouble remembering even close members of the family. He is physically still quite active and has wandered off a number of times. Could someone help with this?*

A. A staff person at a center can advise you about ways you can best care for your parent. You may be referred to a special agency or organization that provides services designed especially to meet the needs of elderly people. The department of public welfare in your county can give you addresses and telephone numbers for both your county and State agencies on aging. These agencies provide information on services and programs for the elderly.

Q. *I have a friend who says she could use some professional help, but she is worried about keeping it confidential.*

A. She needn't worry. Confidentiality is basic to therapy, and the patient has the right to control access to information about her treatment. Professional association guidelines plus Federal and State laws underscore the importance of confidentiality in therapist-client relationships and govern the release of records. Some insurance companies require certain information from the therapist as a condition for payment, but that information can be released only if the patient gives written permission. If your friend wants to know exactly who gets information and what kind of information is released, she should ask her insurance provider and discuss it in detail with the therapist.

Q. *I have a relative with a severe mental problem. Should I urge this person to go to the hospital?*

A. A person who is mentally ill should be in a hospital only if it is absolutely necessary. In general, most mental health professionals believe that persons with mental illness should live in the community and be treated there. That's why mental health centers and community support and rehabilitation programs stress the importance of having many different services available: day, night, and weekend care, and outpatient treatment through regular visits to an office or clinic.

Q. *Do emergency cases wind up as long-term patients in mental hospitals?*

A. Generally no. Mental hospitals are used today for short-term crisis intervention when there are no other community services available or when a person needs extra care to stabilize a drug treatment regimen. Also they serve the small percentage of patients who need long-term, structured, supervised care and treatment in a protective setting.

Q. *I have heard people use the term "involuntary commitment." What does this mean?*

A. In an emergency (for example, where a person is considered a danger to self or others), it is possible for someone to be admitted to a hospital for a short period against his or her will. The exact procedures that must be followed vary from one area to another, according to State and local laws. At the end of the emergency commitment period, the State must release the individual, obtain his or her voluntary consent to extend commitment, or file with the court an extended commitment petition to continue to detain the person involuntarily. Most States require an emergency commitment hearing to be held within 2 to 4 days after hospital admission to justify continued involuntary confinement.

Q. *Whom can I call if I feel that my rights have been violated or if I want to report suspected violation of rights, abuse, or neglect?*

A. Federal law provides that each State have a Protection and Advocacy (P&A) System. These agencies, partially funded by the Center for Mental Health Services, investigate reports of abuse and neglect in public or private mental health or treatment facilities for current residents or those admitted or discharged during the past 90 days. For the name of the P&A agency in your State, contact the National Association of Protection and Advocacy Systems at the address listed at the end of this chapter.

Warning Signals

Many people are not sure how to judge when professional help for mental problems may be needed. There are some behaviors that may be signs of trouble:

1. Is the person acting differently than usual? Could this change be linked to something that has happened recently? Any event,

such as the death of a close relative, loss of a job, marital break-up, or even something positive—like a job promotion—can trigger a troublesome emotional reaction.

2. Does the person complain of episodes of extreme, almost uncontrollable, anxiety or nervousness"? One sign of an emotional problem is "free floating" anxiety that is unrelated to a normal concern, such as a child's illness or a backlog of bills.

3. Does the person become aggressive, rude, and abusive over minor incidents or talk about groups or individuals "out to get me"? If such remarks are made in all seriousness, and if violent behavior occurs, it is likely that help is needed and should be sought.

Any of these symptoms, if they persist or become severe, may suggest a need for professional help. Fortunately, early identification and treatment of the problems causing this behavior often can make these symptoms disappear.

What to Do in Emergency Situations

If a person becomes violent, gets completely out of control, or tries to commit suicide, there are several things to do:

In a dangerous or violent crisis, call the police. Often the police are the best equipped, most available resource, especially when violence has occurred or when there is a strong possibility that the person may do physical injury to self or others.

Once the emergency situation has been brought under control, if the troubled individual is already in treatment, call his or her therapist.

In a nonviolent crisis, contacting other resources may be the best choice. For example, if an individual hasn't eaten for a substantial period of time and has become weak and dehydrated, call his or her physician or therapist. If the person doesn't have one, get him or her to a hospital emergency room where doctors are on duty—even if you have to call an ambulance to get there. Look in the Yellow Pages under "Ambulances," or call the fire department or rescue squad. Look under the list of emergency numbers in the front of your phone book, or call the operator if you can't find a number in a hurry.

Emergency room doctors will treat injuries resulting from violence, a suicide attempt, or a drug or alcohol overdose. They also may be able to provide temporary help for an emotional problem, even if they are not mental health specialists. In addition, they will be able to tell you where and how to get further help. If the person in crisis is a member of a church, synagogue, or temple, you may choose to call the minister, priest, or rabbi. Many members of the clergy are trained to deal with emergencies, or they can refer you to other sources of help.

You may choose to call a mental health or crisis hotline, drug hotline, suicide prevention center, "free clinic," or Alcoholics Anonymous chapter, if your area has such services. Their telephones are often staffed around the clock. Look for a number in the list of emergency or community service numbers in the front of your phone book, or you can find a listing in the white pages under "Suicide," " Mental Health," "Alcoholics Anonymous," or ask the operator for help.

Another option is to call the nearest mental health center. If it's not listed that way in the phone book, look under "Hospitals," "Mental Health Clinics," or "Physicians" in the Yellow Pages. Mental health centers generally provide a wide range of services. Included in these are:

1. 24-hour emergency service—available at hospitals or other mental health clinics any time of the day or night.

2. Outpatient care—a person goes to the center's clinic for treatment that has been set up on a regular appointment basis.

3. Inpatient service—a person stays at the hospital where care is provided.

4. Partial hospitalization—a person might spend occasional days, nights, or weekends at the hospital center, living at home and going to work as much as possible.

5. Consultation, education, and prevention services—assist schools, community organizations, institutions, and businesses in dealing with persons with mental illnesses and in developing programs that help in the understanding and prevention of emotional disorders.

Treatment Methods

The goals of treatment are to reduce symptoms of emotional disorders; improve personal and social functioning; develop and strengthen coping skills; and promote behaviors that make a person's life better. Biomedical therapy, psychotherapy, and behavioral therapy are basic approaches to treatment that may help a person overcome problems. There are many types of therapies that may be used alone or in various combinations.

Biomedical Therapies

Treatment with medications has benefited many patients with emotional, behavioral, and mental disorders and is often combined with other therapy. The medication that a psychiatrist or other physician prescribes depends on the nature of the illness being treated as well as on an assessment of the patient's general medical condition. During the past 35 years, many psychotherapeutic medications have been developed and have made dramatic changes in the treatment of mental disorders. Today there are specific medications to alleviate the symptoms of such mental disorders as schizophrenia, bipolar disorder, major depression, anxiety, panic disorder, and obsessive-compulsive disorder.

Electroconvulsive treatment (ECT) is another biomedical treatment that can help some patients. It is generally reserved for patients with severe mental illnesses who are unresponsive to or unable to tolerate medications or other treatments. While ECT is most commonly indicated in the treatment of major depression, often with psychosis (delusions or hallucinations), it is also used in selected cases of schizophrenia. Severe reduction in food and fluid intake with little physical movement (catatonia), or overwhelming suicidal ideation, where urgency of response is important, are reasons for considering ECT as treatment of choice. Modern methods of administering ECT use low "doses" of electric shock to the brain along with general anesthesia and muscle relaxants to minimize the risk and unpleasantness to patients.

Psychotherapy

Psychotherapy is accomplished through a series of face-to-face discussions in which a therapist helps a person to talk about, define, and resolve personal problems that are troubling. Psychotherapies generally appear to be more effective and appropriate than medications or ECT for less severe forms of emotional distress.

Short-term psychotherapy, lasting for several weeks or months, is used when the problem seems to result from a stressful life event such as a death in the family, divorce, or physical illness. The goal of the therapist is to help the patient resolve the problem as quickly as possible. Often this takes only a few visits. Long-term psychotherapy, lasting from several months to several years, emphasizes the study of underlying problems that started in childhood.

The following is a list of a few types of psychotherapy:

Psychodynamic psychotherapy, which may be either long- or short-term, examines important relationships and experiences from early childhood to the present in an effort to analyze and change unsettling or destructive behaviors and to resolve emotional problems. One form of psychodynamic psychotherapy is psychoanalysis, a long-term, intensive therapy that emphasizes how the patient's unconscious motivations and early patterns of resolving issues are important influences in his or her present actions and feelings.

Interpersonal therapy focuses on the patient's current life and relationships within the family, social, and work environments.

Family therapy involves discussions and problem-solving sessions with every member of a family—sometimes with the entire group, sometimes with individuals.

Couple therapy aims to develop a more rewarding relationship and minimize problems through understanding how individual conflicts get expressed in the couple's interactions.

Group therapy involves a small group of people with similar problems who, with the guidance of a therapist, discuss individual issues and help each other with problems.

Play therapy is a technique used for establishing communication and resolving problems with young children.

Cognitive therapy aims to identify and correct distorted thinking patterns that can lead to troublesome feelings and behaviors. Cognitive therapy is often combined effectively with behavioral therapy.

Behavioral Therapy

Behavioral therapy uses learning principles to change troublesome thinking patterns and behaviors systematically. The individual can learn specific skills to obtain rewards and satisfaction. Such an approach may involve the cooperation of important persons in the individual's life to give praise and attention to desirable changes. Behavioral therapy includes an array of methods such as stress management, biofeedback, and relaxation training.

Other Treatments

Some treatments, called "adjunctive," are used in combination with other therapies, and sometimes they are used alone. They include occupational, recreational, or creative therapies, as well as some that focus on special education. A mental health professional can help a client find the kind of therapy, or combination of therapies, that is best suited to his or her situation.

Rehabilitation Services—Community Support Programs

Many individuals with severe mental illness find it difficult to work, learn, socialize, and live independently outside a controlled setting. To help in these matters, community support programs offer rehabilitation services, either through freestanding programs that are similar to clubs, or through mental health centers. These agencies offer a variety of activities to assist clients in learning skills that will help them to live and work independently and productively in the community. For information on community support programs, contact your local or State mental health agency.

The Helping Professionals—Who They Are and What They Do

Helping professionals work in a variety of settings, such as mental health centers, outpatient clinics, private and group practice, general hospitals, psychiatric hospitals, nursing homes, jails, and prisons. They also work in residential treatment centers, partial care organizations, family or social service agencies, and the psychiatric departments of university medical centers or teaching hospitals.

Psychiatrists

A psychiatrist is a medical doctor who specializes in mental disorders, is licensed to practice medicine, and has completed a year of internship and 3 years of specialty training. A board-certified psychiatrist has, in addition, practiced for at least 2 years and passed the written and oral examinations of the American Board of Psychiatry and Neurology. Psychiatrists can evaluate and diagnose all types of mental disorders, carry out biomedical treatments and psychotherapy, and work with psychological problems associated with medical disorders. Child psychiatrists specialize in working with children; geriatric psychiatrists concentrate on helping older people.

Psychologists

Psychologists who conduct psychotherapy and work with individuals, groups, or families to resolve problems generally are called clinical psychologists, counseling psychologists, or school psychologists. They work in many settings—for example, mental health centers, hospitals and clinics, schools, employee assistance programs, and private practice. In most States, a licensed clinical psychologist has completed a doctoral degree from a university program with specialized training and experience requirements and has successfully completed a professional licensure examination.

The field of psychology also includes those who specialize in such areas as testing, community organization, industrial relations, and laboratory research.

Psychiatric Nurses

Psychiatric nursing is a specialized area of professional nursing practice that is concerned with prevention, treatment, and rehabilitation of mental health-related problems. These nurses are registered professional nurses who have advanced academic degrees at the master's degree level or above. They conduct individual, family, and group therapy and also work in mental health consultation, education, and administration.

Social Workers

Psychiatric (or clinical) social workers have advanced degrees in social work, have completed a field supervision program, and are licensed/certified. In addition to individual, family, and group counseling and psychotherapy, they are trained in client-centered advocacy. This includes information, referral, direct intervention with governmental and civic agencies, and expansion of community resources.

Mental Health Counselors

A clinical mental health counselor provides professional counseling services that involve psychotherapy, human development, learning theory, and group dynamics to help individuals, couples, and families. The promotion and enhancement of healthy, satisfying lifestyles are the goals of mental health counselors, whether the services are rendered in a mental health center, business, private practice, or other community agency. Clinical mental health counselors

215

have earned at least a master's degree, had supervised experience, and passed a national examination before they can be certified by the National Board for Certified Counselors, Inc. (NBCC).

Case Managers and Outreach Workers

These individuals assist persons with severe mental illness, including some who may be homeless, to obtain the services they need to live in the community. Most persons with severe mental illness need medical care, social services, and assistance from a variety of agencies, including those dealing with housing, Social Security, vocational rehabilitation, and mental health. Because such services are fragmented in many areas, case managers provide a critical function to monitor a person's needs and assure that appropriate agencies get involved. In many instances they also act as advocates for the client. Case managers can be nurses, social workers, or mental health workers and can be associated with mental health centers, psychosocial rehabilitation programs, or other agencies. Case management and outreach services are frequently provided by teams that may include people who are recovering from a mental illness who function as peer counselors, case management aides, or outreach workers.

Mental Health Research and Services

The core mission of the National Institute of Mental Health is to understand, treat, and prevent mental illness. Research into the kinds of mental health services that will support this mission plays an important role. The Center for Mental Health Services provides national leadership in mental health care delivery and policy development to facilitate accessible, comprehensive, and quality mental health and support services. The Institute and Center, in cooperation with consumer and family groups, professional organizations, and other Federal and State agencies, work to advance the application of scientific findings and practice-based knowledge to improve the range of effective prevention and treatment services.

Information Resources

If you believe that you, or someone you know, might benefit from the services of a mental health professional, mental health center, or one of the organizations described in this chapter, don't hesitate to take advantage of these useful services.

For referral to a physician, psychiatrist, or psychologist contact your local medical bureau or local department of mental health listed in the telephone book. And remember that your own physician or clergy is usually aware of places in your community to get help.

The following are some excellent information sources:

For Psychiatrists

American Academy of Child and Adolescent Psychiatry
3615 Wisconsin Ave., NW
Washington, DC 20016
(202) 966-7300; (202) 966-2891 FAX

American Medical Association
515 North State St.
Chicago, IL 60610
(312) 464-5000; (312) 464-4184 FAX

American Psychiatric Association
1400 K St. NW, Suite 1101
Washington, DC 20005
(202) 682-6000; (202) 682-6341 FAX

For Psychologists

American Psychological Association
750 First St. NE
Washington, DC 20002-4242
(202) 336-5500; (202) 336-5905 FAX

For Psychiatric Nurses

American Nurses' Association
600 Maryland Ave. SW, Suite 100W
Washington, DC 20024
(202) 651-7000; (202) 561-7001 FAX

American Psychiatric Nurses' Association
1200 19th St., NW, Suite 300
Washington, DC 20036
(202) 857-1133

217

For Social Workers

National Association of Social Workers
750 First St. NE, Suite 700
Washington, DC 20002-4241
(202) 408-8600; 1-800-638-8799
(202) 336-8310 FAX

For Other Mental Health Practitioners

American Mental Health Counselors Association
P.O. Drawer 22370
Alexandria, VA 22304
(703) 823-9800 ext. 383; (703) 751-1696 FAX

American Association for Marriage and Family Therapy
1100 17th St. NW, 10th Floor
Washington, DC 20036
(202) 452-0109; 1-800-374-2638
(202) 223-2329 FAX

National Board for Certified Counselors. Inc.
3-D Terrace Way
Greensboro, NC 27403
(910) 547-0607; (910) 547-0017 FAX

For Psychosocial Rehabilitation Programs

National Rehabilitation Association
633 S. Washington St.
Alexandria, VA 22314
(703) 836-0850; (703) 836-0848 FAX

International Association of Psychosocial Rehabilitation
10025 Governor Warfield Pkwy., Suite 301
Columbia, MD 21044-3357
(410) 730-7190; (410) 730-5965 FAX

For State Mental Health Centers and Programs

National Association of State Mental Health Program Directors
66 Canal Center Plaza, Suite 302
Alexandria, VA 22314-1591
(703) 739-9333; (703) 548-9517 FAX

For Protection and Advocacy

Judge David L. Bazelon Center for Mental Health Law
1101 Fifteenth St., NW, Suite 1212
Washington, DC 20005
(202) 467-5730; (202) 223-0409 FAX

National Association of Protection and Advocacy Systems
900 2nd St. NE, Suite 211
Washington, DC 20002
(202) 408-9514; (202) 408-9520 FAX

For Outpatient Programs and Mental Health Service Facilities

American Association for Partial Hospitalization, Inc.
901 N. Washington St., Suite 600
Alexandria, VA 22314-1535
(703) 836-2274; (703) 836-0083 FAX

National Association of Psychiatric Health Systems
1319 F St. NW, Suite 1000
Washington, DC 20004
(204 393-6700; (202) 783-6041 FAX

National Community Mental Healthcare Council
12300 Twinbrook Pkwy., Suite 320
Rockville, MD 20852
(301) 984-6200; (301) 881-7159 FAX

Consumer Advocacy and Support Organizations

There are also a number of consumer advocacy and support organizations. The underlying philosophy of these organizations is that the best helpers are often those who have experienced similar problems. These groups typically provide emotional support and practical help for dealing with problems that their members share.

Organizations that have chapters in many communities, or can provide referrals and/or educational materials, are:

Alzheimer's Association
919 North Michigan Ave., Suite 1000
Chicago, Illinois 60611
(312) 335-8700; 1-800-272-3900; (312) 335-1110 FAX

Anxiety Disorders Association of America
6000 Executive Blvd., Suite 513
Rockville, MD 20852
(301) 231-8368, (301) 231-7392 FAX

Association for Advancement of Behavior Therapy
305 7th Ave.
New York, NY 10001
(212) 647-1890; (212) 647-1865 FAX

Federation of Families for Children's Mental Health
1021 Prince St.
Alexandria, VA 22314-2971
(703) 684-7710; (703) 836-1040 FAX

The National Alliance for the Mentally III
2101 Wilson Blvd., Suite 302
Arlington, VA 22201
(703) 524-7600; 1-800-950-NAMI (6264); (703) 524-9094 FAX

National Anxiety Foundation
3135 Custer Dr.
Lexington, KY 40517-4001
1-800-755-1576

National Depressive and Manic Depressive Association
730 N. Franklin, Suite 501
Chicago, IL 60610
(312) 642-0049; 1-800-826-3632; (312) 642-7243 FAX

National Mental Health Association
1021 Prince St.
Alexandria, VA 22314-2971
(703) 684-7722; 1-800-969-NMHA (6642); (703) 684-5968 FAX

Pathways to Promise
5247 Fyler Ave.
St. Louis, MO 63139-1494
(314) 644-8400; (314) 644-8834 FAX

Recovery, Inc.
802 North Dearborn St.
Chicago, IL 60610
(312) 337-5661; (312) 337-5756 FAX

Self-Help or Mutual Support Groups

There are many self-help or mutual support groups that provide assistance in particular areas such as phobias, panic, bereavement, obsessive-compulsive disorder, anorexia and bulimia, as well as other disorders such as HIV-dementia and AIDS, cancer, multiple sclerosis, Parkinson's, and many others. Due to space limitations, we are unable to list them all here. Information about self-help groups can be obtained from:

American Self-Help Clearinghouse
St. Claires-Riverside Medical Center
25 Pocono Rd.
Denville, NJ 07834
(201) 625-7101; 1-800-367-6724 (inside NJ)
(201) 625-8848 FAX; (201) 625-9053 TDD

National Self-Help Clearinghouse
Graduate School and University Center
City University of New York
25 West 43rd St., Room 620
New York, NY 10036
(212) 586-5770; (212) 354-5825; (212) 642-1956 FAX

Self-Help Clearinghouse of the Greater Washington Area
7630 Little River Turnpike, #206
Annandale, VA 22003
(703) 941-5465; (703) 642-0803 FAX

Technical Assistance and Information Sharing

Two organizations engage in a variety of technical assistance and information sharing activities. They area:

National Empowerment Center
20 Ballard Rd.
Lawrence, MA 01843-1018
(508) 685-1518; 1-800-769-3728; (508) 681-6426 FAX

National Mental Health Consumers' Self-Help Clearinghouse
311 South Juniper St., Suite 1000
Philadelphia, PA 19107
(215) 735-6082 ext. 317; 1-800-553-4539; (215) 735-8307 FAX

National Institute of Mental Health and Center for Mental Health Services

A list of National Institute of Mental Health publications with information about research into the causes, prevention, and treatment of mental illnesses is available from the:

Information Resources and Inquiries Branch, NIMH
Room 7C-02, 5600 Fishers Lane
Rockville, MD 20857
(301) 443-4513; TDD (301) 443-4449

A list of Center for Mental Health Services publications with information about prevention and treatment of mental illnesses is available from the:

Office of Consumer, Family and Public Information, CMHS
Room 13-103, 5600 Fishers Lane
Rockville, MD 20857
National CMHS Clearinghouse: 1-800-789-CMHS (2647) CMHS
Electronic Bulletin Board: 1-800-790-CMHS (2647)
TDD: (301) 443-9006

Part Three

Medications

Chapter 14

Prescription Medicines and You

Taking Medicines? This Guide Can Help

Taking medicines is not always as simple as swallowing a pill. It can involve many steps and decisions each day. Whether you are using a medicine yourself or helping a child or an adult, it is easy to get off track. Perhaps you:

- did not take all of your medicine because you started feeling better.
- did not have a prescription filled or refilled (and did not tell your doctor).
- forgot to take one or more doses a day.
- took more or less medicine than your doctor told you to take.

This guide can help you avoid errors like these, and get the most from your medicines. It explains:

- How to get and follow a treatment plan that is right for you.
- What you need to do to take your medicines safely.
- How to get help when you need it.

This guide also has tips to make it easier to talk with your health care professionals (doctor, pharmacist, nurse, and others) about your medicines.

Agency for Health Care Policy and Research (AHCPR) Pub. No. 96-0056, August 1996.

Get Involved

Work with your health care professionals before, during, and after taking medicines—to give and get information, and to get help if you need it. Why should you take this active role?

- **Because using medicines in the right way is very important to your health.** With proper use of medicines, you can:

  Get the medicine 's full benefits. For example, if you take too little of a medicine to lower your cholesterol level, you will not reduce your cholesterol as much as you could.

  Avoid dangerous problems. Some people end up at a hospital emergency room because they took too much or too little of a medicine, took it the wrong way, or mixed the wrong medicines, foods, and drinks. Improper medicine use can make you worse instead of better.

  Reduce your chances of having side effects.

- **Because decisions you make about your medicines can affect your schedule, your diet, your finances, and other parts of your daily life.**

- **Because most medicine problems can be avoided or solved—if you talk with your health care professional about what is happening.**

How to Get Involved

Taking an active role in medicine use is a three-step process:

1. Take part in decisions about your treatment.
2. Follow your treatment plan.
3. Watch for problems, and get help in solving them.

Take Part in Decisions about Your Treatment; Talk to Your Health Professionals

Take part in your treatment decisions. Do not be afraid to ask questions and talk about your concerns. You may want to write down questions to ask at your next visit. By taking a moment to ask questions now, you may avoid problems later. Here are some points to cover each time a new medicine is prescribed.

Ask

- about all parts of your treatment, including diet changes, exercise, and medicines.

- about the risks and benefits of each medicine or other treatment you might get.

- how often you or your doctor will have to check your medicine's effects. For example, this means checking your cholesterol level if you are taking a medicine to lower it.

Tell

- all the medicines you are already taking. This includes prescription medicines and the medicines you buy over the counter, like aspirin or laxatives. Then your doctor can avoid giving you a new medicine that may not work well with one you take now.

- what is important to you about your medicines. You may want a medicine with the fewest side effects, or the fewest doses to take each day. You may care most about cost, or how the medicine might affect how you live or work. Or, you may want the medicine your doctor believes will work the best. Telling your doctor will help him or her select the best treatment for you.

- if cost is a concern. There may be a generic drug or another lower-cost medicine you can take.

- if you have any medicine allergies, or if you have had troubling side effects from a medicine.

- if you are or might become pregnant, or if you are nursing a baby.

- any illnesses or problems for which another doctor or health professional is treating you.

Tips: Getting Help

Do not be afraid to "bother" your doctor with your concerns and questions. You need to understand and feel comfortable with your treatment plan.

- Talk to a nurse or a pharmacist. They also can help you get a treatment plan that is right for you.

- Bring a friend or family member with you when you visit your doctor. Talking over your options with someone you trust can help you make better choices, especially if you are not feeling well.

Follow Your Treatment Plan; Talk to Your Health Professionals

To follow the treatment plan you and your doctor agree on, ask questions and tell your health professionals your needs and concerns. The doctor may start by giving you some directions for taking the medicine. If you need more information, you can ask your doctor, pharmacist, or nurse. Here are some points to cover.

Ask

- the name of the medicine and what it is supposed to do.
- how and when to take the medicine, how much to take, and for how long.
- what food, drinks, other medicines, or activities you should avoid while taking the medicine.
- what side effects the medicine may have, and what to do if they occur.
- if you can get a refill, and how often.
- about any terms or directions you do not understand.
- what to do if you miss a dose.
- if there is written information you can take home. Most pharmacies have information sheets on your prescription medicines. Some even offer large print or Spanish versions.

Tell

- any concerns you have about using the medicine.
- any concerns you have about staying with other parts of your treatment.
- if you are not taking your medicine as directed. For example, some people stop taking their medicine as soon as they feel better. Your doctor needs to know about any changes in your treatment plan. Do not let guilty feelings or embarrassment keep you from telling your doctor this important information.

Tips: Getting Help

- When you pick up your medicine, ask your pharmacist any questions you might have about it. If you are in a hurry or would feel more comfortable, call the pharmacist later from home.

- Try to use one pharmacy for all your medicine needs. The next time you are there, take a few minutes to fill out a "profile" form listing all the medicines you take. This will help your pharmacist keep track of your medicines.

- Some pharmacies are open 24 hours a day. Look for any in your area, and keep their phone numbers handy, along with the number of your regular pharmacy.

- Some products (often called compliance aids) can help remind you to take your doses on time and keep track of the doses you take. These aids include check-off calendars, containers with sections for daily doses, and caps that beep when it is time to take a dose. Ask your pharmacist or doctor what is available.

- Friends or family members can also help you follow your treatment plan. For example, they could remind you to take a dose or double check that you did take a dose. But remember: Your medicine was prescribed for you. Never share your prescription medicines with anyone.

Watch for Problems, and Get Help In Solving Them

Keep working with your health professionals while you are taking your medicine.

Ask

- about the results of medical tests that show how the medicine is working. For example, if you are taking a drug for high blood pressure, what is your blood pressure reading now?

- if medicine is still needed.

Tell

- any problems you are having taking your medicine.

- about side effects or any new problems that may be related to the medicine.

229

- any new medicines that another doctor gave you, and any over-the-counter medicines that you started taking since your last doctor's visit. Telling which medicines you take is very important—especially if you have more than one doctor.

- how you are feeling since you started taking the medicine. Do you think it is helping?

Tips: Getting Help

A yearly medicine check-up is a good way to spot hidden problems. Schedule a time with your pharmacist or doctor to look at all the prescription and over-the-counter medicines you take. They can check for duplicate medicines and proper doses. They can also advise you on medicines that are no longer needed, and tell you how to safely get rid of old medicines.

You Can Get Help Wherever You Take Medicines

- At work, there may be a nurse on site. If not, keep the phone numbers of your health professionals with you.

- At school, work with the school nurse to help your child take medicines on time and safely.

- At home, a visiting nurse or pharmacist can help you and your family solve medicine problems.

Stay Involved

Remember, medicines can only help you if you take them the right way. Follow these important steps each time your doctor prescribes a medicine:

1. Take part in decisions about your treatment.
2. Follow your treatment plan.
3. Watch for problems, and get help in solving them.

Medicine Record Form

Write down the name of each medicine you take, the reason you take it, and how you take it. Add new medicines when you get them. You can show the list to your health professionals. You may want to make copies of a blank form [See Figure 14.1] so you can use it again.

Include over-the-counter medicines such as laxatives, diet pills, vitamins, cold medicines, aspirin/other pain, headache, or fever medicine, cough medicine, allergy relief medicine, antacids, sleeping pills.

Prescription Medicines			
Name of medicine	Reason taken	Dosage	Time(s) of day
(example) Penicillin VK 250 mg	To treat my strep throat	1 tablet 4 times a day	9 a.m. 1 p.m. 5 p.m. 9 p.m.

Over-the-Counter Medicines
(Check here if you use any of these)

❏ Laxatives
❏ Diet Pills
❏ Vitamins
❏ Cold medicine
❏ Aspirin/other pain, headache or fever medicine

❏ Cough medicine
❏ Allergy relief medicine
❏ Antacids
❏ Sleeping pills
❏ Others (names)
_____
_____

Figure 14.1. Medicine Record Form. Make a list of medicines you take regularly.

For More Information

You can find many helpful books about medicines in bookstores, pharmacies, and libraries. Ask your pharmacist or librarian for suggestions. The Agency for Health Care Policy and Research (AHCPR) offers single, free brochures about preventing, diagnosing, and treating common health conditions. For a list of topics—including heart failure, acute pain, and smoking cessation—contact:

AHCPR Publications Clearinghouse
P.O. Box 8547
Silver Spring, MD 20907
(800) 358-9295

Chapter 15

Generic Drugs in Prescription Fulfillment

Fast Facts

- Your state has a law that permits pharmacists to select less costly generic drugs instead of brand-name products when filling some of your prescriptions.
- A generic drug is called by its basic chemical name instead of a registered brand-name chosen by the manufacturer.
- A generically equivalent drug product is one that has the same active ingredients, strength, and dosage form as its brand-name counterpart.
- For a drug to be therapeutically equivalent, it must be chemically the same and must also have the same medical effect.

While medical expenses generally continue to go up, your pharmacist can probably help you lower the cost of purchasing prescription drugs. Your state has a drug product selection law that permits pharmacists to select less costly generic drugs instead of brand-name products when filling some of your prescriptions.

What Does the Drug Product Selection Law Mean to You?

The purpose of this law is to give you the opportunity to save money on prescription drugs. Here's how it works. Instead of a prescribed

"Generic Drugs," *Facts for Consumers*, Federal Trade Commission, March 1993 (#5857); Bureau of Consumer Protection, Office of Consumer and Business Education (202) 326-3650.

brand-name drug, your pharmacist frequently can select a less expensive generic equivalent. However, if your doctor writes on the prescription form that a specific brand-name drug is necessary, the prescription must be filled exactly as written.

Many people can save money under their state's drug product selection law. Those who can benefit the most are generally those with the greatest need—older persons and the chronically ill on long-term drug therapy.

What Is a Generic Drug?

A generic drug is called by its basic chemical name instead of a registered brand-name chosen by the manufacturer. Generic drugs have the same active ingredients as brand-name drugs. One difference between them is the name; another, usually, is the price. If your pharmacist gives you a generic drug in place of a brand-name product, good standard practice and most state laws require that it be generically and therapeutically equivalent.

What Does Generically Equivalent Mean?

A generically equivalent drug product is one that has the same active ingredients, strength, and dosage form as its brand-name counterpart.

What Does Therapeutically Equivalent Mean?

For a drug to be therapeutically equivalent, it must be chemically the same and also must have the same medical effect.

Are There Generic Equivalents for All Drugs?

No. Some drugs are protected by patents and are supplied by only one pharmaceutical company. After the original patent expires, other manufacturers may be permitted to produce a generic equivalent, often sold at a lower cost. Presently, about half the drugs on the market are available generically, offering you the possibility of savings.

Will I Get the Medicine My Doctor Prescribed If the Pharmacist Selects a Generic Equivalent?

Your pharmacist is required by law to give you the medicine prescribed by your doctor. However, he or she may select a generic equivalent unless your doctor has asked for a specific brand-name drug as medically necessary.

How Can I Use the Drug Product Selection Law?

You can ask your doctor to write a prescription permitting substitution of a generic drug product, whenever appropriate. You can ask your doctor and your pharmacist whether a generic product will be as effective, and less costly. Or, of course, you can request that only brand-name products be used to fill your prescriptions.

What Is the Pharmacist's Role in Drug Product Selection?

Having studied drugs, their use, and their effects, your pharmacist is highly qualified to compare and evaluate drug products.

Who Should I Talk to about the Drug Product Selection Law?

Talk to your doctor and explain that you want the most effective drug at the best price. Contact your pharmacist and discuss the quality, effectiveness, and the cost of the drug product you will be using. As a trained health care professional, your pharmacist is in an excellent position to explain your prescription and instruct you on how to take it for the best results. If you have any questions about drug product selection, talk to your doctor or pharmacist.

To Contact the Federal Trade Commission

FTC Headquarters
6th & Pennsylvania Avenue, N.W.
Washington, D.C. 20580
(202) 326-2222
TDD (202) 326-2502

FTC Regional Offices:

1718 Peachtree Street, N.W., Suite 1000
Atlanta, Georgia 30367
(404) 347-4836

101 Merrimac Street, Suite 810
Boston, Massachusetts 02114-4719
(617) 424-5960

55 East Monroe Street, Suite 1860
Chicago, Illinois 60603
(312) 353-4423

668 Euclid Avenue, Suite 520-A
Cleveland, Ohio 44114
(216) 522-4207

1999 Bryan Street, Suite 2150
Dallas, Texas 75201
(214) 979-0213

1961 Stout Street, Suite 1523
Denver, Colorado 80294
(303) 844-2271

11000 Wilshire Boulevard, Suite 13209
Los Angeles, California 90024
(310) 235-4000

150 William Street, Suite 1300
New York, New York 10038
(212) 264-1207

901 Market Street, Suite 570
San Francisco, California 94103
(415) 356-5270

2806 Federal Bldg.
915 Second Ave.
Seattle, Washington 98174
(206) 220-6363

Chapter 16

Reading and Understanding Prescriptions

Making It Easier to Read Prescriptions

Sig: 1 tab po qid pc & hs

Unless you have a medical background, that bunch of letters probably looks like gobbledygook. In fact, it's several abbreviations for Latin terms used on prescriptions (see chart), in this case telling the pharmacist, "Label the container for this patient's medication with the following instructions: Take one tablet 4 times a day, after meals and at bedtime."

But if some health professionals get their way, prescriptions may soon be easier to read—and therefore safer, since improved readability helps prevent medication mix-ups.

In separate efforts, the Food and Drug Administration and the American Medical Association recently urged medication prescribers to take new precautions with prescriptions.

Patients should take precautions, too, says Thomas McGinnis, R.Ph., associate director for pharmacy affairs at FDA. "If the directions written on a prescription seem confusing, ask your doctor or pharmacist to explain, until you fully understand how to take the medication."

Text in this chapter is from "Making It Easier to Read Prescriptions," *FDA Consumer*, July-August 1995 and "A Dose of Clear Directions for Prescription Drug Users," *FDA Consumer* July-August 1997.

The Rx

The Drug Enforcement Administration requires that prescriptions for controlled substances (drugs regulated by the Federal Controlled Substances Act) state the patient's name and address, date, name of the prescribed drug, dosage strength and form (such as 10-milligram tablets), amount to be dispensed, directions for use, number of allowed refills, and the prescriber's name, address, DEA registration number, and signature.

States may make additional requirements. And they regulate the information on other prescriptions.

Since September 1993, for instance, all Texas prescriptions have had to include the intended use of the drug, unless the prescriber decides this inclusion is not in the patient's best interest.

"At the same time, we strengthened the confidentiality portion of our statute," says Steve Morse, R.Ph., assistant director of compliance with the Texas State Board of Pharmacy, in Austin. "The law makes it very clear that pharmacists may not share usage information except as the patient directs, or with other health-care professionals when the pharmacist determines that passing this information on would be in the best interest of the patient, or with certain regulators, such as DEA, as required by law."

The Institute for Safe Medication Practices, in Warminster, Pa., also advocates putting the intended use on prescriptions, says pharmacist Michael Cohen, president of the institute. Many prescribers agree with this practice, Cohen says, while others argue against it. A number of states already require the use to be on drug orders for patients in long-term care facilities, he says.

"There's no question in my mind," Cohen says, "that if the doctor generally included the drug's use on the prescription, most drug name mix-ups that occur would never happen."

Look-Alike Names

Mix-ups of drugs whose names look alike in handwriting or sound alike have also been a concern to FDA, which has received numerous reports. Jerry Phillips and other colleagues on FDA's Medication Error Subcommittee began tracking this type of medication error in June of 1992.

"We review each report," Phillips says, "and, if warranted, we may call for the manufacturer to change a product's labeling and packaging, or even its name."

Examples of look-alike names and the approximate number of reports are:

- Norvasc (amiodipine besylate) for high blood pressure, and Navane (thiothixene) for psychosis, 35 reports

- Levoxine (levothyroxine) for low thyroid, and Lanoxin (digoxin) for heart failure, 25 reports

- Prilosec (omeprazole) for duodenal ulcer, and Prozac (fluoxetine) for depression, 12 reports.

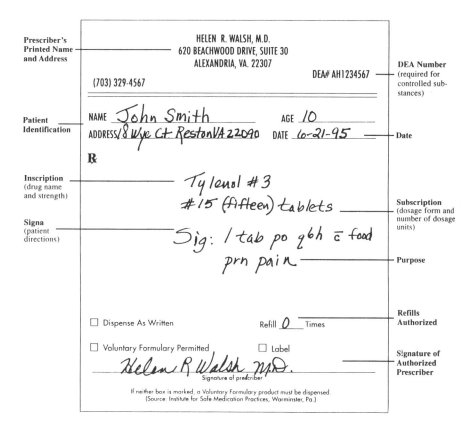

Figure 16.1. Anatomy of a Prescription. *States may vary in what they require on a prescription. This example was made up to show most types of possible information. Latin terms appear only in the patient directions, and ambiguous terms are discouraged.*

In the February 1995 *FDA Medical Bulletin*, the agency advised printing or typing prescriptions for drugs with look-alike names. "It's the handwritten or verbal orders that have been misinterpreted," Phillips says. Including the diagnosis on these prescriptions also could help prevent mix-ups, he says.

At FDA's request, Levoxine's manufacturer changed the name to Levoxyl. Also at FDA's request, Prilosec's name was changed in 1990 from Losec, which was being confused with the diuretic Lasix (furosemide).

In addition, some doctors today may be able to send prescriptions directly to pharmacies by computer, bypassing handwritten prescribing.

More Clarifying

The American Medical Association, at its annual meeting in 1994, recommended ways to make prescription writing clearer. AMA's recommendations include:

- If handwriting is illegible, use a computerized medication order system, if available. Otherwise, print or type prescriptions.

- Write out instructions rather than use ambiguous abbreviations. (For example, write "daily" rather than "qd," an abbreviated Latin term for "every day," which could be misinterpreted as "qid," meaning "4 times a day," or "od," meaning "right eye.")

- Avoid vague instructions, such as "take as directed."

- Use the USAN-approved generic drug name, official name, or trademarked name if a specific product is required, rather than a locally coined name or unestablished abbreviated drug name. (For example, use "didanosine," the generic name of an AIDS drug, or its trade name, "Videx," instead of the abbreviation "DDI." USAN stands for United States Adopted Names, a nonproprietary designation for any compound used as a drug, established by negotiation between the manufacturer and the USAN Council.)

- Avoid apothecary or chemical symbols, such as "K," the chemical symbol for potassium.

- Use a leading "0" in decimals expressing less than one, as in "0.5 mL" (milliliter), but never an ending "0," as in "5.0 mL."

- Avoid decimals when possible. (For example, prescribe "500 mg" [milligrams], rather than "0.5 g" [grams].)

240

- Spell out the word "units" rather than write "u."

- Use the metric system.

When verbal orders are necessary, AMA recommends that they be fully, clearly and articulately dictated, and then read back by the person receiving the order. (For example, say "three times daily," rather than the Latin abbreviation "tid.")

While Latin terms such as "Sig," for signa ("write") or signetur ("let it be labeled"), are still commonly seen on prescriptions, prescribers who follow the new recommendations may soon retire some of these terms and otherwise clarify their drug orders. "Let it be labeled correctly" is the expected result.

Prescription Symbols

Latin served a good purpose on prescriptions when they were first written in the 1400s. Spread widely by Roman soldiers and traders, Latin was the main language of western Europe for hundreds of years. It was unlikely to change, because it was a "dead" language, and it was unlikely to be misinterpreted, because it was exact in its meaning. Of course, the patients who didn't know Latin probably didn't have the vaguest idea what they were taking.

Table 16.2 Common Latin Rx Terms

Latin	Abbreviation	Meaning
ante cibum	ac	before meals
bis in die	bid	twice a day
gutta	gt	drop
hora somni	hs	at bedtime
oculus dexter	od	right eye
oculus sinister	os	left eye
per os	po	by mouth
post cibum	pc	after meals
pro re nata	prn	as needed
quaque 3 hora	q 3 h	every 3 hours
quaque die	qd	every day
quater in die	qid	4 times a day
ter in die	tid	3 times a day

The only part of a prescription where Latin appears today, however, is in the directions for taking the drug. This use has become a kind of medical shorthand. (See chart.) Some of these abbreviated terms have the potential to cause medication errors because they look so similar in handwriting, so their use is on the decline.

Where does the "Rx" for "prescription" come from? Its origins are given variously as an abbreviation of the Latin word "recipe," meaning "take," or as a representation of the astrological sign of Jupiter. This sign was placed on ancient prescriptions to invoke that deity's blessing on the medicine to help the person get well. More recently, the cross at the end of the "R" has been explained as a substitute period.

—by Dixie Farley

Dixie Farley is a staff writer for FDA Consumer.

A Dose of Clear Directions for Prescription Drug Users

More than four centuries ago, doctors were considered omnipotent, and the ethical statutes of England's Royal College of Physicians instructed: "Let no physician teach the people about medicines, or even tell them the names of the medicines, particularly the more potent ones ... for the people may be harmed by their improper use."

While doctors today are more forthcoming, many patients still have a hard time getting important information about the drugs their doctors prescribe. In a time when Corn Flakes, over-the-counter Tylenol, and even Alpo dog food come with easy-to-understand information about proper use, many prescription drugs still come with only a "Use as Directed" sticker for patients. The rest of the labeling is for the medical professional, in language that may be difficult for lay people to understand.

This lack of information for patients may be one reason for the recent finding, published in 1992 in the *Journal of Clinical Pharmacy and Therapeutics*, that about half of prescription drugs don't work as intended because they are improperly used.

Noncompliance can have tragic consequences. Missed doses of heart medications, for example, may lead to cardiac arrest. And missed doses of anti-glaucoma medicines can lead to eye nerve damage and blindness.

To help avoid medication problems, a new "Action Plan for the Provision of Useful Medicine Information" was unveiled in January 1997 to provide more and better information to patients.

Simple, Relevant Information

Under the action plan, health professionals will voluntarily provide prescription drug information to patients in the form of leaflets written in simple language.

Useful prescription drug information must reach at least 75 percent of patients by the year 2000, in keeping with the Department of Health and Human Services goal under its Healthy People 2000 program. By 2006, the information must reach at least 95 percent of patients. If these goals aren't met, FDA may require the information by regulation.

The plan was developed with the input of health professionals and consumer, government and industry representatives.

"Working together and using today's computer technology," said Secretary of Health and Human Services Donna Shalala when she approved the plan, "we can make prescription information more widely available, more understandable, and more relevant for each individual patient."

The action plan calls for the written information to include the condition(s) for which the drug is used, directions for taking the drug correctly, and possible side effects. Doctors or pharmacists can add information about an "off-label" use—a use that is not approved by FDA—if it is written based on an individual patient's needs.

Health professionals are responsible for getting the information to patients. FDA is available for technical assistance and will work to educate the public about the plan, according to Thomas McGinnis, a pharmacist and FDA's associate director of pharmacy affairs.

FDA will survey consumers nationwide in the year 2000 and again in 2006 to determine if the goals have been met. The agency will evaluate samples of the patient labeling to make sure it provides the required information in simple language. (See "Is the Labeling Useful?")

FDA has tried before to provide prescription medicine information to consumers. A rule the agency proposed in 1979 would have required manufacturers to include leaflets known as patient package inserts, or PPIs, with 10 prescription drugs or drug classes. The rule was withdrawn in 1982 to allow private organizations time to provide the information voluntarily.

In the next decade, FDA research showed minimal progress in getting good-quality medication information to patients. So, in 1995, FDA proposed a rule, commonly called MedGuide, that set forth goals for the distribution of useful prescription drug information to consumers and would have required manufacturers to include drug information for the patient when a product posed a serious health risk.

In August 1996, Congress passed legislation that put the MedGuide proposal on hold to provide another opportunity for private achievement of the MedGuide goals. The action plan is the private sector's framework for achieving those goals.

Labeling Lacking

Currently, manufacturers provide patient information for about 40 prescription drugs or drug classes. FDA requires patient information for some drugs, including oral contraceptives and isoproterenol inhalation products used by asthmatics. Manufacturers voluntarily provide FDA-reviewed patient labeling with some other products, such as Accutane (isotretinoin) for acne and Halcion (triazolam) for insomnia.

A 1997 FDA survey found that 67 percent of consumers were getting some written information with their prescription drugs, up from 54 percent in 1994.

But the surveys don't take into consideration the quality of the information. "The materials being given to consumers are very variable," McGinnis says. "Some are very poor, some are very good, and some are in-between. Most of the information out there now is going to have to be beefed up to meet the action plan criteria."

By increasing patients' knowledge about their drug therapies, the action plan aims to help patients take their drugs correctly. Improper use of prescription drugs leads to unnecessary illnesses, emergency room visits, hospital admissions, and deaths. FDA estimates extra health-care costs from preventable drug-related illnesses to be at least $20 billion a year. (See "Medication Mishaps.")

In addition to instructions for proper use, the information sheets will address a drug's risks and side effects, according to McGinnis. By telling patients what to look for and what to do if they see warning signs, the information may help patients recognize side effects earlier, before serious damage is done.

"These drugs are risky—they wouldn't be prescription drugs if they weren't—and patients have a right to know what the risks are," McGinnis says.

Some groups representing the pharmaceutical industry and health professionals have expressed concern to FDA that informing patients of risks and side effects may hurt compliance by scaring consumers out of taking the drug as prescribed. To this, McGinnis replies, "We've heard that argument, but we've never seen it supported scientifically."

Empowering the Patient

Written information sheets cannot replace the advice of a health professional. But there are some barriers to communication between patients and health professionals, according to David Schulke, director of policy and regulatory affairs at the American Pharmaceutical Association. "There are financial pressures that cause doctors and pharmacists to talk to more patients in less time, giving less time to each patient."

Because of the competing demands on health professionals' time, written information is especially important. "The piece of paper becomes a back-up, a safety net that patients can keep with them and refer to for information," says consumer advocate Arthur Levin, director of the Center for Medical Consumers.

Patients sometimes need to take on a very active role in their own health care, according to McGinnis. "FDA is hoping the additional information will help the patient feel less inhibited about asking questions," he says. "We hope it will encourage patients to become more involved, along with their physician, pharmacist or nurse."

Medication Mishaps

Accupril and Accutane. The drug names sound pretty similar, but they are prescribed for very different conditions. Accupril (quinapril hydrochloride) is used to treat high blood pressure and heart failure. Accutane (isotretinoin) is for certain types of severe acne.

You wouldn't want to take Accutane for a heart condition by mistake. But a patient *could* be given the wrong drug by accident. Confusion can arise from similar drug names or packaging, a prescriber's poor handwriting, misinterpretation of an abbreviated drug name, or an incorrect data entry into the computer.

To prevent avoidable accidents, FDA's Center for Drug Evaluation and Research compares drug names to see if a change is needed to avoid confusion.

"FDA's goal is to try to catch the potential for error before the product is marketed," says Sharon Smith Holston, FDA's deputy commissioner for external affairs. "Later, if we get reports of errors, we will work with the manufacturer to correct the problem by making a change in the packaging, labeling or name."

Patients themselves can prevent certain types of drug errors. The National Council on Patient Information and Education recommends asking your health professional at least these six questions about a prescription medication:

- What is the name of the medicine and what is it supposed to do?

- How and when do I take it, and for how long?

- What foods, drinks, other medicines, or activities should I avoid while taking this medicine?

- Are there any side effects, and what should I do if they occur?

- Will this new prescription work safely with the other prescription and nonprescription medicines I am taking?

- Is there any written information available about the medicine?

Patients who get drug information in writing as well as orally, says FDA pharmacist Thomas McGinnis, are much more likely to notice if the drug they got isn't for the condition they went to the doctor about or if it may be dangerous if taken with certain foods or another medication.

If a medication error occurs or is suspected, a health professional may report it, in confidence, to FDA's MedWatch program at (1-800) FDA-0178 or to the U.S. Pharmacopeia's Medication Errors Reporting Program at (1-800) 23-ERROR.

Is the Labeling Useful?

To be acceptable under the action plan, the information given to patients must be scientifically accurate, unbiased, specific, complete, understandable, up-to-date, and useful.

"The criteria aren't set in stone," says FDA pharmacist Thomas McGinnis. For example, the format may have to be adjusted for some populations. For the elderly, whose eyesight may be declining, the type may have to be larger.

How will FDA determine if labeling is "useful"? The agency will look for specific information, including:

- medicine name

- critical warnings (prominently displayed)

- conditions for which the product is used

- circumstances under which the product shouldn't be used and directions about what to do if one of these circumstances applies (for example, "Talk to your health care professional before taking this medication if any of these apply to you.")

- drugs, foods and activities that should be avoided while taking the medication, and other precautions necessary to take the medicine properly

- symptoms of adverse reactions possibly related to the drug

- risk, if any, of developing a drug tolerance or dependence

- instructions for proper use, including the usual doses, instructions if a scheduled dose is missed, special instructions (for example, whether to take with food or water), and what to do in case of an overdose

- storage instructions

- general information, including a statement encouraging discussion with a health-care professional and a statement that the drug should not be given to others.

- a statement that the patient labeling does not contain all possible information about the medicine and that the health-care professional has more information.

To Get a Copy of the Action Plan

Keystone Center
http://www.nyam.org/keystone/
(202) 783-0248

To Get More Information about the Action Plan

Kimberly Edgerly
FDA Office of Consumer Affairs
(HFE-88)
5600 Fishers Lane
Rockville, MD 20857
(1-800) 532-4440
(10 a.m. to 4 p.m. Eastern time, Monday through Friday)

—by Tamar Nordenberg

Tamar Nordenberg is a staff writer for FDA Consumer.

Chapter 17

Nonprescription Medicines

Advice for Americans about Self-Care

Access + Knowledge = Power

American medicine cabinets contain a growing choice of nonprescription, over-the-counter (OTC) medicines to treat an expanding range of ailments. OTC medications often do more than relieve aches, pains and itches. Some can prevent diseases like tooth decay, cure diseases like athlete's foot and, with a doctor's guidance, help manage recurring conditions like vaginitis and the minor pain of arthritis.

The U.S. Food and Drug Administration (FDA) determines whether medicines are prescription or nonprescription. The term prescription (Rx) refers to medicines that are safe and effective when used under a doctor's order. Nonprescription (OTC) drugs are medicines FDA decides are safe and effective for use without a doctor's prescription.

FDA also decides when a prescription drug is safe enough to be sold directly to consumers over the counter. The regulatory process allowing Americans to take a more active role in their health care is known as Rx-to-OTC switch. As a result of this process, more than 600 products sold over the counter today use ingredients or dosage strengths available only by prescription 20 years ago.

This chapter contains text from "Nonprescription Medicines: What's Right for You?" an undated document distributed as a public service by the U.S. Food and Drug Administration and the Nonprescription Drug Manufacturers Association and "Label Literacy for OTC Drugs," *FDA Consumer*, May-June 1997.

Increased access to OTC medicines is especially important for our maturing population. Two out of three older Americans rate their health as excellent to good, but four out of five report at least one chronic condition.

Fact is, today's nonprescription medicines offer greater opportunity to treat more of the aches and illnesses most likely to appear in our later years. As we live longer, work longer and take a more active role in our own health care, the need grows to become better informed about self-care.

The best way to become better informed—for young and old alike—is to read and understand the information on OTC labels. Next to the medicine itself, it's the most important part of self-care with nonprescription medicines.

With new opportunities in self-medication come new responsibilities and a growing need for knowledge. The U.S. Food and Drug Administration and the Nonprescription Drug Manufacturers Association (NDMA) have prepared the following information to help Americans take advantage of self-care opportunities.

It's on the Label

- A description of tamper-resistant feature(s) to check before you buy the product
- The product name
- Ingredients
- Any recent significant product changes
- Indications—What the medicine is for
- Usual Dosage—Directions for use
- Warnings—When to stop taking the medicine; when to see a doctor; possible side effects
- Exp. Date—When to throw it out

OTC Know-How Is on the Label

You wouldn't ignore your doctor's instructions for using a prescription drug; so don't ignore the label when taking a nonprescription medicine.

Some medicines, though, come in small packages—and reading the label is not always that easy. That's why the OTC industry and FDA are working to make medicine labels easier to read—and easier to understand.

You can help yourself too. Always use enough light (it usually takes three times more light to read the same line at age 60 than at age 30) and use your glasses or contact lenses when reading labels!

When it comes to medicines, more does not necessarily mean better. You should never misuse OTC medicines by taking them longer or in higher doses than the label recommends. Symptoms that persist are a clear signal it's time to see a doctor.

Remember, if you read the label and still have questions, talk to a doctor, nurse or pharmacist.

Drug Interactions: A Word to the Wise

Although mild and relatively uncommon, interactions involving OTC drugs can produce unwanted results or make medicines less effective. It's especially important to know about drug interactions if you're taking Rx and OTC drugs at the same time.

Some drugs can also interact with foods and beverages, as well as with health conditions such as diabetes, kidney disease, and high blood pressure.

Here are a few drug interaction cautions for some common OTC ingredients:

- Avoid alcohol if you are taking antihistamines, cough-cold products with the ingredient dextromethorphan, or drugs that treat sleeplessness.

- Do not use drugs that treat sleeplessness if you are taking prescription sedatives or tranquilizers.

- Check with your doctor before taking products containing aspirin if you're taking a prescription blood thinner or if you have diabetes or gout.

- Do not use laxatives when you have stomach pain, nausea or vomiting.

- Do not use cough-cold or weight-control medicines with the ingredient phenylpropanolamine (PPA) if you're being treated for high blood pressure or depression, if you have heart disease, diabetes or thyroid disease, or if you are taking other medicines containing PPA.

- Unless directed by a doctor, do not use a nasal decongestant if you are taking a prescription drug for high blood pressure or depression, or if you have heart or thyroid disease, diabetes or prostate problems.

251

- This is not a complete list. Read the label! Drug labels change as new information becomes available. That's why it's important to read the label each time you take medicine.

Time for a Medicine Cabinet Checkup?

- Be sure to look through your medicine supply at least once a year.

- Always store medicines in a cool, dry place.

- Throw away any medicines that are past the expiration date.

- To make sure no one takes the wrong medicine, keep all medicines in their original containers.

Pregnancy and Nursing

Drugs can pass from a pregnant woman to her unborn baby. A safe amount of medicine for the mother may be too much for the unborn baby. If you're pregnant, always talk with your doctor before taking any drugs, Rx or OTC.

Although most drugs pass into breast milk in concentrations too low to have any unwanted effects on the baby, breast-feeding mothers still need to be careful. Always ask your doctor before taking any medicine while breast-feeding. A doctor can tell you how to adjust the timing and dosing of most medicines so the baby is exposed to the lowest amount possible, or whether the drugs should be avoided altogether.

Kids Aren't Just Small Adults

OTC drugs rarely come in one-size-fits-all. Here are some tips about giving OTC medicines to children:

- Children aren't just small adults, so don't estimate the dose based on their size. Read the label. Follow all directions.

- Know the difference between TBSP. (tablespoon) and TSP. (teaspoon). They are different doses.

- Be careful about converting dose instructions. If the label says two teaspoons, it's best to use a measuring spoon or a dosing cup marked in teaspoons, not a common kitchen spoon.

- Don't play doctor. Don't double the dose just because your child seems sicker that last time.

- Before you give your child two medicines at the same time, talk to your doctor or pharmacist.

- Follow any age limits on the label.

- Never let children take medicines by themselves.

- Never call medicine candy to get your kids to take it. If they come across the medicine on their own, they're likely to remember that you called it candy.

Child-Resistant Packaging

Child-resistant caps are designed for repeated use to make it difficult for children to open. Remember, if you don't re-lock the cap after each use, the child-resistant device can't do its job—keeping children out!

It's best to store all medicines—including vitamins and supplements—where children can neither see nor reach them. Containers of pills should not be left on the kitchen counter as a reminder. Purses and briefcases are among the worst places to hide drugs from curious kids. And since children are natural mimics, it's a good idea not to take medicines in front of them. They may be tempted to play house with your medicine later on.

Be especially careful with iron-containing supplements. Iron is the leading cause of accidental fatal poisonings in children under three.

If you find some packages too difficult to open—and don't have young children living with you or visiting—you should know the law allows one package size for each medicine to be sold without child-resistant features. If you don't see it on the store shelf, ask.

Label Literacy for OTC Drugs

Information on a medicine label should be in "plain English" and larger type and should emphasize side effects and warnings with boldface type and bullets, a sampling of consumers told the Food and Drug Administration. They said this would help them understand how the drug works and would lessen their concerns about any risk from using it.

Their comments, gathered in a 1996 focus group study, as well as several years worth of comments from meetings with industry, health professionals, other consumers, and interested groups, enabled FDA on Feb. 27, 1997 to propose labeling rules for over-the-counter drugs that would make information on the label easier to read and understand.

"We want the label to be easier to read so people will indeed read it," says William Gilbertson, Pharm.D., associate director for FDA's OTC drug monographs. "And we want it to be easier to understand so people will react correctly."

This is especially important as many new potent medicines become available OTC, says Debra Bowen, M.D., director of FDA's division of OTC drug products. "These are pharmacologically active agents that have side effects, as well as beneficial effects. To use them correctly and not get into trouble from using them, people are going to have to read the label and make sure they're appropriately selecting and using them with other drugs they may be taking."

Ilisa Bernstein, a senior science policy advisor with FDA's Office of Policy, compares the proposed changes with those imposed in 1992 for food labeling and a new public-private plan that will give patients better *prescription* drug information.

"Our overall goal is to ensure that consumers read the labels, choose the product that is right for them, and use the product correctly," says Bernstein, who coordinated the agency's efforts to develop the OTC labeling proposal.

Knowing Proper Medicine Use: Ay, There's the Rub

FDA rules already require OTC drug labels to include all the information consumers need for safe and effective use. *But consumers can use the information only if they first read the entire label and understand what they read.*

Most OTC medicines are subject to rules known as monographs, which require certain labeling information for certain types of drugs. For example, there is an antacids monograph for all OTC antacid products.

A few products, such as Ivy Block (bentoquatam) to prevent and treat poison ivy, are marketed under new drug applications, which require certain information on a specific product's label. Other rules require additional labeling information, such as the statement to keep medicine out of children's reach.

Ensuring proper use of these medicines is no small job, as FDA points out in the OTC labeling proposal, because:

- There are about 100,000 OTC drug products on the market.

- Consumers self-treat four times more health problems than doctors treat.

- Sixty to 95 percent of all illnesses are initially treated with self-care, including self-treatment with OTC drugs.

And with health-care costs on the rise, so is the use of OTC medicines. To save money, consumers increasingly treat common ailments themselves instead of seeing a doctor, FDA notes.

Increased use of both prescription and OTC medicines is also partially due to the growing population of older people, who live longer due to improved medical care that often calls for several medicines. Experts estimate that by the year 2000, older people will account for up to half of all medicine use.

Unfortunately, failing eyesight often accompanies old age, putting older people at increased risk for medicine misuse and consequent health risk because they can't read the labels. For example, an arthritic older person who can't see well may catch a cold and decide to use an OTC cough-cold product. If the label has tiny print and cluttered information, the person may not be able to read that the product contains aspirin. And if the person already takes a prescription arthritis drug similar to aspirin, a harmful effect could occur—in this instance, too much of the same type of medicine may cause stomach or intestinal bleeding.

In reviewing studies that looked at whether people could read OTC drug labels, FDA found one in which a significant number of people 60 and older could not read the print on some labels because the letter width was too compressed and the letter height too short. Another study showed that people had to have eyesight *much better* than normal to read most labels on 25 OTC drugs.

The Pharmacists Planning Service Inc., Sausalito, Calif., petitioned FDA in the early 1990s to adopt standards for print size and style on OTC drug labels, stating that most people can't read the small print on some labels.

FDA's Gilbertson agrees that "to include the vast amount of information now required for some medicines, the print could get so small some people may not be able to read it." Required information on an aspirin label, for example, now consists of about 500 words, he says. But about 2,000 words are required if aspirin is added to a cough-cold medicine that also contains a cough suppressant, a nasal decongestant, and an expectorant.

"Yet people should read the entire label," Gilbertson says, "especially when using a medicine the first time. Some people assume if a drug is OTC, it's 100 percent safe. Not true. All drugs pose risk. And risk increases with improper use. If people have questions after reading the label, they should talk to their doctor, pharmacist, or other health-care professional."

Medicine misuse also can occur when important labeling information is difficult to find, says FDA's Bowen.

A person allergic to an ingredient in a drug product needs to know whether the product contains it. Although active ingredients are usually listed on OTC drug products, current rules don't require labels for all drugs to list inactive ingredients. And labels that do list the information about ingredients may include it in any paragraph virtually anywhere on the label, Bowen says. "If it's in tiny print, it's even harder to find."

Proper use of OTC drugs becomes more critical as potent prescription drugs increasingly switch to OTC use, as their safety profiles become more established. (See "Now Available Without a Prescription" originally published in the November 1996 *FDA Consumer*) and reprinted in Chapter 19.

For example, Tagamet (cimetidine) and other drugs of this type are used at prescription strength for ulcer treatment. The OTC versions, approved only for heartburn, are at lower doses. "But Tagamet in particular can have interactions at higher doses with other drugs," Bowen says.

FDA wants to help as many people as possible understand OTC drug labels so they'll use the medicines properly.

The Proposed Solution

The agency proposes an easier-to-read, easier-to-understand OTC drug label that presents important required information as distinct elements in an uncluttered format, using simpler wording in larger type. Most importantly, Bowen says, "the proposal would standardize the order of the required labeling elements and where that information is on the label."

Standardization would eliminate current practices in which product directions, warnings and approved uses appear in different places on the label and the information can appear in varying type styles and with varying graphic features. These practices make it difficult for consumers to compare products to decide which is best for the symptoms they wish to treat.

Confirming the need for national standards, Michael Weintraub, M.D., director of FDA's Office of Drug Evaluation V, says, "No matter what the product, when a consumer in any part of the country turns

Key Aspects of the Proposed OTC Drug Label

This proposed prototype label would make it easier for consumers to read, understand and, it is hoped, follow the important information on OTC drug labels.

The outline format is designed to cue consumers to the information's organization, increasing their attention to the main messages.

Other proposed improvements include easier-to-read 6-point Helvetica type; distinct sections presented in a standard order; and adequate spacing between letters, words and lines of text. The required use of uppercase and lowercase letters and dark type on a light background also would improve readability.

Proposed Format

Active ingredients would be listed alphabetically with their quantity per dosage unit (in this case a tablet). Consumers could clearly see the purpose of each ingredient.

The list of uses in the next section would help consumers readily compare products to find the appropriate medicine for their specific symptoms.

Placing all warnings in one continuous space would help ensure that every warning is noticed.

Headings and subheadings, boldface type, bullets, and simpler, concise language would emphasize and clarify important information.

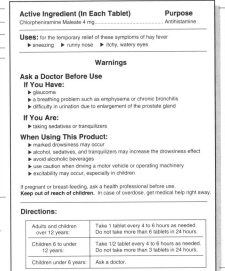

Active Ingredient (In Each Tablet)   **Purpose**
Chlorpheniramine Maleate 4 mg................................. Antihistamine

Uses: for the temporary relief of these symptoms of hay fever
▶ sneezing   ▶ runny nose   ▶ itchy, watery eyes

Warnings

Ask a Doctor Before Use
If You Have:
▶ glaucoma
▶ a breathing problem such as emphysema or chronic bronchitis
▶ difficulty in urination due to enlargement of the prostate gland

If You Are:
▶ taking sedatives or tranquilizers

When Using This Product:
▶ marked drowsiness may occur
▶ alcohol, sedatives, and tranquilizers may increase the drowsiness effect
▶ avoid alcoholic beverages
▶ use caution when driving a motor vehicle or operating machinery
▶ excitability may occur, especially in children

If pregnant or breast-feeding, ask a health professional before use.
Keep out of reach of children. In case of overdose, get medical help right away.

Directions:

Adults and children over 12 years:	Take 1 tablet every 4 to 6 hours as needed. Do not take more than 6 tablets in 24 hours.
Children 6 to under 12 years:	Take 1/2 tablet every 4 to 6 hours as needed. Do not take more than 3 tablets in 24 hours.
Children under 6 years:	Ask a doctor.

Existing Label

Allergy Tablets

INDICATIONS: Provides effective, temporary relief of sneezing, watery and itchy eyes, and runny nose due to hay fever and other upper respiratory allergies.
DIRECTIONS: Adults and children 12 years and over—1 tablet every 4 to 6 hours, not to exceed 6 tablets in 24 hours or as directed by a physician. Children 6 to 11 years—one half the adult dose (break tablet in half) every 4 to 6 hours, not to exceed 3 whole tablets in 24 hours. For children under 6 years, consult a physician.
EACH TABLET CONTAINS: Chlorpheniramine Maleate 4 mg. **May also contain** (may differ from brand): D&C Yellow No. 10, Lactose, Magnesium Stearate, Microcrystalline Cellulose, Pregelatinized Starch.
WARNINGS: May cause excitability especially in children. Do not take this product unless directed by a physician, if you have a breathing problem such as emphysema or chronic bronchitis, or if you have glaucoma or difficulty in urination due to enlargement of the prostate gland. May cause drowsiness; alcohol, sedatives and tranquilizers may increase the drowsiness effect. Avoid alcoholic beverages, and do not take this product if you are taking sedatives or tranquilizers without first consulting your physician. Use caution when driving a motor vehicle or operating machinery. As with any drug, if you are pregnant or nursing a baby, seek the advice of a health professional before using this product. Keep this and all drugs out of the reach of children. In case of accidental overdose, seek professional assistance or contact a Poison Control Center immediately.
Store at controlled room temperature 2°-30°C (36°-86°F).
Use by expiration date printed on package.
Protect from excessive moisture.
For better identification keep tablets in carton until used.

Made in U.S.A.

over an OTC medicine package and reads the label, we want the different types of information to be easy to read and always in the same place. This will increase the likelihood of safe and effective use. Consumers won't have to hunt around anymore for information on the label."

To improve readability, FDA proposes a minimum 6-point type size for required information. (For comparison, newspapers usually use 9- or 10-point type.)

Bowen acknowledges that "the minimum type size is not going to address all people who have eyesight problems. But the larger type, along with a standard location and less clutter, will help."

In its proposal, FDA asks for public comment on whether to require a minimum type size for the principal display panel to improve readability and to require a package insert in larger print to help ensure proper use by people who can't read 6-point type.

Simpler, More Concise Language

To reduce the label information load, FDA proposes simplified wording. For example, three familiar warnings would be simplified to:

- "If pregnant or breast-feeding, ask a health professional before use" instead of "As with any drug, if you are pregnant or nursing a baby, seek the advice of a health professional before using this product."

- "Keep out of reach of children" instead of "Keep this and all drugs out of the reach of children."

- "In case of overdose, get medical help right away" instead of "In case of accidental overdose, seek professional assistance or contact a poison control center immediately." This revision reflects the fact that not all states have poison control centers and that consumers may more readily obtain advice from more accessible medical professionals if the wording is changed.

Also, FDA proposes more than 35 simpler terms or phrases that can be used on the label in lieu of more complex or technical wording. For example, "lung" could be used instead of "pulmonary," "help" or "aid" instead of "assistance," "use(s)" instead of "indication(s)," "drug" instead of "medication," and "hole in" instead of "perforation of."

Other changes under consideration include alternative packaging designs, such as extending a single side panel on small packages to increase label space, and placement of sodium, calcium, magnesium, and potassium contents on the label.

Industry Assistance

Last January, FDA formally recognized the Nonprescription Drug Manufacturing Association (NDMA) for its contributions to the proposal by presenting the group with a Special Recognition Award.

"Industry has been very forthcoming, giving us lots of good suggestions," says FDA's Weintraub. In nominating NDMA, he commended the group's "wholehearted effort in partnership with the agency," stating that its members "provided excellent concepts, promoted the free and collegial exchange of ideas with the agency, and contributed user-friendly wording for the labels."

Said NDMA President James Cope: "Everybody benefits—particularly the consumer—when industry and regulators strive to cooperate."

—by Dixie Farley

Dixie Farley is a staff writer for FDA Consumer.

Comments On the Proposal

The public had until June 27, 1997 to submit written comments on FDA's proposal for more readable labels for OTC drugs.

FDA published its proposal in the Feb. 27, 1997, Federal Register, available in some libraries and on the World Wide Web at http://www.access.gpo.gov/su_docs/aces/aaces002.html. Select "Federal Register, Volume 62 (1997)" in the list of databases, then scroll down the page to submit this search request: "fda" and "february 27" and "otc drugs."

After FDA reviews the comments and other submitted information, it will issue a final rule requiring the new format on nearly all OTC drug products. Consumers can expect to see the new labels on OTC products about two years after that.

Chapter 18

Protect Yourself Against Tampering

U.S. nonprescription, over-the-counter (OTC) medicines are among the most safely packaged consumer products in the world. Most by law are sealed in tamper evident packaging for your protection. But manufacturers cannot make a tamper proof package. They can only make the safest package that technology allows. The rest is up to you.

You Can Help Protect Yourself

Here's how:

- Read the label. OTC medicines with tamper-evident packages tell you on the label what seals and other features you should look for.

- Inspect the outer packaging. Look before you buy it!

- Inspect the medicine itself when you open the package. Look again before you take it! If it looks suspicious, be suspicious.

- Look especially for capsules or tablets that are different in anyway from others in the package.

- Don't use any medicine from a package that shows cuts, slices, tears or other imperfections.

An undated document produced by the U.S. Food and Drug Administration and the Nonprescription Drug Manufacturers Association.

- Never take medicines in the dark.

- Read the label and look at the medicine every time you take a dose.

If in Doubt, Tell Somebody

Not every change in the appearance or condition of a product means that it has been tampered with. But if there is any question in your mind, don't buy it, don't use it, and don't leave it at that. Tell somebody who can do something about it!

Whenever you suspect anything wrong with a medicine or its packaging, take it back to the store. If there is a real problem, the manager will report it to the proper authorities.

Remember

No one can prevent tampering. What tamper-evident packaging does is try to provide evidence of tampering that you can see if you look. What you can do is pay attention to the safety features that the manufacturer has provided. With a little time, a little care, and your own good sense you can be the best safety feature of all.

The information in this chapter was produced in cooperation with the U.S. Food and Drug Administration by the

Nonprescription Drug Manufacturers Association
1150 Connecticut Avenue NW
Washington, DC 20063
(202) 429-9260
(202) 223-6835 fax

Chapter 19

Now Available Without a Prescription

For those who yearn to break their cigarette addiction but don't fancy a trip to the doctor's office, the ability to get the nicotine patch without a physician's prescription may be just what the doctor ordered.

In July 1996, the Food and Drug Administration approved the "switch" of the Nicotrol patch to over-the-counter (OTC) status, following on the heels of a February 1996 switch of another stop-smoking aid containing nicotine, Nicorette gum. Then, on Aug. 2, FDA approved the switch of a second nicotine patch, Nicoderm CQ.

The patch and gum join more than 600 other OTC drugs that, according to the Nonprescription Drug Manufacturers Association, would have required a prescription only 20 years ago. The 600-plus products are now available without a prescription because FDA, in cooperation with panels of outside experts, determined they could be used safely and effectively without a doctor's supervision.

In the last year and a half alone, FDA has given OTC approval to drugs with such household names as Children's Advil and Children's Motrin (ibuprofen), Orudis KT (ketoprofen) and Actron (naproxen sodium), for pain relief and fever reduction; Femstat 3 (butoconazole nitrate) for vaginal yeast infection; Pepcid AC (famotidine), Tagamet HB (cimetidine), Zantac 75 (ranitidine hydrochloride), and Axid AR (nizatidine), for heartburn; and Rogaine (minoxidil) for hair growth.

Over-the-counter switches provide increased access to effective drugs. Eighty-five percent of Americans feel it is important to have

FDA Consumer, November 1996.

OTC medications available to relieve minor medical problems, according to a 1992 Heller Research Group study of "Self Medication in the '90s: Practices and Perceptions."

"There is an important trend toward consumer participation in their own health care," says Debra Bowen, M.D., director of FDA's division of over-the-counter drug products. "It's part of our mission to keep up with the consumers' wish to be more involved."

Switches have a huge impact on the health-care economy. The greater availability of medicines over the counter saves approximately $20 billion each year, according to the 1995 *Physicians' Desk Reference for Nonprescription Drugs*, a book of drug information published annually by Medical Economics in cooperation with drug manufacturers. The $20 billion takes into account prescription costs, doctor visits, lost time from work, insurance costs, and travel.

The Switch Process

The original Federal Food, Drug, and Cosmetic Act of 1938 made no clear-cut distinction between Rx and OTC drugs. The 1951 Durham-Humphrey amendments to the act set up specific standards for classification.

The amendment requires that drugs that cannot be used safely without professional supervision be dispensed only by prescription. Such drugs may be deemed unsafe for nonprescription use because they are habit-forming or toxic, have too great a potential for harmful effects, or are for medical conditions that can't be readily self-diagnosed.

All other drugs can be sold OTC. A drug must be made available without a prescription if, by following the labeling, consumers can use it safely and effectively without professional guidance.

Some drugs are approved initially as OTC drugs. More often, though, medications are first approved Rx and later switched. "While a product is available by prescription, we can learn about the drug's safety profile in a much more controlled environment," Bowen says.

Drugs are commonly switched one of two ways: under the "OTC drug review," or by a manufacturer's submission of additional information to the original drug application.

The OTC drug review is an ongoing assessment by panels of non-government experts of the effectiveness of all drugs approved before 1962, before proof of efficacy was a requirement. The panels also review prescription ingredients to determine if some are appropriate for OTC marketing. About 40 former prescription-only drug ingredients have been switched by this process.

The second common path to OTC approval is submission of data to FDA (almost always by a manufacturer) showing the drug is appropriate for self-administration. Often the submission includes studies showing that the product's labeling can be read, understood and followed by the consumer without the guidance of a health-care provider. FDA reviews the new data, along with any information known about the drug from its prescription use.

In almost every case, the agency has sought the recommendation of a joint advisory committee made up of members of the agency's Nonprescription Drugs Advisory Committee and another advisory committee with expertise in the type of drug being considered. For

Cumulative Rx-to-OTC Switches, 1976 - September 15, 1996

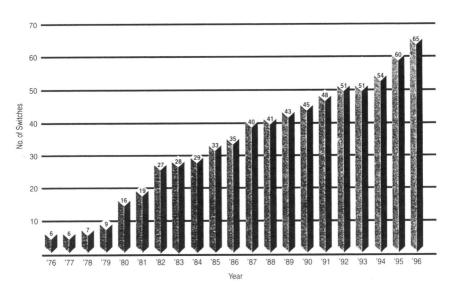

Figure 19.1. Medicines that can be used safely and effectively on the basis of product labeling alone must, by law, be made available to Americans without a doctor's prescription. This chart illustrates the cumulative number of drugs switched from prescription-only to OTC availability by FDA on a yearly basis. The number of switches for 1996 is the total as of Sept. 15, 1996. (Source: Nonprescription Drug Manufacturers Association)

265

example, because Rogaine is for conditions of the hair and scalp, representatives of the Dermatologic and Ophthalmic Drugs Advisory Committee participated.

While not bound by the advisory committee's counsel, FDA almost always follows its recommendation.

Benefit-Risk Comparison

When considering an Rx-to-OTC switch, the key question for FDA is whether patients alone can achieve the desired medical result without endangering their safety.

No drug is absolutely safe. There are risks associated with every medication, so FDA does a benefit-to-risk comparison to determine whether it is appropriate for consumers to self-medicate with a drug for a certain use.

On the safety side, the agency looks at the drug's toxicity—its potential for poisonous effects—when the drug is used according to its labeled directions, and also from foreseeable misuse of the drug.

While misuse by some consumers is inevitable—some people may overmedicate on the mistaken assumption that more is better—the Heller study showed that consumers appreciate the risks of taking any drug. Ninety percent of those surveyed said medications should be used only when absolutely necessary. Seventy percent said they prefer to fight symptoms without any medication.

FDA weighs a drug's safety against its benefit to patients. The agency considers whether consumers will be able to understand and follow label directions, whether patients can diagnose the condition themselves—or at least recognize the symptoms they want to treat—and whether routine medical examinations or laboratory tests are required for continued safe use of a drug.

No easy risk-benefit formula exists. FDA does a case-by-case review of each drug. Recently, the agency considered OTC switch applications for two very different drugs—Rogaine for hair growth and the nicotine patch for smoking cessation. Each raised unique issues, yet the risk-benefit comparison led FDA to the same conclusions in the two assessments—over-the-counter status is appropriate.

Concerns about side effects can sometimes be managed by approving OTC drugs at lower doses than their prescription counterparts. The drugs must still be effective for the short-term symptoms for which they're intended.

The issue of whether a condition can be self-diagnosed was a central one for the Rogaine advisory committee. Most OTC drugs are intended for treatment of symptoms that can be easily recognized, like headache or upset stomach. Others, though, are intended to treat diseases like asthma or vaginal fungal infections, which cannot be consumer-diagnosed.

Consumer-Friendly Labeling

Labeling is an influential element in the OTC risk-benefit comparison. The decision about a drug's safety for OTC use can't be made in a vacuum, by looking only at the drug ingredients. Every drug, used improperly, can cause adverse reactions. Even appropriate use can lead to side effects (antihistamine use may cause drowsiness, for example). And some drugs can be dangerously unsafe or ineffective if taken while using certain other drugs.

Labeling can alert consumers to such potential problems. Labeling of all drugs must be clear and truthful. For OTC drugs, the intended uses, directions and warnings have to be written so consumers, including individuals with low reading comprehension, can understand them.

FDA is working with the pharmaceutical industry to increase the readability of OTC labels by making the language more consumer-friendly and standardizing the format, including where important information is placed.

In some cases, Bowen says, consumers can get more information in the OTC labeling than they would get from their doctors. "For the nicotine patch, we developed a package—a package containing not only a drug that relieves withdrawal symptoms, but also behavioral modification information. The package provides an element of support that studies showed some people weren't getting from their doctors, by telling them when they'll most likely feel the urge to smoke, what they can do in place of smoking, and where they can go for support."

A Popular Alternative

Under the law, OTC drugs may be advertised directly to consumers without the many restrictions placed on Rx products. OTC status provides a greater opportunity for direct communication with the consumer, not only by advertising in magazines and on television, but also with packaging, brochures, and retail displays.

Nicorette gum magazine ads announce, "Nicorette Gum Is Now Available Full Strength Without A Prescription. Hallelujah!" "Hallelujah" may be the victory cry for those who, with the aid of OTC nicotine gum, were able to beat the cravings. But consumers aren't the only ones with something to gain from Rx-to-OTC switches.

Some manufacturers are exclaiming "Hallelujah" as well, over profits gained from direct access to millions of consumers. Pepcid AC for heartburn, for example, had sales topping $200 million in the first year after the product's April 1995 switch approval, making it the most profitable switch to date.

Today's emphasis on self-care fuels the popularity of nonprescription drugs. But OTC products are intended to supplement the medical options of the consumer, not substitute for a prescriber's medical knowledge. If a health problem persists or worsens while using an OTC drug, consult a health-care provider.

"People must be in a partnership with their health-care providers for optimal health," Bowen says. "Many situations aren't appropriate for self-treatment, and others may require professional guidance for self-treatment."

If you do choose OTC treatment, heed Bowen's warning: "Drugs aren't candy; they aren't risk-free. You have to follow the label and take appropriate responsibility for your own self-care."

12-4 Vote for OTC Rogaine

An FDA advisory committee voted "yes" on Nov. 17, 1995, to a prescription-to-OTC switch for Rogaine for treatment of common hereditary hair loss.

This wasn't the first time an FDA advisory committee had considered the switch. A July 1994 meeting ended in a 10-to-4 vote against OTC availability. Ten of fourteen advisory committee members weren't convinced that the benefit of Rogaine outweighed the drug's risks. Mainly, the committee was concerned that consumers would misdiagnose their hair-loss problem, and in some cases dangerously delay needed treatment.

To address this issue, Rogaine's manufacturer, Pharmacia & Upjohn, conducted six studies to see whether consumers could understand the labeling and determine if they had the common hereditary hair loss for which the product is intended. The studies showed, to the second committee's satisfaction, that consumers could self-diagnose their condition and comprehend the directions and other labeling information.

Upjohn also previewed the marketing campaign for the committee. The television ads, the company said, would be designed to educate consumers about whether the product is right for them. A toll-free number for consumers and an educational brochure at the place of purchase would be available, too.

The brochure graphically depicts the hair loss at the top of the head for which the drug is most effective. It states, in bold lettering, "If you have no family history of gradual thinning hair or hair loss, or if you are unsure of the cause of your hair loss, talk to your doctor."

The second time, members voted 12-to-4 in favor of the switch. Following the committee's recommendation, FDA approved OTC Rogaine on Feb. 9, 1996.

The product, which has been marketed since 1988 and used by over 3 million people, is now available over the counter.

9-0 Vote for OTC Nicotrol

Nicotrol was the first nicotine patch for smoking cessation approved by FDA.

It received an advisory committee's unanimous recommendation for a prescription-to-OTC switch on April 19, 1996. Worn for 16 hours a day, the patch reduces nicotine cravings by providing a constant, controlled flow of nicotine into the bloodstream.

The committee concluded that the benefits of the stop-smoking aid outweigh its risks, but only after considering manufacturer McNeil Consumer Products' proposed labeling and marketing plans, and the company's studies comparing quit rates for OTC and prescription patches.

The company presented data showing that prescription and OTC patch users achieved similar quit rates (19 percent of OTC users abstained in weeks 2 through 6, versus 16.6 percent of Rx users) and experienced no serious adverse reactions.

McNeil demonstrated that smokers understood the proposed labeling, including the warning not to smoke while using the patch and directions on how to apply and remove the patch. According to the company, more than 80 percent of consumers used the behavioral modification materials, including handbooks, an audiotape, and toll-free help-line.

The committee was told that abuse was not expected to be a problem, especially for adults. The patches are not to be sold to minors and will not be distributed through vending machines. Advertising will be targeted to adults.

FDA agreed that the benefits of the patch—an increased chance for people to quit smoking—outweighed any slight risks, and approved the product for OTC sale last July 3. The OTC patches became available in retail stores July 18.

—by Tamar Nordenberg

Tamar Nordenberg is a staff writer for *FDA Consumer*.

Chapter 20

A Guide to Nonprescription Pain Relievers

Used to be, aspirin and other salicylates were the only medications available for nonprescription relief of minor ailments—from headaches and fever to muscle strain and minor arthritis.

Today, consumers looking for temporary relief from such garden-variety ills have their pick of what can be a bewildering array of "regular," "extra-strength," and "maximum pain relief" tablets, caplets and gel caps on the drugstore shelf.

Though this cornucopia can seem confusing, the products' pain-relieving ingredients fall into just four categories: aspirin (and other salicylates), acetaminophen, ibuprofen, and naproxen sodium.

For the most part, these over-the-counter (OTC) analgesic ingredients are equally effective. However, some may be more effective for certain types of ailments, and some people may prefer one type to another because of their varying side effects. "Knowing the pros and cons of each type of pain reliever will allow you to choose among them," says William T. Beaver, M.D., professor of pharmacology and anesthesia at Georgetown University School of Medicine in Washington, D.C.

Old Faithful

Americans have been reaching for aspirin for almost 100 years as an all-purpose pain reliever (see "Aspirin: A New Look at an Old Drug" in the January-February 1994 *FDA Consumer*). Aspirin (or acetylsalicylic

This document originally appeared in the January-February 1995 *FDA Consumer*, 1995; reprinted in May 1995.

acid) works in part by suppressing the production of prostaglandins, hormone-like substances that have wide-ranging roles throughout the body, such as stimulating uterine contractions, regulating body temperature and blood vessel constriction, and helping blood clotting. "Regular" strength aspirin contains 325 milligrams (mg) per tablet; "extra" or "maximum" strength, 500 mg per tablet. The usual adult (defined as 12 years and older) dosage is one to two 325-mg aspirin tablets every four hours.

Some manufacturers add caffeine to aspirin. "There is no evidence that caffeine relieves pain, but it can enhance the effects of aspirin, possibly by lifting a person's mood," says Michael Weintraub, M.D., director of FDA's Office of OTC Drug Evaluation. Since a two-tablet dose provides roughly the same amount of caffeine as a cup of coffee, you can get the same effect by taking two plain aspirin with coffee.

To minimize the stomach irritation aspirin can cause, some brands are "buffered" with calcium carbonate, magnesium oxide, and other antacids or coated so the pills don't dissolve until they reach the small intestine. Buffered formulas may offset aspirin's directly irritating effects on the stomach lining. They may be useful for people who get heartburn or stomach pain when they take aspirin, as well as for those with arthritis, who need to take as much as 4,000 mg every day.

Aspirin also causes gastrointestinal (GI) upset indirectly (by inhibiting production of a prostaglandin that protects the stomach lining by stimulating mucus production); buffering does nothing to offset this effect.

The downside of coated aspirin products is that they may take up to twice as long to provide pain relief as plain aspirin, according to Weintraub. Last September, an FDA advisory panel recommended that labels on products containing aspirin warn that heavy drinkers are especially vulnerable to developing GI bleeding.

Aspirin should not be taken by people who have:

- ulcers, because it can worsen symptoms

- asthma, because it can trigger an attack in some asthmatics

- uncontrolled high blood pressure, because of an increased risk of one type of stroke

- liver or kidney disease, because it may worsen these conditions

- bleeding disorders or who are taking anticoagulant medication, because it may cause bleeding. Continual high dosages of aspirin can cause hearing loss or tinnitus—a persistent ringing in the ears.

FDA requires products containing aspirin and other salicylates to carry a label warning that children and teenagers should not use the medicine for chickenpox or flu symptoms because of its association with Reye syndrome, a rare disorder that may cause seizures, brain damage, and death.

The label also alerts pregnant women that use of aspirin in the last trimester may increase the risk of stillbirth and of maternal and fetal bleeding during delivery.

One Aspirin Alternative

Twenty years ago, FDA approved acetaminophen (Tylenol, and other brands and generics) in dosages of 325 mg and 500 mg for OTC use. "Nobody knows exactly how acetaminophen works, but one theory is that it acts on nerve endings to suppress pain," says Weintraub.

Acetaminophen is as effective as aspirin in relieving mild-to-moderate pain and in reducing fever, but less so when it comes to soft tissue injuries, such as muscle strains and sprains, he adds. The usual adult dosage is two 325-mg tablets every four hours.

Acetaminophen-based products to ease menstrual cramps often contain other ingredients, such as pamabrom (a diuretic) or pyrilamine maleate (an antihistamine used for its sedative effects). "While these ingredients are safe, they have not been proven effective against uterine cramps, although they may relieve other symptoms associated with menstrual pain," says Weintraub.

Though acetaminophen is no better or faster at pain relief than aspirin, the drug is gentler on the stomach and reduces fever without the risk of Reye syndrome. However, even at moderate doses, acetaminophen can cause liver damage in heavy drinkers. At press time, FDA was planning to require a warning about this on the labels of OTC products containing the drug.

From Rx to OTC

Like aspirin, ibuprofen and naproxen sodium inhibit prostaglandin production. However, they are more potent pain relievers, especially for menstrual cramps, toothaches, minor arthritis, and injuries accompanied by inflammation, such as tendinitis. FDA approved ibuprofen for OTC marketing in 1984 at a dosage level of 200 mg every 4 to 6 hours, and naproxen sodium in 1994 at a dosage level of 200 mg every 8 to 12 hours.

"Ibuprofen and naproxen sodium were converted to OTC status after their manufacturers did the necessary studies to show that these pain relievers were effective at OTC dosages, which are lower than prescription dosages," explains Weintraub. The lowest dosage strength for prescription-strength ibuprofen (Motrin and others) is 300 mg per tablet, and 275 mg per tablet for the prescription version of naproxen sodium (Anaprox, for example). "In addition, the pharmaceutical companies had to show that these drugs were safe for use by a larger, more varied group of people [than would have received them by prescription only] and that the drugs were safe to use without medical supervision, as is the case with all nonprescription drugs."

Taken at the recommended adult dosage, OTC ibuprofen (Advil and others) and naproxen sodium (Aleve) are somewhat gentler on the stomach than aspirin. However, people who have ulcers or who get GI upset when taking aspirin should avoid both. In addition, asthmatics and people who are allergic to aspirin should avoid ibuprofen and naproxen sodium. An FDA advisory panel has recommended labeling on ibuprofen products like that recommended for aspirin, warning heavy drinkers about increased risk of gastric bleeding and impaired liver function (products with naproxen sodium labels already include this information).

Although ibuprofen and naproxen sodium interfere with blood clotting much less than aspirin does, they should not be used by people who have bleeding disorders or who are taking anticoagulants. Children under 12 should not be given either drug, except under a doctor's supervision, and people over 65 are advised to take no more than one naproxen sodium tablet every 12 hours. Choosing an OTC pain reliever involves balancing effectiveness for a particular ailment with side effects. Often this is a very individual choice, based in part on your health history and how the drug affects you. Regardless of which type of OTC pain reliever you choose, remember that it is intended to be used on a short-term basis, unless directed by a doctor, cautions Weintraub. The warning labels on these products include limitations on duration of use to ensure that chronic or serious illnesses are not masked. Typically, labels advise against taking the product for more than 10 days to relieve pain (for children, the upper limit is five days), or more than three days to reduce fever. If symptoms worsen, pain persists, or there is redness or swelling, medical attention should be sought.

— by Ruth Papazian

Ruth Papazian is a writer in New York City.

Table 20.1. OTC Pain Relief Primer

Type/Dosage	Common Brands	What It Does	Possible Side Effects
aspirin 325 mg 500 mg	Anacin[1] Ascriptin[2] Bayer Bayer Plus[2] Bufferin[2] Ecotrin[3]	Relieves mild to moderate pain from headaches, sore muscles, menstrual cramps, and arthritis; reduces fever.	Prolonged use may cause gastrointestinal bleeding, especially in heavy drinkers; may increase the risk of maternal and fetal bleeding and cause complications during delivery if taken in the last trimester; can cause Reye syndrome if given to children and teenagers who have the flu or chickenpox.
acetaminophen 325 mg 500 mg	Anacin-3 Excedrin[1] Pamprin[4] Midol[4] Tylenol	Relieves mild to moderate pain from headaches and sore muscles; reduces fever.	May cause liver damage in drinkers and those taking excessive amounts (more than 4,000 mg daily) for several weeks.
ibuprofen 200 mg	Advil Motrin-IB Nuprin Pamprin-IB	Relieves mild to moderate pain from headaches, backaches, and sore muscles; relieves minor pain of arthritis; provides good relief of menstrual cramps and toothaches; reduces fever.	Gastrointestinal bleeding, especially in heavy drinkers; stomach ulcers; kidney damage in the elderly, people who have cirrhosis of the liver, and those taking diuretics.
naproxen sodium 200 mg	Aleve	Relieves mild to moderate pain from headaches, backaches, and sore muscles; relieves minor pain of arthritis; provides good relief of menstrual cramps and toothaches; reduces fever.	Gastrointestinal bleeding; stomach ulcers; kidney damage in the elderly, people who have cirrhosis of the liver, and those taking diuretics.

1. Contains caffeine.
2. Contains buffers.
3. Enteric coated.
4. Contains ingredients other than analgesics.

Chapter 21

Taming Tummy Turmoil

A vague queasiness stirs in your stomach. Queasy quickly turns to severely nauseated. A sour bubble rises in your throat, and you dash for the bathroom in a cold sweat.

Whatever the cause, the nausea and vomiting of an upset stomach are nasty. Upset stomachs caused by motion or too much food or drink may respond to over-the-counter (OTC) medicines. For other upset stomachs, professional care and no medication often are best.

Motion Sickness

Paleness, yawning and restlessness often precede the nausea, vomiting and dizziness that occur in motion sickness, which most frequently strikes youngsters ages 2 to 12, but may occur at any age.

The primary culprit in this condition is excess stimulation to the inner ear's maze of fluid-filled canals, responsible for maintaining the body's balance. Poor ventilation, anxiety or other emotional upset, and visual stimuli may contribute to motion sickness.

Because motion sickness is easier to prevent than to treat once it has begun, it may help to take an OTC drug to prevent symptoms 30 to 60 minutes before traveling and then continue doses during travel.

The Food and Drug Administration considers four active ingredients to be safe and effective for use in OTC drugs for motion sickness, says Gerald Rachanow, deputy director of the monograph review staff in FDA's Office of OTC Drug Evaluation. The ingredients are cyclizine

From *FDA Consumer*, June 1995 with revisions made in 1996.

(Marezine and others), dimenhydrinate (Dramamine and others), diphenhydramine (Benadryl and others), and meclizine (Bonine and others).

The active ingredients in these drugs are antihistamines. Their main side effect is drowsiness. Alcohol, tranquilizers and sedatives may increase this effect. Rachanow says anyone taking a drug for motion sickness should use caution when driving a vehicle or operating machinery and should avoid alcoholic beverages.

In large doses, OTC drugs for motion sickness may cause dry mouth and, rarely, blurred vision. "People with breathing problems such as emphysema or chronic bronchitis, glaucoma, or urinating difficulty due to an enlarged prostate should not take these drugs unless directed to do so by a doctor," Rachanow says.

OTC drugs for motion sickness have the following age restrictions:

- cyclizine—not for use under age 6
- dimenhydrinate—not for use under age 2
- diphenhydramine—not for use under age 6
- meclizine—not for use under age 12

Before trying these drugs, or along with them, the following measures may also help stave off motion sickness:

- Don't read during travel.
- Keep your line of vision fairly straight ahead.
- Avoid excess food or alcohol before and during extended travel. Avoid all food and drinks on short trips.
- Stay where motion is felt the least—the front seat of a car, near the wings of an airplane, or amidship (preferably on deck).
- Avoid tobacco smoke and other odors, particularly from food.

Heartburn

In the spring of 1995, FDA approved famotidine and cimetidine as the first drugs for OTC use that work systemically to reduce the amount of stomach acid produced. They are also sold by prescription at higher dosage levels to treat gastrointestinal illnesses such as ulcers.

The drugs are marketed OTC as Pepcid AC Acid Controller (famotidine) and Tagamet HB (cimetidine) to treat occasional heartburn, acid indigestion, and sour stomach in people age 12 and older. Pepcid AC may also be taken as a preventative before consuming food and beverages expected to cause these symptoms.

People should take no more than two Pepcid AC tablets or four Tagamet HB tablets in 24 hours, and should limit use at the maximum dose without consulting a doctor to two weeks. They should consult a doctor if they have swallowing difficulty or persistent abdominal pain, as these symptoms may indicate a more serious condition.

In addition, with Tagamet HB, people should consult their doctor before use if they also take any of these prescription drugs: theophylline (oral asthma medicine), warfarin (blood-thinning medicine), or phenytoin (seizure medicine). If people have questions about whether their medicines contain these drugs or about other drug interactions, they should call the manufacturer, SmithKline Beecham Consumer Affairs, at (1-800) 482-4394.

Most products approved to relieve heartburn, indigestion, or upset stomach from too much food or drink are antacids, which neutralize gastric acidity.

Antacids may contain various active ingredients. The four general categories, with common brands and potential side effects, are:

Sodium salts (Alka-Seltzer, Bromo Seltzer, and others). People on a salt-restricted diet, especially if being treated for high blood pressure, should only take sodium antacids under a doctor's orders. FDA requires labels of all OTC antacids to give the sodium content. Because a risk of stomach rupture has been associated with sodium bicarbonate intended to be dissolved in water, FDA has proposed a "Stomach Warning" in product labeling: "To avoid serious in- jury, do not take until [insert product dosage form, e.g., "tablet," "powder"] is completely dissolved. It is very important not to take this product when overly full from food or drink. Consult a doctor if severe stomach pain occurs after taking this product."

Calcium salts (Alka-2, Rolaids [Calcium Rich], Titralac, Turns, and others). Extended heavy use of calcium antacids (20 grams or more daily for a prolonged period) may cause excess calcium in the blood, which can lead to kidney stones and reduced kidney function. People who already have impaired kidneys may develop milk-alkali syndrome (causing symptoms such as nausea, vomiting, mental confusion, and loss of appetite) with as little as 4 grams a day.

Aluminum salts (ALternaGEL, Amphogel, Rolaids, and others). Aluminum salts can constipate, so they're usually combined with magnesium salts to counter this effect. Overuse can weaken bones, especially in people with impaired kidney function, leading to conditions such as osteomalacia (softening of the bones, which causes symptoms such as tenderness, muscular weakness, and weight loss).

Magnesium salts (Camalox, Gelusil, Maalox, Mylanta, and others). These salts have a laxative effect, so they're usually combined with aluminum salts; Camalox also has calcium salts. Very prolonged use may cause kidney stones. Too much magnesium in the blood can cause heart, central nervous system, and kidney problems.

As this list shows, some antacid products contain a combination of antacid ingredients. Some also contain simethicone, which breaks up gas bubbles, making them easier to eliminate from the body.

"Antacids are fast-acting drugs," says Hugo Gallo-Torres, M.D., a medical officer in FDA's division of gastrointestinal and coagulation drug products. "They should bring relief within 15 to 20 minutes of each episode. If, after several episodes, there is no relief, then something else may be going on, something that requires a physician's evaluation."

Antacids may interact with many drugs. Gallo-Torres advises consulting a doctor before using antacids if you have a condition that requires adjusting sodium in your diet, or if you are taking a prescription medicine.

Overindulgence

Bismuth subsalicylate is recommended for overeating and drinking excessively. Bismuth also has some antibacterial effect. The product, sold as Pepto-Bismol and generic brands, may cause a temporary, harmless darkening of the tongue or stool.

FDA has proposed that products containing bismuth subsalicylate have labeling warning not to give the drug to children and teenagers who have or are recovering from chickenpox, flu symptoms (nausea, vomiting or fever), or flu. The warning is needed because, like aspirin, bismuth subsalicylate is a salicylate and may be associated with an increased risk of Reye syndrome, a rare but serious illness that can occur in children and teenagers with those illnesses.

Other proposed warnings advise users not to take the drug if they're allergic to any salicylate, and to consult a doctor first if they have diabetes, gout or arthritis or if they take blood-thinning medicine.

Users are also advised to stop taking the drug if they have ringing in the ears. Rachanow explains: "This may happen when too much drug is taken or when another salicylate, such as aspirin, is taken at the same time."

Viral Infection

Nausea, vomiting and diarrhea may also be due to mild viral gastrointestinal infection. Children are especially susceptible. A doctor should be consulted if vomiting or diarrhea recur or persist, because dehydration or a chemical imbalance may result and require treatment. It is very important that patients recovering from viral gastrointestinal infection drink plenty of fluids.

Preventing Problems

The best way to deal with heartburn or indigestion is to avoid them in the first place. Simple preventive steps are:

- Avoid big meals. Your stomach must work long and hard to process them, which means it must produce a lot of acid. It helps to eat more frequent, smaller meals.

- After you eat, don't lie down right away. If you do, you're more likely to have heartburn, because gravity is now preventing food from going speedily to the intestines.

- Eat your last full meal at least three hours before bedtime. When you go to sleep, everything slows down, including your digestive system, so food you've eaten right before bedtime will stay in your stomach longer. It won't feel good.

- Sleep with your head and shoulders propped up 6 to 8 inches, so that your body is at a slight angle. This gets gravity working for you and not against you. Digestive juices in your stomach are then more likely to head south, for your intestines, instead of back up into your esophagus to cause a burning sensation.

- Avoid tight-fitting garments. They can literally compress your stomach, making it more likely that the stomach's acid contents will back up into your esophagus.

- Avoid foods that contain a lot of acid, such as citrus fruits and tomatoes, and any other food that gives you problems.

- Cut down on caffeine. It makes your stomach produce more acid. Caffeine-heavy items include coffee, tea, chocolate, and some sodas.

- Cut down on alcohol and smoking. Both irritate the lining of your stomach and tend to lower esophageal sphincter pressure.

281

When this happens, it's easier for the stomach's acid contents to shoot back up your esophagus.

General Advice

With stomach upsets in general, it's a good idea to call the doctor if symptoms last more than a few days. A doctor should be called if symptoms become severe—for instance:

- continuous vomiting or diarrhea
- extreme discomfort or pain in the gastrointestinal tract
- black stool (unless the drug you took, such as Pepto Bismol, contains bismuth subsalicylate)
- visible blood in the stool
- vomiting of blood or material that looks like coffee grounds, but which is actually digested blood.

Prolonged self-treatment may mask a more serious condition, such as an ulcer or cancer.

Women who are pregnant or breast feeding should consult their doctors before taking any drugs.

Fortunately, most upset stomachs get better by themselves or require minimal treatment. As with any medicine, it's important to read an OTC drug's entire label and follow directions carefully. And, as with any illness, it's important to know when to call the doctor.

—by Dixie Farley

Dixie Farley is a staff writer for *FDA Consumer*.

Table 21.1. OTC Drugs for Upset Stomachs

Drug	Common Brands	Possible Side Effects
Motion Sickness (Antihistamines)		
cyclizine	Marezine	drowsiness; dry mouth; rarely, blurred vision
dimenhydrinate	Dramamine	same
diphenhydramine	Benadryl	same
meclizine	Bonine	same
Heartburn, Indigestion, Sour Stomach (Antacids)		
sodium salts	Alka-Seltzer, Bromo Seltzer	interference with salt-restricted diet; with sodium bicarbonate to be dissolved in water, risk of stomach rupture if product is not fully dissolved
calcium salts	Alka-2, Calcium Rich Rolaids, Titralac, Tums	with extended heavy use, kidney stones, reduced kidney function
aluminum salts	ALternaGEL, Amphogel, Rolaids	constipation; with overuse, weakened bones
magnesium salts	Camalox, Gelusil, Maalox, Mylanta	laxative effect; with prolonged use, kidney stones; with excessive blood magnesium, problems of the heart, central nervous system, and kidneys
Heartburn, Indigestion, Sour Stomach (Acid Reducers)		
famotidine	Pepcid AC Acid Controller	headache, dizziness, constipation, diarrhea—mostly at higher prescription dosages
cimetidine	Tagamet HB	drug interactions (especially with theophylline, warfarin or phenytoin); prescription dosages: headache, diarrhea, dizziness, sleepiness
Overindulgence		
bismuth	Pepto-Bismol	temporary, harmless darkening subsalicylate of the tongue or stool, risk of Reye syndrome in children or teenagers who have or are recovering from flu or chickenpox; with overuse, ringing in the ears

Chapter 22

Colds and Flu: Time Only Sure Cure

It's not chicken soup. Believe it or not, a much more unorthodox therapy of warm-and-cold showers has recently been proposed—though not proven—for the prevention of the common cold. Shower therapy joins an ever-growing spectrum of suggested preventers and treatments for the common cold—among them, hand washing, vitamin C, interferon, seclusion, and various over-the-counter cough and cold medications.

"An efficient, practical and inexpensive prophylaxis [preventive measure] against one of the most frequent (and 'expensive') diseases has been identified at last," claims water therapy researcher Edzard Ernst, M.D., in the April 1990 issue of *Physiotherapy*. Though some may doubt his shower theory, Ernst is right about one thing—the common cold is a frequent and expensive disease, striking some people as many as 12 times a year and leading to some 15 million days lost from work annually in the United States. Influenza, or flu, likewise, is a frequent and expensive disease, reaching epidemic levels in the United States each year.

Identify the Enemy

Flu is like the cold in many ways—most basically, they're both respiratory infections caused by viruses. If a cold is misdiagnosed as flu, there's no problem. At worst, a cold can occasionally lead to secondary bacterial infections of the middle ear or sinuses, which can be treated

FDA Consumer October 1996 with revisions made in March 1997; Pub. No. (FDA)97-1264.

with antibiotics. But if the flu is misdiagnosed as a bad cold, potentially life-threatening flu complications like pneumonia may be overlooked.

Some of the symptoms of a cold and flu are similar, but the two diseases can usually be distinguished. (See accompanying table.)

Typically, colds begin slowly, two to three days after infection with the virus. The first symptoms are usually a scratchy, sore throat, followed by sneezing and a runny nose. Temperature is usually normal or only slightly elevated. A mild cough can develop several days later.

Symptoms tend to be worse in infants and young children, who sometimes run temperatures of up to 102 degrees Fahrenheit (39 degrees Celsius). Cold symptoms usually last from two days to a week.

Signs of the flu include sudden onset with a headache, dry cough, and chills. The symptoms quickly become more severe than those of a cold. The flu sufferer often experiences a "knocked-off-your-feet" feeling, with muscle aches in the back and legs. Fever of up to 104 degrees Fahrenheit (40 degrees Celsius) is common. The fever typically begins to subside on the second or third day, and then respiratory symptoms like nasal congestion and sore throat appear. Fatigue and weakness may continue for days or even weeks.

"The lethargy, achiness and fever are side effects of the body doing its job of trying to fight off the infection," according to Dominick Iacuzio, Ph.D., influenza program officer with the National Institutes of Health (NIH).

Table 22.1. Is It a Cold or the Flu?

Symptoms	*Cold*	*Flu*
fever	rare	characteristic, high (102-104F); lasts 3-4 days
headache	rare	prominent
general aches, pains	slight	usual; often severe
fatigue, weakness	quite mild	can last up to 2-3 weeks
extreme exhaustion	never	early and prominent
stuffy nose	common	sometimes
sneezing	usual	sometimes
sore throat	common	sometimes
chest discomfort	mild to moderate	common; can become severe

Source: National Institute of Allergy and Infectious Diseases

Influenza rarely causes stomach upset. What is popularly called "stomach flu"—with symptoms like nausea, diarrhea and vomiting—is technically another malady: gastroenteritis.

Cold and flu-like symptoms can sometimes mimic more serious illnesses like strep throat, measles, and chickenpox. Allergies, too, can resemble colds with their runny noses, sneezing, and general miserable feeling.

If symptoms persist, become severe or localized in the throat, stomach or lungs, or if other symptoms such as vomiting and behavioral changes occur, consult your physician. "With the typical symptoms, it's not necessary to contact your physician immediately," Iacuzio says.

The Treatment Arsenal

There is no proven cure for colds or flu but time. However, over-the-counter medications are available to relieve the symptoms.

"OTC cough-cold products can make you more comfortable while you suffer," says Debbie Lumpkins, a scientist with the Food and Drug Administration's division of over-the-counter drug products. "They are intended to treat the symptoms of minor conditions, not to treat the underlying illness."

Don't bother taking antibiotics to treat your flu or cold; antibiotics do not kill viruses, and they should be used only for bacterial complications such as sinus or ear infections. Overuse of antibiotics has become a very serious problem, leading to a resistance in disease-causing bacteria that may render antibiotics ineffective for certain conditions.

Children and teenagers with symptoms of flu or chickenpox should not take aspirin or products containing aspirin or other salicylates. Use of these products in young flu and chickenpox sufferers has been associated with Reye syndrome, a rare condition that can be fatal. Because cold symptoms can be similar to those of the flu, it's best not to give aspirin to people under 20 with these types of symptoms.

The active ingredients FDA considers safe and effective for relieving certain symptoms of colds or flu fall into the following categories:

- Nasal decongestants open up the nasal passages. They can be applied topically, in the form of sprays or drops, or taken orally. But using sprays or drops longer than three days may cause nasal congestion to worsen.

- Antitussives, also known as cough suppressants, can quiet coughs due to minor throat irritations. They include drugs taken orally, as well as topical medications like throat lozenges and ointments to be rubbed on the chest or used in a vaporizer.

- Expectorants, taken orally, help loosen mucus and make coughs more productive.

Until recently, another category of over-the-counter drugs called "antihistamines" was approved only for use by sufferers of hay fever and some other allergies. In October, clemastine fumarate, the active ingredient in products such as Tavist-1 and Tavist-D, was approved to treat cold symptoms. The effectiveness of other OTC antihistamines for this use is still being studied.

Most nonprescription cough-cold remedies contain a combination of ingredients to attack multiple symptoms. These combination products often contain antipyretics to reduce fever and analgesics to relieve minor aches, pains and headaches.

Users of OTC medicines should carefully follow the labeling instructions and warnings. To help people understand the OTC labels, FDA is working with industry on new labeling that would use more consumer-friendly language and standardize the placement of important information from product to product.

The Cold War

OTC cough and cold medication sales totaled 3.2 billion dollars in 1995, according to a national industry survey. That's no surprise, considering Americans endure about 1 billion colds each year.

Children get the most colds—six or eight a year. By contrast, adults average two to four a year, with a greater frequency in the parents of children.

The high rate in children is blamed on their lack of a built-up resistance to infection and the close contacts with other kids in schools and day care. Women's closer contact with children may also explain the greater prevalence of colds in women than in men.

Adults over 60 usually suffer less than one cold a year, probably because they have built up a natural immunity.

Most colds strike Americans in the fall and winter. Contrary to what many people believe, the increased rate of colds during this time is actually not due to the cold weather. So why do more people feel "under the weather" during the winter months? Probably, say researchers at NIH's National Institute of Allergy and Infectious Diseases, because of the greater time spent indoors in cold weather, increasing the opportunity for viruses to spread among people. Also, the lower humidity during the colder months helps cold-causing viruses to thrive and may dry the lining of the nasal passages, making them more susceptible to infection.

Because the symptoms of the common cold are caused by more than 200 different viruses—most by the so-called "rhinoviruses" (from the Greek rhin, meaning "nose")—the development of a vaccine isn't feasible. To minimize the spread of colds, people should try to keep their defenses up and their exposure down.

First Line of Defense

Cold viruses can be transmitted in one of two ways: by touching respiratory secretions on a person's skin (when shaking hands, for example) or on environmental surfaces (like doorknobs or handrails) and then touching the eyes, nose or mouth, or by inhaling infectious particles in the air (like respiratory secretions from a cough or sneeze).

The best way to break the chain of infection? Hand washing is the key, according to Iacuzio, along with not touching the nose, eyes or mouth.

"Your mucus membranes are your first line of defense against infection," according to Iacuzio. "Interference with the constant passage of mucus raises the chances for entry of the virus." That's why drinking liquids and maintaining a humid environment with a vaporizer may lower susceptibility.

To minimize the spread, other helpful measures include avoiding close, prolonged exposure to people with colds, and always sneezing or coughing into a facial tissue and immediately throwing it away. Cleaning environmental surfaces with a virus-killing disinfectant is also recommended.

The Flu Fighters

Flu typically affects 20 to 50 percent of the U.S. population each winter. It's a highly contagious disease, spreading mostly by direct person-to-person contact. "With the flu, coughing—even more than sneezing—is the most effective method of transmission," Iacuzio says.

The flu virus can linger in the air for as long as three hours. In close quarters, conditions are ripe for the spread of the virus. That explains why the highest incidence of the flu is in 5- to 14-year-olds, who spend much of their time in school, in close contact with their classmates. The most serious complications occur in older adults, however.

Years ago, there were no practical tools to protect people from flu. In 1918-1919, a global flu epidemic, or pandemic, struck half the world's population and claimed the lives of 20 million. Still today, 10,000 to 20,000 Americans—almost all of them elderly, newborns, or chronically ill—die each year from flu complications, usually pneumonia.

The challenge for scientists trying to protect us from the disease is that influenza viruses can change themselves, or mutate, to become different viruses. Scientists have classified flu viruses as types A, B and C. Type A is the most common and leads to the most serious epidemics. Type B can cause epidemics, but usually produces a milder disease than type A. Type C viruses have never been associated with a large epidemic.

Vaccine a Powerful Weapon

The most important tool for fighting the everchanging flu virus is immunization by a killed virus vaccine licensed by FDA. The vaccine is made from highly purified, egg-grown viruses that have been made noninfectious.

Vaccination is available to anyone who wants to reduce their chances of getting the flu. Studies have shown the vaccine's effectiveness rate to be 70 to 90 percent in healthy young adults. In the elderly and in people with certain chronic illnesses, the vaccine sometimes doesn't prevent illness altogether, but it does reduce its severity and the risk of complications.

The government's Advisory Committee on Immunization Practices strongly recommends vaccination for the following high-risk groups:

- people aged 65 or older

- residents of nursing homes and other facilities that provide care for chronically ill persons

- people over the age of 6 months, including pregnant women, who have certain underlying medical conditions that required hospitalization or regular doctors' visits during the preceding year. These conditions include:

    - asthma, anemia, metabolic disease such as diabetes, or heart, lung or kidney disease

    - impaired immune system due to HIV infection, treatment with drugs such as long-term steroids, or cancer treatment with radiation or chemotherapy

- children and teenagers (6 months to 18 years) who must take aspirin regularly and therefore may be at risk of developing Reye syndrome if they get the flu.

To reduce the risk of transmitting flu to high-risk persons—and to protect themselves from infection—the advisory committee recommends flu shots for people with regular close contact with high-risk groups. Such people include health-care workers, nursing home personnel, home-care providers, and children. Police, firefighters, and other community service providers may also find vaccination useful.

Because it takes the immune system about six to eight weeks to respond to vaccination, the best time to get the flu vaccine is mid-October to mid-November, before the December-to-March U.S. flu season hits.

The vaccine's most common side effect is soreness at the vaccination site for up to two days. Some people may experience post-shot fever, malaise, sore muscles, and other symptoms resembling the flu that can last for one to two days. Actually, the flu vaccine can't cause flu because it contains only inactivated viruses.

The vaccine should be repeated annually, since the immunity is believed to last only about a year, and because the vaccine's composition changes each year based on the flu strains scientists expect to be most common.

To decide which strains of influenza virus should be incorporated into the vaccine for the coming flu season, FDA's Vaccines and Related Biologicals Advisory Committee meets in late January each year to consider reports from national and international surveillance systems. A World Health Organization panel meets in Geneva in mid-February to make final recommendations for the next season's flu vaccine.

The strains are labeled by their type (A, B or C) and the place where the strain was isolated. In 1996, the predominant strains were A/Johannesberg, A/Texas, and B/Beijing. The anticipated strains for the 1996-1997 flu season are largely the same: A/Texas, A/Wuhan-like, and B/Beijing.

"In the not-too-distant future," says Iacuzio, "consumers may have alternatives to the flu shot, including different delivery methods like nasal drops or a spray." Major pharmaceutical companies, in cooperation with scientists representing NIH, FDA's Center for Biologics Evaluation and Research, and academia, are making significant strides, also, toward an even more protective vaccine.

Some people—but not many—should avoid the flu shot. People allergic to eggs and people with certain other allergies and medical problems like bronchitis or pneumonia should consult a doctor before getting a flu shot. And those with a high fever should not receive the vaccine until they feel better.

Pregnant women who have a high-risk condition should be immunized regardless of the stage of pregnancy; healthy pregnant women may also want to consult their health-care providers about being vaccinated.

In the rare cases when the vaccine is not advisable, two prescription drugs are available for prevention of type A influenza: Symmetrel (amantadine), approved by FDA in 1976, and Flumadine (rimantadine), approved by FDA in 1993. Either drug also can be used to reduce symptoms and shorten the illness if administered within 48 hours after symptoms appear.

First Do No Harm

If, despite precautions, you do get a cold or flu, besides taking an OTC medication if needed and as directed, drink fluids and get plenty of bed rest. "Your body is trying to attack the virus," Iacuzio says. "Give in, and give your body a chance to fight off the infection. It takes energy to do that."

Many people are convinced that vitamin C can prevent colds or relieve symptoms. There is no conclusive evidence of this, but the vitamin may reduce the severity or duration of symptoms, according to the National Institute of Allergy and Infectious Diseases. But taking vitamin C in large amounts over long periods can be harmful, sometimes causing diarrhea and distorting common medical tests of the urine and blood.

Another proposed therapy, interferon-alpha nasal spray, can prevent infection and illness but causes unacceptable side effects like nosebleeds, according to the institute.

Many patients have their own, unproven theories about what works. "As long as it's not harmful, why not try it?" says Iacuzio. "But be skeptical of something that hasn't been clinically proven in a well-designed, placebo-controlled study." So what about chicken soup? It may soothe a sore throat, unstuff clogged passageways, and hydrate a thirsty body. At the very least, according to Iacuzio, "It's good TLC. Psychologically, that's important when you're sick."

— by Tamar Nordenberg

Tamar Nordenberg is a staff writer for *FDA Consumer*.

Chapter 23

Alcohol and Medicines: Ask Before You Mix

Prescription and nonprescription medicines can help you stay healthy if taken correctly. Taking medicines right requires understanding what foods, beverages and other medicines can prevent a prescription from working properly. Common substances such as caffeine, tobacco, dairy products and alcohol can affect how a medicine works. The text in this chapter looks at one of these: ALCOHOL.

Alcohol and Medicines

About 100 prescription medicines can produce unwanted effects when mixed with alcohol. Alcohol can interact harmfully with some common nonprescription medicines Such as aspirin and allergy medicines. When alcohol and some medicines are mixed the problems can be minor or very severe. It can even be fatal. It's important to understand when, if and how alcohol and medicines can be mixed.

What Can Happen

A few examples of alcohol-medicine interactions are shown in Figure 23.1. This selected listing of medicines by chemical and brand name is only intended to provide examples. The risks cited do not always occur, but be safe, ask your health care professionals whether any of the medicines you take can interact with alcohol.

An undated document produced by the National Council on Patient Information and Education (NCPIE), 666 Eleventh Street, NW, Suite 810, Washington, DC 20001; reprinted with permission.

Mixing Alcohol With:	**Can Cause:**
Analgesic Pain Medication	
• Salicylates (aspirin, such as Bayer, Empirin)	Stomach and intestinal bleeding, bleeding ulcers
• Ibuprofen (such as Advil, Motrin)	
Antidiabetic Agents	
• Chlorpropamide (such as Diabinese)	Altered control of blood sugar, most often hypoglycemia
• Tolbutamide (such as Orinase)	
• Insulin (such as Humulin 70/30)	
Barbiturates	
• Secobarbital (such as Seconal)	Greater sedative effect, drowsiness, confusion
• Phenobarbital (such as Barbita)	
• Pentobarbital (such as Nembutal)	
Benzodiazepines	
• Alprazolam (such as Xanax)	Greater sedative effect, impaired motor coordination, (such as driving ability)
• Diazepam (such as Valium)	
• Triazolam (such as Halcion)	
Monoamine Oxidase (MAO) Inhibitors	
• Isocarboxazid (such as Marplan)	Certain alcoholic beverages contain tryamine that can cause severe high blood pressure that may be fatal
• Phenelzine (such as Nardil)	
• Tranylcypromine (such as Parnate)	

This selected listing of medicines by chemical and brand name is only intended to provide examples. The risks cited do not always occur, but be safe, ask your health care professionals whether any of the medicines you take can interact with alcohol.

Figure 23.1. Common drug/alcohol interactions.

Alcohol, You and Your Medicines

- Alcohol makes some medicines work less effectively. You don't get their full benefit.

- Sometimes alcohol increases the effects and the risks of a medicine to potentially dangerous levels.

Five Factors Determine How Alcohol Affects You and Your Medicines.

1. What medicine or medicines you take.

2. The amount of the medicine you take.

3. How much alcohol you drink.

4. When you take the alcohol and when you take the medicine.

5. How your body processes (metabolizes) medicines.

Be Safe: Ask Your Health Professionals

Talk to your doctor, pharmacist or nurse if you take a prescription, or plan to take medicine such as aspirin or allergy medicines.

Ask. Should you avoid alcohol—or any foods, other beverages such as coffee or caffeinated soft drinks, other medicines?

Get Specifics. Find out what could happen if you mix medicines and these substances.

Learn how you can reduce risks and avoid dangerous effects.

Plan for special occasions or other times when you'd normally drink alcohol or use these other substances.

Don't skip doses of your prescribed medicine. Don't change your schedule or stop taking a medicine without consulting your health care professional. With expert advice, you can avoid harmful interactions and enjoy all the benefits your medicines have to offer.

The information in this chapter was made possible in part by a grant from the Licensed Beverage Information Council. The content is entirely the responsibility of the National Council on Patient Information and Education (NCPIE).

NCPIE encourages professionals and community groups to foster patient professional communication about medicines. However, NCPIE

does not supervise or endorse the activities of any group or professional. Discussion and action concerning medicines are solely the responsibility of the patient and their health care professionals, and not
NCPIE.

Chapter 24

A Parent's Guide for Medicine Use by Children

Medicines can help your children feel better and stay active. Sometimes they even save lives. To work the way they should, medicines must be used properly. When we make mistakes in the way we give medicines, children don't get well. Some mistakes cause problems that can put your child's health—and life—at risk. The common mistakes that hurt children's health include:

- Stopping a medicine too soon or too suddenly.

- Not giving enough of a medicine (forgetting or skipping doses and giving them at the wrong times).

- Letting a child refuse to take a medicine (or deciding on your own not to follow the doctor's advice).

- Giving too much of a medicine (giving larger doses or giving them more often than advised).

How can you be sure that you do what's best for your child? The first step is to speak up. Talk to your health professionals, your children, and the others who take care of your children about every medicine they take.

Undated document produced by the National Council on Patient Information and Education, 666 11th Street, NW, Suite 810, Washington, DC 20001; (202) 347-6711.

Talk to Your Health Professionals

- Discuss the decision to begin or continue use of any medicine. Find out about non-drug approaches that may be used along with medicines.

- Ask your doctor to explain the benefits and the potential risks of medicines he or she prescribes for your child.

- Tell your doctor or pharmacist about other medicines your child is taking, including over-the-counter medicines. This can help prevent drug interactions.

- Ask doctors and pharmacists the 5 questions that appear at the end of this chapter. Take them along when you visit the doctor's office or pharmacy.

- Never stop, or adjust, the dosage of your child's medicine without consulting the doctor.

- Monitor and report on your child's response to the medicine. If you think it is causing side effects, let the doctor know. Don't be afraid of "bothering" him or her. Doctors need feedback to give the best treatment.

- Call the doctor or pharmacist if you have other questions later on. Don't "guess" when it comes to medicines.

Talk to Your Child

- Teach your children that proper use of medicines, is a key to good health, just like eating right or brushing your teeth.

- Explain the difference between legitimate medicines and illegal drugs. Use only the word "medicines" to talk about prescriptions and over-the-counter medicines. Use the term "drugs" to refer to illegal substances.

- Encourage your children to ask questions of the doctor and pharmacist about the medicines they will be taking. Show them how by your example.

- Decide together which responsibilities you and your child will have in following the treatment. A younger child might help you remember each dose; a teenager might take the lead, with you monitoring and providing back up.

- Get your child's help in solving problems that make it hard to follow treatment, such as remembering medicine in a busy schedule, taking medicines in school, and coping with side effects.

Talk to the Others Who Care for Your Children

The Other Parent. Both parents and step-parents should be involved in helping the child take medicine. Share information you get from the health professional. Explain instructions. Clarify the roles each of you will play.

Grandparents, Day Care Helpers, Babysitters. Explain the medicine schedule and treatment details to all those who give your child medicine in your absence. Follow up to be sure your instructions were carried out.

Schools and Teachers. Tell school personnel if your child is taking a long-term medicine or if a dose is needed during school. Involve the teacher or school nurse in watching for side effects, problems in taking medicines, or other problems.

Get The Answers to These Questions from Your Doctor or Pharmacist

1. What is the name of the medicine and what is it supposed to do?

2. How and when do I give the medicine and for how long?

3. What food, beverages, other medicines, or activities should the child avoid while taking the medicine?

4. Are there any side effects, and what do I do if they occur?

5. Is there any written information available about the medicine?

Chapter 25

How to Give Medicine to Children

"Open wide ... here comes the choo-choo." When it comes to giving children medicine, a little imagination never hurts. But what's more important is vigilance: giving the medicine at the right time at the right dose, avoiding interactions between drugs, watching out for tampering, and asking your child's doctor or the pharmacist about any concerns you may have. Whether it's a prescription or over-the-counter (OTC) drug, dispensing medicine properly to children is important. Given incorrectly, drugs may be ineffective or harmful.

Read the Label

"The most important thing for parents is to know what the drug is, how to use it, and what reactions to look for," says Paula Botstein, M.D., pediatrician and acting director of the Food and Drug Administration's Office of Drug Evaluation III. She recommends that a parent should ask the doctor or pharmacist a number of questions before accepting any prescription:

- What is the drug and what is it for?
- Will there be a problem with other drugs my child is taking?
- How often and for how long does my child need to take it?
- What if my child misses a dose?
- What side effects does it have and how soon will it start working?

The text in this chapter originally appeared in the January-February 1996 *FDA Consumer*. The version here is from a reprint of the original article [Publication No. (FDA) 96-3223] and contains revisions made in December 1996.

301

It's also a good idea to check the prescription after it has been filled. Does it look right? Is it the color and size you were expecting? If not, ask the pharmacist to explain. Check for signs of tampering in any OTC product. The safety seal should be intact before opening. Also, parents should be extra careful to read the label of over-the-counter medicines.

"Read the label, and read it thoroughly," says Debra Bowen, M.D., an internist and director of FDA's medical review staff in the Office of OTC Drugs. "There are many warnings on there, and they were written for a reason. Don't use the product until you understand what's on the label."

Make sure the drug is safe for children. This information will be on the label. If the label doesn't contain a pediatric dose, don't assume it's safe for anyone under 12 years old. If you still have questions, ask the doctor or pharmacist.

Children are more sensitive than adults to many drugs. Antihistamines and alcohol, for example, two common ingredients in cold medications, can have adverse effects on young patients, causing excitability or excessive drowsiness. Some drugs, like aspirin, can cause serious illness or even death in children with chickenpox or flu symptoms. Both alcohol and aspirin are present in some children's medications and are listed on the labels.

Younger and Trickier

The younger the child, the trickier using medicine is. Children under 2 years shouldn't be given any over-the-counter drug without a doctor's OK. Your pediatrician can tell you how much of a common drug, like acetaminophen (Tylenol), is safe for babies.

Prescription drugs, also, can work differently in children than adults. Some barbiturates, for example, which make adults feel sluggish, will make a child hyperactive. Amphetamines, which stimulate adults, can calm children.

When giving any drug to a child, watch closely for side effects. "If you're not happy with what's happening with your child, don't assume that everything's OK," says Botstein. "Always be suspicious. It's better to make the extra calls to the doctor or nurse practitioner than to have a bad reaction to a drug."

And before parents dole out OTC drugs, they should consider whether they're truly necessary, Botstein says.

Americans love to medicate—perhaps too much. A study published in the October 1994 issue of the *Journal of the American Medical*

Association found that more than half of all mothers surveyed had given their 3-year-olds an OTC medication in the previous month.

Not every cold needs medicine. Common viruses run their course in seven to 10 days with or without medication. While some OTC medications can sometimes make children more comfortable and help them eat and rest better, others may trigger allergic reactions or changes for the worse in sleeping, eating and behavior. Antibiotics, available by prescription, don't work at all on cold viruses.

"There's not a medicine to cure everything or to make every symptom go away," says Botstein. "Just because your child is miserable and your heart aches to see her that way, doesn't mean she needs drugs."

Aspirin and Children

Remember those orange-flavored baby aspirin tablets? They're not usually for kids anymore. Children and teenagers should never take aspirin, or products containing aspirin or other salicylates, if they have chickenpox or flu symptoms or are recovering from these or other viral illnesses. Such aspirin use has been associated with Reye syndrome, a rare but serious condition that can cause death.

"The incidence of Reye syndrome has dropped dramatically," says Debbie Lumpkins, an FDA microbiologist in the Office of OTC Drugs, "but that doesn't mean it can't still happen."

FDA has proposed adding a more descriptive warning label on aspirin and other products containing salicylates. The label would describe symptoms of Reye syndrome in more detail than it does now.

To reduce fever safely in children, use acetaminophen or ibuprofen products.

Dosing Dilemmas

The first rule of safety for any medicine is to give the right dose at the right time interval.

Prescription drugs come with precise instructions from the doctor, and parents should follow them carefully. OTC drugs also have dosing instruction on their labels. Getting the dosage right for an OTC drug is just as important as it is for a prescription drug.

Reactions and overdosing can happen with OTC products, especially if parents don't understand the label or fail to measure the medicine correctly. Similar problems can also occur when parents give children several different kinds of medicine with duplicate ingredients.

"People should exercise some caution about taking a bunch of medicines and loading them onto a kid," Botstein says.

Pediatric liquid medicines can be given with a variety of dosing instruments: plastic medicine cups, hypodermic syringes without needles, oral syringes, oral droppers, and cylindrical dosing spoons. Whether they measure teaspoons, tablespoons, ounces, or milliliters, these devices are preferable to using regular tableware to give medicines because one type of teaspoon may be twice the size of another. If a product comes with a particular measuring device, it's best to use it instead of a device from another product.

It's also important to read measuring instruments carefully. The numbers on the sides of the dosing instruments are sometimes small and difficult to read. In at least one case, they were inaccurate. In 1992, FDA received a report of a child who had been given two tablespoons of acetaminophen rather than two teaspoons because the cup had confusing measurements printed on it. The incident prompted a nationwide recall of medicines with dosage cups.

The following are some tips for using common dosing instruments:

Syringes. Syringes are convenient for infants who can't drink from a cup. A parent can squirt the medicine in the back of the child's mouth where it's less likely to spill out. Syringes are also convenient for storing a dose. The parent can measure it out for a babysitter to use later. Some syringes come with caps to prevent medicine from leaking out. These caps are usually small and are choking hazards. Parents who provide a syringe with a cap to a babysitter for later use should caution the sitter to remove the cap before giving the medicine to the child. The cap should be discarded or placed where the child can't get at it. There are two kinds of syringes: oral syringes made specifically for administering medicine by mouth, and hypodermic syringes (for injections), which can be used for oral medication if the needles are removed. For safety, parents should remove the needle from a hypodermic syringe. Always remove the cap before administering the medication into the child's mouth. Otherwise, the cap could pop off in the child's mouth and could choke the child. FDA is working with manufacturers to eliminate the safety hazards posed by the caps. Until then, parents must be extra cautious when using capped syringes.

Droppers. These are safe and easy to use with infants and children too young to drink from a cup. Be sure to measure at eye level and administer quickly, because droppers tend to drip.

Cylindrical dosing spoons. These are convenient for children who can drink from a cup but are likely to spill. The spoon looks like a test tube with a spoon formed at the top end. Small children can hold the long handle easily, and the small spoon fits easily in their mouths.

Dosage cups. These are convenient for children who can drink from a cup without spilling. Be sure to check the numbers carefully on the side, and measure out liquid medicine with the cup at eye level on a flat surface.

FDA Proposes New Regulations

FDA is working on changing the labels of over-the-counter medications to make them more eye-catching, easier to read, and consumer-friendly. One such label appears on the recently approved OTC version of children's Motrin.

For prescription drugs, FDA took measures in December 1994 to provide more information to health-care providers about use of those products in children. This rule was final in January 1995.

The agency now lets prescription drug manufacturers base pediatric labeling on data extrapolated from adequate and well-controlled adult studies, together with other information about safety and dosing in children. This is allowed as long as the agency concludes that the course of the disease and the drug's effects are sufficiently similar in children and adults.

Presently, most prescription drugs do not contain pediatric doses on their labels. A 1979 regulation required full clinical trials in children as the basis for pediatric labeling. Doctors who need to prescribe those drugs to children do so based on their own experience and reports in medical literature. The new regulations will give health-care providers more information to prescribe medicine for children safely.

In addition, FDA is taking steps to increase the numbers of drugs being tested in children, and the agency is working closely with the National Institute of Child Health and Human Development to conduct pediatric studies.

The goal of FDA's changes is to help ensure that whenever a child receives medication, it is as safe and effective as possible.

—by Rebecca D. Williams

Rebecca D. Williams is a writer in Oak Ridge, Tenn.

Chapter 26

Using Over-the-Counter Medications Wisely: Advice for Teens

Pharmacy shelves are filled with medicines you can buy without a prescription. But teens should be aware that just because a drug is available over the counter (often abbreviated OTC), that doesn't mean it's always free of side effects.

On the contrary, you need to take OTC drugs with much the same caution as drugs prescribed by your doctor. Special care is necessary if you use more than one of these products at the same time, or if you take an OTC product while also being treated with a prescription product. And there are some OTC drugs that shouldn't be taken by people with certain medical problems. If possible, you should ask your parent, pharmacist or physician for advice before taking any OTC product you haven't used before.

Besides getting expert advice, the most important thing you can do before buying an OTC drug is to read the label. The name of the product isn't always the same as the name of the drug it contains, and some products contain more than one ingredient.

Aspirin and Other Fever Reducers

Reading the label becomes especially important for teens when it comes to products containing aspirin (acetylsalicylic acid) or their chemical cousins, other salicylates, which are used to reduce fever or treat headaches and other pain. Teenagers (as well as children) should not take products containing aspirin or salicylates when they have

A reprint from *FDA Consumer* November 1991, Pub. No. (FDA) 92-3199.

chickenpox, flu, or symptoms that might be the flu (this includes most colds). Children and teenagers who take aspirin and other salicylates during these illnesses may develop a rare but life-threatening condition called Reye syndrome. (Symptoms usually occur near the end of the original illness and include severe tiredness, violent headache, disorientation, belligerence, and excessive vomiting.)

Acetaminophen (sold under brand names such as Datril and Tylenol) can also reduce fever and relieve pain and has not been associated with Reye syndrome. Remember, though, because fevers in most colds don't normally go above 100 degrees Fahrenheit and don't cause much discomfort, you usually don't have to take any drug for the fever. If you think you have a cold but your temperature is running higher, consult your doctor because you might have flu or a bacterial infection.

It's very important to read the label of every OTC medicine. For example, a cough formula or cold medicine may both contain phenylpropanolamine. A person taking both products at the same time might get too much of this ingredient, which is also in some OTC diet pills. The cold medicine may also contain aspirin in the form of acetylsalicylic acid and should not be taken by children and teenagers with symptoms of flu or chickenpox because of the risk of Reye syndrome.

Sniffle and Cough Combination

OTC drugs to relieve stuffy noses often contain more than one ingredient. Some of these products are marketed for allergy relief and others for colds. They usually contain both an antihistamine and a nasal decongestant. The decongestant ingredient unstuffs nasal passages; antihistamines dry up a runny nose. But some of these products may also contain aspirin or acetaminophen, and some contain a decongestant alone. Some of these drugs are "extended-release" or "long-acting" preparations that continue to work for up to 12 hours. Others are immediate-release products and usually work for four to six hours. Again, it's important to read the label—and check with the pharmacist—to be sure you're getting the right product for your symptoms.

Most antihistamines can cause drowsiness, while many decongestants have the opposite effect. Still, it's hard to predict whether any one product will make you sleepy or keep you awake—or neither—because reactions to drugs can vary from one person to another. So it's best not to drive or operate machinery until you find out how the drug affects you. In addition, alcohol, sedatives and tranquilizers intensify the drowsiness effect of antihistamines, so it's best not to take them at the same time unless a doctor tells you to. Some brand names of products containing both antihistamines and decongestants are Allerest, Actifed and Dimetapp.

Brand names of products that contain only antihistamines include Dimetane, Chlor-Trimeton and Benadryl. (But you should be aware that closely related products with similar names may have other ingredients. For example, Dimetane Decongestant contains an antihistamine and a decongestant, and Chlor-Trimeton Decongestant and Benadryl Plus contain both a decongestant and acetaminophen.)

If you decide you want to try to unstuff your nose without pills, there are other medications in the form of nasal drops and sprays sold OTC for this purpose. As with pills, some of these are long acting (up to 12 hours) and some are shorter acting. And, as with pills, most have some side effects. Many of the products contain a nasal decongestant such a oxymetazoline or phenylephrine. When used for more than three days or more often than directed by the label, these drops or sprays can sometimes cause a "rebound" effect, in which the nose gets more stuffy. Other nose drops and sprays are formulated with a saline (salt) solution and can be used for dry nose or to relieve clogged nasal passages.

As you can see, selecting a product to treat a stuffy nose can be tricky. So can choosing a product to treat a cough. In addition to one or more ingredients specifically for coughs, many cold or cough syrups contain the same ingredients that are in pills to treat allergies and colds. This means that if you're taking acetaminophen pills or cold pills, you'll want to read the label or consult the pharmacist to make sure that you're not getting a double dose of the ingredients by taking a cold or cough syrup.

There are several different types of ingredients to treat coughs, depending on the kind of cough you have. Some ingredients make it easier for you to bring up phlegm, while others suppress the cough. Before taking any kind of cough medicine, it's a good idea to first try drinking plenty of liquids and adding moisture to the air by using a vaporizer or boiling water. Sometimes just doing these things will reduce the cough enough that you won't have to take any medicine. If a cough lasts more than a few days, see your doctor.

Diet Pills

FDA recently banned 111 ingredients in OTC weight control products because they had not been proven effective. Among the substances were alcohol, ascorbic acid (vitamin C), caffeine, several forms of sugar, guar gum, phenacetin (a pain reliever), sodium, and yeast. Two other ingredients in OTC diet products, benzocaine and phenylpropanolamine (PPA), are still being reviewed by FDA. PPA can increase blood pressure if taken at too high a dose. In fact, some experts think these products may cause problems for some people at the recommended doses.

Some cold and allergy medicines (both in pills and syrups) also contain PPA. Unless you read the ingredient labeling carefully when you're taking both cold and diet products, you may not realize that you're getting more PPA than is safe.

Most teens are better off avoiding OTC diet pills unless told to take them by a doctor. Researchers have found that getting more exercise is a better way to lose weight over the long run than using pills.

Products Containing Salicylates

The following products don't have aspirin in their brand names but they contain aspirin or other salicylates and shouldn't be taken by teens who have symptoms of flu or chickenpox unless told to do so by a doctor. (Ingestion of salicylates during these illnesses increases children's and teens' risk of Reye syndrome.)

- Alka-Seltzer Effervescent Antacid and Pain Reliever (also the extra-strength version)
- Alka-Seltzer Plus Night-Time Cold Medicine
- Anacin Maximum Strength Analgesic Coated Tablets
- Ascriptin A/D Caplets (also the regular and extra-strength versions)
- BC Powder
- BC Cold Powder Multi-Symptom Formula
- BC Cold Powder Non-Drowsy Formula
- Bayer Children's Cold Tablets
- Bufferin (all formulations)
- Excedrin Extra-Strength Analgesic Tablets and Caplets
- Pepto-Bismol
- Ursinus Inlay-Tabs
- Vanquish Analgesic Caplets

In addition, many products to treat arthritis contain aspirin.

(This list contains many common products, but isn't all-inclusive. So be sure to read the label before purchasing any OTC medication.)

Stomach Help

When your stomach gets upset, it's understandable that you want the quickest relief possible. But unless the problem continues for several days or is severe, drugs are usually not necessary.

If you're constipated, drinking more water, getting more exercise, and eating high-fiber foods, such as fruits and vegetables, will often solve the problem.

Though appropriate for some medical conditions, laxatives can be habit forming and can make constipation worse when overused. Not having a bowel movement every day does not necessarily mean that you're constipated—for some people it's normal.

If you have diarrhea, it's a good idea to rest, eat only small amounts of food at a time, and drink plenty of fluids to prevent dehydration. OTC products marketed to stop diarrhea may contain loperamide (Imodium A-D), or attapulgite (Diasorb, Kaopectate and others), or bismuth subsalicylate (Pepto-Bismol and others). Bismuth subsalicylate is presently being reviewed by FDA, as part of an ongoing evaluation of OTC drugs, to determine its effectiveness against diarrhea. Teens should avoid products with bismuth subsalicylate if they have flu or chickenpox symptoms because of the risk of Reye syndrome mentioned earlier.

If you're running a fever above 100° F, or if your upset stomach symptoms are severe or continue for more than a day or two, consult your doctor, who may recommend one of the many OTC products available for these problems.

Rash Action

Because rashes can be caused by so many different things—including allergies, funguses, and poison oak or ivy—it's often best to get a doctor's opinion about what's causing your rash before treating it.

There are topical OTC products that you apply directly to the skin available specifically to treat poison ivy and oak. Some of these products contain calamine, which protects the skin, and benzocaine, which dulls the pain or itching. Other products contain an antihistamine or hydrocortisone, which relieve itching. Antihistamine creams, such as Benadryl, and hydrocortisone products, such as Cortaid and Caldecort, can also be used for rashes from allergies and insect bites, but you shouldn't use them for more than seven days without seeing a doctor.

Another type of skin problem, pimples or acne, can also be treated with topical OTC products. Many of these lotions (such as Clearasil products and Oxy-5 and-10) contain benzoyl peroxide in strengths of 2.5, 5, or 10 percent. It's best to try the lower dosage level first, to keep your skin from getting too dry. FDA is currently taking another look at the safety data for benzoyl peroxide as part of its ongoing review of OTC drugs.

Other products (including some Clearasil and Oxy products) contain sulfur, sulfur combined with resorcinol, or salicylic acid. (There is no known association between Reye syndrome and the use of topical acne products containing salicylates.) If your face doesn't clear up while using these products, or if your skin gets overly dry or breaks out in a rash, contact your doctor.

Expert Advice

These are just a few of the types of products available over the counter. Their number and uses can be confusing to adults and teens alike. Before buying any product you haven't already used, it's best to read the labeling and, if possible, ask the pharmacist how the product works and what it should be used for. And, if still in doubt, check with your doctor.

— by Judith Levine Willis

Judith Levine Willis is editor of FDA Consumer.

Chapter 27

Medicine Safety for Adults 65 and Older

People over age 65 make up 12 percent of the American population, but they take 25 percent of all prescription drugs sold in this country. As a group, older people tend to have more long-term illnesses—such as arthritis, diabetes, high blood pressure, and heart disease—than do younger people. Because they may have a number of diseases or disabilities at the same time, it is common for older people to take many different drugs.

Drugs can be wonderful tools for the care of people of all ages. Many people over age 65 owe their long lives in part to new and improved medicines and vaccines. But for older adults, drug use may have risks, especially when several medicines are used at one time.

In general, drugs act differently in older people than in younger people. This may be due to normal changes in the body that happen with age. For instance, as you get older, you lose water and lean tissue (mainly muscle) and you gain more fat tissue. This can make a difference in how long a drug stays in your body and how much of the drug your body absorbs.

The kidneys and liver are two important organs that break down and remove most drugs from the body. As you age, these organs may not work as well as they used to, and drugs may leave the body more slowly.

Keep in mind that "drugs" can mean both medicines prescribed by your doctor and over-the-counter (OTC) medicines that you buy without a prescription. OTCs can include vitamins and minerals, laxatives,

"Medicines: Use Them Safely," National Institute on Aging (NIA), *Age Page*, 1995.

cold medicines, and antacids. Both prescription and OTC drugs can cause serious problems. Be very careful to take them exactly the way your doctor advises. To be safe, don't mix them together or with alcohol without first talking to your doctor. You and your family should learn about the drugs you take and their possible side effects. Remember, drugs that are strong enough to cure you can also be strong enough to hurt you if they aren't used right.

The following tips can help you avoid risks and get the best results from your medicines.

- DO take medicine in the exact amount and on the same schedule prescribed by your doctor.

- DO always ask your doctor about the right way to take any medicine before you start to use it.

- DO always tell your doctor about past problems you have had with drugs, such as rashes, indigestion, dizziness, or not feeling hungry.

- DO keep a daily record of all the drugs you take. Include prescription and OTC drugs. Note the name of each drug, the doctor who prescribed it, the amount you take, and the times of day you take it. Keep a copy in your medicine cabinet and one in your wallet or pocketbook.

- DO review your drug record with the doctor at every visit and whenever your doctor prescribes new medicine. Your doctor often gets new information about drugs that might be important to you.

- DO make sure you can read and understand the drug name and the directions on the container. If the label is hard to read, ask your pharmacist to use large type.

- DO check the expiration dates on your medicine bottles. Throw the medicine away if it has passed this date.

- DO call your doctor right away if you have any problems with your medicines.

There are also some things you should remember *not* to do:

- DO NOT stop taking a prescription drug unless your doctor says it's okay—even if you are feeling better. If you are worried that the drug might be doing more harm than good, talk with your doctor. He or she may be able to change your medicine to another one that will work just as well.

- DO NOT take more or less than the prescribed amount of any drug.

- DO NOT mix alcohol and medicine unless your doctor says it's okay. Some drugs may not work well or may make you sick if taken with alcohol.

- DO NOT take drugs prescribed for another person or give yours to someone else.

Questions to Ask Your Doctor

Before leaving the doctor's office, ask these questions:

- What is the name of the drug and what will it do?
- How often should I take it?
- How long should I take it?
- When should I take it? As needed? Before, with, after, or between meals? At bedtime?
- If I forget to take it, what should I do?
- What side effects might I expect? Should I report them?
- Is there any material about this drug that I can take with me?
- If I don't take this drug, is there anything else that would work as well?

Resources

The U.S. Food and Drug Administration (FDA), Consumer Affairs Office has more information about safe use of medicines. Contact the FDA at 5600 Fishers Lane, HFE 88, Rockville, MD 20857, or call: (301) 443-3170.

The Elder Health Program has free information about older people and medications. Contact the Elder Health Program, School of Pharmacy, University of Maryland at Baltimore, 20 North Pine Street, Baltimore, MD 21201, or call: (410) 706-3011.

The National Institute on Aging (NIA) distributes a free booklet, *Talking with Your Doctor: A Guide for Older People*. [For your convenience, this document is reprinted in Chapter 9.] To order this booklet or other free materials on health and aging, contact the NIA Information Center, P.O. Box 8057, Gaithersburg, MD 20898-8057, or call: 1-800-222-2225, or 1-800-222-4225 (TTY).

Chapter 28

Aging and Health:
The Role of Self-Medication

Introduction

Self-medication with nonprescription, over-the-counter (OTC) medicines is one of the most prevalent forms of medical care among older Americans, just as it is among all Americans. It is the first line of personal defense in staying active, well, and independent—and staying that way longer.

Older Americans use at least 25 percent of OTC medicines even though they make up almost 13 percent of the population.[1] One reason for the more common use of OTCs among older adults is that many conditions for which OTC drugs are used, such as arthritis, insomnia and constipation, become more prevalent with advancing age.[2]

As a nation, we have become more aware of the "Aging of America" and its implications for the use and costs of health care. Simultaneously, wellness programs and self-care have emerged as major components of health maintenance, particularly for the older population.

Until recently, very little data have existed on the use of OTCs by older adults. In 1984, the Nonprescription Drug Manufacturers Association (NDMA) released a national study of consumers' health care practices and OTC drug use. In 1992, NDMA conducted another study to update the findings. Although much remains to be learned, we now have some specific data on the use of OTCs by those 65 and older.

Aging and Health: The Role of Self-Medication Fourth Ed. Nonprescription Drug Manufacturers Association, 1995; reprinted with permission.

This text summarizes our current knowledge of the health and self-medication practices of older Americans.

The Health of Older Americans: Myths and Reality

One of every eight Americans, or 12.7 percent of the population, is now age 65 or older. In 1993, older adults numbered 32.8 million persons.

Americans of all ages are healthier today than they were 10 to 20 years ago. Men who reach age 65 can expect to live another 15 years. Women can expect to live another 19 years.[3]

In addition, experts predict the number of people age 65 and up will more than double by 2030. And in the coming years, the 85 and older crowd will make up nearly one-fourth of the older population.[4]

As the number of older persons and their average age increases, the lay public and health care professionals alike have changed their attitudes toward aging. Madison Avenue's recognition of major consumer markets and the power of senior votes give us a new image of older adults as community leaders, statesmen, actors and actresses, musicians, artists, businessmen, and our neighbors. Older adults are recognized as healthy, vibrant, and active.

In fact, less than one-fourth of Americans age 65 to 74 describe themselves as retired, and less than one-third of Americans age 75 and older do.[5]

The majority of older Americans consider themselves to be in good health. In the 1993 National Health Interview Survey (NHIS), almost 40 percent of persons age 65 and older rated their health as excellent or very good. Another 33 percent rated their health as good. Only eight percent said their health was poor.[6]

Three-quarters of those 65 to 74 who are not living in institutions say they are in good health. And even among those 75 and older, two-thirds consider themselves healthy.[7]

Health promotion and self-care are prevalent themes. Hospitals, senior centers and social service agencies across the nation offer educational programs attended weekly by thousands of older Americans. When questioned in an earlier NHIS survey, nine of 10 older adults report they are doing a good job of taking care of their health. Twenty-four percent said they do an excellent job, 32 percent said "very good" and 34 percent said "good." Of the remaining 10 percent, only a few said "poor."[8]

These positive attitudes about health occur despite the prevalence of chronic illnesses. As a person ages, chronic conditions become more common than acute health problems. Most older adults have at least one chronic health condition and many have multiple conditions.

Almost half of all persons age 65 and older have arthritis and about 40 percent have hypertension.[9]

Table 28.1. Common problems for persons age 65 and older at the rate per 100 persons.

Condition	Rate/100
Arthritis	48
Hypertension	36
Hearing Impairment	32
Heart Disease	32
Orthopedic Impairment	19
Cataracts	17
Sinusitis	16
Diabetes	11
Tinnitus (ringing in the ears)	9
Varicose Veins	9

Source: American Association of Retired Persons, 1994.

Older persons use health care services more than younger adults. Individuals age 65 and older see a physician an average of 11 times per year, compared with almost six times per year for younger adults.[10]

Older adults accounted for 35 percent of all hospital stays and 46 percent of all days of care in hospitals in 1992.[11] The average length of a hospital stay was 8.2 days for older people, compared to 5.1 days for people under 65.[12] About 1.6 million elderly persons lived in nursing homes in 1990.[13]

Despite the aggregate statistics, health care professionals, as well as the lay public, have come to appreciate the great variation in the aging process. No two persons age the same physiologically, emotionally, or socially.

Medical researchers and physicians generally agree that health status and medicine use are determined more by physiological age than by chronological age.

Nonprescription Drug Use by Older Americans

No national agency routinely collects data on the use of nonprescription drugs by the age of consumer. Thus, to gather information about the use of OTC medicines by older adults, the NDMA sponsored nationwide surveys in 1984 and 1992.[14] Both surveys were conducted by an independent research organization.

The studies included questions about everyday health problems and self-medication with OTCs. The studies did not attempt to measure responses to life-threatening diseases that require prompt and often continuous medical attention or that indicate the use of prescription medicines. The objectives of the study were to discover the type of common, minor health problems people experience and to learn what people do about these problems, and, if they use OTC medicines, with what results.

The 1992 study findings showed:

- Adults age 65 and older reported experiencing an average of 5.1 everyday health problems during a two-week period. This compares with an average of seven problems reported by the total adult population. This lower level of problems may partly reflect a higher tolerance of minor symptoms by older adults, perhaps because they suffer more painful, chronic illnesses causing them to overlook minor health problems.

- The most frequently reported everyday health problems of older Americans are arthritis and rheumatism, sleeping problems, muscle aches and pains, upset stomach, being overweight, headaches, colds and bunions/corns/calluses.

- Twenty-eight percent of their reported problems were not treated at all, while an additional 20 percent were treated with home remedies (e.g., salt water gargles for sore throats). A doctor or dentist was telephoned or visited for 21 percent of the reported problems, while a previously prescribed medicine was used 17 percent of the time. Twenty-eight percent of the time, older adults treated their everyday problems with OTC medicines, compared to 38 percent in the younger population.

- When nonprescription medicines are used for everyday problems, usually only one medication is used and only for a brief period, generally a day or two. Long-term and multiple drug consumption are rare for treatment of the everyday problems reported in the survey.

- Older consumers using nonprescription medicines reported successful and safe use of these products. When asked why a nonprescription medicine was discontinued, 88 percent said they stopped using the medicine because the problem had been resolved. Only three percent reported that the OTC medicine failed to work, two percent said they ran out of the medicine, and one percent noted that their physician advised a change or discontinuation of medication. Less than one percent reported an unfavorable or allergic reaction to the OTC medicine.

- Older individuals were satisfied with the performance of nonprescription medicines they used: 93 percent expressed satisfaction with the products and 95 percent indicated that they would use the same type of nonprescription medicine again if the health problem recurred.

In summary, most older adults do not see themselves as vastly different from other Americans in personal health matters. Despite more chronic illnesses, they use self-medication responsibly and express a high degree of satisfaction with nonprescription medicines.

The Economic Factor: Costs and Benefits

The economic cost-effectiveness of self-medication with nonprescription medicines is especially important in this time of soaring health care expenditures, particularly for older Americans. Persons 65 and older accounted for more than one-third of the nation's total personal health care expenditures in 1987.[15]

In 1987 (the latest data currently available), the average health care cost per person over age 65 was $5,360, more than three times the $1,776 spent by younger persons.[16]

Not including health costs of nursing home and other institutional residents, older Americans' out-of-pocket health costs were projected to average more than $2,800 per person in 1994, up 112 percent from 1987.[17]

Like health care status, individual expenses vary widely. The major reasons for high health care expenditures are the presence of a chronic, disabling disease or an acute episode of serious illness. Those persons in nursing homes for an extended period of time and those in their last year of life incur far greater expenses for medical care than healthy older adults.

Self-Medication Helps Contain Costs

The U.S. Bureau of Labor Statistics reports that in 1993, the average household headed by an individual age 65 or older spent $460 on prescription drugs. In contrast, only $108 was spent on nonprescription drugs.[18]

Of the estimated $938 billion spent on health care in 1994 in the United States, almost $14 billion is paid for nonprescription medicines—less than two cents of every health care dollar.[19]

For a single dose treatment with OTC medicines, Americans pay an average of 11 cents for an OTC pain reliever, 12 cents for an upset stomach remedy, 17 cents for a laxative and 20 cents for a cough-cold treatment. The cost to treat these conditions for three days (12 to 18 treatments) ranges from $1.69 to $2.54.[20]

A typical OTC medicine costs about $4, while the average prescription drug is $25 and the average doctor visit about $40. Thus, for typical, self-treatable ailments, consumers save about $60 in out-of-pocket and insurance costs by practicing self-medication.[21]

Self-Medication Acts as a Screening Mechanism

When properly practiced, self-medication operates as a selective screening mechanism that sorts out everyday and self-treatable disorders from those requiring professional medical care.

The "New Era" of Self-Care

Increased science, technology, and government review of OTC medicines allow today's consumers, including older adults, to be increasingly assured of the safety and effectiveness of modern nonprescription drugs.

As a result, today we are well launched into a new era of self-medication. This "new era," coupled with a new interest in personal self-reliance and a new sophistication in health matters, appears to be paving the way for entrusting the consumer with more of the medicines previously available only by prescription.

Rx-to-OTC Switch Empowers Consumers

Present U.S. law provides for the transfer of selected prescription-only products to OTC status by the Food and Drug Administration (FDA). An increasingly self-reliant society needs and wants new OTC medicines; and the spiraling costs of health care demand it. Progress is apparent: More than 50 prescription drug ingredients and/or dosages have been transferred to direct consumer availability by the FDA in the last two decades.[22] Many commonly used OTC medicines on the market today were available only by prescription just a few years ago.

Industry, consumers, health professionals and government officials are working to provide continued opportunity for the transfer of established, safe prescription ingredients to OTC status. Such transfers will continue to occur if current science, technology, and experience can assure safe and appropriate use of the products by consumers. Products that can help older Americans treat their special health needs merit particular attention.

The Value of Information and Independence

A major goal of most older adults is to remain independent. Health care professionals support measures that enable older persons to maintain their ability to function on their own in their own environment. Likewise, older adults, the majority of whom are healthy, demand that the health care system provide not only sophisticated technology when they are in the hospital, but also sophisticated tools to enable them to stay well when they are at home.

Nonprescription drugs are among these invaluable resources.

Public demand for information naturally follows public interest in self-medication. However, consumers must be informed and responsible in their use of OTCs. Next to safe and effective medicines, consumer information is the most important element in any successful self-medication system.

Information Begins with Good Labeling

Labeling information is there when the product is bought and also when it is used, perhaps months later.

The importance of reading and understanding product labels is crucial. Health care professionals should emphasize this in their work with older consumers. Furthermore, this message can form the basis for cooperative educational programs. (NOTE: Many consumers don't use enough light when reading the product label. It is important to remember that it usually takes three times more light to read the same line at age 60 than at age 30.)

Another major source of information is advertising. Consumers have a right to be informed of the availability of products they can use in self-care— advertising provides that information.

A third source of information is education and consultation from professionals. Education programs for older adults frequently include information about how to use and store medicines properly and possible problems caused by drug interactions. Many hospitals and senior centers offer regular "brown bag screenings" and invite seniors to bring their medicines for review by health care professionals.

In brief, industry, health professionals, government, and consumers work together to make self-medication safe and effective, maximizing the ability of older persons to stay independent longer.

A Shared Responsibility

In conclusion, America's young and old find nonprescription medicines to be a familiar, convenient, inexpensive, and satisfactory way of handling minor illnesses and injuries that cause discomfort and interfere with the tasks and the fun of daily living. Self-medication is an act of independence, an expression of personal autonomy, a means for individuals in our complex society to recapture a measure of control over their personal health and well-being.

Self-medication is valuable as a self-reliance strategy for the individual. It is essential as a contribution to a successful and affordable health care system for the nation.

References

1. Schondelmeyer, Steven W., "Estimates of Nonprescription Drug and Supplies Expenditures by the Elderly: 1986 to 1991," *PRIME Institute*, University of Minnesota, Minneapolis, MN: 1992.

2. Coons, Johnson, Chandler, "Sources of Self-Treatment Information and Use of Home Remedies and OTC Medications Among Older Adults," *Journal of Geriatric Drug Therapy*, Vol. 7(1), 1992, p. 72.

3. American Association of Retired Persons, *A Profile of Older Americans*, 1994, Washington, D.C.

4. U.S. Department of Commerce, Bureau of the Census, *Profiles of America's Elderly*, No. 2. Washington, D.C.: July 1992.

5. American Association of Retired Persons, *America's Changing Work Force—Statistics in Brief.* Washington, D.C.: 1993

6. U.S. Department of Health and Human Services, National Center for Health Statistics, *National Health Interview Survey*, "Number of persons and percent distribution by respondent-assessed health status," Series 10, No. 190, Table 70, 1993.

7. U.S. Department of Commerce, Bureau of the Census, "A Demographic Portrait of America's Oldest Old." Washington, D.C.: 1992.

8. U.S. Department of Health and Human Services, National Center for Health Statistics, "Aging in the Eighties: Advance Data from Vital and Health Statistics," No. 115, DHHS Pub. No. 86-1250, 1986.

9. American Association of Retired Persons, *A Profile of Older Americans*, 1994, Washington, D.C.

10. U.S. Department of Health and Human Services, National Center for Health Statistics, *National Health Interview Survey*, "Number per person per year and number of physician contacts," Series 10, No. 190, Table 71, 1993.

11. American Association of Retired Persons, *A Profile of Older Americans*, 1994, Washington, D.C.

12. American Association of Retired Persons, *A Profile of Older Americans*, 1994, Washington, D.C.

13. U.S. Department of Commerce, Bureau of the Census, *We the American...Elderly*, Figure 10, page 6, Washington, D.C.: September 1993.

14. Heller Research Group and Nonprescription Drug Manufacturers Association, Self-Medication in the '90s: Practices and Perceptions. Washington, D.C.: 1992.

15. Waldo, Sonnefeld, McKusick and Arnett, "Health expenditures by age group, 1977 and 1987." *Health Care Financing Review*, Vol. 10, Number 4, Table 3: summer 1989.

16. Waldo, Sonnefeld, McKusick and Arnett, "Health expenditures by age group, 1977 and 1987." *Health Care Financing Review*, Vol. 10, Number 4, Table 3: summer 1989.

17. American Association of Retired Persons/Public Policy Institute and The Urban Institute, "Coming Up Short: Increasing

Out-of-Pocket Health Spending by Older Americans." Washington, D.C.: April 1994.

18. U.S. Department of Labor, Bureau of Labor Statistics, "Average annual expenditures and characteristics." *Consumer Expenditure Survey*, 1994, Table 1300. Washington, D.C.: November 1994.

19. Nielsen North America; U.S. Department of Health and Human Services, Health Care Financing Administration, Pub. No. 03361, November 1995.

20. Nielsen North America, Schaumburg, Ill: April 1995.

21. Nonprescription Drug Manufacturers Association; Pharmaceutical Research and Manufacturers of America; American Medical Association, 1993.

22. Nonprescription Drug Manufacturers Association, "Ingredients and Dosages Transferred from Rx-to-OTC Status." Washington, D.C.: July 1994.

Chapter 29

Self-Medication in the '90s: Practices and Perceptions

Introduction

This text summarizes key findings of nationally representative consumer research conducted in early 1992 for the Nonprescription Drug Manufacturers Association (NDMA). By design, this research closely parallels a study commissioned by NDMA nine years earlier. Both surveys were conducted by the Heller Research Group.

In 1983, NDMA commissioned a national survey on the role of self-treatment in the U.S. health care system. *Health Care Practices and Perceptions* answered many questions about self-medication and helped substantiate the kinds of health problems consumers experience and how they respond to those problems.

Until then, a major gap in our knowledge existed on how Americans treated the temporary aches and ailments of daily living, as well as the chronic and recurring illnesses individuals manage by themselves or with professional guidance.

Health Care Practices and Perceptions (Heller I) was a unique attempt to go to the American people directly with an independent study to find out what *they* knew and what *they* did about self-medication.

The Heller study for the first time provided hard data which could be used to assess the role played by nonprescription, over-the-counter (OTC) medicines in our health care system.

Self-Medication in the '90s: Practices and Perceptions, Highlights of a Survey on Consumer Uses of Nonprescription Medicines, Prepared by the Nonprescription Drug Manufacturers Association, May 1992; reprinted with permission.

The 1983 study provided evidence that Americans, based on their own experience, found OTC medicines both safe and effective in the treatment of common, everyday health problems. The study demonstrated that Americans were conservative in self-medication, were using OTC medications responsibly, and felt that OTC medications played an important role in their health care.

That Was Then, This Is Now

The OTC industry has continued to grow and change since the Heller I study was conducted. New ingredients and products are available over the counter to consumers. Entire new product categories now enable consumers to treat an expanding range of temporary and chronic conditions.

Self-Medication in the '90s: Practices and Perceptions (Heller II) updates and builds on the data uncovered in 1983. It also explores new areas of consumer practices and perceptions significant in the 1990s and beyond. The study answers questions such as:

- How often do Americans experience everyday health problems (as opposed to serious, even life-threatening illness or injury)?
- What are these problems?
- To what extent do Americans take care of common, everyday health problems without seeking professional help?
- What problems do they choose to treat themselves?
- How often do they tolerate rather than treat health complaints?
- How often and under what circumstances do they use OTC medicines?
- What is their perception of the results they get from using OTC medicines?
- Do Americans practice responsible, informed self-care with OTC medicines?

How The Study Was Done

The Heller Research Group was selected again to conduct the survey in early 1992. As in 1983, the objective was an independent consumer survey large enough and comprehensive enough to represent the health care practices of the total U.S. population.

Households of potential respondents were selected at random and contacted by telephone. Quota groups were established so the sample would represent the actual composition of the U.S. population. Once a respondent agreed to participate, he or she was sent detailed explanations and background materials by mail, then interviewed a week later by telephone. Following this, most respondents completed written questionnaires.

The questions dealt with health status, health habits, and personal attitudes toward medicines. Dr. Heller and his staff tabulated and analyzed the data. The final survey consisted of responses from almost 1,500 Americans.

This summary highlights the survey's findings and provides a brief analysis by NDMA.

Major Findings

What Do People Do About Health Problems?

The first question the survey undertook to answer was: What are people doing about self-treatable health problems? After noticing they have a problem, people can respond in five basic ways:

- They can decide to ignore the problem and tolerate it without treatment.
- They can use a home remedy, like baking soda on bee stings or salt water gargles for sore throats.
- They can take an OTC drug.
- They can use a prescription drug already in the home.
- They can call or visit a doctor or dentist.

Naturally, they can do more than one of these things.

Table 29.1. What Was Done in 1983 vs. 1992.

Action	1983	1992
Did not treat	37%	30%
Used a home remedy	14%	16%
Used an OTC medication	35%	38%
Used Rx medication in home	11%	13%
Called/went to doctor/dentist	9%	17%

Totals add to over 100% because more than one thing could have been done.

As shown in Table 29.1, in 1983 nonprescription medicines were used to treat 35% of all problems while 37% were not treated. Prescription medicines in the home accounted for 11%, and doctors and dentists were called or visited 9% of the time. Home remedies at 14% was the largest method of treatment other than OTCs.

When looking at 1992 compared to 1983, there are fewer people electing not to treat their problems, dropping from 37% to 30%. There seems to be less inclination to tolerate problems—more people are treating and fewer are "toughing it out." The use of OTC medicines inched up to 38% compared to the 35% seen in the past. Home remedies and prescriptions at home also showed marginal increases.

The proportion of people making use of health professionals has increased substantially since 1983. Seventeen percent contacted doctors or dentists, compared to 9% in the prior study. This increase in professional consultation could be linked to insurance coverage—62% of people claim they have insurance that pays for prescription drugs compared to 47% in 1983. For doctor bills, insurance covered 74% compared to 61% in 1983. Membership in Health Maintenance Organizations has also shown an increase.

When looking at people's actions on the first day and what they had done on subsequent days, there is no evidence that increased doctor visits are the result of dissatisfaction with the performance of OTC medicines.

Table 29.2. Top Ten Problems Suffered in Past Two Weeks (%)

Problem	%
Common Cold	32
Muscle aches/pain	29
Headache	29
Lip problems	29
Minor cuts/scratches	26
Upset stomach	25
Overweight problems	24
Acne/pimples	22
Sinus problems	22
Sleeping problems	20

What Are America's Self-Treatable Health Problems?

The 1992 survey also determined what health problems were occurring and which problems were most likely to be treated by an OTC
medicine. Respondents averaged six problems per person per
two-week period.

The common cold topped the list of the most frequently reported
problems, with muscle aches/pain, headache, lip problems and minor
cuts/scratches closely behind (Table 29.2). The top problems did not
differ significantly from those reported in 1983.

In Table 29.3, headaches top the list of problems most likely to be
treated by OTCs, followed by athlete's foot, lip problems, the common
cold, chronic dandruff, menstrual problems, upset stomach, painful
dry skin, and sinus conditions.

This order did not change much from 1983, although there were
minor shifts in rank. Headaches are still number one and menstrual
problems moved up in rank. Migraine headaches, number six in 1983,
did not make the top 10. The survey found that more sufferers of migraine headaches tend to treat their pain with prescription drugs.
Upset stomach, which didn't make the top 10 last time, does appear,
although lower on the list.

Table 29.3. Top Ten Problems Most Likely to be Treated by OTC
Medications

1992 Problem	1992 %
Headache	76
Athletes Foot	69
Lip Problems	68
Common Cold	63
Chronic Dandruff	59
Pre-Menstrual	58
Menstrual	57
Upset Stomach	57
Painful Dry Skin	56
Sinus Problems	54

Generally speaking, consumers are using slightly more OTC medicines in 1992 than they did in 1983. The larger increases are seen in digestive conditions, pain problems and in the feminine category. Treatment of feminine problems and respiratory conditions, which showed no change, garner the highest OTC use at 50%. OTC use for skin problems also remained steady, while there was a marginal increase in eye/ear/mouth problems.

For ailments treated by a doctor, it is clear that consumers are making the appropriate choices. Doctors are treating infections, teeth problems, ulcers, bronchitis, ear problems and viruses. When they do self-treat, consumers are selecting medicines appropriate to their ailments.

Satisfaction With OTC Medications

Of those consumers who discontinued using an OTC medication, 90% did so because the problem had gone away. Only 3% indicated that the medication didn't work, the same response as 1983. For problems treated with an OTC, 94% of consumers said they would use the same type of product again, compared with 93% in Heller I. The overall satisfaction with OTC medicines is 92%, still at the same high level as in 1983.

What Are Consumer Attitudes about Self-Care with OTCs?

All individuals surveyed were asked to say whether they agree or disagree with statements reflecting attitudes toward medicines and self-medication. In summary, here is what they said:

- Almost seven in 10 respondents said, if at all possible, they prefer to fight symptoms without taking medications.

- Close to nine in 10 consumers said they know medication should *only* be taken when absolutely necessary.

Although these are very high levels, there is a slight drop from 1983. This appears to confirm that consumers today are less willing than in 1983 to "tough it out."

- Eighty-five percent said it is important to have nonprescription medications to help relieve minor medical problems (77% in 1983).

- Eighty-eight percent disagreed that "only prescription medications are effective," and 73% agreed that "for some medical problems, nonprescription medications are just as effective as prescription medications."

- Three statements dealt with sources of information about OTCs. Eighty-seven percent said that reading package labels is one way they decide which OTC to take; 81 % said a pharmacist is a good source of information; and 73% said advertising helps them learn what medicines are available for what problems.

There is a great deal of consistency in the last two points with the 1983 results.

Prescription to OTC Switch

Specific questions were included in 1992 to focus on prescription to OTC medicine switches—the process by which a medicine formerly available only by prescription is allowed by the Food and Drug Administration on OTC status.

Consumers reported using Rx-to-OTC switch medicines about one-fourth of the time in categories where Rx-to-OTC switch products exist.

As seen in Figure 29.5, in 1992 almost 60% of all menstrual problems treated with OTCs were medicines that contained switched ingredients. Switch ingredients were also highly used for treatment of hay fever and pre-menstrual problems.

Table 29.4. Attitudes Toward the Use of Medicines

Attitude	Percent of adults who agree
Even though a medication is available without a prescription, one should take care when using it.	94
I read the instructions before taking a nonprescription medication for the first time.	93
If I am at all unsure about a situation, I do not self-medicate. I call or go to a doctor.	70
It is perfectly safe to take as many nonprescription medications as you wish.	95% disagree

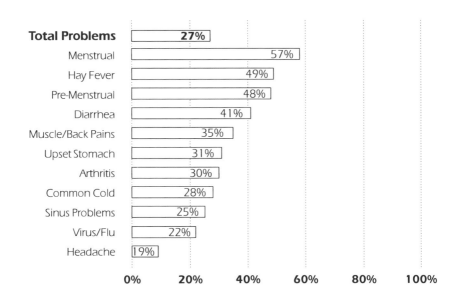

Figure 29.5. *Prescription to OTC Switch.*

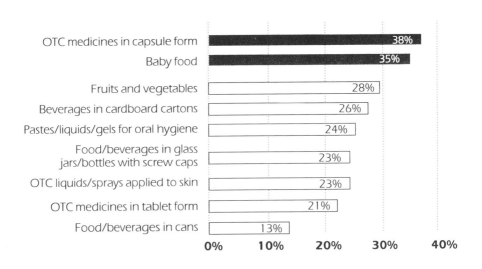

Figure 29.6. *Concern about Product Tampering*

The survey also gauged consumer attitudes about the Rx-to-OTC switch trend in this country:

- More than half of all consumers (54%) believe the availability of Rx-to-OTC switch products has made it possible to save the time and expense of going to a doctor.

- Close to 60% believe switches have made it possible to save money when purchasing medication on their own.

- Two of every three consumers say they are in favor of the Rx-to-OTC switch process and 64% agreed with the statement: "I prefer that prescription medications which can safely be self-administered be made available without a prescription."

- When asked their preference if two products, one formerly prescription and one not, were available, respondents chose the one that used to be prescription by more than a 2 to 1 margin.

Level of Concern about Product Tampering

The survey also measured consumer concern about tampering with nonprescription medicines compared with other product categories.

Figure 29.6 shows that consumers are most concerned about tampering in connection with nonprescription capsules and baby food. However, OTC medicines such as liquids and tablets do not stand out relative to other products. The level of concern is no higher for non-capsule OTCs than for other product categories sold when measured.

In an attempt to understand the public's views on solutions to tampering, respondents were asked to choose among five potential alternatives— specifically, which solutions they preferred (Table 29.7).

Table 29.7. Preferred Solutions for Tampering Problem

Solution	Percent
TRP packaging	54%
Consumer education	33%
Tamper-prone products sold behind the counter	3%
Vigilance/inspection by store personnel	3%
Ban selected product forms	3%

TRP=Tamper Resistant Packaging; Percentage does not equal 100% because 4% did not offer an answer.

As to the tampering problem, it is clear that consumers are opting for solutions that industry can implement. They are not in favor of banning products or placing them behind the pharmacist's counter. Almost nine in 10 consumers feel that tamper-resistant packaging (TRP) and increased education are the better route; more than half think packaging will help, and one-third favor increased education.

The more intrusive solutions—banning products, selling behind the counter and relying on store personnel—garnered very little support from consumers. None of these options rose above 3%.

Part Four

Cautions for Health Care Consumers

Chapter 30

A Guide to Choosing Medical Treatments

Medical treatments come in many shapes and sizes. There are "home remedies" shared among families and friends. There are prescription medicines, available only from a pharmacist, and only when ordered by a physician. There are over-the-counter drugs that you can buy—almost anywhere—without a doctor's order. Of growing interest and attention in recent years are so-called alternative treatments, not yet approved for sale because they are still undergoing scientific research to see if they really are safe and effective. And, of course, there are those "miracle" products sold through "back-of-the-magazine" ads and TV infomercials.

How can you tell which of these may really help treat your medical condition and which will only make you worse off—financially, physically, or both?

Many advocates of unproven treatments and cures contend that people have the right to try whatever may offer them hope, even if others believe the remedy is worthless. This argument is especially compelling for people with AIDS or other life-threatening diseases with no known cure.

Clinical Trials

Before gaining Food and Drug Administration marketing approval, new drugs, biologics, and medical devices must be proven safe and effective by controlled clinical trials.

Pub. No. (FDA) 97-1223, reprinted from *FDA Consumer*, June 1995.

In a clinical trial, results observed in patients getting the treatment are compared with the results in similar patients receiving a different treatment or placebo (inactive) treatment. Preferably, neither patients nor researchers know who is receiving the therapy under study.

To FDA, it doesn't matter whether the product or treatment is labeled alternative or falls under the auspices of mainstream American medical practice. (Mainstream American medicine essentially includes the practices and products the majority of medical doctors in this country follow and use.) It must meet the agency's safety and effectiveness criteria before being allowed on the market.

In addition, just because something is undergoing a clinical trial doesn't mean it works or FDA considers it to be a proven therapy, says Donald Pohl, of FDA's Office of AIDS and Special Health Issues. "You can't jump to that conclusion," he says. A trial can fail to prove that the product is effective, he explains. And that's not just true for alternative products. Even when the major drug companies sponsor clinical trials for mainstream products, only a small fraction are proven safe and effective.

Many people with serious illnesses are unable to find a cure, or even temporary relief, from the available mainstream treatments that have been rigorously studied and proven safe and effective. For many conditions, such as arthritis or even cancer, what's effective for one patient may not help another.

Real Alternatives

"It is best not to abandon conventional therapy when there is a known response in the effectiveness of that therapy," says Joseph Jacobs, M.D., former director of the National Institutes of Health's Office of Alternative Medicine, which was established in October 1992. As an example he cites childhood leukemia, which has an 80 percent cure rate with conventional therapy.

But what if conventional therapy holds little promise?

Many physicians believe it is not unreasonable for someone in the last stages of an incurable cancer to try something unproven. But, for example, if a woman with an early stage of breast cancer wanted to try shark cartilage (an unproven treatment that may inhibit the growth of cancer tumors, currently undergoing clinical trials), those same doctors would probably say, "Don't do it," because there are so many effective conventional treatments.

Jacobs warns that, "If an alternative practitioner does not want to work with a regular doctor, then he's suspect."

Alternative medicine is often described as any medical practice or intervention that:

- lacks sufficient documentation of its safety and effectiveness against specific diseases and conditions

- is not generally taught in U.S. medical schools

- is not generally reimbursable by health insurance providers.

According to a study in the January 28, 1993, *New England Journal of Medicine*, 1 in 3 patients used alternative therapy in 1990. More than 80 percent of those who use alternative therapies used conventional medicine at the same time, but did not tell their doctors about the alternative treatments. The study's authors concluded this lack of communication between doctors and patients "is not in the best interest of the patients, since the use of unconventional therapy, especially if it is totally unsupervised, may be harmful." The study concluded that medical doctors should ask their patients about any use of unconventional treatment as part of a medical history.

Many doctors are interested in learning more about alternative therapies, according to Brian Berman, M.D., a family practitioner with the University of Maryland School of Medicine in Baltimore. Berman says his own interest began when "I found that I wasn't getting all the results that I would have liked with conventional medicine, especially in patients with chronic diseases.

"What I've found at the University of Maryland is a healthy skepticism among my colleagues, but a real willingness to collaborate. We have a lot of people from different departments who are saying, let's see how we can develop scientifically rigorous studies that are also sensitive to the particular therapies that we're working with."

Anyone who wants to be treated with an alternative therapy should try to do so through participation in a clinical trial. Clinical trials are regulated by FDA and provide safeguards to protect patients, such as monitoring of adverse reactions. In fact, FDA is interested in assisting investigators who want to study alternative therapies under carefully controlled clinical trials. Some of the alternative therapies currently under study with grants from NIH include:

- acupuncture to treat depression, attention-deficit hyperactivity disorder, osteoarthritis, and postoperative dental pain

- hypnosis for chronic low back pain and accelerated fracture healing

341

- Ayurvedic herbals for Parkinson's disease. (Ayurvedic medicine is a holistic system based on the belief that herbals, massage, and other stress relievers help the body make its own natural drugs.)

- biofeedback for diabetes, low back pain, and face and mouth pain caused by jaw disorders. (Biofeedback is the conscious control of biological functions, such as those of the heart and blood vessels, normally controlled involuntarily.)

- electric currents to treat tumors

- imagery for asthma and breast cancer. (With imagery, patients are guided to see themselves in a different physical, emotional or spiritual state. For example, patients might be guided to imagine themselves in a state of vibrant health and the disease organisms as weak and destructible.)

While these alternative therapies are the subject of scientifically valid research, it's important to remember that at this time their safety and effectiveness are still unproven.

Avoiding Fraud

FDA defines health fraud as the promotion, advertisement, distribution, or sale of articles, intended for human or animal use, that are represented as being effective to diagnose, prevent, cure, treat, or mitigate disease (or other conditions), or provide a beneficial effect on health, but which have not been scientifically proven safe and effective for such purposes. Such practices may be deliberately deceptive, or done without adequate knowledge or understanding of the article.

Health fraud costs Americans an estimated $30 billion a year. However, the costs are not just economic, according to John Renner, M.D., Kansas City-based champion of quality health care for the elderly. "The hidden costs—death, disability—are unbelievable," he says.

To combat health fraud, FDA established its National Health Fraud Unit in 1988. The unit works with the National Association of Attorneys General and the Association of Food and Drug Officials to coordinate federal, state and local regulatory actions against specific health frauds.

Regulatory actions may be necessary in many cases because products that have not been shown to be safe and effective pose potential hazards for consumers both directly and indirectly. The agency's priorities for regulatory action depend on the situation; direct risks to health come first.

Unproven products cause direct health hazards when their use results in injuries or adverse reactions. For example, a medical device called the InnerQuest Brain Wave Synchronizer was promoted to alter brain waves and relieve stress. It consisted of an audio cassette and eyeglasses that emitted sounds and flashing lights. It caused epileptic seizures in some users. As a result of a court order requested by FDA, 78 cartons of the devices, valued at $200,000, were seized by U.S. marshals and destroyed in June 1993.

Indirectly harmful products are those that do not themselves cause injury, but may lead people to delay or reject proven remedies, possibly worsening their condition. For example, if cancer patients reject proven drug therapies in favor of unproven ones and the unproven ones turn out not to work, their disease may advance beyond the point where proven therapies can help.

"What you see out there is the promotion of products claiming to cure or prevent AIDS, multiple sclerosis, cancer, and a list of other diseases that goes on and on," says Joel Aronson, director of FDA's Health Fraud Staff, in the agency's Center for Drug Evaluation and Research. For example, he says, several skin cream products promise to prevent transmission of HIV (the virus that causes AIDS) and herpes viruses. They are promoted especially to healthcare workers. Many of the creams contain antibacterial ingredients but, "there is no substantiation at all on whether or not (the skin creams) work" against HIV, says Aronson. FDA has warned the manufacturers of these creams to stop the misleading promotions.

People at Risk

Teenagers and the elderly are two prime targets for health fraud promoters.

Teenagers concerned about their appearance and susceptible to peer pressure may fall for such products as fraudulent diet pills, breast developers, and muscle-building pills.

Older Americans may be especially vulnerable to health fraud because approximately 80 percent of them have at least one chronic health problem, according to Renner. Many of these problems, such as arthritis, have no cure and, for some people, no effective treatment. He says their pain and disability lead to despair, making them excellent targets for deception.

Arthritis

Although there is no cure for arthritis, the symptoms may come and go with no explanation. According to the Arthritis Foundation, "You may think a new remedy worked because you took it when your symptoms were going away."

Some commonly touted unproven treatments for arthritis are harmful, according to the foundation, including snake venom and DMSO (dimethyl sulfoxide), an industrial solvent similar to turpentine. FDA has approved a sterile form of DMSO called Rimso-50, which is administered directly into the bladder for treatment of rare bladder condition called interstitial cystitis. However, the DMSO sold to arthritis sufferers may contain bacterial toxins. DMSO is readily absorbed through the skin into the bloodstream, and these toxins enter the bloodstream along with it. It can be especially dangerous if used as an enema, as some of its promoters recommend.

Treatments the foundation considers harmless but ineffective include copper bracelets, mineral springs, and spas.

Cancer and AIDS

Cancer treatment is complicated because in some types of cancer there are no symptoms, and in other types symptoms may disappear by themselves, at least temporarily. Use of an unconventional treatment coinciding with remission (lessening of symptoms) could be simply coincidental. There's no way of knowing, without a controlled clinical trial, what effect the treatment had on the outcome. The danger comes when this false security causes patients to forgo approved treatment that has shown real benefit.

Some unapproved cancer treatments not only have no proven benefits, they have actually been proven dangerous. These include Laetrile, which may cause cyanide poisoning and has been found ineffective in clinical trials, and coffee enemas, which, when used excessively, have killed patients.

Ozone generators, which produce a toxic form of oxygen gas, have been touted as being able to cure AIDS. To date this is still unproven, and FDA considers ozone to be an unapproved drug and these generators to be unapproved medical devices. At least three deaths have been connected to the use of these generators. Four British citizens were indicted in 1991 for selling fraudulent ozone generators in the United States. Two of the defendants fled to Great Britain, but the other two pleaded guilty and served time in U.S. federal prisons.

The bottom line in deciding whether a certain treatment you've read or heard about might be right for you: Talk to your doctor. And keep in mind the old adage: If it sounds too good to be true, it probably is.

Tip-Offs to Rip-Offs

New health frauds pop up all the time, but the promoters usually fall back on the same old clichés and tricks to gain your trust and get your money. According to FDA, some red flags to watch out for include:

- claims the product works by a secret formula. (Legitimate scientists share their knowledge so their peers can review their data.)

- publicity only in the back pages of magazines, over the phone, by direct mail, in newspaper ads in the format of news stories, or 30-minute commercials in talk show format. (Results of studies on bona fide treatments are generally reported first in medical journals.)

- claims the product is an amazing or miraculous breakthrough. (Real medical breakthroughs are few and far between, and when they happen, they're not touted as "amazing" or "miraculous" by any responsible scientist or journalist.)

- promises of easy weight loss. (For most people, the only way to lose weight is to eat less and exercise more.)

- promises of a quick, painless, guaranteed cure.

- testimonials from satisfied customers. (These people may never have had the disease the product is supposed to cure, may be paid representatives, or may simply not exist. Often they're identified only be initials or first names.)

Approaching Alternative Therapies

The NIH Office of Alternative Medicine recommends the following before getting involved in any alternative therapy:

- Obtain objective information about the therapy. Besides talking with the person promoting the approach, speak with people who have gone through the treatment—preferably both those who were treated recently and those treated in the past. Ask about the advantages and disadvantages, risks, side effects, costs, results, and over what time span results can be expected.

345

- Inquire about the training and experience of the person administering the treatment (for example, certification).

- Consider the costs. Alternative treatments may not be reimbursable by health insurance.

- Discuss all treatments with your primary care provider, who needs this information in order to have a complete picture of your treatment plan.

For everyone—consumers, physicians and other health-care providers, and government regulators—FDA has the same advice when it comes to weeding out the hopeless from the hopeful: Be open-minded, but don't fall into the abyss of accepting [just] anything at all. For there are—as there have been for centuries—countless products that are nothing more than fraud.

Resources

Whether looking for an alternative therapy or checking the legitimacy of something you've heard about, some of the best sources are advocacy groups, including local patient support groups. Those groups include:

American Cancer Society
1599 Clifton Road, N.E.
Atlanta, GA 30329
(404) 320-3333; (800) ACS-2345

Arthritis Foundation
P.O. Box 19000
Atlanta, GA 30326
(800) 283-7800

National Multiple Sclerosis Society
733 Third Ave.
New York, NY 10017-3288
(212) 986-3240; (800) 344-4867

HIV/AIDS Treatment Information Service
P.O. Box 6303
Rockville, MD 20849-6303.
(800) 448-0440; TDD/Deaf Access: (800) 243-7012

Federal government resources on health fraud and alternative medicine are:

FDA (HFE-88)
Rockville, MD 20857
(800) 532-4440

Office of Alternative Medicine
NIH Information Center
6120 Executive Blvd., EPS
Suite 450
Rockville, MD 20852
(301) 402-2466

U.S. Postal Inspection Service
(monitors products purchased by mail)
Contact your local post office.

Federal Trade Commission
(regarding false advertising)
Room 421
6th St. and Pennsylvania Ave., N.W.
Washington, DC 20580
(202) 326-2222

Other agencies that may have information and offer assistance include local Better Business Bureaus, state and municipal consumer affairs offices, and state attorneys general offices.

—by Isadora B. Stehlin

Chapter 31

Fraudulent Health Claims: Don't Be Fooled

Billions of consumer dollars are wasted on unproven, fraudulently marketed, and sometimes useless health care products and treatments. In addition to wasting their money, consumers with serious medical problems may be wasting valuable time before they seek proper treatment. Even worse, some products may cause serious harm and endanger lives.

Fortunately, there are ways to tell which health-related claims are likely to be legitimate. This chapter will help you spot false and unsubstantiated claims. It describes some typical areas where fraud flourishes and suggests how you can protect yourself.

How to Spot False Claims

Remember the first rule of thumb for evaluating health claims: If it sounds too good to be true, it probably is. Also, learn to recognize the typical phrases and marketing techniques used to deceive consumers:

- The product is advertised as a quick and effective cure-all for a wide range of ailments or for an undiagnosed pain.

- The promoters use key words, such as *scientific breakthrough, miraculous cure, exclusive product, secret ingredient* or *ancient remedy*.

Federal Trade Commission, Bureau of Consumer Protection, Office of Consumer and Business Education (202) 326-3650; produced in cooperation with the U.S. Food and Drug Administration; Pub. No. 96-1249, March 1996.

- The promoter claims the medical profession or research scientists have conspired to suppress the product.

- The advertisement includes undocumented case histories claiming amazing results.

- The product is advertised as available from only one source, and payment in advance is required.

In addition, health care clinics that require patients to travel away from home to receive treatment may be suspect. While many clinics offer effective treatments, some prescribe untested, unapproved, ineffective, and possibly dangerous "cures." Moreover, physicians who work in such clinics may be unlicensed or lack appropriate specialization. For these reasons, you should contact state or local health authorities where the clinic is located before you arrange to go.

Finally, don't rely on promises of a "money-back guarantee." Be aware that many fly-by-night operators will not be around to respond to a refund request.

Why Health Fraud Schemes Work

Health fraud is a business that sells false hope. It preys on people who are victims of diseases that have no medical cures, such as AIDS, arthritis, multiple sclerosis, and certain forms of cancer. It also thrives on the wishful thinking of those who want short-cuts to weight loss or improvements to personal appearance. It makes enormous profits because it promises quick cures and easy solutions to better health or personal attractiveness.

Some Medical Problems That Attract Health Fraud Schemes

Cancer

A diagnosis of cancer can bring feelings of fear and hopelessness. Many people may be tempted to turn to unproven remedies or clinics that promise a cure. Although some cancer patients have been helped by participating in legitimate clinical trials of experimental therapies, many others have wasted time and money on fraudulently marketed, ineffective treatments.

When you are evaluating cancer-cure claims, keep in mind that no single device or remedy is capable of treating all types of cancer. Cancer is a name given to a wide range of diseases that require different forms of treatment best determined by a medical doctor.

For more information about cancer, contact the American Cancer Society office listed in your yellow pages. To order free publications on cancer research and treatment, call the National Cancer Institute's Cancer Information Service: 1-800-422-6237.

AIDS and HIV

People diagnosed with AIDS and HIV infection also may feel pressured to try untested "experimental" drugs or treatments. Although there are legitimate treatments that can extend life and improve the quality of life for AIDS patients, there is, so far, no cure for AIDS. Trying unproven products or treatments can be dangerous, and may delay proper medical care. It also can be expensive and usually is not covered by insurance.

Don't be pressured into making an immediate decision about trying an untested product. Ask for time to get more information from a knowledgeable physician or health care professional. Legitimate health care providers will not object to your seeking additional information. The U.S. Government has established a toll-free HIV-AIDS Treatment Information Service, 1-800-HIV-0440. This information help line is staffed by health information specialists who are fluent in English and Spanish.

Arthritis

If you are among the estimated 37 million Americans who suffer from one of the many forms of arthritis, be aware that this disease invites a flood of fraudulent products and services. This is because medical science has not yet found a cure for arthritis. The Arthritis Foundation advises that symptoms should be monitored by a doctor because the condition can worsen if it is not properly treated.

An estimated $2 billion is spent annually on unproven arthritis remedies. Thousands of dietary and natural "cures" are sold for arthritis—mussel extract, vitamin pills, desiccated liver pills, and honey and vinegar mixtures. Many scientists believe there is insufficient medical evidence to suggest that a lack of vitamins or minerals causes arthritis or that taking dietary supplements can give relief. For a free brochure about unproven remedies, call the Arthritis Foundation, toll-free, 1-800-283-7800 (9:00 a.m.-7:00 p.m., Eastern Time, Monday-Friday), or write: Arthritis Foundation, P.O. Box 19000, Atlanta, Georgia 30326.

Precautions for Taking Dietary Supplements

There are thousands of dietary supplements on the market. Many contain vitamins and minerals to supplement the amounts of these nutrients that people get from the food they eat. There also are many products on the market that contain substances such as high-potency free amino acids, botanicals, enzymes, herbs, animal extracts, and bioflavanoids.

Some dietary supplements have documented benefits; the advantages of others are unproven and claims about those products may be false or misleading. For example, claims that you can eat all you want and lose weight effortlessly are not true. To lose weight, you must lower your calorie intake or increase your calorie use through exercise. Most experts recommend doing both. Similarly, no body building product can "tone you up" effortlessly or build muscle mass without exercise. Claims to the contrary are false. Other questionable claims may involve products advertised as effective in curing insomnia, reversing hair loss, relieving stress, curing impotency, improving memory or eyesight, and slowing the aging process.

In addition to lacking documented effectiveness, some dietary supplements may be harmful under some conditions of use. Reports of adverse reactions to dietary supplements are monitored by the U.S. Food and Drug Administration to identify emerging safety issues.

According to the FDA, the following substances in dietary supplements are among those that raise serious safety issues at certain concentrations: chaparral, comfrey, yohimbe, lobelia, germander, willow bark, guar gum, jin bu huan, ma huang, L-tryptophan, phenylalanine, and germanium. In addition, some vitamins and minerals can cause problems for some people when taken in excessive doses. These include vitamin A, niacin, vitamin B_6, vitamin D, iron, and folic acid. And remember, a label of "natural" is no guarantee of a product's safety or effectiveness.

Consumers who use dietary supplements should always read product labels to determine the % daily value for various nutrients contained in the product. Also, it's a good idea to seek advice from a health professional before taking dietary supplements, particularly for children, adolescents, older or chronically ill persons, and women who are pregnant or breast-feeding.

For More Information or to Report a Problem

- To determine the value of a health care product or treatment, consult a pharmacist, doctor, or other health professional.

- To report a company you believe may be making false advertising claims, write to: Correspondence Branch, Federal Trade Commission, Washington, DC 20580.

- To report a company for falsely labeling its products or to report a serious adverse effect associated with the use of a dietary supplement, call your local Food and Drug Administration office.

- For information about a particular hospital, clinic, or treatment center, contact state or local health authorities where the facility is located. If it is in a foreign country, contact that government's health authority to see that the facility is properly licensed and equipped to handle the procedures involved.

- In addition, you may wish to contact your state Attorney General's office or a local consumer agency to get more information or to report problems. (Consult your telephone directory.)

To Contact the Federal Trade Commission

FTC Headquarters
6th & Pennsylvania Avenue, N.W.
Washington, D.C. 20580
(202) 326-2222
TDD (202) 326-2502

FTC Regional Offices

1718 Peachtree Street, N.W., Suite 1000
Atlanta, Georgia 30367
(404) 347-4836

101 Merrimac Street, Suite 810
Boston, Massachusetts 02114-4719
(617) 424-5960

55 East Monroe Street, Suite 1860
Chicago, Illinois 60603
(312) 353-4423

668 Euclid Avenue, Suite 520-A
Cleveland, Ohio 44114
(216) 522-4207

1999 Bryan Street, Suite 2150
Dallas, Texas 75201
(214) 979-0213

1961 Stout Street, Suite 1523
Denver, Colorado 80294
(303) 844-2271

11000 Wilshire Boulevard, Suite 13209
Los Angeles, California 90024
(310) 235-4000

150 William Street, Suite 1300
New York, New York 10038
(212) 264-1207

901 Market Street, Suite 570
San Francisco, California 94103
(415) 356-5270

2806 Federal Bldg.
915 Second Ave.
Seattle, Washington 98174
(206) 220-6363

Chapter 32

Quackery Targets Teens

Quackery, an age-old business, costs Americans billions of dollars each year and immeasurable losses suffered from harmful products and delayed medical treatment. The quack's victims are usually thought of as the aged or chronically ill.

But quacks are quick to spot new markets, so it's not surprising that they have discovered teenagers. These youths and their impatience with the blossoming process are fertile ground for quacks. Teenagers are ready to experiment with products that promise to speed their development and ease growing pains.

And many of these junior and senior high school age children have money enough to do the experimenting. In fact, a study by Teenage Research Unlimited revealed that 27.6 million teenagers spent an average of $93 a month on personal items in 1989 for a total of nearly $31 billion.

Further, in families in which both parents work, teens take on more of the family shopping responsibilities. The U.S. Labor Department reports that as of March 1988, 62.4 percent of families with teenagers had two working parents. And a 1987 report by Teen Research Unlimited showed that teens do the shopping in 70 percent of the households with working mothers.

These young shoppers often have access to mom or pop's credit card. And, like their parents, they are buying more through the mail, a medium that offers a cloak of anonymity under which quacks thrive.

Department of Health and Human Services (DHHS) Pub. No. (FDA) 90-1147; revised April 1990; reprinted 1995.

The teen years are often insecure years, filled with questions like: "Am I beautiful (or handsome)?" "Will my breasts ever develop?" "Shouldn't I be more muscular?" "Am I too fat?" "Would a tan give me more sex appeal?"

Quacks love such questions. And they're ready with answers that have been—according to them—"overlooked or ignored by the established scientific community."

Time is of such essence to the young that they grasp at straws and don't recognize the quack's deceptions for what they really are.

Take a look at some of the advertisements in teen magazines. There's a "space age diet" that allows you to "eat all day and still lose weight," a beauty cream that will ensure "gorgeous, proportioned breasts," and a pill to provide a tan overnight. Sound unlikely? Impossible is a better word. But, fond of superlatives and driven by desire, teenagers are ready to believe such ads.

Here are some of the dubious products that teenagers today are asked to believe in:

Breast Developers

For decades, millions of dollars have been spent on devices, creams and lotions advertised as breast developers. All wasted. There is no device or system of exercise that will increase the size of the breasts. At best, devices promoted as breast developers merely strengthen and develop the muscles that support the breasts, and exercising these muscles will not appreciably increase breast size.

Creams and lotions advertised as breast developers don't work either. Some contain the hormone estrogen. Estrogen can increase breast size, but in order to be sold without a prescription these products must contain such a small amount of the hormone that its effect is insignificant. (Estrogen is used in birth control pills and to treat symptoms of menopause. FDA approval for estrogen does not include use for breast development.)

The only proven method of increasing breast size is breast augmentation surgery, which carries some risks and is hardly recommended for teenagers.

Weight Loss

Teenagers—especially girls—are not exempt from the American penchant for dieting. One expert says that as many as three-fourths of high school girls are on a diet at any one time. Writing in the May-

June 1987 issue of *Nutrition Today*, Dr. Kelly Brownell of the University of Pennsylvania School of Medicine said that some children begin dieting as early as the fourth grade.

Those figures may startle some people, but not the quacks. They know them well and have pounced on that audience, offering "magical" diets and pills to keep the pounds off. Most of the diets and virtually all of the pills are worthless; some are even dangerous. At times, some diets will achieve a temporary weight loss that is usually unrelated to the "magical" food or pill.

The dieting craze may be particularly questionable for adolescents, since a well-balanced diet is vital during the teen years when the body goes through dramatic change and growth.

Depending on the ingredients, some pills promoted for weight loss can cause side effects such as nervousness, nausea and insomnia, and can also be addictive. The recognized active ingredient in most nonprescription diet pills is either phenylpropanolamine (PPA) or benzocaine. The effectiveness of these two ingredients for weight loss has yet to be determined by FDA. However, too much PPA has been associated with elevated blood pressure. Benzocaine is supposed to work by numbing the inside of the mouth to make food less appetizing.

Most weight-loss products sold as part of a diet-and-pill plan are harmless. The products don't work, but the plan may. Of course, the plan would work just as well without the product, which is nothing more than a psychological crutch.

Some devices are also promoted for weight loss. Electrical muscle stimulators, for example, have a legitimate use for physical therapy treatment, but FDA has had to take a number of such devices off the market because they were promoted for weight loss and "body toning." These stimulators can be dangerous when used incorrectly. Hazards include electrical shocks and burns.

Body wraps are another favorite gimmick of the quacks. They're touted as a means of "burning fat." The wraps are worn around part or all of the body, sometimes preceded by the application of a cream or lotion. Temporary weight loss may occur as the result of sweating and loss of water in the tissues, but when the water content of the tissue returns to normal, the "lost" weight reappears. The wraps do not "burn" or dissolve fat. Furthermore, experts consider them dangerous because they can cause severe dehydration and circulatory problems.

There are no magic foods, pills, wraps, diets or wands for losing weight. The only way to lose weight is to consistently eat fewer calories than the body needs and uses. But teenagers should be cautioned about excessive dieting. Their growing bodies can't tolerate the nutrient loss that comes with eating too little.

Steroids and Growth Hormone

Our sports-loving nation loves a winner, and it's fair to say that most of the 5 million boys and girls who compete in high school sports love to win. Some of them will go to great lengths to do so. That may mean using performance-enhancing drugs such as anabolic steroids and human growth hormone.

Anabolic steroids—compounds similar to the male hormone testosterone—are too often used by athletes, both boys and girls, to build muscle. They are also used by young men who just want to look better. They are prescription drugs, but most of those who use them obtain them illegally, often from the black market. Steroids have a lot of unwanted side effects—that's why they are supposed to be sold only by prescription. They may well build muscle, but it's a losing proposition, because their use—particularly in the large doses that athletes take—can stunt growth, lead to cancer, ruin the liver, and bring on other complications, including enlarged breasts in boys. For girls, the side effects include developing masculine traits that may be irreversible.

Black-market steroids often are produced in another country or by clandestine domestic manufacturers under questionable conditions and may be contaminated. The quacks have also moved in with phony steroids and phony pills that they say—falsely—will counter some of the side effects of steroids.

In 1988, FDA warned that a counterfeit version of the hormone human chorionic gonadotropin, or HCG, was being sold to weight lifters and other athletes. The bogus hormones were contaminated with a substance that causes infections and fever.

A black market has also sprung up for human growth hormone. This prescription drug is legitimately given to children who suffer from pituitary dwarfism or growth hormone deficiency, but it, too, has dangerous side effects. Nevertheless, athletes seeking to benefit from added growth are buying the hormone on the black market. Quacks are also marketing "growth tablets" that, in fact, contain no hormones or any other ingredients that can promote growth.

Tanning and Tanning Pills

Tanning is never harmless, regardless of the source: the sun, a sunlamp, a tanning bed, or a pill. Exposure to ultraviolet radiation from the sun or other sources leads to premature aging of the skin. It is also the number one cause of skin cancer.

Many teenagers get their tans at tanning parlors, where they may be told that the type of ultraviolet radiation from the lamps will not be harmful. That's not true. Ultraviolet radiation from *any* source can be harmful.

Other youths may turn to tanning pills. But they're not safe either. They generally contain a color additive that has not been approved by FDA for coloring the body. Advertisements claim that the pills produce "a rich, golden-bronze, natural-looking tan" that makes one look "healthy, energetic, and attractive" all year. But the pills actually produce a distinct orange tinge on the skin. The pills may also leave fatty deposits in the blood, liver and skin, and on the eye's retina, where they may interfere with night vision. Further, the "tan" the pills produce is no protection against sunburn.

Hair: Removal and Growth

The only effective way to remove hair permanently is with electrolysis—a process by which hair roots are destroyed with an electrified needle. Electrolysis should only be performed by a physician or professional electrologist, according to the American Medical Association (AMA). While it is safe when done correctly, it can be tedious, painful and expensive, the AMA adds. Scarring may result and regrowth is possible.

Effective means of temporarily removing hair include shaving, tweezing, waxing, and using cream or lotion depilatories. But FDA cautions that there is no risk-free method of removing hair. Waxing, for example, can be painful, and creams can cause rashes and swelling.

There is limited good news about removing hair, however. According to the AMA, hair removal does not make renewed growth thicker or stiffer, nor does it quicken regrowth.

While girls struggle to remove hair, some teenage boys worry that they won't be able to keep theirs. Since most baldness is hereditary, young men may take a look at their long-since bald fathers and fear that they will soon be watching the tops of their heads get smoother. All of the over-the-counter hair creams, lotions, and other products sold to prevent baldness or grow hair are worthless. But that doesn't bother quacks at all. The health fraud artists are ready with a variety of baldness "cures," and their intended victims include those worried youngsters. FDA has banned the sale of these phony products, but the quacks often stay one step ahead of the law.

There is only one drug approved by FDA to grow hair. It is a drug called minoxidil, available only by prescription. Minoxidil does not work for everyone and is not a cure. It is best at filling patchy gaps on the top of the head that appear when baldness first begins. It does not work on the front of the head. Also, minoxidil must be used twice daily for a lifetime. Hair thins out within a few months if treatment is stopped.

"Look-Alike" Drugs

The widespread use of illegal drugs among teenagers has helped generate a market for "fake" drugs. These "look-alike" drugs are intentionally made to look like amphetamines, barbiturates, or other often-abused drugs. They are sold on the street and by mail order, and the seller often implies that they are the illegal drugs they resemble.

The look-alikes generally contain decongestants, caffeine, and other stimulants in what FDA has called "dangerous, illogical combinations." Some contain alarmingly high doses of one ingredient. When taken in excess or mixed with alcohol, the look-alikes have caused strokes and death. They are extremely dangerous when mixed with, or replaced by, real "uppers" or "downers."

The availability and use of look-alikes make it harder for health professionals and law enforcement officials to combat the problem of illegal drug use. The AMA points out the following problems caused by look-alikes:

- School children and others who don't normally abuse drugs are told that the "look-alikes" are okay to use because they are legal and safe (in fact, they are neither).

- Look-alike drugs may make youngsters believe that the illegal drugs they mimic aren't as potent and dangerous as they really are.

- Traditional drug abuse education programs are hampered by the wide availability of the imitation drugs.

- Physicians and poison centers are deceived by the fake drugs, which makes drug-related diagnoses difficult.

- The look-alikes make it even more difficult for law enforcement officials to stop illegal drug traffic.

Most states have banned the manufacture and marketing of look-alikes, and the federal government has taken action against some manufacturers. But the availability of look-alike drugs is still a threat to the health and safety of teenagers.

Recognizing Quackery

It is during the teenage years that people start to become serious consumers, and there's no better time to learn how to avoid quackery. Here are some tips:

- Be wary if immediate, effortless or guaranteed results are promised.

- Look for telltale words and phrases such as "breakthrough," "miracle," "secret remedy," "exclusive," and "clinical studies prove that ... ."

- Beware of promotions for a single product claimed to be effective for a wide variety of ailments.

- Don't forget that, unlike scientists and health professionals, quacks do not subject their products to the scrutiny of scientific research. The quack simply thrusts a product onto the market in order to get your money.

- Be cautious of money-back guarantees, for a guarantee is only as good as the company that backs it.

- If it sounds too good to be true—it probably is.

For More Information

If you have questions about a product or company, get answers before you make a purchase. For information, contact:

- the Better Business Bureau
- the nearest Food and Drug Administration office
- your local consumer office or state attorney general's office
- your doctor.

The text in this chapter was prepared jointly by FDA and the Council of Better Business Bureaus.

Chapter 33

Life Extension: Science or Science Fiction?

Explorers once searched for the fountain of youth, and old legends tell of magic potions that keep people young. The ancient questions— Why do people grow old? How can we live longer?—still fascinate people, including the scientists who study aging (gerontologists). But their most important question is this: how can people stay healthy and independent as they grow older?

Recently, researchers have begun to find certain chemicals in our bodies that may someday answer these questions. As a result, some stores and catalogs now sell products that are similar to these chemicals. However, the advertising claims that these products can extend life are very much exaggerated. Here are some of the chemicals being studied and what scientists have learned about them so far.

Antioxidants

These are natural substances that may help prevent disease. Antioxidants fight harmful molecules called oxygen free radicals, which are created by the body as cells go about their normal business of producing energy. Free radicals also come from smoking, radiation, sunlight, and other factors in the environment.

Some antioxidants, such as the enzyme SOD (superoxide dismutase), are produced in the body. Others come from food; these include vitamin C, vitamin E, and beta carotene, which is related to vitamin A.

National Institute on Aging (NIA), *Age Page*, 1994.

The body's antioxidant defense system prevents most free-radical damage, but not all. As people grow older, the damage may build up. According to one theory of aging, this build-up eventually causes cells, tissues, and organs to break down.

There is some evidence to support this theory. For instance, the longer an animal lives, the more antioxidants it has in its body. Also, some studies show that antioxidants may help prevent heart disease, some cancers, cataracts, and other health problems that are more common as people get older.

Most experts think that the best way to get these vitamins is by eating fruits and vegetables (five helpings a day) rather than by taking vitamin pills. SOD pills have no effect on the body. They are broken up into different substances during digestion. More research is needed before specific recommendations can be made.

DNA and RNA

DNA (deoxyribonucleic acid) is the material in every cell that holds the genes. Every day some DNA is damaged and most of the time it is repaired. But more and more damage occurs with age, and it may be that DNA repair, never 100-percent perfect, falls further and further behind. If so, the damage that does not get repaired and builds up could be one of the reasons that people age.

As a result, pills containing DNA and RNA (ribonucleic acid, which works with DNA in the cells to make proteins) are on the market. But DNA and RNA are like SOD tablets. When they are taken by mouth, they are broken down into other substances and cannot get to cells or do any good.

DHEA

Short for dehydroepiandrosterone, DHEA is a hormone that has turned back some signs of aging in animals. When given to mice, it has boosted the immune system and helped prevent some kinds of cancer.

DHEA travels through the body in the blood in a special form, called DHEA sulfate, which turns into DHEA when it enters a cell. Levels of DHEA sulfate are high in younger people but tend to go down with age. Substances labeled DHEA are being sold as a way to extend life, although no one knows whether they are effective.

Other Hormones

In a recent study with a small number of men, injections of growth hormone boosted the size and strength of the men's muscles and seemed to reverse some signs of aging. Now, larger studies are testing growth hormone and other hormones, such as estrogen and testosterone, to find out whether they can prevent weakness and frailty in older people. However, it is much too early to know whether any of these hormones will work. Moreover, the side effects of hormones could be very serious; high amounts of some hormones have been linked to cancer.

The Bottom Line

Currently no treatments, drugs, or pills are known to slow aging or extend life in humans. Check with a doctor before buying pills or anything else that promises to slow aging, extend life, or make a big change in the way you look or feel.

Ten Tips for Healthy Aging

No known substance can extend life, but the chances of staying healthy and living a long time can be improved:

1. Eat a balanced diet, including five helpings of fruits and vegetables a day.

2. Exercise regularly (check with a doctor before starting an exercise program).

3. Get regular health check-ups.

4. Don't smoke (it's never too late to quit).

5. Practice safety habits at home to prevent falls and fractures. Always wear your seatbelt in a car.

6. Stay in contact with family and friends. Stay active through work, play, and community.

7. Avoid overexposure to the sun and the cold.

8. If you drink, moderation is the key. When you drink, let someone else drive.

9. Keep personal and financial records in order to simplify budgeting and investing. Plan long-term housing and money needs.

10. Keep a positive attitude toward life. Do things that make you happy.

Resources

The National Institute on Aging offers a free booklet on the biology of aging and other information on health and aging. Write or call:

NIA Information Center
P.O. Box 8057
Gaithersburg, MD 20898-8057
800-222-2225
800-222-4225 (TTY)

Chapter 34

Hope or Hoax: Unproven Cancer Treatments

People who have just been told they have cancer must decide quickly what to do about treatment—their lives may depend on it. When conventional, mainstream treatments don't promise total cures, thousands of cancer patients turn to questionable, untested, possibly fraudulent treatments.

The promises of the practitioners of these treatments can be seductive, not unlike the pitch of the used car salesman offering the "deal of a lifetime." But the stakes are much higher.

Unproven cancer treatments may sound good at first to patients faced with the possibility of side effects from conventional cancer treatments, including chemotherapy, radiation and surgery. In contrast, promoters often describe questionable, untested treatments outside mainstream medicine as natural, nontoxic and noninvasive. However, while some—such as herbal treatments and some diets—may sound "natural," others are not, and are made up of unknown substances and possibly toxic contaminants. Others may appear harmless, but, because they are ineffective and cause people to delay or forego beneficial treatments, they, too, are dangerous. Manufacturing standards typically do not exist. Theories underlying the treatments vary widely, but one thing they have in common is the absence of scientific proof that they work.

The Office of Technology Assessment, an agency that serves the U.S. Congress, recently published a report on questionable (or, as OTA calls them, unconventional) cancer treatments, defining them as those

FDA Consumer, March 1992.

treatments that fall outside the bounds of mainstream medicine and have not been proven safe or effective by scientific standards that balance benefit and risk.

This is in contrast to experimental therapies within mainstream medicine, which are new products under investigation or approved products being tested for new uses. These products are tested in a way that allows duplication of the results by others and that controls for other factors that may influence the results. FDA does not test products itself, but permits the human testing of new therapies. Before such testing can begin, the product's sponsor (a pharmaceutical company, private organization, government agency, or individual) needs to show scientific evidence that the product may work and that precautions will be taken to protect patients on whom it is tested.

Once the results of the clinical trials have been submitted to FDA by the sponsor, FDA must decide whether a treatment's benefits outweigh its risks. For example, cancer drugs often have serious side effects. But the condition they treat is also serious, as cancer patients well know. FDA wants to make sure that new treatments provide benefits outweighing their risks before permitting them on the market. As part of the review process, FDA also approves a labeling insert that accompanies approved products and allows physicians to prescribe the drug safely and effectively at the appropriate doses.

All reviews of new products for cancer (as well as other life-threatening diseases) are done as quickly as possible, with most approval decisions taking a year or less.

Promoters of questionable treatments rarely submit information to FDA about their products, let alone reliable and accurate data. Marketers or promoters of questionable, unconventional treatments for cancer can be prosecuted for violating federal and state laws.

According to Barrie R. Cassileth, Ph.D., of Chapel Hill, N.C., a researcher in the field of unproven cancer treatments, current popular treatments are often lifestyle-oriented remedies with a "do-it-yourself" quality. These treatments may especially appeal to consumers who want an active role in their own care. They include the popular so-called metabolic therapy, which, depending on the practitioner, may combine special diets, "detoxification" by internal cleanings or enemas, spiritual or emotional "healing," and high-dose vitamins and minerals. Other questionable therapies have names that sound like current mainstream cancer treatments. For example, one questionable treatment is called "immuno-augmentive therapy" (IAT), which sounds like immunotherapy, a mainstream treatment that manipulates a patient's immune system to fight cancer.

OTA Report

Because of the popularity of many unconventional treatments, Congress commissioned OTA to study them. After four years of research, OTA concluded in a 300-page report that "effectiveness [of unconventional treatments] is unknown, and relevant information on adverse effects is nonexistent." According to OTA, certain psychological and behavioral approaches may have some benefit when they are used *in addition* to mainstream treatments. For example, psychological support groups can benefit those patients who want to try them.

People frightened by a diagnosis of cancer may want to believe in the existence of "a miracle cure." Extravagant claims for questionable cancer treatments are often found in testimonials in the media. These messages can be quite convincing to someone facing the life-and-death issues of cancer. But people should view claims for questionable cancer treatments with the following in mind:

- If it sounds too good to be true, it probably is.
- Don't believe you have nothing to lose.
- Scientific medicine is accountable.
- Real hope is found in mainstream cancer treatment.

If It Sounds Too Good to Be True

A recent *Wall Street Journal* cartoon pictured a hiker encountering a guru on top of a hill who tells him, "I found the secret to happiness, but the FDA won't let me release it."

The punchline might have had him say he found a cure for cancer. Such extravagant claims are common for treatments for cancer and other chronic and sometimes fatal diseases for which medical science has yet to find a cure. But real "breakthroughs" in medicine are few and far between, and when they do occur, the medical community is quick to take advantage of them.

An example of a claim "too good to be true" is found in the promotional literature for Cancell, a currently popular cancer treatment that looks like a dark brown liquid and is made up of ordinary chemicals, including nitric acid, sodium sulfite, potassium hydroxide, sulfuric acid, and catechol. The literature for Cancell states that the product is nontoxic and has no side effects. Although the Cancell booklet says no claims are made for the treatment, it also says that the treatment "digests" cancer cells and then, "the cancer no longer exists." No scientific evidence supports the use of Cancell for any disease, and no

369

data have been submitted to FDA on Cancell's safety or effectiveness. FDA has conducted numerous regulatory investigations of Cancell, and has taken its promoters to court to try to stop its distribution.

William Jarvis, M.D., professor of Preventive Medicine at Loma Linda University and president of the National Council Against Health Fraud, Inc., says that advocates of unconventional therapies have one major characteristic in common: They exude self-confidence about their treatments. In his opinion, they offer an illusion of effectiveness, like a magician's act.

Testimonials may seem convincing, but many times, according to Jarvis, the patients quoted never had cancer in the first place. Another important fact is that physicians can't predict with certainty how long a cancer patient will live. When people live longer than expected, they may attribute their survival to an unconventional treatment, just as people who live to be 100 may claim that a glass of wine a day kept them alive. In reality, the cancer patients may have tried many different treatments, including mainstream therapies, and no one knows why they lived longer than expected. A certain number of people do beat the odds. The people who don't aren't around to refute the testimonials.

The choices in conventional cancer medicine—most often involving surgery, chemotherapy and radiation—do involve risk and discomfort, but in return, the patient has a chance of real, proven benefit.

Nothing to Lose

Freedom of choice is often mentioned as a reason why cancer patients should have access to any treatment they think might be helpful, especially if no conventional treatments exist that offer much hope for prolonging their lives. However, patients may have a lot to lose.

Jarvis calls it the "Gambler's fallacy." He says that "patrons of questionable cancer care expose themselves to incompetent practitioners, unsanitary clinical conditions, improper clinical management that may interfere with the drugs they are taking, and more." As examples, he cites Laetrile treatment, which exposed patients to possible cyanide poisoning, and coffee enemas, which, when used excessively, have killed patients.

In addition, many of these products are manufactured in a haphazard way without standards to ensure that the ingredients found in them and their amounts are the same each time. For example, an FDA inspection revealed that Cancell was manufactured in the back yard with kitchen utensils.

A patient's quality of life may suffer from unconventional, untested therapies. Cassileth recently compared the quality of life of patients at the Livingston-Wheeler Medical Clinic, an unconventional cancer clinic in San Diego, to that of patients at the University of Pennsylvania Cancer Center. The Livingston-Wheeler program includes special diets, enemas, and a vaccine that is supposed to boost the immune system. None of the patients was expected to live more than a year, but the researchers thought that quality of life, as measured by a self-report scale, would be better with the unconventional treatment due to an absence of side effects from chemotherapy and other factors. Although survival times between the two groups did not differ, patients at the unconventional treatment center reported a lower quality of life at all times during treatment—the opposite of what was expected.

Cassileth points out, in addition, that even seemingly innocuous treatments like vitamin or diet therapies can interfere with the effectiveness of chemotherapy or create nutritional problems.

One of the most dangerous outcomes of some unconventional treatments is that they can discourage or prevent people from using conventional care that offers real hope. Various types of cancer may be symptomless, especially when a person is in remission, and people may feel that an unconventional treatment helped them. This can cause patients to miss the chance of effectively treating the disease with a treatment that has shown real benefit.

And questionable treatments can be very expensive. Practitioners of these treatments often charge exorbitant fees for them. But patients cannot be charged for treatments under investigation within mainstream medicine: Researchers must supply them free.

Scientific Medicine Is Accountable

Another difference between scientific medicine and unconventional therapy is accountability.

Jarvis asks: "What advice can we give to a patient who is struggling with decisions about whom to trust?"

His answer is to use accountability as the criterion. People or institutions whose work is done openly and who are prominent medical specialists can be ruined if they use deceptive practices. They are required to tell patients about possible side effects and risks, not just possible benefits.

The American Cancer Society publishes information that explains in detail how proponents of unproven cancer treatments can be identified by their lack of accountability. For example, they are often isolated from established scientists and claim that mainstream medicine and the government conspire against them. Their clinical and scientific record-keeping is weak to nonexistent. They often maintain that their treatments are "secrets," or secretly prepared. They may have multiple, unusual degrees from obscure institutions. Their chief supporters are usually outside mainstream medicine.

In contrast, experimental therapies within mainstream medicine are critically reviewed within the medical community and held up to scientific scrutiny as they are being evaluated for safety and effectiveness. The results of studies are published in established medical journals after review by other scientists. The study methods are outlined in the report so that others can try to verify the results by duplicating them.

Though the burden of proof is on manufacturers to show FDA that a given drug is safe and effective, Helene Brown, at UCLA's Jonsson Comprehensive Cancer Center, says proponents of unconventional therapies try to put the burden of proof on others to show that their therapies don't work. They are not willing to submit data for FDA to review. As Brown says, "It's like putting you in a dark, windowless room and asking you to prove that it's not raining outside."

Contrary to claims of some proponents of questionable treatments, FDA welcomes applications from product sponsors who want to investigate new drugs, and the National Cancer Institute is willing to investigate promising new therapies from researchers whether or not they are affiliated with major institutions.

Real Hope

More than ever, real hope for people with cancer exists in mainstream medicine, with increasing reports of new treatments either being approved or being studied under strict scientific conditions.

For example, in 1991 FDA approved a genetically engineered biologic product, G-CSF, that reduces the number of infections in cancer patients undergoing chemotherapy. Late in 1990, FDA gave permission for the National Cancer Institute to begin using human gene therapy for advanced melanoma, a skin cancer that is difficult to treat. And scientists announced in May 1991 a new cancer diagnostic test, developed through genetic engineering, to identify a gene in urine that, when present, may signal the onset of many types of cancer. This discovery may help in prevention and early treatment of cancer.

Under its "treatment IND" (investigational new drug) program, FDA makes certain experimental drugs available to cancer patients before final approval. For example, more than 40,000 patients received levamisole before it was approved in 1990 as a combination therapy along with fluorouracil, a drug previously approved for other conditions, as a therapy for Dukes' C colon cancer. The combination therapy was shown by NCI clinical trials to reduce the death rate by about one-third and the recurrence rate by about 40 percent. Based on the data it had, FDA allowed the manufacturer to make the drug available to many patients before the FDA review process was complete.

A diagnosis of cancer can make people feel as if they don't have control over their lives and bodies. Prevention and early, effective treatment often can be the key to a good outcome. Time is a precious commodity, especially for cancer patients—and it is sad when it's wasted on unproven treatments with questionable benefits that may cause harm. Effective, safe, innovative care is best found within mainstream medicine.

Get the Facts

For reliable information about therapy options for cancer patients, contact:
National Cancer Institute
Office of Cancer Communications
Bethesda, Md. 20892
Call toll-free: 1-800-4-CANCER

Upon request, NCI will send the booklet *What Are Clinical Trials All About?*, which explains how clinical trials work for patients considering experimental treatment. Other cancer publications are also available.

Information on currently popular unconventional treatments is available from:
American Cancer Society
1599 Clifton Road, N.E.
Atlanta, Ga. 30329
Call toll-free: 1-800-ACS-2345, or your local chapter.

—by Lenore Gelb

Lenore Gelb is editor of the *FDA Medical Bulletin*, a publication for health professionals.

Chapter 35

Unproven Medical Treatments Lure Elderly

Americans spend upwards of $20 billion each year on unproven medical treatments. Sixty percent of those who try untested therapies are over 65 and spend an estimated $10 billion on them, according to a 1984 House Subcommittee on Health and Long-Term Care report, "Quackery: A $10 Billion Scandal."

Approximately 80 percent of older Americans have one or more chronic health problems, according to John Renner, M.D., a Kansas City-based champion of quality health care for the elderly. He says their pain and disability lead to despair, making them excellent targets for deception.

"Despite disappointments with promised cures, they continue to hold out hope that the next quick 'cure' will work," says anti-fraud activist Stephen Barrett, M.D.

Frightened of losing a parent or grandparent, family members, too, encourage them to "try everything," especially unproven remedies, according to Barrie R. Cassileth, Ph.D., writing in *CA-A Cancer Journal for Clinicians*.

And, indeed, sometimes people get better when using unproven treatments. But because these therapies have not passed scientific muster, it is impossible to know if improvement is associated with the treatment, represents spontaneous change, or is due to the "placebo" effect. (A placebo is an inactive substance with no known therapeutic value. The "placebo effect" is the phenomenon of people getting better while taking an inactive substance they believe to be therapeutic.)

Pub. No. (FDA) 94-1218; this article originally appeared in the March 1994 *FDA Consumer*.

"It's important to remember," says Barrett, "that many conditions get better on their own, or appear to get better if we believe they will."

What's the Danger?

Taking a chance on unproven treatments is not simply useless, it is often dangerous, according to the Food and Drug Administration, which divides such products into two categories: direct health hazards and indirect health hazards.

Direct health hazards are likely to cause serious injuries. For example, muscle stimulators, promoted falsely as muscle toners, carry a risk of severe electric shock.

Indirectly harmful products are those that cause people to delay or reject proven remedies, according to FDA. For example, if cancer patients reject proven therapies in favor of unproven ones, their disease may advance beyond the point where proven therapies can help.

All types of unproven therapies can be economically harmful, often draining precious dollars from older Americans' limited resources.

FDA's Health Fraud Staff, in its Center for Drug Evaluation and Research, investigates any product for which a disease claim is made. Joel Aronson, director of the Health Fraud Staff, points out that once a manufacturer claims a product can treat or prevent a disease or condition, "whether that product is bottled water or an herb, it is considered a drug and falls under FDA jurisdiction." A product is also considered a drug if it claims to alter the structure or function of the body.

FDA's Center for Food Safety and Applied Nutrition becomes involved with issues such as health claims for herbs, vitamins, and other dietary supplements (see "Dietary Supplements: Making Sure Hype Doesn't Overwhelm Science" in the November 1993 *FDA Consumer*). For a reprint of this article, contact your local FDA office, or write to FDA, HFE-88, 5600 Fishers Lane, Rockville, MD 20857.

FDA's Promotion and Advertising Staff, in its Center for Devices and Radiological Health, investigates health and disease claims made about devices. Byron Tart, acting director, explains that such devices fall into two main categories: devices approved for some medical use but promoted for an unapproved use, and devices not approved for any medical use at all.

Targeting Older Americans

Commonly, unproven products are pushed zealously on the elderly. Promoters often claim their products prevent aging and such conditions as arthritis, Alzheimer's disease, heart disease, and impotence.

According to the National Institute on Aging, however, "while a healthy lifestyle will help delay many of the conditions associated with aging processes, no preparation or device can stop aging." The 1984 House Subcommittee report estimated that people spent at least $2 billion per year on anti-aging remedies. Some anti-aging products are also promoted to either prevent or treat Alzheimer's disease. According to JoAnn McConnell, Ph.D., of the Alzheimer's Association, "so-called new 'cures' for Alzheimer's surface constantly."

But there are no cures, which may cause Alzheimer's patients and their families to be susceptible to products holding out false hope.

There is, however, one approved treatment for Alzheimer's disease: the drug Cognex (tacrine hydrochloride), which was approved in September of 1993 specifically to treat the symptoms of Alzheimer's disease. "It is not a cure for Alzheimer's disease," says FDA Commissioner David A. Kessler, M.D., "but it provides some relief for patients and their families."

Particularly susceptible to deception are the 37 million Americans—many of them over 65—who have arthritis. One reason is that arthritis symptoms come and go, causing people to associate their spontaneous relief with a new "remedy." The Arthritis Foundation says that older Americans spend an estimated $2 billion annually for unproven arthritis remedies.

A Closer Look

Here's a closer look at some unproven therapies promoted for a variety of ills common in older people:

Cellular therapy promoters claim an extract from animal hearts can strengthen human hearts, eye extracts can cure eye disease, and so on. FDA says there are no scientific studies demonstrating the safety and effectiveness of cellular therapy for any medical purpose and warns of health problems, including severe allergic reactions and death.

Chaparral is an herb used in teas, capsules and tablets that promoters purport delays aging, cleanses the blood, and treats cancer. In early 1993, FDA warned consumers not to use it because it had caused serious liver and kidney troubles. Most manufacturers voluntarily withheld chaparral-containing products from sale, and consumers are advised not to use remaining products.

Coenzyme Q-10, a synthetically produced version of a naturally occurring enzyme, is promoted to slow aging by enhancing the immune system. Not only is there no proven benefit, but it may be dangerous for people with poor circulation, according to Edward L. Schneider, M.D., of the National Institute on Aging. Overall, there is no evidence that "boosting" the immune system delays aging, nor is there any evidence that it's possible to do so, according to Schneider.

DHEA (dehydroepiandrosterone) is a naturally occurring chemical. Because levels decline with aging, some scientists speculate it may play some role in aging processes. But there is no proof that DHEA delays aging, according to Schneider.

DMSO, or dimethyl sulfoxide, is a solvent similar to turpentine promoted for arthritis relief. In a sterile form called Rimso-50, it is approved by FDA for treating a rare bladder condition called interstitial cystitis. For this approved use, it is instilled into the bladder for short times (20 to 30 minutes). This is the only approved human use. There are no controlled studies demonstrating its safety and effectiveness in relieving swollen, inflamed arthritic joints, and in an impure form it can harbor bacterial toxins that can enter the bloodstream even when applied topically. It is one of the few compounds rapidly absorbed through the skin. It can be especially dangerous if used as an enema, as recommended by its promoters.

Electrical stimulators are approved by FDA when prescribed by physicians for various conditions, including after-stroke therapy. However, FDA has not approved them for wrinkle removal and face lifts.

Germanium, an inorganic, nonessential element sold as a dietary supplement. Promoters claim it prevents and treats Alzheimer's, and advise users to apply bandage wraps with it to treat arthritis and headaches. Not only is germanium ineffective, but it has caused serious irreversible kidney damage and death, according to FDA.

Gerovital-H3, originating in Romania more than 30 years ago, was brought here illegally and sold as a cure for arthritis, atherosclerosis, angina pectoris, hypertension, deafness, Parkinson's disease, depression, diabetes, and impotence. One of its ingredients is procaine hydrochloride, an anesthetic approved for dental use. No health claims for Gerovital have been substantiated, and FDA considers it an unapproved new drug. It has caused low blood pressure, respiratory difficulties, and convulsions in some users.

Herbal products are centuries-old, but mostly unproven, "cures" for everything from constipation to anxiety. They are available in various forms, including teas, capsules and tablets. Some are potentially dangerous. Chamomile tea, for example, can cause a severe allergic reaction in people allergic to ragweed. Lobelia can cause vomiting, breathing problems, convulsions, and even coma and death when used in large amounts; people with heart disease are especially susceptible. Comfrey has caused severe and even fatal liver disease. (See "Beware the Unknown Brew: Herbal Teas and Toxicity" in the May 1991 *FDA Consumer*.)

Lecithin, a naturally occurring component of certain body tissues, is touted for lowering cholesterol and treating Alzheimer's disease. There's no proof that it's effective for either one.

Low-intensity lasers are promoted to relieve arthritis pain, but FDA has not approved them for this or any other use.

Magnetism: Pressure dots with tiny magnets affixed to adhesive strips that are worn over the arthritic area are promoted for curing arthritis; a magnet in men's briefs is purported to cure impotence; and a magnet used as a suppository is promoted for curing hemorrhoids. There is no scientific basis for any of these claims.

Retin-A has been approved by FDA as a topical treatment for acne. The agency, however, has not determined whether it is safe and effective as a wrinkle remover.

RIFE generator promoters claim that they can insert a person's photograph into their device and diagnose medical conditions. FDA has not approved the marketing of this device, nor is there any scientific basis for this claim.

RNA, or ribonucleic acid, a natural body chemical that carries genetic information, is a common ingredient in anti-aging compounds and is also promoted for Alzheimer's. Promoters claim it rejuvenates old cells, improves memory, and prevents wrinkling. But there have been no controlled scientific studies to back up these claims.

Superoxide dismutase (SOD) is a normal body chemical that is promoted as being able to slow aging and treat Alzheimer's disease. According to the National Institute on Aging's Schneider, writing in the *New England Journal of Medicine*, some studies have shown higher tissue levels of SOD in longer-living species. A survey of a large number of different animal species revealed, in fact, that the longest-lived species,

379

human beings, had the highest tissue levels of superoxide dismutase. But there is no evidence that SOD works to delay aging or prolong life, nor is there any evidence that taking SOD tablets raises blood or tissue levels of SOD.

Avoiding Fraud

According to FDA, these red flags should make you think twice about remedies not prescribed by your doctor:

- celebrity endorsements
- inadequate labeling (a legitimate nonprescription medication is labeled with indications for use, as well as how to use it and when to seek medical help)
- claims that the product works by a secret formula
- promotion of the treatment only in the back pages of magazines, over the phone, by direct mail, in newspaper ads in the format of news stories, or 30-minute commercials in talk show format.

The Arthritis Foundation says the following claims are also warning signs that a "cure" has but questionable therapeutic value:

- It's effective for a wide range of disorders, such as cancer, arthritis and sexual dysfunction. ("But," says FDA's Aronson, "don't misinterpret this and believe a product promoted for only one disease is safe and effective.")
- It's all natural.
- It's inexpensive and has no side effects.
- It works immediately and permanently, making a visit to the doctor unnecessary.

Older Americans, along with younger folks, should remember that falling victim to health fraud is "not a matter of being weaker or foolish," says Renner. "It is a matter of being in pain or having more than one chronic illness—or both."

Barrett offers a final word of advice: "When you feel your physician isn't doing enough to help, don't stray from scientific health care in a desperate attempt to find a solution." Instead, ask your physician to provide a more detailed explanation or to refer you to another doctor.

Hearing Aids

FDA is taking action to improve the patient care of people who buy hearing aids. Though hearing aids have significantly improved the quality of life for many older Americans, the agency is concerned that some manufacturers are making unsubstantiated claims about their devices and are giving inaccurate portrayals of their devices' risks and benefits.

The agency last November (1994) proposed changes to hearing aid regulations to require a hearing assessment in all cases before a person is sold a hearing aid. The regulation will also require that this assessment be done by a qualified health professional licensed by the state. A public hearing on the proposal was held Dec. 6 and 7 near FDA headquarters in Rockville, Md.

Although a 1977 regulation restricts hearing aid sales to people who have had a hearing evaluation by a doctor within six months, FDA Commissioner Kessler pointed out that the "regulation also included a provision allowing fully informed adult patients to waive the medical examination." Kessler said this waiver has been "overused and misrepresented."

Before proposing the regulation changes, FDA reviewed promotional materials for a number of hearing aids and found that several manufacturers were making unsubstantiated and misleading claims that created unrealistic expectations about the performance of the devices. In addition, the materials failed to disclose significant information and did not accurately disclose the device's potential risks and benefits.

At press time, FDA was reviewing public comments on the proposed regulation changes.

— by Kristine Napier

Kristine Napier is a registered dietitian and writer in Mayfield Village, Ohio.

For More Information

FDA
HFE-88
5600 Fishers Lane
Rockville, MD 20857

U.S. Postal Inspection Service (monitors products purchased by mail)
Office of Criminal Investigation
Washington, DC 20260-2166

Federal Trade Commission (regarding false advertising)
Room 421
6th St. and Pennsylvania Ave., N.W.
Washington, DC 20580

National Institute on Aging
NIA Information Center
P.O. Box 8057
Gaithersburg, MD 20898-8057

Arthritis Foundation
P.O. Box 19000
Atlanta, GA 30326
(ask for their free brochure "Unproven Remedies")

Alzheimer's Association
919 North Michigan Ave.
Suite 1000
Chicago, IL 60611
1-800-272-3900

Chapter 36

Dietary Supplements: More Is Not Always Better

Many people are attracted by ads for vitamins and minerals that imply a supplement will improve appearance, give sex life a boost, prevent or cure diseases, and even lengthen life. But there is, as yet, little scientific evidence to back most of these claims.

Doctors occasionally prescribe dietary supplements to correct nutrient deficiencies diagnosed in their patients. For example, people who are at high risk of developing osteoporosis—a condition causing thin, brittle bones—may be advised by their physicians to take calcium supplements. Dieters, heavy drinkers, and those who are recovering from surgery or an illness may also need certain supplements.

Too often, people take high-dose supplements of various vitamins and minerals without a doctor's advice in the hope of preventing or curing a disease or condition. This can be a waste of money or, worse, a threat to health.

What Do We Know About Supplements?

Scientists still have much to learn about the special nutritional needs of older people. At present, there is no reason to believe that large amounts of vitamins and minerals in supplement form will help prevent or treat health problems or slow aging processes. Multivitamin and mineral pills (often referred to as "one-a-day" type pills) contain either the full recommended dietary allowances (RDAs) established by the National Academy of Sciences National Research Council or,

National Institute on Aging, *Age Page*, 1993.

in some cases, less. Many people take these pills as a form of "insurance" that their daily nutritional needs are met. Daily multivitamin tablets may be beneficial for some people, but the value of any dietary supplement depends on many factors, including eating habits and overall health.

Scientists have identified a large number of nutrients that are vital to health, but supplements contain only some of these. A well-balanced diet—one that contains a wide variety of foods—provides all the necessary nutrients. In addition, there are other substances in foods, such as fiber, that are not essential for life but benefit health. Foods may also contain some essential nutrients that have not yet been identified.

Large amounts of some supplements may upset the natural balance of nutrients that the body normally maintains. Too much of some of them can affect the way others act. Although extra amounts of some nutrients are not absorbed and pass out of the body, others can build up to dangerous levels.

Getting the Nutrients You Need

Most older people can get the nutrients they need by eating a wide range of nutritious foods each day. As a guide, a well-balanced diet should include the following: at least two servings of low-fat milk or dairy products such as cheese, cottage cheese, or yogurt; two servings of protein-rich foods such as poultry, fish, eggs, beans, nuts, or lean meat; four servings of fruit and vegetables, including a citrus fruit or juice and a dark green leafy vegetable; and four servings of breads and cereal products (made with whole grain or enriched flours), rice, or pasta. (These are only general guidelines. Some people may have conditions that restrict their intake of certain foods.)

Some older people may not get the vitamins and minerals they need from their daily diet. In some cases this is because they find it hard to get or prepare the foods they know they need. Digestive problems, chewing difficulties, and the use of certain drugs can also interfere with good nutrition. People with these problems may benefit from a dietary supplement.

If you are taking a supplement, or thinking about taking one, ask your doctor or a registered dietitian (R.D.) if it's really necessary. He or she can check your health and diet, and decide if any steps should be taken to improve your nutrition. If so, a simple dietary change may be all that is needed. If you have been taking an unprescribed supplement, ask for advice about stopping. It may be better to slowly reduce the amount you take than to stop suddenly.

Some Popular Dietary Practices and Fads

The use of megavitamins and the high-potency formulas are of current concern among scientists. These supplements contain 10 to 100 times the RDA for some vitamins and minerals. People may take them because they think the RDAs are only minimum requirements and that, if a little is good, a lot will be better. The allowances, however, are set high enough to cover the needs of healthy people.

Large doses of some nutrients can act like drugs, often with serious results. Large amounts of either vitamin A or D are particularly dangerous. Too much vitamin A can cause headaches, nausea, diarrhea, and eventually liver and bone damage. High doses of vitamin D can cause kidney damage and even death. When taken in excessive amounts, supplemental iron can build up to harmful levels in the liver and other body organs.

Some supplements are of no value to anyone. One example is vitamin B_{15} or pangamic acid (calcium pangamate). Sold for the treatment of heart disease, diabetes, glaucoma, allergies, and "aging," this substance is not needed in the human diet, and it has no medical usefulness.

Another useless supplement currently sold in pill form is SOD (superoxide dismutase). Scientists have found that animals with long lifespans have more of this enzyme in their bodies than do shorter-lived species. Although this knowledge may lead to a better understanding of aging processes, it is not likely to lead to an "anti-aging" pill. SOD is a protein. When taken by mouth, it breaks down into component parts—called amino acids—which are not reassembled. Therefore, SOD does not enter body cells and has no effect.

Steps You Can Take

Consider checking with your doctor before taking any over-the-counter dietary supplement, particularly if you have illnesses such as diabetes, high blood pressure, or arthritis.

Resources

The National Institute on Aging offers a variety of resources on aging. Contact the NIA Information Center, P.O. Box 8057, Gaithersburg, MD 20898-8057.

Part Five

Managing Common Health Risks in the Home

Chapter 37

Fitness and Health

Recommendation Regarding Counseling to Promote Physical Activity

Counseling patients to incorporate regular physical activity into their daily routines is recommended to prevent coronary heart disease, hypertension, obesity, and diabetes. This recommendation is based on the proven benefits of regular physical activity; the effectiveness of clinician counseling to promote physical activity is not established.

Burden of Suffering

In 1985, national survey data revealed that 56% of men and 61% of women in the U.S. either never engaged in physical activity or did so on an irregular basis. Surveillance data from 1991 suggests the prevalence of sedentary lifestyle (58% overall) has not changed. Coronary heart disease (CHD), the predominant risk associated with a sedentary lifestyle, is the leading cause of mortality in the U.S. In the sedentary, an estimated 35% of the excess CHD could be eliminated by becoming more physically active. The excess CHD risk attributable to sedentary lifestyle, and the societal costs of this excess

Excerpted from *Guide to Clinical Preventive Services, Second Edition*, report of the U.S. Preventive Services Task Force, U.S. Department of Health and Human Services, Office of Public Health and Science, Office of Disease Prevention and Health Promotion, 1996.

risk, are higher than those attributed individually to obesity, hypertension, and smoking. The total burden of suffering attributable to sedentary lifestyle in the U.S. is unknown but is probably large.

Efficacy of Risk Reduction

Evidence exists that physical activity and fitness reduce morbidity and mortality for at least six chronic conditions: coronary heart disease, hypertension, obesity, diabetes, osteoporosis, and mental health disorders. Evidence linking sedentary lifestyle with other conditions exists but is not reviewed here. Moderate physical activity comprises activities that can be comfortably sustained for at least 60 minutes (e.g., walking, slow biking, raking leaves, cleaning windows, light restaurant work). Vigorous activity describes those of an intensity sufficient to result in fatigue within 20 minutes (e.g., shoveling snow).

Coronary Heart Disease

There are no prospective intervention trials of physical activity for the primary prevention of CHD. Evidence from cohort studies, however, has shown a consistent association between physical activity and reduced incidence of CHD. A relative risk of death from CHD of 1.9 (95% confidence interval, 1.6 to 2.2) for sedentary persons compared with the physically active was calculated in a meta-analysis of studies on primary prevention of CHD. A relative risk of 1.9 was also reported in an earlier comprehensive review. In a cohort of men, beginning moderately vigorous sports activity was associated with a 41% lower risk of death from CHD, which was comparable to the risk reduction associated with smoking cessation (44%). In another cohort study, initially unfit men who subsequently became fit had a 52% reduction in cardiovascular disease mortality compared with those who remained unfit. The absolute reduction in the age-adjusted death rate from cardiovascular disease was 34/10,000 man-years. Similar benefits from exercise have been reported in older men. Physiologically, the response to physical activity in women appears similar to that in men. Epidemiologic data sufficient to confirm a primary preventive role of physical activity for CHD in women are not yet available, however.

One reason that those who are physically active may be at decreased risk for CHD is self-selection—persons who choose to exercise may be healthier and have fewer overall risk factors for CHD. Studies controlling for such confounding variables, however, have found that the effects of exercise are independent of other CHD risk factors, and that the cardiovascular benefits may even be augmented in the presence of other risk factors for CHD. Moreover, the type of individual who adopts athletic behavior is not protected from CHD if regular exercise is discontinued (e.g., college athletes who are sedentary later in adult life).

Although observational data cannot prove causal associations, the strength, consistency, and coherence of the evidence and presence of a biologic gradient, clearly suggest that both physical activity and fitness influence risk for CHD. Inference of a causal relationship between increased physical activity and decreased CHD is supported by demonstrated physiologic effects which suggest plausible biologic mechanisms (e.g., enhanced fibrinolysis, decreased platelet adhesiveness, improved lipoprotein profile, and lessened adrenergic response to stress).

Hypertension

Cohort studies suggest that physically inactive persons have a 35-52% greater risk of developing hypertension than those who exercise, independent of other risk factors for hypertension. A graded inverse relationship between increasing fitness quartile and blood pressure was noted in a large cohort. Randomized controlled trials of primary prevention of hypertension to date, however, have been either non-specific (i.e., exercise grouped together with diet and weight loss) or limited in sample size. Inconsistencies in results between studies of secondary prevention suggest that certain subsets of individuals (e.g., women and individuals with diastolic elevations) may be more responsive to the blood pressure-lowering effects of physical activity than others. A meta-analysis of controlled longitudinal studies found a weighted net drop in systolic over diastolic blood pressure with endurance training of 3/3, 6/7, and 10/8 mm Hg in normotensive, borderline, and hypertensive subjects, respectively. A similar effect on blood pressure appears across ages 15-80 years, in different social groups, and in both men and women. Low- to moderate-intensity endurance training or circuit weight training may be at least as effective in lowering blood pressure as are high-intensity endurance training and resistance training primarily for muscle strength. A sigmoidal relationship between physical activity and blood pressure benefit may exist, and the threshold of activity necessary for significant effect may be lower than that necessary for cardiovascular fitness or improvement in lipid profile. A possible mechanism is the attenuation of elevated sympathetic nervous system activity from hyperinsulinemia via the effects of exercise.

Obesity

Data from prospective population studies suggest an increased risk for the development of significant weight gain for persons in lower leisure-time physical activity categories compared to those in higher physical activity categories. Experimental data on secondary prevention of obesity confirm such a relationship. Physical activity can influence the development of obesity (e.g., assist in long-term maintenance of isocaloric or balanced energy state) and increase the chances of success in initial and long-term weight loss. This influence stems from increased total energy output, preservation of lean body mass, changes in substrate utilization and fat distribution, and possible reversal of diet-induced suppression of basal metabolic rate, as well as psychologic reinforcement. An association between low levels of leisure time physical activity and insulin resistance with resultant hyperinsulinemia may link obesity (especially abdominal) with hypertension, hyperlipidemia, and CHD in some individuals. Morbidity and mortality in prospective cohort data have been lower in overweight individuals who are physically active even if they remain overweight. Normalization of the metabolic profile (e.g., glucose tolerance, insulin, lipids) is a plausible mechanism for such a decrease in morbidity and mortality.

Non-Insulin-Dependent Diabetes Mellitus

Prospective cohort data reveal an inverse relationship between the level of physical activity and the risk of developing non-insulin-dependent diabetes mellitus (NIDDM). This effect is pronounced among overweight men, but it is also seen in women. The age-adjusted risk of NIDDM is reduced by 6% for each 500-kcal increment in energy expenditure per week. The protective effect of physical activity is especially pronounced in persons at highest risk for NIDDM (i.e., those with positive family history, obesity, or hypertension). In one cohort study, cardiopulmonary fitness appeared to attenuate mortality at each level of glycemic control. Possible mechanisms for these primary and secondary preventive effects are reviewed elsewhere, but decreased insulin resistance seems to play an important role. Both the onset of positive effects of physical activity on glycemic control and the loss of these effects upon its discontinuation are rapid.

Osteoporosis

Nonrandomized controlled interventional data, confirmed by limited randomized controlled trial data, support earlier studies suggesting that postmenopausal women can retard bone loss through physical activity. Cross-sectional studies examining exercise history and fitness level reveal higher bone mass in the more active and fit, respectively. Some prospective data, along with cross-sectional data comparing the bone density of athletic women with that of nonathletic premenopausal women, suggest that physical activity can also reduce the rate of bone loss in premenopausal women with a normal hormonal milieu.

Direct evidence that physical activity reduces the incidence of hip fractures includes a recent large case-control study. This study found a reduction in the risk of hip fracture in women who were active in the past, as well as in those with recent moderate activity. Prior studies focused on recent activity or were cross-sectional in study design. A plausible biologic mechanism is suggested by a large cohort study that substantiated an inverse relationship between bone mineral density and hip fractures. Some studies have suggested that skeletal loads generating muscle pull or resistance rather than gravity or weight bearing alone may provide greater benefit to bone mineral density. Inconsistencies in the literature exist, however. Important questions remain unanswered, such as the role and relative impact of physical activity with respect to estrogen replacement. Furthermore, the percentage of variance in bone mineral density attributable to differences in activity is thought to be modest (20%) compared with the genetic contribution.

Mental Health Disorders

Some consistent findings have emerged from controlled trials assessing problems with affect, such as depression and anxiety, before and after various forms of physical activity. First, improvements are greatest in those who are more depressed and more anxious at the onset of the study. Second, improved cardiovascular fitness is not necessary for mood enhancement. Third, several recent studies have shown diminished gain at high intensity compared to moderate intensity physical activity. Prospective cohort data suggest physical activity also has a preventive effect. Study methodologies to date may lack the sensitivity to detect decreased prevalence in those without preexisting affect disorders, however. Healthy individuals may derive a preventive effect from physical activity, while those with mild to moderate affect disorders derive a therapeutic benefit.

General well-being can apparently be enhanced with physical activity. Research on self-esteem and physical activity has been criticized as being overly simplistic. A more complex model was postulated, giving rise to several new terms that may be considered dimensions of self-esteem, e.g., self-efficacy (capacity to produce a desired effect), self-acceptance, self-concept, physical competence. Exercise-induced increases in self-efficacy may have an important role in successful maintenance of physical activity habits. Study results are mixed as to whether aerobic or anaerobic exercise imparts a greater increase in these components of self-esteem. Furthermore, the relative importance of perceived improvements in areas of life not quantified by standard psychometric batteries (e.g., sleep patterns, sex life) remains to be determined. Cognition does not appear to be improved significantly with physical activity. Mechanisms for psychologic benefit remain undefined, and the role of ß-endorphins requires further study.

Quantity and Intensity of Physical Activities

To improve cardiovascular fitness, exercise cannot be performed occasionally or seasonally, nor can one expect protection from CHD simply by having exercised regularly in the past. Beginning moderately vigorous physical activity during adulthood, however, may reduce the risk of CHD to the level of those who have been active for many years. Among previously unfit men, achieving fitness, which requires regular physical activity, substantially reduces the risk of both all-cause and cardiovascular disease mortality. In a recent cohort study, participating in increasing levels of vigorous activity was associated with decreasing total mortality in a graded relationship. Clearly, regular vigorous physical activity sufficient to achieve physical fitness is associated with important health benefits.

While regular vigorous physical activity is likely to be most beneficial, prior recommendations for developing and maintaining cardiorespiratory fitness may inadequately address the potential benefits of low to moderate levels of physical activity and subsequent risk factor modification, particularly for unfit and sedentary individuals. Moderate physical activities have higher compliance rates than vigorous exercise activities, mesh better with daily lifestyle, and are well maintained over time. Studies with at least three levels of physical activity exposure uniformly reveal a reduction in CHD risk from the lowest to the next-to-lowest activity level. It is not that more modest amounts of physical activity will provide the maximum reduction in CHD risk, but rather that those at greatest risk (i.e., the sedentary and least fit) may derive substantial benefits from initiating even some activity. No clear minimal intensity of physical activity required for benefit has been defined. Intensity can convey an absolute or relative amount (e.g., what might be low intensity to one might be high intensity to another). A linear dose-response relationship (except for the most vigorous levels or more than 3,000 kcal/week) seems to exist between physical activity and health (both lower incidence of disease and improved functional capability). Modifications in the physical activity message may be required to accommodate those with differing interests, limitations, or cultural milieu as well as those with disability (especially when mobility is reduced).

A trial of middle-aged men compared the training effect of 30 minutes of moderate physical activity with three 10-minute bouts per day of equivalent activity separated by at least 4 hours. Over an 8-week study period, both groups achieved similar results. Also, cohort studies of physical activity exposure have assessed the amounts of activity performed per day and time devoted per week, not duration of specific workouts, and achieved significant results. Thus, attention to total energy expenditure per day and per week is warranted. How the expenditure is accumulated is secondary and dependent more on personal preference, musculoskeletal tolerance, and available facilities.

Potential Adverse Effects of Physical Activity

The benefits of physical activity must be weighed against its potential adverse effects, which include injury, osteoarthritis, myocardial infarction, and, rarely, sudden death. Data remain scarce on the incidence of injury during most noncompetitive physical activity. One exception is running, with an annual risk of injury of 35-65%; risk is positively related to the level of exposure to the activity and to prior injury. Aerobic dance participation also carries a relatively high risk, which increases with the frequency of classes. One trial randomly assigned 70–79-year-old men and women to strength training, walk/jog, or control groups. Injury rates were 8.7% for the strength training group during the full 26 weeks, 4.8% for the walk group during weeks 1-13, and 57% for those who jogged during weeks 14-26 and had walked during the first 14 weeks. In cohort data, physical activity in men and women was also associated with an increased risk of orthopedic problems. Most exercise-induced injuries are preventable. They often occur as a result of excessive levels of physical activity, sudden dramatic increases in activity level (especially in persons with poor baseline fitness), and improper exercise techniques or equipment. Intense exercise training can also result in the interruption of menstrual function, bone loss (partly reversible), and an increased fracture risk.

Long-term physical activity probably does not accelerate the development of osteoarthritis (OA) in major weight-bearing joints (e.g., hips, knees). Case-control data revealed no significant difference in knee OA among groups with varying leisure-time physical activity; OA patients were significantly more likely to have been obese at 20 years of age or had prior knee injury. In a 5-year longitudinal cohort with a mean age of 63, runners were matched with controls and followed radiographically and clinically; acceleration of OA in runners was not found. Graduated activity that allows cartilage adaptation is less likely to induce OA than painful or mechanically improper motion that places infrequent but excessive stress on joints. Available data suggest that moderate physical activity performed within the limits of comfort while putting joints through normal motions will not, in the absence of joint abnormality, inevitably lead to joint injury.

Adverse cardiovascular events are perhaps the greatest concern about vigorous exercise. Two recent large studies provide estimates of the relative risk of triggering myocardial infarctions within 1 hour of heavy physical activity compared with less strenuous or no exertion. These relative risks are 2.1 (95% confidence interval, 1.6 to 3.1) and 5.9 (4.6-7.7), respectively. A protective effect was seen with regular physical activity in both studies, however. As the frequency of exercise per week increased, the relative risk of infarction during vigorous activity dropped. The risk of sudden death is known to be increased during vigorous physical activity. This risk appears greater in sedentary persons who engage in vigorous activity as compared to those who are habitually active. In those over 35 years of age, more than 80% of sudden deaths during or shortly after exercise are from CHD. Exercise as a cause of sudden cardiac death was reviewed recently. The overall risk of sudden death is lower, however, for those who are habitually active, despite the transient increase in risk during the actual physical activity, when compared with sedentary counterparts.

Effectiveness of Counseling

The rationale and evidence for effectiveness of physical activity counseling have been reviewed. Prior studies that have demonstrated benefits from counseling provide little information about long-term compliance and are of limited generalizability, because the form of counseling, delivery (e.g., inclusion of community health promotion), type of patients, or clinical setting have not been representative of typical primary care clinician counseling of healthy patients. A recent randomized controlled trial contained similar limitations; the frequency of physical activity was not significantly increased and follow-up was limited to 1 month. A nonrandomized controlled trial of brief physician counseling plus one brief follow-up phone call demonstrated significant increases in both self-reported and objectively measured (using an electronic monitor) physical activity; there were important study limitations, however, including self-selection to the intervention group, use of patient volunteers, and follow-up of only 4–6 weeks. A multicenter cohort study using pre- and post-intervention surveys to assess changes in several behaviors over 1 year did find an increase in beginning regular physical activity. Thus, sufficient published evidence concerning the efficacy of physical activity counseling is lacking.

Recommendations of Other Groups

The American College of Sports Medicine and the Centers for Disease Control and Prevention recommend that every adult accumulate 30 minutes or more of moderate-intensity physical activity on most, preferably all, days of the week. The American Heart Association and the American Academy of Family Physicians (AAFP) recommend that physicians counsel patients in selecting an exercise program and promote regular exercise. The policy of the AAFP is currently under review. The American College of Obstetricians and Gynecologists has issued guidelines on counseling women about regular exercise. The Canadian Task Force on the Periodic Health Examination (CTF) recommends that moderate-level physical activity be performed consistently to accumulate 30 minutes or more most days of the week. The CTF found insufficient evidence to recommend for or against including physical activity counseling in the periodic health examination. The American Academy of Pediatrics recommends teaching the importance of regular, moderate to vigorous physical activity as a way to prevent illness in adult life, and encouraging parents to serve as role models by participating in regular physical activity. The Bright Futures guidelines recommend that children and adolescents participate in regular physical activity, and that parents encourage such activity. The American Medical Association recommends that all adolescents receive annual guidance about the benefits of exercise and encouragement to engage in safe exercise on a regular basis.

Discussion

Direct evidence is limited that clinician counseling can increase the physical activity of asymptomatic patients, but other considerations warrant devoting time to this intervention. First, given the sizable independent relative risk for impaired health in sedentary individuals together with the large population at risk, even modest increases in physical activity levels could have great public health impact. Second, consideration of the total societal cost associated with the sedentary lifestyle and its disproportionate burden is also relevant. Third, the success of counseling in other settings and for other behavioral risk factors deserves consideration. Clinician counseling may reinforce several other important interventions (e.g., school-based emphasis on lifelong activity patterns, reduction of barriers to physical activity at work and in the community) that can change sedentary behavior.

Clinical Intervention

Counseling to promote regular physical activity is recommended for all children and adults. This recommendation is based on the proven efficacy of regular physical activity in reducing the risk for coronary heart disease, hypertension, obesity, and diabetes, although there is currency insufficient evidence that counseling asymptomatic primary care patients to incorporate physical activity into their daily routines will have a positive effect on their behavior. Clinicians should determine each patient's activity level, ascertain barriers specific to that individual, and provide information on the role of physical activity in disease prevention. The clinician may then assist the patient in selecting appropriate types of physical activity. Factors that should be considered include medical limitations and activity characteristics that both improve health (e.g., increased caloric expenditure, enhanced cardiovascular fitness, low potential adverse effects) and enhance compliance (e.g., low perceived exertion, minimal cost, and convenience).

An emphasis on regular, moderate-intensity physical activity rather than on vigorous exercise is reasonable in sedentary persons. This emphasis encourages a variety of self-directed, moderate-level physical activities (e.g., walking or cycling to work, taking the stairs, raking leaves, mowing the lawn with a power mower, cycling for pleasure, swimming, racket sports) that can be more easily incorporated into an individual's daily routine. An appropriate short-term goal is activity that is a small increase over current levels. Over a period of several months, progression to a level of activity that achieves cardiovascular fitness (e.g., 30 minutes of brisk walking most days of the week) would be ideal. Development and maintenance of muscular strength and joint flexibility is also desirable. Sporadic exercise, especially if extremely vigorous in an otherwise sedentary individual, should be discouraged in favor of moderate-level activities performed consistently.

—The draft update of this chapter was prepared for the U.S. Preventive Services Task Force by John Burress, MD, MPH, David Christiani, MD, MPH, and Donald M. Berwick, MD, MPP.

Chapter 38

An Action Guide for Healthy Eating

Most people are busy these days. They have less time than they used to for shopping and for planning what to eat. The text in this chapter is designed to make it easy to fit low-fat, high-fiber eating into busy schedules.

Much research in the last few years has shown that the way people eat has a lot to do with how healthy they are—and how healthy they stay. This research has also shown that eating a healthy diet, low in fat, high in fiber, with plenty of fruits and vegetables, may help to lower cancer risk.

People have heard the message. They've begun to make changes in the foods they choose and the ways these foods are cooked and served. Still, most people are eating too much fat and not enough fiber and fruits and vegetables. And people have questions about which choices to make. Do some of these questions sound familiar?

What Can I Eat to Help Stay Healthy and Lower Cancer Risk?

Experts agree that the best choice is a healthy, balanced diet that is low in fat, moderate in calories, and rich in fiber. It means:

- Eat lots of fruit and vegetables, grains, and beans.

U.S. Department of Health and Human Services, Public Health Service, National Institutes of Health, National Cancer Institute, NIH Publication No. 95-3877, May 1995.

- Include some lean meats and low-fat dairy products.
- Go easy on fats.

How Can I Do This Easily? I Want to Eat Right, But I Don't Want to Give Up a Lot of Foods that I Like.

You don't have to change your whole life's eating habits. A few small actions can make a difference. Here are two examples:

- Switch to reduced or nonfat salad dressing. Regular salad dressing has about 160 calories and 18 grams of fat in a modest 2-tablespoon serving!

- Next time you have toast, try whole wheat with jelly, fruit spread, or jam instead of white bread with butter. You'll cut back on fat, and you'll get more than twice the fiber.

How Do I Get Started?

This chapter shows you how to make a few easy changes in the foods you choose. You will find three action lists that suggest new ways to choose and serve the foods you know and like. The lists follow the dietary guidelines of the National Cancer Institute (NCI). These guidelines are also consistent with the USDA/DHHS Dietary Guideline for Americans.

Choose healthy eating actions to:

- Cut back on fat.
- Increase the fruits, vegetables, and grains you eat.
- Increase the fiber in your diet.

As you read through the lists, you may find that you already are following some of the suggestions. If so, try actions that are new for you. Start with two or three actions that you think you can do easily, and repeat them over time.

They will soon become second nature, and you can add others from the lists. If it helps, keep the action list posted as a reminder.

Action List for Fat

Did you know there are four great reasons to eat less fat?

1. It can assist in weight loss or weight maintenance because you'll be eating fewer calories.

2. It can help reduce your risk of heart disease by reducing saturated fat, which will help lower blood cholesterol levels.

3. It may help reduce your risk of cancer.

4. Eating fewer high-fat foods means more room for fruits, vegetables, grains, and beans.

Here are some actions to get you started and keep you going. Check off two or three actions now and more later.

- Use reduced-fat or nonfat salad dressings.

- Use nonfat or lower fat spread, such as jelly or jam, fruit spread, apple butter, nonfat or reduced-calorie mayonnaise, nonfat margarine, or mustard.

- To top baked potatoes, use plain nonfat or low-fat yogurt, nonfat or reduced-fat sour cream, nonfat or low-fat cottage cheese, nonfat margarine, nonfat hard cheese, salsa, or vinegar.

- Use a little lemon juice, dried herbs, thinly sliced green onions, or a little salsa as a nonfat topping for vegetables or salads.

- Use small amounts of high-fat toppings. For example, use only 1 tsp butter or mayonnaise; 1 tbsp sour cream; 1 tbsp regular salad dressing.

- Switch to 1 percent or skim milk and other nonfat or lower fat dairy products (low-fat or nonfat yogurt, nonfat or reduced-fat sour cream).

- Cut back on cheese by using small (1 oz.) amounts on sandwiches and in cooking or use lower fat and fat-free cheeses (part-skim mozzarella, 1 percent cottage cheese, or nonfat hard cheese).

- Save french fries and other fried foods for special occasions; have a small serving; share with a friend.

- Save high-fat desserts (ice cream, pastries) for special occasions; have small amounts; share a serving with a friend.

- Choose small portions of lean meat, fish, and poultry; use low-fat cooking methods (baking, poaching, broiling); trim off all fat from meat and remove skin from poultry.

- Choose lower fat luncheon meats, such as sliced turkey or chicken breast, lean ham, lean sliced beef.

Cutting Back on Fat

- Use lower fat versions of high-fat foods.
- Use only small amounts of high-fat foods.
- Use high-fat foods only sometimes.
- Choose more low-fat and nonfat foods.

What's a recommended serving size for meat? Experts suggest 3 oz. of cooked meat which is the size of:

- a deck of cards
- a hamburger bun

Table 38.1. One Ounce (1 oz.) of Cheese Equals

1 inch cube of hard cheese
3 tbsp of grated cheese
1 and a half slices of wrapped cheese (brands differ; check label)

How Are You Doing on Fat?

These days, everyone is talking about the importance of cutting back on fat. Surveys show that we're eating less fat than we used to, but we still are getting about 34 percent of our calories that should come from fat.

The number of calories you need each day varies depending on your body size and activity levels. But someone who needs about 2, 000 calories a day should be eating no more than 65 grams of fat a day on average.

Guide to Determining Dietary Fat

Check below to figure out how to determine your fat intake. Please note that the example below is for someone who needs a total of 2,000 calories a day. But the way you calculate how much fat you should eat is the same for people needing other amounts of daily calories.

1. Take the number of calories you eat each day and multiply it by 30 percent (.30). For example: calories X .30 = 600 calories from fat

2. Divide your answer by 9 because there are 9 calories in each gram of fat. This will give you the number of grams of fat per day that should be your goal. 600/9 = 65 grams

3. You can use the information food labels to keep track of the fat you eat each day. By planning your meals in advance and balancing higher fat choices with lower fat ones, you can keep you day's total at the recommended 30 percent of calories or less from fat. Use the Nutrition Facts Section of the food label to compare the fat content of products before you buy foods. Compare serving sizes when comparing total fat content.

Action List for Fruits and Vegetables

Did you know that there are four great reasons to eat fruits and vegetables?

1. It is easy to do.
2. Almost all are low in calories and fat.
3. They are a good source of vitamins and minerals and provide fiber.
4. They may help reduce cancer risk.

Here are some actions to get you started and keep you going. Check off two or three actions now and add more later:

• Buy many kinds of fruits and vegetables when you shop, so you have plenty of choices, and you don't run out. Buy frozen, dried, and canned as well as fresh fruits and vegetables.

• First, use the fruits and vegetables that go bad easily (peaches, asparagus).

• Save hardier varieties (apples, acorn squash) or frozen and canned types for later in the week.

• Use the salad bar to buy cut-up fruits/vegetables if you're in a hurry.

• Keep a fruit bowl, small packs of applesauce, raisins, or other dried fruit on the kitchen counter, table, or in the office.

• Pack a piece of fruit or some cut-up vegetables in your briefcase or backpack; carry moist towelettes for easy cleanup.

• Keep a bowl of cut-up vegetables on top shelf of the refrigerator.

- Add fruit to breakfast by drinking 6 oz. of 100 percent fruit juice or by having them in soup, salad, or cut-up raw.

- Add fruits and vegetables to dinner by microwaving or steaming vegetables and having a special fruit dessert.

- Increase portions when you serve vegetables and fruits. Season them the low-fat way with herbs, spices, lemon juice. If sauce is used, choose a nonfat or low-fat sauce.

- Choose fruit for dessert. For a special dessert, try a fruit parfait with low-fat yogurt or sherbet topped with berries.

- Add extra varieties of vegetables when you prepare soups, sauces, and casseroles (for example, grate carrot and zucchini into spaghetti sauce).

- Add more fruits and vegetables as a snack anytime: mid-morning, after school, before dinner, while watching TV.

- Try canned varieties of beans and peas such as kidney beans or black-eyed peas. It's a fast and easy way to use beans and peas without cooking them from scratch.

These ideas and tips should get you started and keep you going with beans:

- Once a week or more, try a low-fat meatless meal or main dish that features beans (tacos or burritos stuffed with pinto beans; chili with kidney beans; black beans over rice).

- Use beans as a dip for vegetables or filling for sandwiches.

- Serve soup made from beans or peas—minestrone, split-pea, black bean, or lentil (once week or more).

- Try black-eyed peas or black beans as a vegetable side dish with meat or fish.

- Add beans to salads. Many salad bars feature kidney beans, three-bean salad, or chickpeas (garbanzo beans).

How Are You Doing on Fruits and Vegetables?

Most people know that fruits and vegetables are good-for-you foods. That's confirmed by the recommendation of many groups, including the National Cancer Institute. NCI suggests that Americans eat 5 or more servings of fruits and vegetables every day.

Table 38.2. What's a Fruit or Vegetable Serving?

- 6 oz. juice
- one half cup cut-up fruit or vegetable
- 1 cup leafy vegetable
- one half cup cooked dried peas or beans
- one fourth cup dried fruit

Did You Know that Dried Peas and Beans Are Vegetables Too?

What are dried peas and beans? Kidney, lima, black, and pinto beans; chickpeas; split peas; and lentils are just a few examples. They are vegetables, just like carrots and squash, but they have some special qualities, too. Here's why you should make them a regular part of your healthy eating:

1. They are high in fiber and rich in vitamins and minerals.
2. They are low in fat.
3. They are high in protein and minerals. For these reasons, dried peas and beans also qualify as part of the meat group in the USDA/DHHS Food Guide Pyramid.
4. They are easy to fix and go well with lots of other foods.

Action List for Whole Grains

Did you know that there are some great reasons to eat more whole grain breads and cereals?

1. They are low in fat.
2. They are good sources of fiber, vitamins, minerals, and protein.
3. They can be fixed and eaten in many ways.

Here are some actions to get you started and keep you going. Check off two or three actions now and add more later:

- Choose whole grain varieties of bread, muffins, bagels, and rolls (whole wheat, bran, oatmeal, multigrain).

- Choose a whole grain (oatmeal, wheatena) variety when you have hot cereal, or a cold breakfast cereal that provides at least 4 grams of fiber per serving.

- Have whole wheat varieties of pancakes or waffles.

407

- In recipes that call for flour, use at least half whole wheat flour.

- For dinner at least twice a week, serve whole wheat noodles, brown rice, or bulgur (cracked wheat).

- Try higher fiber cracker varieties, such as whole rye crackers, whole grain flatbread, or some of the new multigrain crackers. Check the label to make sure you're choosing a low-fat variety.

- Once a week or more, try a low-fat meatless meal or main dish that features whole grains (spinach lasagna, red beans over brown rice, brown rice and vegetable stir-fry).

What's a whole grain? It's a grain that still has its outer covering, which contains the grain's fiber and many of its vitamins and minerals.

How Are You Doing with Fiber?

The National Cancer Institute recommends that you increase the amount of fiber in your diet to 20-30 grams of fiber a day. Fiber is found in fruits, vegetables, whole grains, cereals, dried beans, and peas. When shopping, read the food label. Foods that are high in fiber contain 5 or more grams of fiber in a serving. Use the Nutrition Facts section of the food label to compare the dietary fiber content of products before you buy foods. Compare serving sizes when comparing dietary fiber content of foods.

National Cancer Institute Dietary Guidelines

The National Cancer Institute has published dietary guidelines for the public. They are geared to cancer prevention but also are consistent with the USDA/DHHS Dietary Guidelines for Americans. The NCI Dietary Guidelines are:

- Reduce fat intake to 30 percent of calories or less.
- Increase fiber to 20-30 grams/day with an upper limit of 35 grams
- Include a variety of fruits and vegetables in the daily diet.
- Avoid obesity.
- Consume alcoholic beverages in moderation, if at all.
- Minimize consumption of salt-cured, salt-pickled, and smoked foods.

For more information on diet and cancer, call the Cancer Information Service at 1-800-4-CANCER.

Table 38.3. Counting Up Fiber

Hereís how quickly some simple food choices within a day can add up to at least 20 grams of fiber.

	Grams of fiber
Breakfast choices:	
1 oz bran flake cereal	4.0
1 medium banana	2.4
6 oz. orange juice	0.5
Lunch choices:	
1 sandwich (2 slices whole wheat bread)	3.0
2 cookies (fig bars)	2.0
1 large pear, with skin	6.2
Dinner choices:	
spaghetti (1 cup pasta)	1.1
1 and three fourths cup salad (mixed greens with carrots, broccoli, and kidney beans)	7.1

Total: 26.3

This is not intended to be a complete dayís menu, but rather, selected choices. These choices include 5 and servings of fruits and vegetables and 6 servings of grains.

Chapter 39

Can Your Kitchen Pass the Food Safety Test?

What comes to mind when you think of a clean kitchen? Shiny waxed floors? Gleaming stainless steel sinks? Spotless counters and neatly arranged cupboards?

They can help, but a truly "clean" kitchen—that is, one that ensures safe food—relies on more than just looks: It also depends on safe food practices.

In the home, food safety concerns revolve around three main functions: food storage, food handling, and cooking. To see how well you're doing in each, take this quiz, and then read on to learn how you can make the meals and snacks from your kitchen the safest possible.

Quiz

Choose the answer that best describes the practice in your household, whether or not you are the primary food handler.

1. The temperature of the refrigerator in my home is:

a. 50 degrees Fahrenheit (10 degrees Celsius)
b. 41 degrees Fahrenheit (5 degrees Celsius)
c. I don't know; I've never measured it.

FDA Consumer, October 1995 with revisions made in December 1995, Pub. No. (FDA) 96-1229.

2. The last time we had leftover cooked stew or other food with meat, chicken or fish, the food was:

a.   cooled to room temperature, then put in the refrigerator
b.   put in the refrigerator immediately after the food was served
c.   left at room temperature overnight or longer

3. The last time the kitchen sink drain, disposal and connecting pipe in my home were sanitized was:

a.   last night
b.   several weeks ago
c.   can't remember

4. If a cutting board is used in my home to cut raw meat, poultry or fish and it is going to be used to chop another food, the board is:

a.   reused as is
b.   wiped with a damp cloth
c.   washed with soap and hot water and sanitized with a mild chlorine bleach solution

5. The last time we had hamburgers in my home, I ate mine:

a.   rare
b.   medium
c.   well-done

6. The last time there was cookie dough in my home, the dough was:

a.   made with raw eggs, and I sampled some of it
b.   store-bought, and I sampled some of it
c.   not sampled until baked

7. I clean my kitchen counters and other surfaces that come in contact with food with:

a.   water
b.   hot water and soap
c.   hot water and soap, then bleach solution
d.   hot water and soap, then commercial sanitizing agent

8. When dishes are washed in my home, they are:

a. cleaned by an automatic dishwasher and then air-dried
b. left to soak in the sink for several hours and then washed with soap in the same water
c. washed right away with hot water and soap in the sink and then air-dried
d. washed right away with hot water and soap in the sink and immediately towel-dried

9. The last time I handled raw meat, poultry or fish, I cleaned my hands afterwards by:

a. wiping them on a towel
b. rinsing them under hot, cold or warm tap water
c. washing with soap and warm water

10. Meat, poultry and fish products are defrosted in my home by:

a. setting them on the counter
b. placing them in the refrigerator
c. microwaving

Answers

1. Refrigerators should stay at 41 degrees Fahrenheit (5 degrees Celsius) or less, so if you chose answer B, give yourself two points. If you didn't, you're not alone. According to Joseph Madden, Ph.D., strategic manager for microbiology in the Food and Drug Administration's Center for Food Safety and Applied Nutrition, many people overlook the importance of maintaining an appropriate refrigerator temperature.

   "According to surveys, in many households, the refrigerator temperature is above 50 degrees Fahrenheit (10 degrees Celsius)," he said. His advice: Measure the temperature with a thermometer and, if needed, adjust the refrigerator's temperature control dial.

   A temperature of 41 degrees Fahrenheit (5 degrees Celsius) or less is important because it slows the growth of most bacteria. The temperature won't kill the bacteria, but it will keep them

413

from multiplying, and the fewer there are, the less likely you are to get sick from them.

Freezing at zero degrees Fahrenheit (minus 18 degrees Celsius) or less stops bacterial growth (although it won't kill all bacteria already present).

2. Answer B is the best practice; give yourself two points if you picked it.

Hot foods should be refrigerated as soon as possible within two hours after cooking. But don't keep the food if it's been standing out for more than two hours. Don't taste test it, either. Even a small amount of contaminated food can cause illness.

Date leftovers so they can be used within a safe time. Generally, they remain safe when refrigerated for three to five days. If in doubt, throw it out, says former FDA microbiologist Jeffery Rhodehamel, now with W.R. Grace and Co.. "It's not worth a food-borne illness for the small amount of food usually involved."

3. If answer A best describes your household's practice, give yourself two points. Give yourself one point if you chose B.

According to FDA's Madden, the kitchen sink drain, disposal and connecting pipe are often overlooked, but they should be sanitized periodically by pouring down the sink a solution of 1 teaspoon (5 milliliters) of chlorine bleach in 1 quart (about 1 liter) of water or a solution of commercial kitchen cleaning agent made according to product directions. Food particles get trapped in the drain and disposal and, along with the moistness, create an ideal environment for bacterial growth.

4. If answer C best describes your household's practice, give yourself two points. Washing with soap and hot water and then sanitizing with a mild bleach solution is the safest practice, said Dhirendra Shah, Ph.D., director of the division of microbiological studies in FDA's Center for Food Safety and Applied Nutrition.

If you picked A, you're violating an important food safety rule: Never allow raw meat, poultry and fish to come in contact with other foods. Answer B isn't good, either. Improper washing, such as with a damp cloth, will not remove bacteria.

5. Give yourself two points if you picked answer C.

    The safest way to eat hamburgers is to cook them until they are no longer red in the middle and the juices run clear. That doesn't happen with rare-cooked meats, and it may not happen with medium-cooked ones. Cooking food, including ground meat patties, to an internal temperature of at least 160° F (71° C) usually protects against food-borne illness. Well-done meats reach that temperature.

    To be on the safe side, check cooked meat, fish and poultry with a meat thermometer to ensure that they have reached a safe internal temperature.

    For microwaved food, follow directions, including the standing time, either in or out of the microwave, after cooking. Microwave cooking creates pockets of heat in the food, but allowing the food to stand before eating allows the heat to spread to the rest of the food.

6. If you answered A, you may be putting yourself at risk for infection with *Salmonella enteritidis*, a bacterium that can be in shell eggs. Cooking the egg or egg-containing food product to at least 140° F (60° C) kills the bacteria. So answer C—eating the baked product—will earn you two points.

    You'll get two points for answer B, also. Foods containing raw eggs, such as homemade ice cream, cake batter, mayonnaise, and eggnog, carry a Salmonella risk, but their commercial counterparts don't. Commercial products are made with pasteurized eggs; that is, eggs that have been heated sufficiently to kill bacteria, and also may contain an acidifying agent that kills the bacteria. Commercial preparations of cookie dough are not a food hazard.

    If you want to sample homemade dough or batter or eat other foods with raw-egg-containing products, consider substituting pasteurized eggs for raw eggs. Pasteurized eggs are usually sold in the grocer's refrigerated dairy case.

7. Answers C or D will earn you two points each; answer B, one point.

    According to FDA's Madden, bleach and commercial kitchen cleaning agents are the best sanitizers—provided they're diluted according to product directions. They're the most effective at getting rid of bacteria. Hot water and soap does a good job, too, but may not kill all strains of bacteria. Water may get rid of visible dirt, but not bacteria.

Also, be sure to keep dishcloths and sponges clean because, when wet, these materials harbor bacteria and may promote their growth.

8. Answers A and C are worth two points each. There are potential problems with B and D. When you let dishes sit in water for a long time, it "creates a soup," FDA's Madden said. "The food left on the dish contributes nutrients for bacteria, so the bacteria will multiply." When washing dishes by hand, he said, it's best to wash them all within two hours. Also, it's best to air-dry them so you don't handle them while they're wet.

9. The only correct practice is answer C. Give yourself two points if you picked it.

   Wash hands with warm water and soap for at least 20 seconds before and after handling food, especially raw meat, poultry and fish. If you have an infection or cut on your hands, wear rubber or plastic gloves. Wash gloved hands just as often as bare hands because the gloves can pick up bacteria. (However, when washing gloved hands, you don't need to take off your gloves and wash your bare hands, too.)

10. Give yourself two points if you picked B or C. Food safety experts recommend thawing foods in the refrigerator or the microwave oven or putting the package in a water-tight plastic bag submerged in cold water and changing the water every 30 minutes. Changing the water ensures that the food is kept cold, an important factor for slowing bacterial growth that may occur on the outer thawed portions while the inner areas are still thawing.

    When microwaving, follow package directions. Leave about 2 inches (about 5 centimeters) between the food and the inside surface of the microwave to allow heat to circulate. Smaller items will defrost more evenly than larger pieces of food. Foods defrosted in the microwave oven should be cooked immediately after thawing. Do not thaw meat, poultry and fish products on the counter or in the sink without cold water; bacteria can multiply rapidly at room temperature.

Rating Your Home's Food Practices

20 points: Feel confident about the safety of foods served in your home.

12 to 19 points: Reexamine food safety practices in your home. Some key rules are being violated.

11 points or below: Take steps immediately to correct food handling, storage and cooking techniques used in your home. Current practices are putting you and other members of your household in danger of food-borne illness.

Home-Based Food-Borne Illness

When several members of a household come down with sudden, severe diarrhea and vomiting, intestinal flu is often considered the likely culprit. But food poisoning may be another consideration.

A true diagnosis is often never made because the ill people recover without having to see a doctor.

Health experts believe this is a common situation in households across the country, and because a doctor is often not seen for this kind of illness, the incidence of food-borne illness is not really known.

A task force of the Council for Agricultural Science and Technology, a private organization of food science groups, estimated in 1994 that 6.5 million to 33 million cases of food-borne illness occur in the United States each year. While many reported cases stem from food prepared by commercial or institutional establishments, sporadic cases and small outbreaks in homes are considered to be far more common, according to the April 1995 issue of *Food Technology*.

Cases of home-based food-borne illness may become a bigger problem, some food safety experts say, partly because today's busy family may not be as familiar with food safety issues as more home-focused families of past generations. A 1993 FDA survey found that men respondents tended to be less safe about food practices than women respondents and that respondents younger than 40 tended to be less safe than those over 40.

For example, when asked if they believed that cooked food left at room temperature overnight is safe to eat without reheating—a very unsafe practice—12 percent of the men respondents (but only 5 percent of the women respondents) said yes.

And, in looking at age differences, the survey found that nearly 40 percent of respondents younger than 40 indicated they did not adequately wash cutting boards, while only 25 percent of those 60 and over indicated the same. The increased use of convenience foods, which often are preserved with special chemicals and processes, also complicates today's home food safety practices, said Joseph Madden, Ph.D., strategic manager for microbiology in FDA's Center for Food Safety and Applied Nutrition. These foods, such as TV dinners, which are specially preserved, give consumers a false idea that equivalent home-cooked foods are equally safe, he said.

To curb the problem, food safety experts recommend food safety education that emphasizes the principles of HACCP (Hazard Analysis Critical Control Point), a new food safety procedure that many food companies are now incorporating into their manufacturing processes. Unlike past practices, HACCP focuses on preventing food-borne hazards, such as microbial contamination, by identifying points at which hazardous materials can be introduced into the food and then monitoring these potential problem areas. (See HACCP: Patrolling for Food Hazards in the January-February 1995 *FDA Consumer*.)

"It's mainly taking a common-sense approach towards food safety in the home," said FDA microbiologist Jeffery Rhodehamel.

"Basically, consumers need to make sure they're not defeating the system by contaminating the product."

More Information

FDA's Office of Consumer Affairs
HFE-88
Rockville, MD 20857

FDA Seafood Hotline
(1-800) FDA-4010
(202) 205-4314 in the Washington, D.C., area
24 hours a day

USDA's Meat and Poultry Hotline
(1-800) 535-4555
(202) 720-3333 in the Washington, D.C., area
Recorded messages available 24 hours a day. Home economists and registered dietitians available 10 a.m. to 4 p.m. Eastern time, Monday through Friday.

Also check with:
- your supermarket or its consumer affairs department
- your local county extension home economist
- local health departments
- food manufacturers

Food safety educators may contact:
Foodborne Illness Education Information Center
Food and Nutrition Information Center
National Agricultural Library/USDA
Beltsville, MD 20705-2351
Facsimile (301) 504-6409
E-mail: croberts@nalusda.gov
World Wide Web site: http://www.nalusda.gov/fnic.html

Other Kitchen Contaminants

Lead

Lead leached from some types of ceramic dinnerware into foods and beverages is often consumers' biggest source of dietary lead, says John Jones, Ph.D., strategic manager for pesticides and chemical contaminants in FDA's Center for Food Safety and Applied Nutrition. (See "Lead Threat Lessens, But Mugs Pose Problem" in the April 1993 *FDA Consumer* and "An Unwanted Souvenir: Lead in Ceramic Ware" in the December 1989-January 1990 *FDA Consumer*.) Here are some tips to reduce your exposure:

- Don't store acidic foods, such as fruit juices, in ceramic containers.

- Avoid or limit to special occasions the use of antique or collectible housewares for food and beverages.

- Follow label directions on ornamental ceramic products labeled "Not for Food Use—May Poison Food" or "For Decorative Purposes Only," and don't use these items for preparing or storing food.

- Also, don't store beverages in lead crystal containers for extended periods.

419

Microwave Packaging

High temperature use of some microwave food packaging material may cause packaging components, such as paper, adhesives and polymers, to migrate into food at excessive levels. For that reason, choose only microwave-safe cooking containers. Never use packaging cartons for cooking unless the package directs you to do so. (See "Keeping Up with the Microwave Revolution" in the March 1990 FDA Consumer.)

Aluminum

According to FDA's Jones, there has been speculation linking aluminum to Alzheimer's disease. The link has never been proved, he said, but if consumers are concerned, they should avoid cooking acidic foods, such as tomato sauce, in aluminum pans. For other uses, well-maintained aluminum pans—as well as stainless steel, copper and iron pots and pans—present no apparent hazards.

Insect and Rodent Droppings, and Dirt

Avoid storing food in cabinets that are under the sink or have water, drain and heating pipes passing through them. Food stored here can attract insects and rodents through openings that are difficult to seal adequately. Wash the tops of cans with soap and water before opening.

—by Paula Kurtzweil

Paula Kurtzweil is a member of FDA's public affairs staff.

Chapter 40

Preventing Childhood Poisoning

Most people regard their home as a safe haven, a calming oasis in an often stormy world.

But home can be a dangerous place when it comes to accidental poisoning, especially accidental poisoning of children. One tablet of some medicines can wreak havoc in or kill a child.

Childhood poisonings caused by accidental overdoses of iron-containing supplements are the biggest concern of poison control experts, consumer protection groups, and health-care providers. Iron-containing supplements are the leading cause of pediatric poisoning deaths for children under 6 in the United States. According to the American Association of Poison Control Centers, from 1986 to 1994, 38 children between the ages of 9 months and 3 years died from accidentally swallowing iron-containing products. The number of pills consumed by these children varied from as few as five to as many as 98.

In the Jan. 15, 1997, *Federal Register*, FDA published final regulations that will make it harder for small children to gain access to high-potency iron products (30 milligrams of iron or more per tablet). FDA has also taken steps to ensure that health-care providers and consumers are alerted to the dangers associated with accidental overdoses of iron-containing products, including pediatric multivitamin supplements that contain iron.

This article originally appeared in the March 1996 *FDA Consumer*. The version reproduced here is from a reprint of the original article [Publication No. (FDA) 97-1233] and contains revisions made in June 1997.

Although iron poisoning is the biggest concern when it comes to childhood poisoning, there is also concern about other drugs.

"Over-the-counter diet pills have the potential to be lethal to children, as do OTC stimulants used to keep you awake and decongestant tablets," says George C. Rodgers, M.D., Ph.D., medical director of the Kentucky Regional Poisoning Center. "Tofranil [imipramine], an antidepressant drug also used for childhood bedwetting, and Catapres [clonidine], a high blood pressure medicine, can be very hazardous because it takes very little to produce life-threatening problems in children. One tablet may do it.

"Antidepressant drugs have a high degree of toxicity," he continues. "They are cardiac and central nervous system toxins, and it doesn't take much of them to do harm, particularly in children. They are prescribed fairly ubiquitously. One of the things we look at when we get kids' poisonings is who had the medicine, and why."

Rodgers also urges extra caution when antidepressant drugs are prescribed for teenage patients who may have behavioral or emotional problems.

"Antidepressant drugs are commonly given to adolescents with behavioral problems, and often a month or two-month supply is prescribed. Teens should not be given more than a week's supply to begin with, and parents need to monitor their usage," he says.

The marketing of pediatric vitamins is also a cause of concern for Rodgers.

"Because they're marketed to look like candy or cartoon characters, it looks like candy and doesn't seem like medicine," he explains.

In addition, children frequently mimic the behavior of their parents. Children who watch their parents take pills may want to do it, too—with potentially fatal results.

Poison-Proofing Your Home

Poison-proofing your home is the key to preventing childhood poisonings. In the case of iron-containing pills or any medicine:

- Always close the container as soon as you've finished using it. Properly secure the child-resistant packaging, and put it away immediately in a place where children can't reach it.

- Keep pills in their original container.

- Keep iron-containing tablets, and all medicines, out of reach— and out of sight—of children.

- Never keep medicines on a countertop or bedside table.

- Follow medicine label directions carefully to avoid accidental overdoses or misdoses that could result in accidental poisoning.

For other substances, buy the least hazardous products that will serve your purposes. When buying art supplies, for example, look for products that are safe for children. For hazardous products such as gasoline, kerosene, and paint thinners that are often kept on hand indefinitely, buy only as much as you need and safely get rid of what you don't use. Never transfer these substances to other containers. People often use cups, soft-drink bottles, or milk cartons to store left-over paint thinner or turpentine. This is a bad idea because children associate cups and bottles with food and drink.

The kitchen and bathroom are the most likely unsafe areas. (Medicines should never be stored in the bathroom for another reason: a bathroom's warm, moist environment tends to cause changes or disintegration of the product in these rooms.) Any cabinet containing a potentially poisonous item should be locked.

"Bathrooms with medicines, kitchens with cleaning products, even cigarette butts left out, can be toxic to kids," Rodgers explains." And remember that child-resistant caps are child-resistant, not childproof. The legal definition is that it takes greater than five minutes for 80 percent of 5-year-olds to get into it: that means 20 percent can get in in less time! Kids are inventive, and can often figure it out. And left-over liquor in glasses on the counter after parties? Don't do it!"

Alcohol can cause drunkenness as well as serious poisoning leading to seizures, coma, and even death in young children. Children are more sensitive to the toxic effects of alcohol than are adults, and it doesn't take much alcohol to produce such effects. Alcohol-laced products, such as some mouthwashes, aftershaves or colognes, can cause the same problems.

Garages and utility rooms should also be checked for potential poison hazards. Antifreeze, windshield washing fluid, and other products should be stored out of children's reach in a locked cabinet. Childproof safety latches can be purchased at your local hardware store.

In the living room or family room, know your plants' names and their poison potential. Although most houseplants are not poisonous, some are. To be on the safe side, keep houseplants out of the reach of young children. Although much has been made of problems with poinsettias (blamed for a death as early as 1919), recent studies indicate it is not as highly toxic as was once believed. Although ingesting it may cause some stomach irritation and burning in the mouth, it's unlikely to be fatal.

"Plants are mostly a problem for children, since it's a natural response for children to taste things. Few adults eat houseplants," Rodgers points out. "Plants have a high capacity for making you sick, but they are usually low-risk for producing life-threatening symptoms."

After poison-proofing your home, prepare for emergencies. Post the numbers of your regional poison control center (which can be found on the inside cover of the Yellow Pages or in the white pages of your phone directory) and your doctor by the phone. Keep syrup of ipecac on hand—safely locked away, of course. (See "Antidotes.") Never administer any antidote without first checking with your doctor or poison control center.

Lead Poisoning

Although lead levels in food and drink are the lowest in history, concern remains about lead leaching into food from ceramic ware. Improperly fired or formulated glazes on ceramic ware can allow lead to leach into food or drink.

Long recognized as a toxic substance, adverse health effects can result from exposure to lead over months or years.

After a California family suffered acute lead poisoning in 1969 from drinking orange juice stored in a pitcher bought in Mexico, FDA established "action levels" for lead in ceramic ware used to serve food. Over the years, these original action levels have been revised as research has shown that exposure to even small amounts of lead can be hazardous. The last revision for ceramic foodware was in 1991. On Jan. 12, 1994, FDA published a regulation for decorative ceramic ware not intended for food use, requiring a permanently affixed label on high-lead-leaching products.

"Most lead toxicity comes from multiple exposure and is a slow accumulation over time," says Robert Mueller, a nurse and poison information specialist at the Virginia Poison Center, headquartered at The Medical College of Virginia Hospitals in Richmond. "Refusing to eat, vomiting, convulsions, and malaise can all be symptoms of lead poisoning." Because lead poisoning occurs over time, such symptoms may not show up right away. A blood test is the surest way to determine that your child has not been exposed to significant amounts of lead.

"In general, if a consumer purchases ceramic ware in the U.S. marketplace today, it meets the new action levels," says Julia Hewgley, public affairs specialist with FDA's Center for Food Safety and Applied Nutrition. "But if you travel abroad and buy ceramic ware, be aware that each country has its own safety regulations. Safety can be terribly variable depending on the type of quality control and whether the piece is made by a hobbyist." To guard against poisonings, Hewgley advises that ceramic ware not be used to store foods. Acidic foods—such as orange, tomato and other fruit juices, tomato sauces, vinegar, and wine—stored in improperly glazed containers are potentially the most dangerous. Frequently used products, like cups or pitchers, are also potentially dangerous, especially when used to hold hot, acidic foods.

"Stop using any item if the glaze shows a dusty or chalky gray residue after washing. Limit your use of antique or collectible housewares for food and beverages," she says.

"Buy one of the quick lead tests available at hardware stores and do a screening on inherited pieces."

Iron Poisoning

Iron-containing products remain the biggest problem by far when it comes to childhood poisoning. Between June 1992 and January 1993, five toddlers died after eating iron supplement tablets, according to the national Centers for Disease Control and Prevention's *Morbidity and Mortality Weekly Report* of February 19, 1993. The incidents occurred in a variety of ways: Children ate tablets from uncapped or loosely capped bottles, swallowed tablets found spilled on the floor, and, in one case, a 2-year-old fed an 11-month-old sibling tablets from a box found on the floor.

Iron is always included in prenatal vitamins prescribed for pregnant women, and is often included in multivitamin formulas and children's supplements. Usually available without prescription, iron supplements can be found in grocery stores, drugstores, and health food stores in a wide variety of potencies, ranging from 18 milligrams (mg) to 150 mg per pill. For a small child, as little as 600 mg of iron can be fatal.

Because iron supplements are typically brightly colored, some people are concerned they may look like candy, and, therefore, are particularly attractive to children. In 1993, the Nonprescription Drug Manufacturers Association (NDMA), which manufactures about 95 percent of nonprescription OTC medicines available to Americans today, adopted formulation provisions for iron products containing 30 mg or more of elemental iron per solid dosage form. These provisions also stipulated that such products would not be made with sweet coatings. That same year, NDMA manufacturers also independently agreed to develop new voluntary warning labels for these products. The voluntary labels read: "Warning: Close tightly and keep out of reach of children. Contains iron, which can be harmful or fatal to children in large doses. In case of accidental overdose, seek professional assistance or contact a poison control center immediately."

FDA's new rules, effective July 15, 1997, require unit-dose packaging for iron-containing products with 30 milligrams or more of iron per dosage unit. Because of the time and effort needed to open unit-dose products, FDA believes unit-dose packaging will discourage a youngster, or at least limit the number of tablets a child would swallow, reducing the potential for serious illness or death. This requirement is in addition to existing U.S. Consumer Product Safety Commission regulations, which require child-resistant packaging for most iron-containing products.

The new rules also now require that labels for all iron-containing products taken in solid oral dosage forms contain the following: "Warning: Accidental overdose of iron-containing products is a leading cause of fatal poisoning in children under 6. Keep this product out of reach of children. In case of accidental overdose, call a doctor or poison control center immediately." Iron is an essential nutrient sometimes lacking in people's diets, which is why iron is often recommended for people with conditions such as iron-deficiency anemia. Taken as indicated, iron is safe. But when tablets are taken beyond the proper dose in a short period, especially by toddlers or infants, serious injury or death may result.

Children poisoned with iron face immediate and long-term problems. Within minutes or hours of swallowing iron tablets, nausea, vomiting, diarrhea, and gastrointestinal bleeding can occur. These problems can progress to shock, coma, seizures, and death. Even if a child appears to have no symptoms after accidentally swallowing iron, or appears to be recovering, medical evaluation should still be sought since successful treatment is difficult once iron is absorbed from the small intestine into the bloodstream. And children who survive iron poisoning can experience other problems, such as gastrointestinal obstruction and liver damage, up to four weeks after the ingested poisoning.

FDA regulates iron-containing products as either drugs or foods, depending on the product formulation and on intended use, as defined by labeling and other information sources.

Some iron-containing products have been regulated as prescription drugs because they included pharmacologic doses of folic acid and usually were prescribed to meet high nutritional requirements during pregnancy.

Signs of Poisoning

How can you tell if your child has ingested something poisonous? "Most poisons, with the exception of lead, work fairly quickly. A key is when the child was otherwise well and in a space of hours develops unusual symptoms: They can't follow you with their eyes, they're sleepy before it's their nap time, their eyes go around in circles. Any unusual or new symptoms should make you think of poisoning as a possibility," Rodgers advises. "Poisonings typically affect the stomach and central nervous system. If a child suddenly throws up, that can be more difficult to diagnose."

Other signs of poison ingestion can be burns around the lips or mouth, stains of the substance around the child's mouth, or the smell of a child's breath. Suspect a possible poisoning if you find an opened or spilled bottle of pills.

If you suspect poisoning, remain calm. For medicines, call the nearest poison control center or your physician. For household chemical ingestion, follow first-aid instructions on the label, and then call the poison control center or your doctor. When you call, tell them your child's age, height and weight, existing health conditions, as much as you know about the substance involved, the exposure route (swallowed? inhaled? splashed in the eyes?), and if your child has vomited. If you know what substance the child has ingested, take the remaining solution or bottle with you to the phone when you call. Follow the instructions of the poison control center precisely.

Progress Against Poisonings

The nation's first poison control center opened in Chicago in 1953, after a study of accidental deaths in childhood reported a large number were due to poisoning. Since that time, a combination of public education, the use of child-resistant caps, help through poison control centers, and increased sophistication in medical care have lowered overall death rates.

Often, calling a poison center simply reassures parents that the product ingested is not poisonous. In other cases, following phone instructions prevents an emergency room trip.

427

Children are not the only victims of accidental poisonings: Older people in particular are at risk because they generally take more medicines, may have problems reading labels correctly, or may take a friend's or spouse's medicine.

In June 1995, the U.S. Consumer Product Safety Commission voted unanimously to require that child-resistant caps be made so adults—especially senior citizens—will have a less frustrating time getting them off. Because many adults who had trouble with child-resistant caps left them off, or transferred their contents to less secure packaging that endangers children, officials say the new caps will be safer for children.

"Childhood poisoning will always be a focus, because children are so vulnerable, especially children under age 5," says Ken Giles, public affairs spokesman for the Consumer Product Safety Commission. "The first two or three years of a child's life are the highest-risk time for all kinds of injuries, so there is a special need to educate new parents. It's essential we keep raising these safety messages that medicines and chemicals can be poisonous."

Antidotes

If you suspect childhood poisoning, **call the nearest poison control center or your physician first**, and follow their instructions precisely.

To induce vomiting in case of accidental poisoning, experts recommend keeping on hand syrup of ipecac—safely stored away from children, of course! Syrup of ipecac induces vomiting, thus ridding the body of the swallowed poison. It usually works within a half-hour of ingestion.

Some medical experts also recommend that parents keep activated charcoal on hand as well. You may have to ask your druggist for it, because it may not be on store shelves. Although some poison control experts recommend having activated charcoal on hand, there is a difference of opinion on its use by consumers. The U.S. Consumer Product Safety Commission, for example, does not recommend that consumers use activated charcoal because it is less palatable to young children.

Activated charcoal (or charcoal treated with substances that increase its absorption abilities) absorbs poison, preventing it from spreading throughout the body. One advantage of activated charcoal is that it can be effective for a considerable time after the poison is swallowed. But activated charcoal should never be used at the same time you administer syrup of ipecac: The charcoal will absorb the ipecac.

For children ages 1 to 12, give one tablespoon of syrup of ipecac followed by one or two glasses of water. Children ages 12 and over should get two tablespoons, followed by one or two glasses of water.

Activated charcoal is usually found in drugstores in liquid form in 30-gram doses. For children under 5, give one gram per every two pounds of body weight. Older children and adults may require much higher doses.

Both antidotes should only be used on conscious poison victims; an unconscious victim should always be treated by professionals.

"Remember to call your local poison control center first before giving your child any at-home antidote," says Robert Mueller, poison information specialist at the Virginia Poison Center in Richmond, Va.

— by Audrey T. Hingley

Audrey T. Hingley is a writer in Mechanicsville, Va.

Chapter 41

Protect Your Family from Lead-Related Hazards

Simple Steps To Protect Your Family From Lead Hazards

If you think your home has high levels of lead:

- Get your young children tested for lead, even if they seem healthy.

- Wash children's hands, bottles, pacifiers, and toys often.

- Make sure children eat healthy, low-fat foods.

- Get your home checked for lead hazards.

- Regularly clean floors, window sills, and other surfaces.

- Wipe soil off shoes before entering house.

- Talk to your landlord about fixing surfaces with peeling or chipping paint.

- Take precautions to avoid exposure to lead dust when remodeling or renovating (call 1-800-424-LEAD for guidelines).

- Don't use a belt-sander, propane torch, dry scraper, or dry sandpaper on painted surfaces that may contain lead.

- Don't try to remove lead-based paint yourself.

U.S. Environmental Protection Agency, U.S. Consumer Product Safety Commission, and U.S. Department of Housing and Urban Development, Publication No. EPA747-K-94-001, May 1995.

Are You Planning to Buy, Rent, or Renovate a Home Built Before 1978?

Many houses and apartments built before 1978 have paint that contains lead (called lead-based paint). Lead from paint, chips, and dust can pose serious health hazards if not taken care of properly. By 1996, federal law will require that individuals receive certain information before renting, buying, or renovating pre-1978 housing:

Landlords will have to disclose known information on lead-based paint hazards before leases take effect. Leases will include a federal form about lead-based paint.

Sellers will have to disclose known information on lead-based paint hazards before selling a house. Sales contracts will include a federal form about lead-based paint in the building. Buyers will have up to 10 days to check for lead hazards.

Renovators will have to give you appropriate information before starting work.

If you want more information on these requirements, call the National Lead Information Clearinghouse at 1-800-424-LEAD.

Important

Lead From Paint, Dust, and Soil Can Be Dangerous If Not Managed Properly

FACT: Lead exposure can harm young children and babies even before they are born.

FACT: Even children that seem healthy can have high levels of lead in their bodies.

FACT: People can get lead in their bodies by breathing or swallowing lead dust, or by eating soil or paint chips with lead in them.

FACT: People have many options for reducing lead hazards. In most cases, lead-based paint that is in good condition is not a hazard.

FACT: Removing lead-based paint improperly can increase the danger to your family.

If you think your home might have lead hazards, read this text to learn some simple steps to protect your family.

Lead Gets in the Body in Many Ways

One out of every 11 children in the United States has dangerous levels of lead in the bloodstream. Even children who appear healthy can have dangerous levels of lead. People can get lead in their body if they:

- Put their hands or other objects covered with lead dust in their mouths.
- Eat paint chips or soil that contain lead.
- Breathe in lead dust (especially during renovations that disturb painted surfaces).

Lead is even more dangerous to children than adults because:

- Babies and young children often put their hands and other objects in their mouths. These objects can have lead dust on them.
- Children's growing bodies absorb more lead.
- Children's brains and nervous systems are more sensitive to the damaging effects of lead.

Lead's Effects

If not detected early, children with high levels of lead in their bodies can suffer from:

- Damage to the brain and nervous system
- Behavior and learning problems (such as hyperactivity)
- Slowed growth
- Hearing problems
- Headaches

Lead is also harmful to adults. Adults can suffer from:

- Difficulties during pregnancy
- Other reproductive problems (in both men and women)
- High blood pressure
- Digestive problems
- Nerve disorders
- Memory and concentration problems
- Muscle and joint pain

Checking Your Family for Lead

Get your children tested if you think your home has high levels of lead. A simple blood test can detect high levels of lead. Blood tests are important for:

- Children who are 6 months to 1 year old (6 months if you live in an older home that might have lead in the paint).

- Family members that you think might have high levels of lead.

If your child is older than 1 year, talk to your doctor about whether your child needs testing. Your doctor or health center can do blood tests. They are inexpensive and sometimes free. Your doctor will explain what the test results mean. Treatment can range from changes in your diet to medication or a hospital stay.

Where Lead-Based Paint Is Found

In general, the older your home, the more likely it has lead-based paint. Many homes built before 1978 have lead-based paint. In 1978, the federal government banned lead-based paint from housing. Lead can be found:

- In homes in the city, country, or suburbs.

- In apartments, single-family homes, and both private and public housing.

- Inside and outside of the house.

- In soil around a home. (Soil can pick up lead from exterior paint, or other sources such as past use of leaded gas in cars.)

Where Lead Is Likely to Be a Hazard

Lead from paint chips, which you can see, and lead dust, which you can't always see, can both be serious hazards. Lead-based paint that is in good condition is usually not a hazard. Peeling, chipping, chalking, or cracking lead-based paint is a hazard and needs immediate attention.

Lead-based paint may also be a hazard when found on surfaces that children can chew or that get a lot of wear-and-tear. These areas include:

- Windows and window sills.
- Doors and door frames.
- Stairs, railings, and banisters.
- Porches and fences.

Lead dust can form when lead-based paint is dry scraped, dry sanded, or heated. Dust also forms when painted surfaces bump or rub together. Lead chips and dust can get on surfaces and objects that people touch. Settled lead dust can reenter the air when people vacuum, sweep, or walk through it.

Lead in soil can be a hazard when children play in bare soil or when people bring soil into the house on their shoes. Call your state agency (see below) to find out about soil testing for lead.

Checking Your Home for Lead Hazards

Just knowing that a home has lead-based paint may not tell you if there is a hazard. You can get your home checked for lead hazards in one of two ways, or both:

- A paint inspection tells you the lead content of every painted surface in your home. It won't tell you whether the paint is a hazard or how you should deal with it.

- A risk assessment tells you if there are any sources of serious lead exposure (such as peeling paint and lead dust). It also tells you what actions to take to address these hazards.

Have qualified professionals do the work. The federal government is writing standards for inspectors and risk assessors. Some states might already have standards in place. Call your state agency for help with locating qualified professionals in your area (see below).

Trained professionals use a range of methods when checking your home, including:

- Visual inspection of paint condition and location.
- Lab tests of paint samples.
- Surface dust tests.
- A portable x-ray fluorescence machine.

Home test kits for lead are available, but the federal government is still testing their reliability. These tests should not be the only method used before doing renovations or to assure safety.

What You Can Do Now to Protect Your Family

If you suspect that your house has lead hazards, you can take some immediate steps to reduce your family's risk:

- If you rent, notify your landlord of peeling or chipping paint.

- Clean up paint chips immediately.

- Clean floors, window frames, window sills, and other surfaces weekly. Use a mop or sponge with warm water and a general all-purpose cleaner or a cleaner made specifically for lead. **REMEMBER: NEVER MIX AMMONIA AND BLEACH PRODUCTS TOGETHER SINCE THEY CAN FORM A DANGEROUS GAS.**

- Thoroughly rinse sponges and mop heads after cleaning dirty or dusty areas.

- Wash children's hands often, especially before they eat and before nap time and bed time.

- Keep play areas clean. Wash bottles, pacifiers, toys, and stuffed animals regularly.

- Keep children from chewing window sills or other painted surfaces.

- Clean or remove shoes before entering your home to avoid tracking in lead from soil.

- Make sure children eat nutritious, low-fat meals high in iron and calcium, such as spinach and low-fat dairy products. Children with good diets absorb less lead.

How to Significantly Reduce Lead Hazards

Removing lead improperly can increase the hazard to your family by spreading even more lead dust around the house. Always use a professional who is trained to remove lead hazards safely.

In addition to day-to-day cleaning and good nutrition:

- You can temporarily reduce lead hazards by taking actions like repairing damaged painted surfaces and planting grass to cover soil with high lead levels. These actions (called "interim controls") are not permanent solutions and will not eliminate all risks of exposure.

436

- To permanently remove lead hazards, you must hire a lead "abatement" contractor. Abatement (or permanent hazard elimination) methods include removing, sealing, or enclosing lead-based paint with special materials. Just painting over the hazard with regular paint is not enough. Always hire a person with special training for correcting lead problems—someone who knows how to do this work safely and has the proper equipment to clean up thoroughly. If possible, hire a certified lead abatement contractor. Certified contractors will employ qualified workers and follow strict safety rules as set by their state or by the federal government.

Call your state agency (see below) for help with locating qualified contractors in your area and to see if financial assistance is available.

Remodeling or Renovating a Home with Lead-Based Paint

If not conducted properly, certain types of renovations can release lead from paint and dust into the air. Take precautions before you begin remodeling or renovations that disturb painted surfaces (such as scraping off paint or tearing out walls):

- Have the area tested for lead-based paint.

- Do not use a dry scraper, belt-sander, propane torch, or heat gun to remove lead-based paint. These actions create large amounts of lead dust and fumes. Lead dust can remain in your home long after the work is done.

- Temporarily move your family (especially children and pregnant women) out of the apartment or house until the work is done and the area is properly cleaned. If you can't move your family, at least completely seal off the work area.

- Follow other safety measures to reduce lead hazards. You can find out about other safety measures by calling 1-800-424-LEAD. Ask for the brochure "Reducing Lead Hazards When Remodeling Your Home." This brochure explains what to do before, during, and after renovations.

If you have already completed renovations or remodeling that could have released lead-based paint or dust, get your young children tested and follow the steps outlined above in this text.

Other Sources of Lead

While paint, dust, and soil are the most common lead hazards, other lead sources also exist.

Drinking water. Your home might have plumbing with lead or lead solder. Call your local health department or water supplier to find out about testing your water. You cannot see, smell, or taste lead, and boiling your water will not get rid of lead. If you think your plumbing might have lead in it:

- Use only cold water for drinking and cooking.

- Run water for 15 to 30 seconds before drinking it, especially if you have not used your water for a few hours.

The job. If you work with lead, you could bring it home on your hands or clothes. Shower and change clothes before coming home. Launder your clothes separately from the rest of your family's.

Toys. Old painted toys and furniture.

Food. Food and liquids stored in lead crystal or lead-glazed pottery or porcelain.

Industry. Lead smelters or other industries that release lead into the air.

Hobbies. Hobbies that use lead, such as making pottery or stained glass, or refinishing furniture.

Folk Remedies. Folk remedies that contain lead, such as "greta" and "azarcon" used to treat an upset stomach.

For More Information

The National Lead Information Center

Call 1-800-LEAD-FYI to learn how to protect children from lead poisoning.

For other information on lead hazards, call the center's clearinghouse at 1-800-424-LEAD. For the hearing impaired, call, TDD 1-800-526-5456 (FAX: 202-659-1192, Internet: EHC@CAIS.COM).

EPA's Safe Drinking Water Hotline

Call 1-800-426-4791 for information about lead in drinking water.

Consumer Product Safety Commission Hotline

To request information on lead in consumer products, or to report an unsafe consumer product or a product-related injury call 1-800-638-2772. (Internet: info@cpsc.gov). For the hearing impaired, call TDD 1-800-638-8270.

State and Environmental Agencies

Some cities and states have their own rules for lead-based paint activities. Check with your state agency (listed below) to see if state or local laws apply to you. Most state agencies can also provide information on finding a lead abatement firm in your area, and on possible sources of financial aid for reducing lead hazards.

State/Region	Phone Number	State/Region	Phone Number
Alabama	(205) 242-5661	Montana	(406) 444-3671
Alaska	(907) 465-5152	Nebraska	(402) 471-2451
Arkansas	(501) 661-2534	Nevada	(702) 687-6615
Arizona	(602) 542-7307	New Hampshire	(603) 271-4507
California	(510) 450-2424	New Jersey	(609) 633-2043
Colorado	(303) 692-3012	New Mexico	(505) 841-8024
Connecticut	(203) 566-5808	New York	(800) 458-1158
Washington, DC	(202) 727-9850	North Carolina	(919) 715-3293
Delaware	(302) 739-4735	North Dakota	(701) 328-5188
Florida	(904) 488-3385	Ohio	(614) 466-1450
Georgia	(404) 657-6514	Oklahoma	(405) 271-5220
Hawaii	(808) 832-5860	Oregon	(503) 248-5240
Idaho	(208) 332-5544	Pennsylvania	(717) 782-2884
Illinois	(800) 545-2200	Rhode Island	(401) 277-3424
Indiana	(317) 382-6662	South Carolina	(803) 935-7945
Iowa	(800) 972-2026	South Dakota	(605) 773-3153
Kansas	(913) 296-0189	Tennessee	(615) 741-5683
Kentucky	(502) 564-2154	Texas	(512) 834-6600
Louisiana	(504) 765-0219	Utah	(801) 536-4000
Massachusetts	(800) 532-9571	Vermont	(802) 863-7231
Maryland	(410) 631-3859	Virginia	(800) 523-4019
Maine	(207) 287-4311	Washington	(206) 753-2556
Michigan	(517) 335-8885	West Virginia	(304) 558-2981
Minnesota	(612) 627-5498	Wisconsin	(608) 266-5885
Mississippi	(601) 960-7463	Wyoming	(307) 777-7391
Missouri	(314) 526-4911		

EPA Regional Offices

Your Regional EPA Office can provide further information regarding regulations and lead protection programs.

EPA Regional Offices

Region 1 (CT, MA, ME, NH, RI, VT)
John F. Kennedy Federal Bldg.
One Congress Street
Boston, MA 02203
(617) 565-3420

Region 2 (NJ, NY, PR, VI)
Building 5
2890 Woodbridge Avenue
Edison, NJ 08837-3679
(908) 321-6671

Region 3 (DE, DC, MD, PA, VA, WV)
841 Chestnut Building
Philadelphia, PA 19107
(215) 597-9800

Region 4 (AL, FL, GA, KY, MS, NC, SC, TN)
345 Courtland Street, NE
Atlanta, GA 30365
(404) 347-4727

Region 5 (IL, IN, MI, MN, OH, WI)
77 West Jackson Boulevard
Chicago, IL 60604-3590
(312) 886-6003

Region 6 (AR, LA, NM, OK, TX)
First Interstate Bank Tower
1445 Ross Avenue, 12th Floor, Suite 1200
Dallas, TX 75202-2733
(214) 665-7244

Region 7 (IA, KS, MO, NE)
726 Minnesota Avenue
Kansas City, KS 66101
(913) 551-7020

Region 8 (CO, MT, ND, SD, UT, WY)
999 18th Street, Suite 500
Denver, CO 80202-2405
(303) 293-1603

Region 9 (AZ, CA, HI, NV)
75 Hawthorne Street
San Francisco, CA 94105
(415) 744-1124

Region 10 (ID, OR, WA, AK)
1200 Sixth Avenue
Seattle, WA 98101
(206) 553-1200

CPSC Regional Offices

Eastern Regional Center
6 World Trade Center
Vesey Street, Room 350
New York, NY 10048
(212) 466-1612

Central Regional Center
230 South Dearborn Street
Room 2944
Chicago, IL 60604-1601
(312) 353-8260

Western Regional Center
600 Harrison Street, Room 245
San Francisco, CA 94107
(415) 744-2966

440

Chapter 42

Protect Your Family and Yourself from Carbon Monoxide Poisoning

Carbon Monoxide Can Be Deadly

You can't see or smell carbon monoxide, but at high levels it can kill a person in minutes. Carbon monoxide (CO) is produced whenever any fuel such as gas, oil, kerosene, wood, or charcoal is burned. If appliances that burn fuel are maintained and used properly, the amount of CO produced is usually not hazardous. However, if appliances are not working properly or are used incorrectly, dangerous levels of CO can result. Hundreds of people die accidentally every year from CO poisoning caused by malfunctioning or improperly used fuel-burning appliances. Even more die from CO produced by idling cars. Fetuses, infants, elderly people, and people with anemia or with a history of heart or respiratory disease can be especially susceptible. Be safe. Practice the DO's and DON'Ts of carbon monoxide.

CO Poisoning Symptoms

Know the symptoms of CO poisoning. At moderate levels, you or your family can get severe headaches, become dizzy, mentally confused, nauseated, or faint. You can even die if these levels persist for a long time. Low levels can cause shortness of breath, mild nausea, and mild headaches, and may have longer term effects on your health. Since many of these symptoms are similar to those of the flu, food

United States Environmental Protection Agency, Indoor Environments Division, Office of Air and Radiation, EPA-402-F-96-005, October 1996.

poisoning, or other illnesses, you may not think that CO poisoning could be the cause.

Play it Safe

If you experience symptoms that you think could be from CO poisoning:

- DO GET FRESH AIR IMMEDIATELY. Open doors and windows, turn off combustion appliances and leave the house.

- DO GO TO AN EMERGENCY ROOM and tell the physician you suspect CO poisoning. If CO poisoning has occurred, it can often be diagnosed by a blood test done soon after exposure.

- DO BE PREPARED TO ANSWER the following questions for the doctor: Do your symptoms occur only in the house? Do they disappear or decrease when you leave home and reappear when you return?

  1. Is anyone else in your household complaining of similar symptoms? Did everyone's symptoms appear about the same time?

  2. Are you using any fuel-burning appliances in the home?

  3. Has anyone inspected your appliances lately? Are you certain they are working properly?

Prevention Is the Key to Avoiding Carbon Monoxide Poisoning

- DO have your fuel-burning appliances—including oil and gas furnaces, gas waterheaters, gas ranges and ovens, gas dryers, gas or kerosene space heaters, fireplaces, and wood stoves—inspected by a trained professional at the beginning of every heating season. Make certain that the flues and chimneys are connected, in good condition, and not blocked.

- DO choose appliances that vent their fumes to the outside whenever possible, have them properly installed, and maintain them according to manufacturers' instructions.

- DO read and follow all of the instructions that accompany any fuel-burning device. If you cannot avoid using an unvented gas or kerosene space heater, carefully follow the cautions that come with the device. Use the proper fuel and keep doors to the rest of the house open. Crack a window to ensure enough air for ventilation and proper fuel-burning.

• DO call EPA's IAQINFO Clearinghouse (1-800-438-4318) or the Consumer Product Safety Commission (1-800-638-2772) for more information on how to reduce your risks from CO and other combustion gases and particles.

• DON'T idle the car in a garage—even if the garage door to the outside is open. Fumes can build up very quickly in the garage and living area of your home.

• DON'T use a gas oven to heat your home, even for a short time.

• DON'T ever use a charcoal grill indoors—even in a fireplace.

• DON'T sleep in any room with an unvented gas or kerosene space heater.

• DON'T use any gasoline-powered engines (mowers, weed trimmers, snow blowers, chain saws, small engines or generators) in enclosed spaces.

• DON'T ignore symptoms, particularly if more than one person is feeling them. You could lose consciousness and die if you do nothing.

A Few Words about CO Detectors

Carbon Monoxide Detectors are widely available in stores and you may want to consider buying one as a back-up—BUT NOT AS A REPLACEMENT for proper use and maintenance of your fuel-burning appliances. However, it is important for you to know that the technology of CO detectors is still developing, that there are several types on the market, and that they are not generally considered to be as reliable as the smoke detectors found in homes today. Some CO detectors have been laboratory-tested, and their performance varied. Some performed well, others failed to alarm even at very high CO levels, and still others alarmed even at very low levels that don't pose any immediate health risk. And unlike a smoke detector, where you can easily confirm the cause of the alarm, CO is invisible and odorless, so it's harder to tell if an alarm is false or a real emergency.

So what's a consumer to do?

First, don't let buying a CO detector lull you into a false sense of security. Preventing CO from becoming a problem in your home is better than relying on an alarm. Follow the checklist of DOs and DON'Ts.

Second, if you shop for a CO detector, do some research on features and don't select solely on the basis of cost. Non-governmental organizations such as Consumers Union (publisher of Consumer Reports), the American Gas Association, and Underwriters Laboratories (UL) can help you make an informed decision. Look for UL certification on any detector you purchase.

Carefully follow manufacturers' instructions for its placement, use, and maintenance.

If the CO detector alarm goes off:

• Make sure it is your CO detector and not your smoke detector.

• Check to see if any member of the household is experiencing symptoms of poisoning.

• If they are, get them out of the house immediately and seek medical attention. Tell the doctor that you suspect CO poisoning.

• If no one is feeling symptoms, ventilate the home with fresh air, turn off all potential sources of CO—your oil or gas furnace, gas water heater, gas range and oven, gas dryer, gas or kerosene space heater and any vehicle or small engine.

• Have a qualified technician inspect your fuel-burning appliances and chimneys to make sure they are operating correctly and that there is nothing blocking the fumes from being vented out of the house.

Chapter 43

A Guide to Protecting Yourself and Your Family from Radon

Surgeon General Health Advisory

"Indoor radon gas is a national health problem. Radon causes thousands of deaths each year. Millions of homes have elevated radon levels. Homes should be tested for radon. When elevated levels are confirmed, the problem should be corrected."

The U.S. Environmental Protection Agency (EPA) Recommends

- Test your home for radon—it's easy and inexpensive.

- Fix your home if your radon level is 4 picocuries per liter(pCi/L) or higher.

- Radon levels less than 4 pCi/L still pose a risk, and in many, cases may be reduced.

Radon is estimated to cause thousands of cancer deaths in the U.S. each year. Radon is estimated to cause about 14,000 deaths per year— however, this number could range from 7,000 to 30,000 deaths per year.

A Citizen's Guide To Radon (Second Edition), United States Environmental Protection Agency, U.S. Department of Health and Human Services, and U.S. Public Health Service, September 1994.

Overview

Radon is a cancer-causing, radioactive gas. You can't see radon. And you can't smell it or taste it. But it may be a problem in your home.

Radon is estimated to cause many thousands of deaths each year. That's because when you breathe air containing radon, you can get lung cancer. In fact, the Surgeon General has warned that radon is the second leading cause of lung cancer in the United States today. Only smoking causes more lung cancer deaths. If you smoke and your home has high radon levels, your risk of lung cancer is especially high.

Radon comes from the natural (radioactive) breakdown of uranium in soil, rock, and water and gets into the air you breathe. Radon can be found all over the U.S. It can get into any type of building—homes, offices, and schools—and build up to high levels. But you and your family are most likely to get your greatest exposure at home. That's where you spend most of your time.

You should test for radon. Testing is the only way to know if you and your family are at risk from radon. EPA and the Surgeon General recommend testing all homes below the third floor for radon. EPA also recommends testing in schools.

Testing is inexpensive and easy—it should only take a few minutes of your time. Millions of Americans have already tested their homes for radon.

You can fix a radon problem. There are simple ways to fix a radon problem that aren't too costly. Even very high levels can be reduced to acceptable levels.

How Does Radon Get Into Your Home?

Radon is a radioactive gas. It comes from the natural decay of uranium that is found in nearly all soils. It typically moves up through the ground to the air above and into your home through cracks and other holes in the foundation. Your home traps radon inside, where it can build up. Any home may have a radon problem. This means new and old homes, well-sealed and drafty homes, and homes with or without basements.

Radon from soil gas is the main cause of radon problems. Sometimes radon enters the home through well water. In a small number of homes, the building materials can give off radon, too. However, building materials rarely cause radon problems by themselves.

Nearly 1 out of every 15 homes in the U.S. is estimated to have elevated radon levels. Elevated levels of radon gas have been found in homes in your state. Contact your state radon office (see the list at the end of this chapter) for general information about radon in your area. While radon problems may be more common in some areas, any home may have a problem. The only way to know about your home is to test.

Radon can be a problem in schools and workplaces, too. Ask your state radon office about radon problems in schools and workplaces in your area.

Radon Gets in Your Home Through

- Cracks in solid floors
- Construction joints
- Cracks in walls
- Gaps in suspended floors
- Gaps around service pipes
- Cavities inside walls
- The water supply

How to Test Your Home

You can't see radon, but it's not hard to find out if you have a radon problem in your home. All you need to do is test for radon. Testing is easy and should only take a few minutes of your time.

The amount of radon in the air is measured in "picocuries per liter of air," or "pCi/L." Sometimes test results are expressed in Working Levels (WL) rather than picocuries per liter (pCi/L). There are many kinds of low-cost "do it yourself" radon test kits you can get through the mail and in hardware stores and other retail outlets. Make sure you buy a test kit that has passed EPA's testing program or is state-certified. These kits will usually display the phrase "Meets EPA Requirements." If you prefer, or if you are buying or selling a home, you can hire a trained contractor to do the testing for you. Make certain you hire an EPA-qualified or state-certified radon tester. Call your state radon office for a list of these testers.

There are Two General Ways to Test for Radon

Short-Term Testing. The quickest way to test is with short-term tests. Short-term tests remain in your home for two days to 90 days, depending on the device. "Charcoal canisters," "alpha track," "electret ion chamber," "continuous monitors," and "charcoal liquid scintillation" detectors are most commonly used for short-term testing.

447

Because radon levels tend to vary from day to day and season to season, a short-term test is less likely than a long-term test to tell you your year-round average radon level. If you need results quickly, however a short-term test followed by a second short-term test may be used to decide whether to fix your home.

Long-Term Testing. Long-term tests remain in your home for more than 90 days. "Alpha track" and "electret" detectors are commonly used for this type of testing. A long-term test will give you a reading that is more likely to tell you your home's year-round average radon level than a short-term test.

How To Use a Test Kit

Follow the instructions that come with your test kit. If you are doing a short-term test, close your windows and outside doors and keep them closed as much as possible during the test. (If you are doing a short-term test lasting just 2 or 3 days, be sure to close your windows and outside doors at least 12 hours before beginning the test, too. You should not conduct short-term tests lasting just 2 or 3 days during unusually severe storms or periods of unusually high winds.) The test kit should be placed in the lowest lived-in level of the home (for example, the basement if it is frequently used, otherwise the first floor). It should be put in a room that is used regularly (like a living room, playroom, den or bedroom) but **not** your kitchen or bathroom. Place the kit at least 20 inches above the floor in a location where it won't be disturbed—away from drafts, high heat, high humidity, and exterior walls. Leave the kit in place for as long as the package says. Once you've finished the test, reseal the package and send it to the lab specified on the package right away for study. You should receive your test results within a few weeks.

EPA Recommends the Following Testing Steps

Step 1. Take a short-term test. If your result is 4 pCi/L or higher (0.02 Working Levels—WL—or higher) take a follow-up test (Step 2) to be sure.

Step 2. Follow up with either a long-term test or a second short-term test: For a better understanding of your year-round average radon level, take a long-term test; if you need results quickly, take a second short-term test. The higher your initial short-term test result, the more certain you can be that you should take a short-term rather than a long-term follow up test. If your first short-term test result is several times the action level—for example, about 10 pCi/L or higher— you should take a second short-term test immediately.

Step 3. If you followed up with a long-term test: Fix your home if your long-term test result is 4 pCi/L or more (0.02 WL or higher). If you followed up with a second short-term test: The higher your short-term results, the more certain you can be that you should fix your home. Consider fixing yow home if the average of your first and second test is 4pCi/L (0.02 WL) or higher.

What Your Test Results Mean

The average indoor radon level is estimated to be about 1.3 pCi/L, and about 0.4 pCi/L of radon is normally found in the outside air. The U.S. Congress has set a long-term goal that indoor radon levels be no more than outdoor levels. While this goal is not yet technologically achievable in all cases, most homes today can be reduced to 2 pCi/L or below.

Sometimes short-term tests are less definitive about whether or not your home is above 4 pCi/L. This can happen when your results are close to 4 pCi/L. For example, if the average of your two short-term test results is 4.1 pCi/L, there is about a 50% chance that your year-round average is somewhat below 4 pCi/L. However, EPA believes that any radon exposure carries some risk—no level of radon is safe. Even radon levels below 4 pCi/L pose some risk, and you can reduce your risk of lung cancer by lowering your radon level. If your living patterns change and you begin occupying a lower level of your home (such as a basement) you should retest your home on that level. Even if your test result is below 4 pCi/L, you may want to test again some-time in the future.

Radon and Home Sales

More and more, home buyers and renters are asking about radon levels before they buy or rent a home. Because real estate sales happen quickly, there is often little time to deal with radon and other is-sues. The best thing to do is to test for radon NOW and save the results in case the buyer is interested in them. Fix a problem if it exists so it won't complicate your home sale. If you are planning to move, call your state radon office for EPA's pamphlet "Home Buyer's and Seller's Guide to Radon," which addresses some common questions. During home sales:

• Buyers often ask if a home has been tested, and if elevated levels were reduced.

• Buyers frequently want tests made by someone who is not involved in the home sale. Your state office has a list of qualified testers.

• Buyers might want to know the radon levels in areas of the home (like a basement they plan to finish) that the seller might not otherwise test.

Today many homes are built to prevent radon from coming in. Your state or local area may require these radon-resistant construction features. Radon-resistant construction features usually keep radon levels in new homes below 2 pCi/L. If you are buying or renting a new home, ask the owner or builder if it has radon-resistant features.

Radon in Water

Compared to radon entering the home through soil, radon entering the home through water will in most cases be a small source of risk. Radon gas can enter the home through well water. It can be released into the air you breathe when water is used for showering and other household uses. Research suggests that swallowing water with high radon levels may pose risks, too, although risks from swallowing water containing radon are believed to be much lower than those from breathing air containing radon.

While radon in water is not a problem in homes served by most public water supplies, it has been found in well water. If you've tested the air in your home and found a radon problem, and your water comes from a well, contact a lab certified to measure radiation in water to have your water tested. If you're on a public water supply and are concerned that radon may be entering your home through the water, call your public water supplier.

Radon problems in water can be readily fixed. The most effective treatment is to remove radon from the water before it enters the home. This is called point-of-entry treatment. Treatment at your water tap is called point-of-use treatment. Unfortunately, point-of-use treatment will not reduce most of the inhalation risk from radon.

Call your state office or the EPA Drinking Water Hotline (800-426-4791) for more information on radon in water.

How to Lower the Radon Level in Your Home

Since there is no known safe level of radon, there can always be some risk. But the risk can be reduced by lowering the radon level in your home.

A variety of methods are used to reduce radon in your home. In some cases, sealing cracks in floors and walls may help to reduce radon. In other cases, simple systems using pipes and fans may be used to reduce radon. Such systems are called "sub-slab depressurization," and do not require major changes to your home. These systems remove radon gas from below the concrete floor and the foundation before it can enter the home. Similar systems can also be installed in houses with crawl spaces. Radon contractors use other methods that may also work in your home. The right system depends on the design of your home and other factors.

Ways to reduce radon in your home are discussed in EPA's "Consumer's Guide to Radon Reduction." You can get a copy from your state radon office.

The cost of making repairs to reduce radon depends on how your home was built and the extent of the radon problem. Most homes can be fixed for about the same cost as other common home repairs like painting or having a new hot water heater installed. The average house costs about $1,200 for a contractor to fix, although this can range from about $500 to about $2,500.

Lowering high radon levels requires technical knowledge and special skills. You should use a contractor who is trained to fix radon problems. The EPA Radon Contractor Proficiency (RCP) Program tests these contractors. EPA provides a list of RCP contractors to state radon offices. A contractor who has passed the EPA test will carry a special RCP identification card. A trained RCP contractor can study the radon problem in your home and help you pick the right treatment method.

Check with your state radon office for names of qualified or state certified radon contractors in your area. Picking someone to fix your radon problem is much like choosing a contractor for other home repairs—you may want to get references and more than one estimate.

If you plan to fix the problem in your home yourself, you should first contact your state radon office for EPA's technical guide, "Radon Reduction Techniques for Detached Houses." You should also test your home again after it is fixed to be sure that radon levels have been reduced. Most radon reduction systems include a monitor that will alert you if the system needs servicing. In addition, it's a good idea to retest your home sometime in the future to be sure radon levels remain low.

Radon and Home Renovations

If you are planning any major structural renovation, such as converting an unfinished basement area into living space, it is especially important to test the area for radon before you begin the renovation. If your test results indicate a radon problem, radon-resistant techniques can be inexpensively included as part of the renovation. Because major renovations can change the level of radon in any home, always test again after work is completed.

The Risk of Living with Radon

Radon gas decays into radioactive particles that can get trapped in your lungs when you breathe. As they break down further, these particles release small bursts of energy. This can damage lung tissue and lead to lung cancer over the course of your lifetime. Not everyone exposed to elevated levels of radon will develop lung cancer. And the amount of time between exposure and the onset of the disease may be many years.

Like other environmental pollutants, there is some uncertainty about the magnitude of radon health risks. However, we know more about radon risks than risks from most other cancer-causing substances. This is because estimates of radon risks are based on studies of cancer in humans (underground miners). Additional studies on more typical populations are under way.

Smoking combined with radon is an especially serious health risk. Stop smoking and lower your radon level to reduce your lung cancer risk.

Children have been reported to have greater risk than adults of certain types of cancer from radiation, but there are currently no conclusive data on whether children are at greater risk than adults from radon.

Your chances of getting lung cancer from radon depend mostly on:

- How much radon is in your home
- The amount of time you spend in your home
- Whether you are a smoker or have ever smoked

It's never too late to reduce your risk of lung cancer. Don't wait to test and fix a radon problem. If you are a smoker, stop smoking.

Radon Myths

MYTH: Scientists aren't sure radon really is a problem.

FACT: Although some scientists dispute the precise number of deaths due to radon, all major health organizations (like the Centers for Disease Control, the American Lung Association and the American Medical Association) agree with estimates that radon causes thousands of preventable lung cancer deaths every year. This is especially true among smokers, since the risk to smokers is much greater than to non-smokers.

MYTH: Radon testing is difficult, time-consuming and expensive.

FACT: Radon testing is inexpensive and easy—it should take only a little of your time.

MYTH: Radon test kits are not reliable and are difficult to find.

FACT: Reliable test kits are available through the mail, in hardware stores and other retail outlets. Call your state radon office for a list of test kit companies that have met EPA requirements for reliability or are state certified.

MYTH: Homes with radon problems can't be fixed.

FACT: There are simple solutions to radon problems in homes. Thousands of homeowners have already fixed radon problems in their homes. Radon levels can be readily lowered for about $500 to $2,500. Call your state radon office for a list of contractors that have met EPA requirements or are state certified.

MYTH: Radon only affects certain kinds of homes.

FACT: House construction can affect radon levels. However, radon can be a problem in homes of all types: old homes, new homes, drafty homes, insulated homes, homes with basements, homes without basements.

MYTH: Radon is only a problem in certain parts of the country.

FACT: High radon levels have been found in every state. Radon problems do vary from area to area, but the only way to know your radon level is to test.

MYTH: A neighbor's test result is a good indication of whether your home has a problem.

FACT: It's not. Radon levels vary from home to home. The only way to know if your home has a radon problem is to test it.

MYTH: Everyone should test their water for radon.

FACT: While radon gets into some homes through the water, you should first test the air in your home for radon. If you find high levels and your water comes from a well, contact a lab certified to measure radiation in water to have your water tested.

MYTH: It's difficult to sell homes where radon problems have been discovered.

FACT: Where radon problems have been fixed, home sales have not been blocked or frustrated. The added protection is sometimes a good selling point.

MYTH: I've lived in my home for so long, it doesn't make sense to take action now.

FACT: You will reduce your risk of lung cancer when you reduce radon levels, even if you've lived with a radon problem for a long time.

MYTH: Short-term tests can't be used for making a decision about whether to fix your home.

FACT: A short-term test followed by a second short-term test may be used to decide whether to fix your home. However, the closer the average of your two short-term tests is to 4 pCi/L, the less certain you can be about whether your year-round average is above or below that level. Keep in mind that radon levels below 4 pCi/L still pose some risk. Radon levels can be reduced in most homes to 2 pCi/L or below.

State Radon Contacts

Alabama	(800) 582-1866	Colorado	(800) 846-3986
Alaska	(800) 478-8324	Connecticut	(203) 566-3122
Arizona	(602) 255-4845	Delaware	(800) 554-4636
Arkansas	(501) 661-2301	District of Columbia	(202) 727-5728
California	(800) 745-7236	Florida	(800) 543-8279

Georgia	(800) 745-0037	New Jersey	(800) 648-0394
Hawaii	(808) 586-4700	New Mexico	(505) 827-4300
Idaho	(800) 445-8647	New York	(800) 458-1158
Illinois	(800) 325-1245	North Carolina	(919) 571-4141
Indiana	(800) 272-9723	North Dakota	(701) 221-5188
Iowa	(800) 383-5992	Ohio	(800) 523-4439
Kansas	(913) 296-6183	Oklahoma	(405) 271-1902
Kentucky	(502) 564-3700	Oregon	(503) 731-4014
Louisiana	(800) 256-2494	Pennsylvania	(800) 237-2366
Maine	(800) 232-0842	Puerto Rico	(809) 767-3563
Maryland	(800) 872-3666	Rhode Island	(401) 277-2438
Massachusetts	(413) 586-7525	South Carolina	(800) 768-0362
Michigan	(800) 723-6642	South Dakota	(800) 438-3367
Minnesota	(800) 798-9050	Tennessee	(800) 232-1139
Mississippi	(800) 626-7739	Texas	(512) 834-6688
Missouri	(800) 669-7236	Utah	(800) 536-4250
Montana	(406) 444-3671	Vermont	(800) 640-0601
Nebraska	(800) 334-9491	Virginia	(800) 468-0138
Nevada	(702) 687-5394	West Virginia	(800) 922-1255
New Hampshire	(800) 852-3345 x4674	Wisconsin	(608) 267-4795
		Wyoming	(800) 458-5847

Indian Nations

All Indian Pueblo Council	(505) 881-2254
Cherokee Nation	(918) 458 5496
Chickasaw Nation	(405) 436-2603
Hopi Tribe	(602) 734-2441
Inner Tribal Council	(602) 248-0071
Jicarilla Apache Tribe	(505) 759-3242
Navajo Nation	(602) 871-7754
Oneida Indian Nation	(315) 361-6300
Seneca Nation	(716) 532-0024
St. Regis Mohawk Tribe	(518) 358-3141

For Indian Nations in the States of MN, WI, IL, MI, IN, and OH, call (312) 886-6063

For Further Information

For more information on how to reduce your radon health risk, ask your state radon office to send you these guides:

455

- Home Buyer's and Seller's Guide to Radon
- Radon in Schools
- Radon: A Physician's Guide
- Consumer's Guide to Radon Reduction
- Technical Support Document

If you plan to make repairs yourself, be sure to contact your state radon office for a current copy of EPA's technical guidance on radon mitigation, "Application of Radon Reduction Techniques for Detached Houses."

Chapter 44

Protect Your Family from Fire and Electrical Hazards

Introduction

The United States has one of the highest fire death and injury rates in the world. Fire—in the form of flames and smoke—is the second leading cause of accidental death in the home.

More than 4,000 people die each year in home fires. Every year, there are more than 500,000 residential fires serious enough to be reported to fire departments. More than 90 percent of residential fire deaths and injuries result from fires in one and two family houses and apartments. Property losses exceed 4 billion dollars annually, and the long term emotional damage to victims and their loved ones is incalculable.

The U.S. Consumer Product Safety Commission (CPSC) has targeted the principal consumer products associated with fires, namely home heating devices, upholstered furniture, bedding, cigarette lighters, matches, and wearing apparel. The Commission is participating in a special Congressionally authorized study of cigarette-ignited fires, which cause more deaths than any other kind of fire. The Commission continues to push for extensive use of smoke detectors. With the help of concerned consumers, the number of residential fires has declined about 30 percent since 1980.

This chapter contains text excerpted from "Your Home Fire Safety Checklist," an undated publication of the U.S. Consumer Product Safety Commission, and "Electrical Safety," information provided by the National Electrical Safety Foundation (Rosslyn, Virginia), reprinted with permission.

457

The CPSC is fulfilling its role to make products inherently more fire safe. We recognize that much more can be done to cut down on the needlessly high and tragic fire toll by an alert and informed public. Many of the injuries associated with flammable products result from hazards that are overlooked. Fire experts agree that one key to fewer fires is a greater awareness of how accidents can be prevented. By spotting these hazards and taking some simple precautions, many fires and fire-related injuries can be prevented.

Use the checklist in this chapter as a safety guide to spot possible fire safety problems which may be present in your home. It is a first step in reducing the risk of fire. Answer YES or NO to answer each of the following questions. If you answer NO to any question, the potential hazard should be corrected to avoid the risk of injury or death.

Sources of Fire

Supplemental Home Heating

The use of supplemental room heaters, such as wood and coal burning stoves, kerosene heaters, gas space heaters and electrical heaters, has decreased, along with the number of residential fires.

Even though there has been a decrease in fires associated with supplemental heaters, it is important to remember that about 120,000 residential fires still occur annually with the use of these heaters, or about 22 percent of all residential fires. These fires kill more than 600 people. Annually there are thousands of contact burn injuries and hundreds of carbon monoxide poisonings.

Wood Stoves

You should be able to respond "yes" to the following safety statements.

1. The wood stove or fireplace has been installed according to existing building codes and manufacturer's instructions.

2. The chimney and stovepipe are checked frequently during the heating season for creosote buildup and are cleaned when necessary.

3. The stove sits on a non-combustible or on a code-specified or listed floor protector.

4. Combustibles such as curtains, chairs, firewood, etc., are at least three feet away from the stove.

5. Only proper fuel is used in the stove.

6. A metal container with a tight-fitting lid is used for ash removal.

Recommendations:

- Do not use wood burning stoves and fireplaces unless they are properly installed and meet building codes.

- Follow the label instructions on the stove which recommends an inspection twice monthly. Have chimneys inspected and cleaned by a professional chimney sweep. Creosote is an unavoidable product of wood burning stoves. Creosote builds up in chimney flues and can cause a chimney fire. To cut down on creosote buildup, avoid smoldering fires.

- Use a code-specified or listed floor protector. It should extend 18 inches beyond the stove on all sides. This will reduce the possibility of the floor being ignited.

- Follow the instructions on the stove label for proper location of the stove from combustible walls.

- Never burn trash in a stove because this could over heat the stove. Gasoline and other flammable liquids should never be used to start wood stove fires. Gasoline will ignite and explode. Use coal only if designated as appropriate by the manufacturer.

Kerosene Heaters

You should be able to respond "yes" to the following safety statements.

1. Only 1-K kerosene is used and it is bought from a dealer who can certify that the product is 1-K kerosene.

2. The heater is placed out of the path of traffic areas such as doorways and hallways.

3. Kerosene is stored outdoors, and out of the reach of children in a tightly sealed, preferably blue plastic or metal container, labeled "kerosene."

4. No attempt is to be made to move the heater if flare-up (flames outside the heater cabinet) occurs. The fire department is called immediately.

459

5. The heater is used in well ventilated rooms.

6. The heater is turned off while sleeping and is never left operating unattended.

7. The heater is placed at least three feet away from anything that might catch fire such as clothing, furniture, curtains, etc.

Recommendations:

- Check with your local fire marshal regarding local and state codes and regulations for using a kerosene heater.

- NEVER USE GASOLINE. Even small amounts of gasoline mixed with kerosene can increase the risk of fire.

- Use properly labeled containers. It reduces the likelihood of mistaking gasoline for kerosene.

- Place heater so it will not be knocked over or trap you in case of fire.

- Use 1-K kerosene because grades other than 1-K contain much more sulfur and will increase sulfur dioxide emissions, posing a possible health problem. If you buy kerosene from a gasoline station make sure you and/or the attendant are using the kerosene pump, not the gasoline pump.

- Never fill the heater while it is operating. Always refuel the heater outdoors to prevent spillage on floors and rugs which could later result in fire ignition.

- Keep the room in which the heater operates ventilated (e.g. door open or the window ajar). This will prevent an indoor air pollution problem and minimize health problems. Kerosene heaters are not usually vented.

- Keep flammable liquids and fabrics away from an open flame.

- Never try to move the heater or try to smother the flames with a rug or a blanket if a flare-up occurs. Activate the manual shut-off switch and call the fire department. Moving the heater may increase the height of the flames and cause leakage resulting in personal injury.

Gas-Fired Space Heaters

You should be able to respond "yes" to the following safety statements.

1. Only vented heaters are installed or used in sleeping quarters.

2. Vented heaters are properly vented to the outside.

3. The unvented gas-fired room heater has a warning label and instructions that are followed.

4. The unvented gas-fired room heater has a label stating it has a "pilot safety system" which turns off the gas if not enough fresh air is available.

5. The vented heater has a label stating that is equipped with a vent safety shutoff system.

6. If the heater uses liquefied petroleum (LP) gas, the container is located outside the house.

7. The manufacturer's instructions for lighting the pilot are followed.

8. Matches are lighted before turning on the gas if pilot lighting is required.

9. Flammable materials and liquids are kept away from gas heating appliances.

Recommendations:

*   Follow the manufacturer's instructions regarding where and how to use gas space heaters. Unvented heaters should not be used in small enclosed areas, especially bedrooms because of the potential for carbon monoxide poisoning.

*   Do not use a propane heater (LP) which has a gas cylinder stored in the body of the heater. Its use is prohibited in most states and localities in the United States.

*   Follow the manufacturer's instructions for lighting the pilot. Gas vapors may accumulate and ignite explosively, burning your hand or face.

*   Light matches, if needed for lighting the pilot, before turning on the gas to prevent gas buildup.

*   Do not operate a vented style heater unvented. It could allow combustion products, including carbon monoxide, to reach dangerous levels which will result in illness and death.

Portable Electric Heaters

The Commission estimates that half the deaths and one-third of the injuries resulting from electric heater fires occurred at night when family members were asleep and the heater unattended. The Commission is also concerned about the use of power or extension cords which can be too small to supply the amount of current required by the typical portable electric heater.

You should be able to respond "yes" to the following safety statements.

1. The heater is operated at least three feet away from upholstered furniture, drapes, bedding and other combustible materials.

2. The extension cord (if used) is marked #14 or #12 American Wire Gauge (AWG).

3. The heater is used on the floor.

4. The heater is turned off when family members leave the house or are sleeping.

Recommendations:

*   Operate heater away from combustible materials. Do not place heaters where towels or the like could fall on the appliance and trigger a fire.

*   Avoid using extension cords unless absolutely necessary. If you must use an extension cord with your electric heater, make sure it is marked with a power rating at least as high as that of the heater itself. Keep the cord stretched out. Do not permit the cord to become buried under carpeting or rugs. Do not place anything on top of the cord.

*   Never place heaters on cabinets, tables, furniture or the like. Never use heaters to dry wearing apparel or shoes.

Cooking Equipment

Cooking equipment is estimated to be associated with more than 100,000 fires annually, and almost 400 deaths, and 5,000 injuries. Gas cooking equipment accounts for about 30,000 fires, and electric cooking equipment for about 55,000 fires.

You should be able to respond "yes" to the following safety statements.

1. The storage area above the stove is free of flammable and combustible items.

2. Short or tight fitting sleeves, and tight fitting shirts, robes, gowns, etc., are worn while cooking.

3. Items that could attract children (e.g. cookies and candy) are not kept above the range and are kept out of the immediate area.

4. The stove is not left unattended when cooking especially when the burner is turned to a high setting.

Recommendations:

*   Never place or store pot holders, plastic utensils, towels and other non-cooking equipment on or near the range because these items can be ignited.

*   Roll up or fasten long loose sleeves with pins or elastic bands while cooking. Do not reach across a range while cooking. Long loose sleeves are more likely to catch on fire than are short sleeves. Long loose sleeves are also more apt to catch on pot handles, overturning pots and pans and cause scalds.

*   Do not place candy or cookies over top of ranges. This will reduce the attraction kids may have for climbing on cooking equipment, thus reducing the possibility of their clothing catching fire.

*   Keep constant vigilance on any cooking that is required above the "keep warm" setting.

Cigarette Lighters and Matches

Each year more than 200 deaths are associated with fires started by cigarette lighters. About two thirds of these result from children playing with lighters. Most of the victims are under five years old.

You should be able to answer "yes" to the safety statements below.

1. Cigarette lighters and matches are kept out of the reach of children.

2. Cigarette lighters are never used to entertain a child.

Recommendations:

*   Keep lighters and matches out of sight and out of the reach of children. Children as young as two years old are capable of lighting cigarette lighters and matches.

- Never encourage or allow a child to play with a lighter or to think of it as a toy. Do not use it as a source of amusement for a child. Once their curiosity is aroused, children may seek out a lighter and try to light it.

- Always check to see that cigarettes are extinguished before emptying ashtrays. Stubs that are still burning can ignite trash.

Materials That Burn

Your home is filled with materials and products that will burn if ignited. Upholstered furniture, clothing, drapery fabrics, and liquids such as gasoline and volatile solvents are involved in many injury-causing fires each year. Most of these fires could be prevented.

Upholstered Furniture

In 1989, there were 18,600 residential fires associated with upholstered furniture; about 900 people lost their lives. About one half of these fires were caused by smoking materials. Property losses amounted to over $100 million from fires started by cigarette ignition of upholstered furniture.

You should be able to respond "yes" to the safety statements below.

1. Upholstered furniture fabrics made from vinyl, wool or thermoplastic fibers are generally selected for safety reasons.

2. I check thoroughly after parties for ashes or unextinguished cigarettes that may have fallen behind and between cushions and under furniture.

Recommendations:

- Look for furniture designed to reduce the likelihood of furniture fire from cigarettes. Much of the furniture manufactured today has significantly greater resistance to ignition by cigarettes than upholstered furniture manufactured 10 to 15 years ago. This is particularly true of furniture manufactured to comply with the requirements of the Upholstered Furniture Action Council's (UFAC) Voluntary Action Program. Such upholstered furniture may be identified by the gold colored tag on the furniture item. The legend on the front of the tag in red letters states—"Important Consumer Safety Information from UFAC."

- Always check the furniture where smokers have been sitting for improperly discarded smoking materials. Ashes and lighted cigarettes can fall unnoticed behind or between cushions or under furniture.

- Do not place or leave ashtrays on the arms of chairs where they can be knocked off.

- Look for fabrics made predominantly from thermoplastic fibers (nylon, polyester, acrylic, olefin) because they resist ignition by burning cigarettes better than cellulosic fabrics (rayon or cotton). In general, the higher the thermoplastic content, the greater the resistance to cigarette ignition.

Mattresses and Bedding

Smoldering fires in mattresses and bedding materials caused by cigarettes are a major cause of deaths in residential fires. In 1989 over 35,000 mattress/bedding fires caused about 700 deaths.

You should be able to respond "yes" to the following safety statements.

1. "No smoking in bed" is a rule that is practiced in my home.

2. Heaters, ash trays, smoking materials and other fire sources are located away from bedding.

Recommendations:

- DO NOT smoke in bed. Smoking in bed is a major cause of accidental fire deaths in homes.

- Locate heaters or other fire sources three feet from the bed to prevent the bed catching on fire.

- Consider replacing your old mattress with a new one if you are a smoker. Mattresses manufactured since 1973 are required to resist cigarette ignition.

Wearing Apparel

Most fibers used in clothing can burn, some more quickly than others. A significant number of clothing fires occur in the over 65 age group principally from nightwear (robes, pajamas, nightgowns). In 1989 about 200 clothing fire deaths were reported; about three fourths occurred in the 65 and older age group. The severity of apparel burns is high. Hospital stays average over one month.

Small open flames, including matches, cigarette lighters, and candles are the major sources of clothing ignition. These are followed by ranges, open fires and space heaters. The most commonly worn garments that are associated with clothing ignition injuries are pajamas, nightgowns, robes, shirts/blouses, pants/slacks and dresses.

You should be able to respond "yes" to the following statements.

1. When purchasing wearing apparel I consider fiber content and fabric construction for safety purposes.

2. I purchase garments for my children that are intended for sleepwear since they are made to be flame resistant.

Recommendations:

• Consider purchasing fabrics such as 100% polyester, nylon, wool and silk that are difficult to ignite and tend to self extinguish.

• Consider the flammability of certain fabrics containing cotton, cotton/polyester blends, rayon, and acrylic. These are relatively easy to ignite and burn rapidly.

• Look at fabric construction. It also affect ignitability. Tight weaves or knits and fabrics without a fuzzy or napped surface are less likely to ignite and burn rapidly than open knits or weaves, or fabrics with brushed or piled surfaces.

• Consider purchasing garments that can be removed without having to pull them over the head. Clothes that are easily removed can help prevent serious burns. If a garment can be quickly stripped off when it catches fire, injury will be far less severe or avoided altogether.

• Follow manufacturer's care and cleaning instructions on products labeled "flame resistant" to ensure that their flame resistant properties are maintained.

Flammable Liquids

One of the major causes of household fires is flammable liquids. These include gasoline, acetone, benzene, lacquer thinner, alcohol, turpentine, contact cements, paint thinner, kerosene, and charcoal lighter fluid. The most dangerous of all is gasoline.

You should be able to respond "yes" to the following safety statements.

1. Flammable liquids are stored in properly labeled, tightly closed non-glass containers.

2. These products are stored away from heaters, furnaces, water heaters, ranges, and other gas appliances.

3. Flammable liquids are stored out of reach of children.

Recommendation:

• Take extra precautions in storing and using flammable liquids, such as gasoline, paint thinners, etc. They produce invisible explosive vapors that can ignite by a small spark at considerable distances from the flammable substance. Store outside the house.

Early Warning and Escape

Even when you have complied with every item in this Home Fire Safety Checklist, you still need to have a plan for early warning and escape in case a fire does occur. Many fire deaths and fire injuries are actually caused by smoke and gases. Victims inhale smoke and poisonous gases that rise ahead of the flames. Survival depends on being warned as early as possible and having an escape plan.

Smoke Detectors

You should be able to respond "yes" to the following statements.

1. At least one smoke detector is located on every floor of my home.

2. Smoke detectors are placed near bedrooms, either on the ceiling or 6-12 inches below the ceiling on the wall. Locate smoke detectors away from air vents or registers; high air flow or "dead" spots are to be avoided.

3. Smoke detectors are tested according to manufacturer's instructions on a regular basis (at least once a month) and are kept in working condition at all times.

4. Batteries are replaced according to manufacturer's instructions, at least annually.

5. Batteries are never disconnected.

6. The detector has a distinct warning signal that can be heard whether asleep or awake.

Recommendations:

• Purchase a smoke detector if you do not have one. Smoke detectors are inexpensive and are required by law in many localities. Check local codes and regulations before you buy your smoke detector because some codes require specific types of detectors. They provide an early warning which is critical because the longer the delay, the deadlier the consequences.

• Read the instructions that come with the detector for advice on the best place to install it. As a minimum detectors should be located near bedrooms and one on every floor.

• Follow the manufacturer's instructions for proper maintenance. Smoke detectors can save lives, but only if properly installed and maintained.

• Never disconnect a detector. Consider relocating the detector rather than disconnecting it if it is subject to nuisance alarms, e.g. from cooking.

• Replace the battery annually, or when a "chirping" sound is heard.

• Follow the manufacturer's instructions about cleaning your detector. Excessive dust, grease or other material in the detector may cause it to operate abnormally. Vacuum the grill work of your detector.

Escape Plan

Planning ahead, rehearsing, thinking, and acting clearly are keys to surviving a fire. How prepared are you?

You should be able to respond "yes" to the following statements.

1. The family has an escape plan and an alternate escape plan.

2. Escape routes and plans are rehearsed periodically.

3. The escape plan includes choosing a place safely outside the house where the family can meet to be sure everyone got out safely.

4. At least two exits from each part of the house are established.

5. The fire department number is posted on every telephone.

Recommendations:

- Establish advanced family planning for escape. It is an important partner with smoke detectors and it will prepare you for a fire emergency.

- Include small children as a part of the discussion and rehearsal. It is especially important to make sure they understand that they must escape; they can't hide from fire under a bed or in a closet.

Your life and that of your family can be saved by foresight, planning, discussing and rehearsal.

Electrical Safety

Each year many Americans are injured in and around their homes. Unsafe conditions such as overloaded circuits and damaged insulation as well as the misuse of extension cords and electrical products create fire hazards and may result in electrocutions.

The U.S. Consumer Product Safety Commission estimates that in 1993 the electrical system in homes was involved in 43,300 fires and 330 deaths and 1720 injuries. In 1992, the most recent year for which data is available, there were an estimated 530 electrocution deaths.

Take a few minutes to look for and correct electrical safe hazards in your home. It does not take too long to check the insulation on a cord, move an appliance away from water, check for correct wattage light bulbs or install a GFCI (Ground Fault Circuit Interrupter).

Invest your time. It could prevent an electrical safety hazard and save lives.

Have Your Electrical System Inspected

Consumer Product Safety Commission studies of residential electrical fires show that the majority of serious fires need not have occurred. The conditions that caused the fires probably would have been detected by an electrical inspection. These problems were not detected or corrected because no inspection had been made for several years. In a number of cases investigated by CPSC, homes ranging from 40 to 100 years old had not been inspected since they were built. A safety inspection should be performed by a qualified electrical or licensed electrical inspector.

To insure the electrical safety of your home, your electrical inspection should be up-to-date and defects corrected. There are no hard-and-fast rules about frequency of inspection but here are some suggestions.

To determine when your electrical system was last inspected, examine the door and cover of your electrical panel(s). The panel should contain a label or tag with a date, a signature, or initials on it. If there is more than one date, the most recent one should be the date of the last inspection. DO NOT remove the service-panel cover. This is a job for a qualified electrician.

Circuit Breaker Panel

Potential Electrical Hazards and Their Symptoms

- **Power Outages.** Fuses need replacement or circuit breakers need resetting frequently.

- **Overrated Panel.** Electrical panel contains fuses or circuit breakers rated at higher currents than the ampacity (current capacity) of their branch circuits, some times called "over-amped" or "overfused"

- **Dim/Flickering Lights.** Lights dim or the size of your television picture shrinks often.

- **Arcs/Sparks.** Bright light flashes or showers of sparks anywhere in your electrical system.

- **Sizzles/Buzzes.** Unusual sounds from the electrical system.

- **Overheating.** Parts of your electrical system, such as switch plates, wall outlet covers, cords and plugs may be warm. These should never be hot-painful to touch, or discolored from heat.

- **Permanently Installed Extension Cords.** Used to extend the home wiring system for a long period, instead of being used temporarily to connect some appliance with a cord too short to reach the wall outlet.

- **Loose Plugs.** Attachment plugs that wobble or pull out of a wall outlet easily.

- **Damaged Insulation.** Cut, broken, or cracked insulation.

If your last inspection was 40 or more years ago, inspection is overdue.

If your last inspection was 10-40 years ago, inspection is advisable, especially if substantial electrical loads (high-wattage appliances, lights and wall outlets or extension cords) have been added or if some of the warning signs discussed are present.

If your last inspection was less than 10 years ago, inspection may not be needed, unless some of the warning signs, described are present or temporary wiring has been added.

You may live in an area that is not served by state or local electrical inspectors, so that no inspection record will be found on your electrical panel. In that case, use the age of the house as a guide to the probable need for an inspection.

Appliance Power Budget

Circuits can only handle a specified total wattage of all the electrical products connected to that circuit. If too much wattage is plugged into a circuit, serious electrical problems can result. Here is a guide to knowing what a circuit can handle:

- 15 ampere branch circuit can carry 1500 watts.
- 20 ampere branch circuit can carry 2000 watts.

Find the nameplate on each appliance indicating its power (watts) rating. Add up the total watts for appliances that you may use at the same time on the same branch circuit. Examples:

- Hair Dryer: 1400 watts
- Iron: 1000 watts
- Portable Heater: 1200 watts
- Vacuum Cleaner: 600 watts
- Deep Fat Fryer: 1300 watts
- Portable Fan: 150 watts

Most home lighting and wall outlet branch circuits may carry as much as 1500 watts (15 ampere branch); some kitchen circuits, as much as 2000 watts (20 ampere).

Cords

Q. Are lamp, extension, telephone and other cords placed out of the flow of traffic?

Cords stretched across walkways may cause someone to trip. Whenever possible, arrange furniture so that outlets are available for lamps and appliances without the use of extension cords. Extension cords should not be used as a substitute for permanent wiring. If you must use an extension cord, place it on the floor against a wall where people cannot trip over it. Move the phone so that telephone cords will not lie where people walk.

Q. Are cords out from beneath furniture and rugs or carpeting?

Furniture resting on cords can damage them. Electric cords which run under carpeting can overheat and cause a fire. Remove cords from under furniture or carpeting. Replace damaged or frayed cords.

Q. Are cords attached to the walls, baseboards, etc. with nails or staples?

Nails or staples can damage cords, presenting fire and shock hazards. Remove nails and staples from cords after disconnecting power. Check wiring for damage. Use tape if necessary to attach cords to walls or floors.

Q. Are electrical cords in good condition, not frayed or cracked?

Damaged cords may cause a shock or fire. Replace frayed or cracked cords. Do not use frayed electrical cords.

Q. Do extension cords carry no more than their proper load, as indicated by the ratings labeled on the cord and the appliance?

Overloaded extension cords may cause fires. Replace No. 18 gauge cords with No. 16 gauge cords. Older extension cords using small (No. 18 gauge) wires can overheat at 15 amps or 20 amps. Change the cord to a higher rated one or unplug some appliances, if the rating on the cord is exceeded because of the power requirements of one or more appliances being used on the cord. Use an extension cord having a sufficient amp or wattage rating, if an extension cord is needed.

Light Bulbs

Q. Are the light bulbs the appropriate size and type for the lamp or fixture?

A bulb of too high wattage or the wrong type may lead to fire through overheating. Ceiling fixtures, recessed lights, and "hooded" lamps will trap heat. Replace with a bulb of the correct type and wattage. (If you do not know the correct wattage, contact the manufacturer of the fixture.) Place halogen lamps away from curtains. These lamps become very hot and can cause a fire hazard.

Space Heaters

Q. Are heaters which come with a 3-prong plug being used in a 3-hole outlet or with a properly attached adapter?

The grounding feature provided by a 3-hole receptacle or an adapter for a 2-hole receptacle is a safety feature designed to lessen the risk of shock. Never defeat the grounding feature. Use an adapter to connect the heater's 3-prong plug, if you do not have a 3-hole outlet. Make sure the adapter ground wire or tab is attached to the outlet.

Q. Are heaters placed where they can not be knocked over, and away from furnishings and flammable materials, such as curtains or rugs?

Heaters can cause fires or serious burns if they cause you to trip, if they are knocked over or if they are placed near home furnishings. Relocate heaters away from passageways and flammable materials such as curtains, rugs, furniture or newspaper.

Circuit Breaker Receptacle Plug-In

A Ground Fault Circuit Interrupter (GFCI) detects any loss (leakage) of electrical current in a circuit that might be flowing through a person using an electrical product. When such a loss is detected, the GFCI turns electricity off before severe injuries or electrocution can occur. (However, you may receive a painful shock during the time that it takes for the GFCI to cut off the electricity.) GFCI wall outlets can be installed in place of standard outlets to protect against electrocution for just that outlet, or a series of outlets in the same branch.

A GFCI Circuit Breaker can be installed on some circuit breaker electrical panels to protect against electrocution, excessive leakage current and overcurrent for an entire branch circuit. Plug-in GFCIs can be plugged into wall outlets where appliances will be used.

Q. Have you tested your GFCIs to be sure they still offer protection from fatal electrical shock?

A GFCI can provide power without giving an indication that it is no longer providing shock protection. Be sure your GFCI still provides protection from fatal electric shock. Test monthly. First plug a night light or lamp into the GFCI-protected wall outlet (the light should be turned on), then depress the "TEST" button on the GFCI. If the GFCI is working properly, the light should go out. There will be an indicator to show if it is working properly or not. If it is working, it will disconnect the power from the protected circuit or plug. If not, have the GFCI replaced. Reset the GFCI to restore power.

If the "RESET" button pops out but the light does not go out, the GFCI has been improperly wired and does not offer shock protection at that wall outlet. Contact a qualified electrician to correct any wiring errors.

PROBLEM: Electric shocks can be more serious in certain locations of the home such as bathrooms, kitchens, basements and garages where people can contact heating radiators, water pipes, electric heaters, electric stoves and water in sinks and bathtubs. If a person touches one of these and a faulty electrical appliance at the same time, they can receive a shock and may be electrocuted.

If you have a home without GFCIs, consult with a qualified electrician about adding this protection. If you want to install some GFCI protection yourself, use plug-in units to protect individual wall outlets. Both two-conductor and three-conductor receptacle outlets can be protected with plug-in units. You may have a newer home that is equipped with GFCIs in the home areas mentioned above.

Fuses/Circuit Breakers

Fuses and circuit breakers are safety devices located on your electrical panel to prevent over-loading and fires. They stop the electrical current if it exceeds the safe level for some portion of the home electrical system. Overloading means that the appliances and lighting in the home regularly demand more electrical current than the home electrical system can safely deliver. If the demand for electrical current exceeds the safety level, a fuse opens once and must be replaced to reconnect the circuit. A circuit breaker "trips" its switch to open the circuit, and the circuit is reconnected by closing the switch manually.

There are at least two different types of circuit breakers. One has a control handle that swings all the way to "OFF" when it is tripped. The other has an intermediate position, close to "ON" (sometimes it is difficult to see that it has tripped). Both types of circuit breakers must be reset with the hand control after the problem has been eliminated. The first type should simply be moved back to "ON," the second moved first to "OFF" and then to "ON."

Q. If fuses are used, are they the correct size for the circuit?

Replacing a correct size fuse with a larger size fuse can present a serious fire hazard. If the fuse in the box is rated higher than that indicated for the circuit, excessive current will be allowed to flow and possibly overload the outlet and house wiring to the point that a fire can begin. Be certain that correct-size fuses are used. (If you do not know the correct sizes, plan to have a qualified electrician identify and label the sizes to be used.)

NOTE: Most of the screw-based fuses used should be 15 amp. If all, or nearly all, fuses used are 30 amp, these fuses may be rated too high for the circuits.

PROBLEM: Your fuse panel has Edison-base plug fuses (screw base like a light bulb) installed. Fuses of different ratings will fit in Edison sockets. Consumers sometimes replace a fuse that repeatedly "blows" with a higher ampere rated fuse. Although the new fuse may not open, it also may not protect the branch circuit. Overloading can lead to fire. To prevent future installation of fuses that allow currents too high for your wiring, your fuse panel should be converted to S-type sockets that accept only fuses of the correct amperage rating. If you have Edison-base fuse sockets, have them fitted with the S-type socket inserts.

PROBLEM: If your home has a four-fuse panel (60-ampere) service, most of the fuses will be rated at 15 or, at most, 20 amperes. If you do not know for certain, have your electrical panel inspected to determine which branches should be protected at a 15-ampere level and which, if any, are adequate for 20 ampere safety devices. If it has one or more fuses rated above 20 amperes, someone may have tried to avoid power outages by substituting higher amperage fuses. Your wiring may be exposed to overloading that can lead to fire. Reduce the fuses to 15-ampere rated ones, unless you are absolutely certain that a special circuit is wired for 20 amperes. If fuses continue to "blow," keep track of which branch circuits are affected and which appliances are in use when the power outage occurs. Consult a qualified electrician to resolve the problem.

Receptacle Outlets

Switches are used to turn the power on and off. Receptacle outlets are usually mounted on a wall or floor to supply electricity to appliances through a cord and plug.

Q. Are there outlets or switches which are unusually warm or hot to the touch?

Unusually warm or hot outlets or switches may indicate that an unsafe wiring condition exists. Unplug cords from these outlets and do not use the switches. Have a qualified electrician check the wiring as soon as possible.

Q. Do all outlets and switches have cover plates so that no wiring is exposed?

Exposed wiring presents a shock hazard. Add a cover plate.

Small Appliances and Tools

Q. Are small electrical appliances such as hair dryers, shavers, curling irons, unplugged when not in use?

Even an appliance that is not turned on, such as a hairdryer, can be potentially hazardous if it is left plugged in. If it falls into water in a sink or bathtub while plugged in, it could electrocute you. Install ground fault circuit interrupter (GFCI) protection near your kitchen and bathroom sinks to protect against electric shock. For more information, see the section on GFCIs. Unplug all small appliances when not in use. Never reach into water to get an appliance that has fallen in without being sure the appliance is unplugged.

Q. Do you make sure that there is nothing covering your electric blanket when in use, and do you avoid "tucking in" the sides or ends of your electric blanket?

"Tucking in" an electric blanket or placing additional coverings on top of it can cause excessive heat buildup which can start a fire. Do not tuck in electric blankets. Use electric blankets according to the manufacturer's instructions. Don't allow anything on top of the blanket while it is in use. (This includes other blankets or comforters, even pets sleeping on top of the blanket.) Do not use electric blankets on children.

Q. Do you turn off your heating pad before you go to sleep?

Sleeping with a heating pad that is turned on can cause serious burns even at relatively low settings. Never go to sleep with a heating pad that is turned on. Do not use a heating pad if you are diabetic or obese.

Q. Are power tools equipped with a 3-prong plug or marked to show they are double insulated?

These safety features reduce the risk of an electric shock. Use a properly connected 3-prong adapter for connecting a 3-prong plug to a 2-hole receptacle. Consider replacing old tools that have neither a 3-prong plug nor are double insulated.

Q. Are power tool guards in place?

Power tools used with guards removed pose a serious risk of injury from sharp edges or moving parts. Replace guards that have been removed from power tools.

Q. Are the grounding features of any 3-prong plugs being properly used i.e., the grounding pin has not been removed?

The third prong is there because the appliance must be grounded to avoid electric shock.

The few minutes you took to check your home using this text could prevent a safety hazard and save a life!

The National Electrical Safety Foundation

The National Electrical Safety Foundation is a not-for-profit (501(c)(3)) organization whose board of directors and officers serve without compensation. This text was originally published as a public service by the National Electrical Safety Foundation in cooperation with the U.S. Consumer Product Safety Commission and the Consumer Information Center, U.S. General Services Administration. No endorsement of any particular product, company or service is implied by their mention in this publication.

For more information about electrical safety and the Foundation, please contact:

National Electrical Safety Foundation
1300 North 17th Street, Suite 1847
Rosslyn, Virginia 22209
Phone: 703-841-3211
Fax: 703-841-3311

Part Six

Caring for Chronically or Terminally Ill Patients and Making End-of-Life Decisions

Chapter 45

Older Adults Examine Health-Care Options

At the end of the movie "The Wizard of Oz," Dorothy clicks the heels of her ruby slippers together and repeats, "There's no place like home" until she magically returns to the safe haven of her bedroom in Kansas.

Like Dorothy, many ailing older adults feel there's no place like home.

Surveys reveal that most older adults would rather be cared for in the comfort of their own homes than in a nursing home. Some studies have shown that people heal more quickly at home than in an institution and that home care often is the less expensive alternative. These factors, combined with the swelling ranks of the graying sector, have made home health care a growing concern in this country. The number of elderly receiving home health care in 1988 was more than double that in 1977, according to the National Association for Home Care.

Fortunately, various agencies are rising to meet the burgeoning need for home-based care of senior citizens, and thanks to technological advances in portable medical equipment, many treatments previously possible only in a hospital (such as kidney dialysis and intravenous feeding) can now be given at home. The Food and Drug Administration is responsible for ensuring that the new home medical devices used for these treatments are safe and effective.

In addition, emergency response devices such as "Lifeline" provide instant access to emergency care if necessary. The development of

FDA Consumer, January-February 1991.

specialized gadgets, such as grab bars and stove mirrors, have also made the home environment safer and more accommodating for older people.

Home Improvements

A number of health impairments that often accompany old age— such as limited mobility and strength, and vision or hearing loss— make modifications to the home imperative. Often, simple devices such as loop handles instead of door knobs on cabinets can spell the difference between dependent and independent living for an older person.

A number of changes may also be necessary to improve the safety of the home. Falls are the most common cause of fatal injury for older people. In 1982 alone, more that 2,500 people 65 and older were treated in hospital emergency rooms for injuries that resulted from tripping over rugs. Double-faced adhesive carpet tape or rubber matting applied to the backs of rugs can help prevent these accidents. Changes in floor levels should also be clearly marked with white or reflecting tape, and stairways should be well-lit.

Wet, soapy tile or porcelain surfaces are slippery, making the bathroom a hazardous area for the older adult. Textured strips applied to bathroom floors and to the bottoms of tubs and showers can help prevent falls. Many elders find grab bars on the wall adjacent to the toilet and in the tub or shower helpful. Tub seats are good for people in wheelchairs or those with loss of strength who have difficulty lowering themselves to the floor of the tub.

Knob-type faucet or tub hardware should be replaced with single-lever faucets, which can be easily operated by arthritic hands. To avoid burns, anti-scald temperature controls can be installed to prevent the water temperature from rising above an established limit. Settings can also be lowered on hot water heaters.

Narrow doorways can pose a problem for senior citizens who use walkers or wheelchairs. Removal of a door can often provide the needed clearance. If this isn't feasible, "swing-clear" hinges can enlarge a door opening nearly two inches. Lever latches instead of standard doorknobs alleviate the problem arthritics have with gripping or twisting. Likewise, slide bolts are easier to operate than deadbolts and provide nearly the same security.

As people age, they generally find that background noises interfere with their ability to hear and participate in conversations. Carpeted floors and curtained windows can reduce noise levels and distracting echoes.

482

Because it takes older people longer to focus vision when moving between light and dark areas, light levels should be kept consistent in bedrooms and hallways, and night lights should be used.

The kitchen can pose particular problems for senior citizens. For those with impaired hand dexterity, simple devices can aid food preparation. Cutting boards with spikes, for example, hold foods such as vegetables in place for cutting, and boards with indentations hold mixing bowls in place.

A mirror above the stove allows a person in a wheelchair to see what's cooking in pots, and sling belts attached to the counter can support someone unable to stand for long periods. Items can be moved safely between the kitchen and serving area on wheeled storage carts.

To avoid fires, store flammable items such as potholders, dish towels, or plastic utensils away from the range. Roll up long, loose sleeves securely before cooking. The Consumer Product Safety Commission estimates that nearly three-quarters of all people who die from clothing fires are over 65. Many of these fires start when long sleeves ignite while the person is working over the stove.

Because some older people have lowered immunity, they need to be especially careful about exposure to food-borne microorganisms that can cause serious—even fatal—infections. (See "Food Safety Crucial for People with Lowered Immunity" in the July-August 1990 *FDA Consumer*.) Senior citizens, therefore, should avoid unpasteurized milk or raw or undercooked eggs, poultry, fish, shellfish, or meat. Hands, utensils, counters, and cutting surfaces should be washed with hot soapy water between preparation of different foods, particularly after handling raw eggs, meat, poultry, or fish. Plastic or glass cutting boards should be used, rather than wooden ones, which are difficult or impossible to clean adequately. When handling raw meat, poultry, or fish, cover any cuts or open sores on the hands with a plastic sealing bandage or plastic gloves.

Emergency Response Devices

A number of emergency response devices help ensure that an older person who lives alone will get needed help when an emergency arises, whether it's an inability to get out of the tub or a heart attack. These small devices, available at local hospitals, are worn around the neck. The wearer simply pushes a button and is connected to an experienced operator. This operator, who has access to the caller's medical history and numbers of people to contact in an emergency, summons help.

Home-Care Helpers

Some senior citizens require home care to live comfortably and safely. When friends and family are unable to provide that help, professionals can often meet those needs, which vary considerably from person to person.

A man or woman severely disabled by arthritis, for example, can hire a part-time homemaker to shop and clean. Meals on Wheels, a service available in most communities, can provide hot meals. Someone recovering from a stroke or other illness may temporarily need physical, occupational or speech therapy as well as a home health aide to assist with personal care.

The mainstays of home care are nurses, homemakers or health aides, social workers, therapists, and physicians. Visiting nurses provide hands-on care such as changing bandages and checking blood pressure, heart rate, and other vital signs. Nurses also teach patients or family members how to do some of the medical tasks, such as giving injections. In most home health-care situations, the nurse also identifies any additional services a client may need, such as physical therapy.

Homemakers shop, cook and clean for their clients. Home health aides provide additional help such as bathing, walking, dressing, and administering oral medications. Sometimes, all that's needed to avoid a nursing home is help with bathing and dressing.

Social workers help geriatric patients and their families find the services and agencies they need. They also help patients and their families cope with the stresses of illness and disability.

Physical therapists provide home patients with exercise and other therapies they need to relieve pain and restore muscle strength. Occupational therapists pinpoint home devices such as grab bars that enable more independence. They also teach techniques that aid in daily living activities, such as how to dress with the use of just one hand. Speech pathologists teach hearing-impaired individuals how to read lips and help stroke patients and other speech-impaired individuals recover their ability to talk.

Physicians authorize the home health-care plan. They periodically review the effectiveness of home-care services and recommend any necessary changes.

Some home health-care services are covered under Medicare or private insurance policies. Your local Social Security office can tell you what services are covered by Medicare.

High Tech at Home

Recent advances in technology have reduced many types of bulky medical equipment to a more portable size, enabling many patients to leave the hospital more quickly following a major illness. For those afflicted with chronic ailments, home medical equipment can also prevent a hospital stay.

Cardiac patients' heart rhythms can be monitored at home, for example, by portable devices consisting of an electrode placed on the chest and attached to a small electronic box worn in a pocket or pouch by the patient.

Some cardiac patients' lives have been saved in their own homes by a telephone defibrillator system. If the patient has symptoms such as chest pain, palpitations, or shortness of breath, the patient or caregiver places a defibrillator pad containing electrodes on the patient's chest. The electrodes detect the patient's heartbeat pattern, and an electrocardiogram (EKG) is sent to a base station through the telephone lines. Medical personnel at the base station evaluate the EKG and, if necessary, activate the defibrillator on the patient's chest so that it gives brief electric shocks. These shocks can help stabilize or restore a patient's heartbeat until emergency medical personnel arrive on the scene.

There are a number of portable oxygen systems that help ease the chronic shortness of breath characteristic of emphysema and chronic bronchitis. These chronic obstructive pulmonary diseases are second only to heart disease as a cause of disability, according to the Social Security Administration.

Usually people with these respiratory conditions receive oxygen from large tanks or a device that concentrates the oxygen in room air. Oxygen is delivered to the patient through a tube that is either placed in the nose or surgically inserted into the neck. When they need to leave their homes, people can also sling a handbag-like sack of oxygen over their shoulders. This convenient oxygen container is filled from a tank of oxygen kept at home.

After initial training, many people can administer their own supplemental oxygen without supervision. The frequency of administration varies with the severity of the disability.

"Some people need oxygen constantly," says FDA's Marcia Withiam-Wilson, M.S.N., a nurse consultant to FDA, "whereas other people just need it whenever they exert themselves—when they walk some distance, for example, but not when they are sitting in a chair."

Intravenous (IV) care equipment is also available for home use. Some people can receive cancer chemotherapy intravenously in their own homes with the instruction and supervision of a home nurse. IV equipment can also be used in the home to give antibiotics to people with infections such as pneumonia or osteomyelitis, a bone infection common in the elderly. Home use of IV antibiotics can allow an earlier hospital discharge of some patients with pneumonia, for example.

A number of ailments that commonly afflict the elderly require tube feeding, which often can be done at home. Some people receiving chemotherapy, for example, may need to supplement their meals with a nutritional solution given in a tube inserted through the nose and into the stomach or surgically inserted directly into the stomach or small intestine. Stroke patients having difficulty swallowing may also need such tube feeding, as may some patients with oral cancers or various gastrointestinal diseases. Health practitioners can teach patients and their caregivers how to administer tube feedings at home, and how to record intake, output, and the patients' weight so their nutritional status can be assessed.

Some people receiving radiation therapy, which can impede the gut's ability to digest or absorb food, and others with certain disorders need to be fed a nutritional solution via a catheter inserted surgically in a vein near the collar bone. This type of intravenous feeding, too, can be done at home after initial training by a health professional. Products used for intravenous feedings at home are called home total parenteral nutrition. FDA, which regulates these products as drugs, ensures their safety and effectiveness.

Kidney failure afflicts many older adults, particularly those with high blood pressure or diabetes. Patients with kidney failure can be treated in the home with peritoneal dialysis, in which the patient's blood is purified by a solution (dialysate) inserted into the abdominal cavity through a surgically inserted catheter. (See "Kidney Disease—When Those Fabulous Filters Are Foiled" in the March 1990 *FDA Consumer*.)

A process known as continuous ambulatory peritoneal dialysis allows the patient to go about normal activities during the day. Peritoneal dialysis is usually continued at night with the aid of a machine that allows dialysis to be performed while the patient sleeps. Home peritoneal dialysis is not difficult and can be done without supervision after initial training by health personnel at a dialysis center, according to Ruth Hubbard, R.N., a scientific reviewer at FDA.

Some patients with kidney failure are also treated at home with hemodialysis, in which their blood is channeled through a device that removes impurities and excess fluids. This procedure takes about three or four hours and is usually done about three times a week. In addition, hemodialysis at home requires the assistance of a trained partner to help the patient set up the equipment and monitor progress during treatment.

Both hemodialysis and peritoneal dialysis can be done in the hospital, but "the advantage of home dialysis," says Hubbard, "is that it doesn't restrain the patient to a strict schedule and people are able to participate in their own care and have more control."

Other portable equipment used in the home include blood transfusion devices and home x-ray units that are brought to the home and operated by trained personnel. Many laboratory tests, in addition, can now be done in mobile labs that drive right up to the patient's door.

Avoiding Medication Hazards

Usually, one of the most important parts of home care for older people is the medications they take on a regular basis. The various ailments to which senior citizens succumb often require them to take several medications simultaneously. Mixing medications can have serious consequences, and older adults may be especially prone to side effects from medications. New guidelines developed by FDA request drug companies to study drugs in older patients. (See "Testing Drugs in Older People" in the November 1990 *FDA Consumer*.)

To avoid harmful reactions to medications, people over 65 should be sure to let their doctors know every drug they are taking, including over-the-counter drugs. Pharmacists can also help trouble-shoot damaging combinations of drugs. Senior citizens should be alert to any drug side effects and report them to their doctors immediately.

The key to a medication's effectiveness is taking it properly. Medications should be taken as instructed—at the proper time and according to other instructions, such as only taking the drug on an empty stomach or with meals. A medication schedule that indicates, in a chart-like fashion, which medications should be taken and when can help ensure that medicines are taken properly. The schedule should be posted where it can be consulted often and where the patient can easily mark off drug doses as they are taken.

Many older people find the childproof caps on drug bottles difficult, if not impossible, to open. You can ask your pharmacist to give you regular caps, but be sure to keep the medication away from children.

By being conscientious about taking their medications, and seeking out the devices and personal services they need, older people can live long and comfortable lives in the familiar surroundings of their own homes.

Home-Care Resources

The following publications or organizations can provide additional information on home care for older people:

- American Association of Retired Persons, 1909 K St., N.W., Washington, D.C. 20049, (202) 728-4355. This organization puts out a booklet called "The Do-able Renewable Home," which details how to adapt a home to fit special needs.

- Area Agencies on Aging. The phone numbers for these agencies can be found under the local or county government listings in the phone book. They provide referrals to local organizations or services that cater to the elderly.

- National Association for Home Care, 519 C St., N.E., Washington, D.C. 20002,(202) 547-7424. This organization provides referrals to home-care agencies.

—by Margie Patlak

Margie Patlak is a free-lance writer who specializes in medicine and health.

Chapter 46

What You Need to Know about Advance Medical Directives

What Is a Health Care Advance Directive?

A health care advance directive is a document in which you give instructions about your health care if, in the future, you cannot speak for yourself. You can give someone you name (your "agent" or "proxy") the power to make health care decisions for you. You also can give instructions about the kind of health care you do or do not want.

In a traditional Living Will, you state your wishes about life-sustaining medical treatments if you are terminally ill. In a Health Care Power of Attorney, you appoint someone else to make medical treatment decisions for you if you cannot make them for yourself.

The Health Care Advance Directive described in this text combines and expands the traditional Living Will and Health Care Power of Attorney into a single, comprehensive document.

Why Is It Useful?

Unlike most Living Wills, a Health Care Advance Directive is not limited to cases of terminal illness. If you cannot make or communicate

This chapter contains text from *Shape Your Health Care Future with Health Care Advance Directives,* ©1995 American Association of Retired Persons, the ABA Commission on Legal Problems of the Elderly, and American Medical Association. All rights reserved under International and Pan American Copyright Conventions; reprinted with permission; and "Advance Directives: 49 Things That Are Known And 9 Things That Are Not Known," *Briefing Paper Series, Ethics and Decision-Making Issue No. 3*, University of Minnesota Institute for Health Services Research, March 1996; reprinted with permission.

decisions because of a temporary or permanent illness or injury, a Health Care Advance Directive helps you keep control over health care decisions that are important to you. In your Health Care Advance Directive, you state your wishes about any aspect of your health care, including decisions about life-sustaining treatment, and choose a person to make and communicate these decisions for you.

Appointing an agent is particularly important. At the time a decision needs to be made, your agent can participate in discussions and weigh the pros and cons of treatment decisions based on your wishes. Your agent can decide for you whenever you cannot decide for yourself, even if your decision-making ability is only temporarily affected.

Unless you formally appoint someone to decide for you, many health care providers and institutions will make critical decisions for you that might not be based on your wishes. In some situations, a court may have to appoint a guardian unless you have an advance directive.

An advance directive also can relieve family stress. By expressing your wishes in advance, you help family or friends who might otherwise struggle to decide on their own what you would want done.

Are Health Care Advance Directives Legally Valid in Every State?

Yes. Every state and the District of Columbia has laws that permit individuals to sign documents stating their wishes about health care decisions when they cannot speak for themselves. The specifics of these laws vary, but the basic principle of listening to the patient's wishes is the same everywhere. The law gives great weight to any form of written directive. If the courts become involved, they usually try to follow the patient's stated values and preferences, especially if they are in written form. A Health Care Advance Directive may be the most convincing evidence of your wishes you can create.

What Does a Health Care Advance Directive Say?

There are two parts to the Health Care Advance Directive.

The most important part of the advance directive is the appointment of someone (your agent) to make health care decisions for you if you cannot decide for yourself. You can define how much or how little authority you want your agent to have. You also can name persons to act as alternate agents if your primary agent cannot act for you, and disqualify specific persons whom you do not want to make decisions for you.

If there is no one whom you trust fully to serve as your agent, then you should not name an agent. Instead, you can rely on the second part of the Advance Directive to make your wishes known.

In the second part of the Advance Directive, you can provide specific instructions about your health care treatment. You also can include a statement about donating your organs. Your instructions in the second part provide evidence of your wishes that your agent, or anyone providing you with medical care, should follow.

You can complete either or both parts of the Health Care Advance Directive.

How Do I Make a Health Care Advance Directive?

The process for creating a Health Care Advance Directive depends on where you live. Most states have laws that provide special forms and signing procedures.

Most states also have special witnessing requirements and restrictions on whom you can appoint as your agent (such as prohibiting a health care provider from being your agent). Follow these rules carefully.

Typically, states require two witnesses. Some require or permit a notarized signature. Some have special witnessing requirements if you live in a nursing home or similar facility. Even where witnesses are not required, consider using them anyway to reinforce the deliberate nature of your act and to increase the likelihood that care providers in other states will accept the document.

If I Change My Mind, Can I Cancel Or Change a Health Care Advance Directive?

Yes, you can cancel or change your Health Care Advance Directive by telling your agent or health care provider in writing of your decision to do so. Destroying all copies of the old one and creating a new one is the best way. Make sure you give a copy of the new one to your physician and anyone else who received the old one.

What Do I Need to Consider Before Making a Health Care Advance Directive?

There are at least four important questions to ask yourself:

First—What Are My Goals for Medical Treatment? The Health Care Advance Directive may determine what happens to you over a period of disability or at the very final stage of your life. You can help others respect your wishes if you take some steps now to make your treatment preferences clear.

While it is impossible to anticipate all of the different medical decisions that may come up, you can make your preferences clear by stating your goals for medical treatment. What do you want treatment to accomplish? Is it enough that treatment could prolong your life, whatever your quality of life? Or, if life-sustaining treatment could not restore consciousness or your ability to communicate with family members or friends, would you rather stop treatment?

Once you have stated your goals of treatment, your family and physicians can make medical decisions for you on the basis of your goals. If treatment would help achieve one of your goals, the treatment would be provided. If treatment would not help achieve one of your goals, the treatment would not be provided.

In formulating your goals of treatment, it is often helpful to consider your wishes about different end-of-life treatments and then asking yourself why do you feel that way. If you would not want to be kept alive by a ventilator, what is it about being on a ventilator that troubles you? Is it the loss of mobility, the lack of independence, or some other factor? Would it matter if you needed a ventilator for only a few days rather than many months? The answers to these kinds of questions will reflect important values that you hold and that will help you shape your goals of treatment.

Another way to become clear about your goals of treatment is to create a "Values History." In doing a Values History, you examine your values and attitudes, discuss them with loved ones or advisors and write down your responses to questions such as:

- How do you feel about your current health?

- How important is independence and self-sufficiency in your life?

- How do you imagine handling illness, disability, dying, and death?

- How might your personal relationships affect medical decision-making, especially near the end of life?

- What role should doctors and other health professionals play in such decisions?

- What kind of living environment is important to you if you become seriously ill or disabled?

- How much should the cost to your family be a part of the decision-making process?

- What role do religious beliefs play in decisions about your health care?

- What are your thoughts about life in general in its final stages: your hopes and fears, enjoyments and sorrows?

Once you have identified your values, you can use them to decide what you want medical treatment to accomplish.

Second—Who Should Be My Agent? Choosing your agent is the most important part of this process. Your agent will have great power over your health and personal care if you cannot make your own decisions. Normally, no one oversees or monitors your agent's decisions.

Choose one person to serve as your agent to avoid disagreements. If you appoint two or more agents to serve together and they disagree, your medical caregivers will have no clear direction. If possible, appoint at least one alternate agent in case your primary agent is not available.

Speak to the person (and alternate agents) you wish to appoint beforehand to explain your desires. Confirm their willingness to act for you and their understanding of your wishes. Also be aware that some states will not let certain persons (such as your doctor) act as your agent. If you can think of no one you trust to carry out this responsibility, then do not name an agent. Make sure, however, that you provide instructions that will guide your doctor or a court-appointed decision-maker.

Third—How Specific Should I Be? A Health Care Advance Directive does not have to give directions or guidelines for your agent. However, if you have specific wishes or preferences, it is important to spell them out in the document itself. Also discuss them with your agent and health care providers. These discussions will help ensure that your wishes, values and preferences will be respected. Make sure to think about your wishes about artificial feeding (nutrition and hydration), since people sometimes have very different views on this topic.

At the same time, be aware that you cannot cover all the bases. It is impossible to predict all the circumstances you may face. Simple statements like "I never want to be placed on a ventilator" may not reflect your true wishes. You might want ventilator assistance if it were temporary and you then could resume your normal activities. No matter how much direction you provide, your agent will still need considerable discretion and flexibility. Write instructions carefully so they do not restrict the authority of your agent in ways you did not intend.

493

Fourth—How Can I Make Sure That Health Care Providers Will Follow My Advance Directive? Regardless of the laws about advance directives in your state, some physicians, hospitals, or other health care providers may have personal views or values that do not agree with your stated desires. As a result, they may not want to follow your Health Care Advance Directive.

Most state laws give doctors the right to refuse to honor your advance directive on conscience grounds. However, they generally must help you find a doctor or hospital that will honor your directive. The best way to avoid this problem is to talk to your physician and other health care providers ahead of time. Make sure they understand the document and your wishes, and they have no objections. If there are objections, work them out, or change physicians.

Once you sign a Health Care Advance Directive, be sure to give a copy of it to your doctor and to your agent, close relatives, and anyone else who may be involved in your care.

What Happens If I Do Not Have an Advance Directive?

If you do not have an advance directive and you cannot make health care decisions, some state laws give decision-making power to default decision-makers or "surrogates." These surrogates, who are usually family members in order of kinship, can make some or all health care decisions. Some states authorize a "close friend" to make decisions, but usually only when family members are unavailable.

Even without such statutes, most doctors and health facilities routinely consult family, as long as there are close family members available and there is no disagreement. However, problems can arise because family members may not know what the patient would want in a given situation. They also may disagree about the best course of action. Disagreement can easily undermine family consent. A hospital physician or specialist who does not know you well may become your decision-maker, or a court proceeding may be necessary to resolve a disagreement.

In these situations, decisions about your health care may not reflect your wishes or may be made by persons you would not choose. Family members and persons close to you may go through needless agony in making life and death decisions without your guidance. It is far better to make your wishes known and appoint an agent ahead of time through a Health Care Advance Directive.

Who Can Help Me Create a Health Care Advance Directive?

You do not need a lawyer to make a Health Care Advance Directive. However, a lawyer can be helpful if your family situation is uncertain or complex, or you expect problems to arise. Start by talking to someone who knows you well and can help you state your values and wishes considering your family and medical history.

Your doctor is an important participant in creating your Health Care Advance Directive. Discuss the kinds of medical problems you may face, based on your current health and health history. Your doctor can help you understand the treatment choices your agent may face. Share your ideas for instructions with your doctor to make sure medical care providers can understand them.

You can obtain up-to-date state-by-state information about advance directives, along with statutory forms, if they exist in your state, from:

Legal Counsel for the Elderly (LCE)
American Association of Retired Persons
P.O. Box 96474
Washington, DC 20090-6474

LCE has state-specific guidebooks about advance directives. If you want to order a booklet, send $5 per booklet (for shipping and handling) to the above address.

Choice In Dying, Inc.
200 Varick Street
New York, NY 10014-4810
Telephone: 1-800-989-WILL

Choice In Dying, Inc. is a non-profit educational organization.

Hospital associations, medical societies or bar associations in your state or county, or your local area agency on aging (AAA) may provide forms for your state.

If your state has a statutory form, remember that preprinted forms may not meet all your needs. Take the time to consider all possibilities and seek advice, so that the document you develop meets your special needs.

If you want legal help, contact your state or local Office on Aging. These offices usually are quite familiar with health care issues and local resources for legal assistance. You also can contact the bar association for your state or locality. Its lawyer referral service may be able to refer you to an attorney who handles this type of matter.

Finally, organizations that deal with planning for incapacity, such as your local Alzheimer's Association chapter, may be able to provide advice or referrals.

49 Things That Are Known about Advance Directives

Introduction

As case managers and other long-term care professionals find themselves increasingly helping clients plan and prepare for their long-term care needs, the topic of advance directives and an understanding of what this topic involves becomes more relevant. As such, long-term care professionals need to not only understand what advanced directives are and how they are created, but also whether a client has an advance directive, and whether the client has informed his or her health care provider and family about the contents of the advanced directive. Moreover, in cases where a client does not have an advanced directive, which will be the majority of cases, long-term care professionals need to be prepared to thoroughly discuss the option of advanced directives with the client. This section describes 49 things that are known and 9 things that are not known about advanced directives. Meant as an educational reference tool, this brief should serve as a useful starting point in educating long-term care professionals and others about advance directives. The body of this brief was prepared by ethicist Steven Miles, M.D., a faculty member of the University of Minnesota Center for Biomedical Ethics and the National Long-Term Care Resource Center. Each assertion is based on a study that is on file at the University of Minnesota Center for Biomedical Ethics. A copy of the supporting bibliographies and citations can be obtained by contacting the Center for Biomedical Ethics at (612) 626-9762, or writing to Dr. Steve Miles, University of Minnesota, Center for Biomedical Ethics, University Office Plaza, Suite 110, 2221 University Avenue S.E., Minneapolis, MN 55455.

What Is an Advance Directive?

1. An advance directive is a health directive made while cognitively intact in order to guide a person's health care, if he or she becomes temporarily or permanently unable to make a decision. Two types of advance directives exist: a living will and a durable power of attorney. These documents are legally recognized in all states but may not be legally required for a

person to retain or exercise any right pertaining to the use or non-use of life sustaining treatments.

2. A "living will" is a document that enables a person to tell caregivers the circumstances under which life-sustaining treatment is to be provided, withheld, or foregone in the event the agent becomes unable to make decisions.

3. A "durable power of attorney for health care" is a document that enables a person to appoint a fully legally empowered guardian to direct his or her care in the event that the person is unable to decide or communicate on their own behalf.

Who Writes Advance Directives?

4. People with more than average education and with strong views about not wanting life-sustaining treatment are more likely to accept, prefer, and use advance directives to express treatment preferences.

5. People from racial minorities are more reluctant and less likely to fill out living wills perhaps because of difficulties in cross-cultural trust or communication.

6. Lack of interest, procrastination, uncertainty about how to explicitly express or document preferences, a preference for discussion rather than documentation to convey personal preferences, fears about the irrevocability of the directive, discomfort with the topic, and the belief that family will and should decide or would be upset by the process of planning are some of the most common reasons why individuals do not complete advance directives.

7. Few health care providers have advance directives.

Facts about Living Wills

8. Most people fail to understand the standardized preference options on living wills and seem to prefer less aggressive treatment than what is provided by these options (i.e., wanting all available treatment unless permanently unconscious).

9. Many want treatment preferences expressed in their living will to be interpreted in accordance with the patient's interest, and with a great deal of flexibility by their friends, families, and health care providers.

10. Commonly held over-estimates of the efficacy of CPR, cause people to say they want CPR much more often than they do when accurately informed.

11. Individual preferences set forth in advance directives are generally stable over time but some do change them.

Facts about Durable Power of Attorney for Health

12. Older people prefer for family to make decisions on their behalf, over trying to express those preferences in a living will.

13. Older persons, however, may prefer group decision-making by several family members.

14. Many persons with AIDS prefer for non-family members to serve as their health care proxy.

15. Nearly 50% of individuals with advance directives have discussed their preferences with their proxy.

Identifying and Increasing the Use of Advance Directives

16. Advance directives are often mislaid, lost, or forgotten.

17. Routine inquiry by health care providers of whether or not persons have advance directives will help to identify advance directives in a few instances of which providers have previously been unaware.

18. Routine provision of information about advance directives in clinics has not been shown to be an efficient way to substantially increase the number of advance directives.

19. Community-based educational presentations can increase the number of advance directives completed.

20. Mailings of simple brochures can increase the number of Durable Power of Attorney Assignments.

21. Multi-modal (written, video, and face-to-face) educational interventions on advanced directives increase the completion of advance directives.

Family Members as Proxy Decision-Makers

22. Family members' estimates of patients' views are not much more accurate than chance when compared to those of the

patients. However, family members estimations are generally more on target than providers' estimations.

23. Conflicts among family members about a patient's views in a hospital setting are infrequent and usually resolved in a few days.

24. Asking proxies to decide as the patient would decide appears to slightly improve agreement between proxy choice and patients' preferences in some studies.

Health Care Provider's Knowledge of a Person's Treatment Preferences

25. Although only 10% of primary care physicians never raise or discuss advance planning, few (20%) physicians ask about the preferences of newly admitted intensive care unit patients.

26. In approaching a dialogue on advance directives, professionals may usefully propose and confirm that a person would not be inclined to want prolonged life-sustaining treatment, including tube feeding, in the circumstances of terminal illness, irreversible dementia (or coma), and irreversible dependence on life-support.

27. With or without discussion, providers know about the advance directives their patients have only 25% of the time.

28. Health care providers are not able to guess a person's health care preferences with any more precision than a family member, no matter how intense their conviction.

People's Preferences for Discussions with Health Care Providers about Advance Directives

29. Nearly all people want to be informed and involved in decisions about the use of life-sustaining treatments.

30. Most people want health care professionals to lead the decision-making process and make recommendations, fully informing them of the decision, and giving an option to refuse or modify those proposals.

31. Treatment descriptions with the same facts will elicit a different decision depending on whether the professional frames them negatively or positively. For example, if the success rate

is emphasized, fewer people will want the treatment than if the death rate is emphasized.

32. People want health care providers to bring the issue of advance directives up before they become gravely sick.

33. Individuals with advance directives are more likely to engage in an advance planning discussion with health care providers.

Health Care Provider's Initiation and Conduct of Discussions about Treatment Preferences

34. Providers feel more comfortable discussing these issues with proxies (i.e., families) than with patients themselves.

35. Providers say that administrative barriers (availability of forms and time for discussion) limits use of these documents.

36. Providers in hospital and outpatient settings often delay raising this issue until persons lose decision-making ability, though this is improving for persons with cancer and AIDS and, to a lesser degree, with other progressive terminal illnesses, like congestive heart failure.

37. A general discussion of advance treatment options (when the physician is not also explaining and counseling about an actual treatment situation) usually takes about 15 minutes.

38. A substantial minority of providers have very limited knowledge of advance directives and many have reservations about the specificity and usefulness of these documents.

39. Providers do not raise this issue when they anticipate that it may have a negative effect on patient outcomes.

Effect of Advance Treatment Discussions on Patients

40. Negative effects of these discussions are experienced by few; such effects include fear of worsening health or abandonment.

41. A high majority of people experience these discussions as relieving uncertainty, and making them feel cared for and in control.

42. Positive effects appear to be greater for better educated individuals and those with longer provider-patient relationships. Also, beneficial effects tend to persist for months following the discussion, as the discussion leaves individuals with the impression

that their provider understands their preferences, as well as helps to ease future advance planning discussions with proxies.

Recording of Advance Directives

43. Advance directives are present in a small, but increasing, minority of health care records and are referred to in a very small number of health care records. In context, limited treatment decisions are present in about 15% of hospital records, precede 75% of hospital deaths, 50% of intensive care unit deaths, and 85% of nursing home deaths.

44. Advance directives may cause undocumented oral communications that influence clinical decisions, especially when hospital staff can identify the individuals with lost advance directives.

Effect of Advance Directives on Health Care Decisions

45. Given the high frequency of decisions to limit the use of life-sustaining treatments by providers and the simultaneous high frequency of preferences that such treatments be limited by people with advance directives, an additive effect of advance directives on patient care is difficult to find.

46. The impact of advance directives on the course of treatment of a hospitalized nursing home resident transferred to the hospital is very small. This is due, in part, to the low rate of communication between nursing homes and hospitals regarding the existence of residents' advance directives.

47. The effect of advance directives on the course of nursing home use, as opposed to treatment use, is small. The location of treatment has a very large effect on the kind of treatment done. Remaining in a nursing home is very likely to result in much less aggressive treatment, regardless of the content of an advance directive. Being in a hospital is more likely to result in more aggressive treatment, regardless of an advance directive.

Effect of Advance Directives on the Cost of Care

48. The cost savings of advance directives will vary according to the institution, population, degree to which the course of medical care is changed, and nature of cost-accounting. Still,

cost savings to the whole health care system for end-of-life care is relatively small.

49. In studies of intensive care units, advance directives have a small, favorable effect on decreasing costs of hospital care. However, in hospital-clinic system based studies, advance directives have no significant effect on use of resources.

9 Things That Are Not Known

1. How can one formally solicit accurate written expressions of treatment or proxy preferences from people prior to the development of strong treatment preferences and beliefs about the desirability of written directives?

2. What are the best designs, or wording, for advance directives (e.g., living wills, durable power of attorney for health) to accurately capture or convey a person's preferences?

3. Is the person named as a proxy decision maker the person whose views would most closely approximate those of the patient?

4. How does the type and amount of face-to-face or individualized educational counseling, as well as site and circumstance of completion, affect the quality and accuracy of advance directives?

5. How can the abilities of proxies to represent the views of the individuals be enhanced?

6. How does a health care provider's knowledge of a person's treatment preferences affect the medical care provided, including ordinary prevention treatment.

7. How are health care providers' discussions about treatment preferences actually conducted?

8. How does advance planning affect caregivers during end-of-life treatment, treatment withdrawal, and bereavement?

9. What is the additive effect of advance directives on the total lifetime cost of health care?

—Based on a study by Steve A. Miles, M.D.
Summarized by University of Minnesota
National LTC Resource Center Staff.

Chapter 47

Caring for an Ill Spouse

Question. For the past two years, I've been taking care of my elderly husband, who suffered a debilitating stroke and also has diabetes. His health has gradually been deteriorating, and I'm not sure how long I'll be able to take care of him by myself. Where can I turn for some assistance? And how do I know if I'm doing all that I could?

Answer. If you haven't already, let your husband's doctor know that you need some help. There are several agencies and programs that can assist you in caring for your husband. Also, you can ask your local social service agency and Office on Aging for some help in assessing your needs and arranging for any services you may be eligible for.

Depending on your insurance and your husband's medical condition, you may be able to have a visiting nurse come to your home periodically to assess and help treat your husband's medical problems. Or you may be able to have a home health aide spend several hours a day assisting you or giving you a break from your responsibilities.

Many hospitals and health care agencies have home care programs designed to provide a variety of services, especially after you're discharged from the hospital. You may be able to have physical therapy, intravenous medications, parenteral nutrition (liquid nutrition fed through a tube into a vein) and so forth. In fact, there are few medical services that can't be provided at home these days.

"Caring for an Ill Spouse," by Jay Siwek, MD, Professor and Acting Chair, Department of Family Medicine, Georgetown University Medical Center. *The Washington Post*, HEALTH Page Z28, July 23, 1996; reprinted with permission.

If you need help with food, you may qualify for Meals on Wheels, which will deliver nutritionally balanced meals to your home. And if you can afford it, you could hire a private duty nurse to help you or let you have some time to attend to other duties.

Do you have any family in the area or a support group from your church? It's important to get some relief now and then so that you don't suffer from what's known as caregiver burnout. In Great Britain, for example, homebound patients can be admitted to the hospital periodically for "respite care," the chief purpose of which is giving the caregiver a break.

With the aging of our society and the shift of care outside the hospital, caregiver stress has become a growing problem that carries a double burden. Because of the interdependent relationship involved, caregiver stress can claim two casualties, the caregiver and the ill spouse, parent or loved one. Many health professionals realize that supporting the caregiver may be the most important intervention they make in caring for patients.

Another option is adult day care, a growing area of service for people not sick enough to be in a hospital or long-term care facility but in need of care beyond what can be provided at home. Adult day care facilities offer families the opportunity to have a loved one cared for in a supervised setting where they can socialize and participate in rehabilitative programs.

An important thing to realize is that you're not alone in caring for an ill or frail loved one. Millions of spouses or adult children serve as primary caregivers. For information, ideas and support, there are many self-help groups available.

Nationally, the Well Spouse Foundation provides emotional support through local chapters, as well as a bimonthly newsletter. Write to P.O Box 801, New York, NY 10023; (800) 838-0879.

Children of Aging Parents is another national self-help group for caregivers of the elderly. This organization provides advice, support through local chapters, and a bimonthly newsletter. Write to 1609 Woodbourne Rd. #302A, Levittown, Pa. 19057; (800) 227-7294.

There are more than a dozen local support groups for caregivers, sponsored by individuals, hospitals, social service agencies, churches, nursing homes and so forth. Check with one of the national organizations, or your local social service agency.

For more information, there are several books that address the concerns of a spouse caring for an ill loved one. Check your local library or bookstore for "Caregiver Books."

Chapter 48

Questions and Answers about Assisted Living or Residential Care Facilities

The aging of America, together with extended life expectancy, is resulting in an unprecedented demand for all kinds of long term care services. For many, aging means a very active time of independence, but for many more, it means a time of decreased functioning and dependence on others. Now more than ever before, a wide array of long term care options is being offered by private and public organizations to help people live independently for as long as possible. Whatever the case may be, choosing the appropriate setting can make all the difference in an individual's mental, physical, and social well-being.

This guide focuses on an exciting and growing phenomenon in long term care known as assisted living. Whether you need care for a loved one or yourself, this text is designed to help you learn about assisted living, determine whether it is appropriate, and make a wise selection.

The facility you select depends on the needs of the individual. It is also a good idea to consult with individuals best qualified to discuss those needs with you, including your personal physician, case manager, social worker, and even your financial planner.

What Is Assisted Living?

Assisted living is part of a spectrum of long term care services that provides a combination of housing, personal services, and health care designed to respond to individuals who need help with normal daily activities in a way that promotes maximum independence.

Throughout the United States, assisted living is known by 26 different names. Some of the most common are:

- Residential care,
- Adult congregate living care,
- Personal care, and
- Boarding home.

Regardless of which name is used, assisted living represents an option of care that is less than that provided and required by skilled nursing facilities but something more than independent living apartment complexes.

Assisted living services can be provided in freestanding facilities, near or integrated with skilled nursing facilities, as components of continuing care retirement communities, or at independent housing complexes.

Services and Activities

The services and activities rendered in assisted living facilities generally include:

- 24-hour protective oversight,

- Three meals a day in a group dining room, and

- The provision and/or coordination of a range of services that promote the quality of life of the individual, that may include:
  - Personal care services, such as help with eating, bathing, dressing, and toileting,
  - Provision and/or coordination of required social services.
  - Supervision and oversight for persons with cognitive disabilities,
  - Medication administration,
  - Social and religious activities,
  - Exercise and recreational activities,
  - Transportation,
  - Laundry and linen service, and
  - Housekeeping and maintenance.

Check with your local area agency on aging to find out whether there are formal approval requirements or standards for assisted living facilities in your locality. The most important thing is to find a facility that meets your needs and standards.

Each resident receives individualized services to help him/her function within the facility and within the community. Upon admission, a service plan is developed by the facility to coordinate the delivery of services to each resident. The plan includes an assessment of the resident's physical and psychosocial capabilities. The plan is reviewed and updated regularly by the facility, and as the resident's condition indicates. The resident, family, or responsible party should have a role in the development of the service plan.

A facility service coordinator is designated to be responsible for the process of developing, implementing, and evaluating the progress of the service plan.

A copy of the service plan often is given to the resident, family, or responsible party.

Health Services

Assisted living facilities provide supervision or assistance with activities of daily living (ADLs); coordination of services by outside agencies; and monitoring of activities of the resident to ensure his or her health, safety, and well-being. Assistance with ADLs may include the administration or supervision of medication by a qualified staff person. Assisted living facilities typically do not provide continuous skilled nursing care.

The facility should assure that prompt and appropriate medical, health, and dental care services are obtained when required. The health care of each resident is under the supervision of a physician of his/her choice.

Residents suffering from temporary periods of incapacity due to illness, injury, or recuperation from surgery may be allowed to remain in the facility or be readmitted from a hospital if appropriate services can be provided.

Resident Needs and Accommodations

Accommodations and options vary greatly from one assisted living facility to the next. The availability of particular accommodations and amenities (private rooms, private baths, kitchenettes, etc.) may or may not be regulated by the state. Consumer needs and preferences should be the primary criteria for selection of a facility and its amenities.

Typically, an assisted living facility ranges in size from 40 to 120 units. It should be constructed and equipped in compliance with all applicable codes and state and federal regulations. However, a facility is not defined by the number of residents it can serve, but by the scope of services it provides. The availability of services and limitations of a facility to provide those services, as well as the facility's discharge criteria, should be clearly understood by residents and their representatives prior to admission.

Assisted living facilities should be designed, operated, staffed and maintained in a manner appropriate to the needs and desires of the population served. Treating residents with dementia, Alzheimer's or other disabilities requires a facility design and philosophy that will assure resident safety and autonomy. Such services should be provided in an appropriate and safe setting that is in compliance with any state and federal regulations.

A Philosophy of Consumer Choice

The philosophy of residential care is the emphasis on the right of the individual to choose the setting in which he/she would like to have care and services provided. Residents' rights should include at a minimum the right to:

- Privacy,
- Be treated at all times with dignity and respect,
- Be informed of services available and the limits of those services,
- Manage his or her personal funds,
- Retain and have use of his or her personal possessions,
- Interact freely with others both within the home and in the community,
- Practice the religion of his or her choice or to abstain from religious practice,
- Control his or her receipt of health-related services, and
- Be free from abuse and neglect.

Most facilities post a listing of residents' rights in a conspicuous place and provide residents with a copy upon admission.

In addition to observing the personal rights of residents, residential care facilities usually have guidelines for the accommodation of visitors. Usually access to the residents and to the facility by approved advocates and community organizations is permitted, but at reasonable times. Most facilities establish house rules pertaining to, but not limited to, the use of personal property and the use of tobacco and alcohol.

Personnel

The number and type of staff employed by assisted living facilities varies greatly and depends on the number of residents and their service requirements. Staff are either employed directly by the facility or obtained through coordination with outside agencies, and include:

- Administrators, who manage the facility;
- Nurses, who may assist residents with medication administration and other nursing services allowed by state regulation;
- Direct care staff, who assist residents with personal needs, such as feeding, dressing, bathing, transferring, and toileting;
- Food service personnel, who prepare and serve nutritional meals to the residents;
- Activities coordinators, who organize activities and programs for residents; and
- Maintenance personnel, who ensure the upkeep and maintenance of the buildings and grounds.

In general, it is up to the management of the assisted living facility to ensure that appropriate staff are on duty at all times to properly provide for the health, safety, and well-being of the residents and upkeep of the buildings and grounds.

At a minimum, each assisted living facility has an administrator who is responsible for the overall operation of the facility. He/she ensures that all staff are qualified to care for the residents and are competent in performing their duties consistent with applicable state and federal regulations. The administrator's role is to assure each resident receives all services indicated in the resident's service plan.

Some states require the administrator to complete a state-approved (depending on the state) certification program. In addition, many administrators annually accumulate continuing education units (CEUs) appropriate to the size of the facility and scope of services provided. These CEUs may be approved by the state's board of nursing home administrators, board of nursing, board of social work, or other appropriate state agency.

Paying for Assisted Living

Costs for assisted living facilities vary greatly, and depend on the size of units, services provided, and location. While assisted living is not covered by Medicare, some services are covered by Supplemental Security Income, state Medicaid programs, the Older Americans Act, and Social Services Block Grants. In addition, several private health and long term care insurance policies do include assisted living/ residential care coverage. The majority of assisted living costs are paid for through personal finances of residents and/or their families.

For information on Medicaid program coverage, contact your state health or welfare department. You also should contact your state and local housing departments for information on housing subsidies.

Finding an Assisted Living Facility

After you have determined the kind of services you need, obtain a list of assisted living facilities in your area offering those services.

Your hospital discharge planner, personal physician, case manager, clergy, social worker, financial planner, and friends may be familiar with area facilities. Other sources of information include the American Health Care Association, your area agency on aging, state health or welfare departments, and your state long term care ombudsman.

By telephoning the facilities on your initial list, you will be able to narrow the field to two or three offering the specific services, location, and price range you desire. Talk with the administrators and tour the facilities. Plan to visit each of these facilities on several occasions and at different times of day or on the weekend. This will give you a better feel for what life will be like in a facility. Don't be afraid to ask questions!

A Guide to the Right Choice

Remember the most important consideration is the individual's specific situation. Each resident has different needs, preferences, and desires that should be taken into account in choosing an appropriate facility. Although the value you place on any question is up to you, remember that you can't change the resident to fit the facility. You must select the facility that meets the needs and choices of the resident.

Chapter 49

Consumer Protection and Quality-of-Care Issues in Assisted Living

Many view assisted living as a promising option for providing care and help to an increasing number of frail elderly persons in a less costly and more homelike setting than nursing homes. Assisted living facilities (ALF) are similar to other residential care settings, such as board and care facilities, that offer housing, meals, protective oversight, and personal assistance to persons with physical or cognitive disabilities. Unlike nursing homes or many board and care settings, however, assisted living attempts to provide consumers with greater autonomy and control over their living and service arrangements.

Consumer demand for assisted living appears to be high, and *Fortune* magazine has identified it as one of the top three potential growth industries for 1997. However, recent media accounts and other reports have highlighted instances where assisted living residents have been harmed or died as a result of alleged inadequate care and supervision.

Results in Brief

A number of federal agencies have some jurisdiction over consumer protection and quality of care in ALFs. However, states have the primary responsibility for developing standards and monitoring care provided in ALFs. A recent compilation of state assisted living activities shows that state approaches to oversight vary. Some states regulate these facilities under standards previously developed for the

Excerpted from *Long-Term Care: Consumer Protection and Quality-of-Care Issues in Assisted Living*, U.S. General Accounting Office, HEHS-97-93, May 1997.

board and care industry; some have developed standards and licensing requirements specifically for ALFs; others are in the process of developing them. But little is known about the effectiveness of the various state approaches to regulation and oversight or about the extent of problems assisted living residents may be experiencing. Moreover, some stakeholders are concerned that the rapid rate of assisted living market development may be outpacing many states' ability to monitor and regulate care furnished by providers.

Not only do state approaches to regulation of ALFs vary, the level and intensity of services provided in ALFs may also vary. According to some experts, consumers can find themselves in a facility unable to meet their expected needs. To determine whether the ALF setting is appropriate for them, prospective residents rely on facility-supplied information including contracts that set forth residents' rights and provider responsibilities. But one recent limited study found that contracts varied in detail and, in some cases, were vague and confusing. For example, a number of contracts stated only that services would be provided as the facility deemed appropriate, and few specified what occurs if a resident's health status declines. Overall, little is known about the accuracy and adequacy of information furnished to individuals and their families who are considering assisted living.

Many of these concerns about consumer protection and quality of care in assisted living have been identified by state governments, providers, and consumer advocates. Although several research efforts are under way currently, further research may be needed to determine (1) the nature and extent of problems related to consumer protection and quality of care that may be occurring, (2) the effectiveness and adequacy of existing models of oversight and regulation, and (3) the accuracy and adequacy of information provided to consumers and whether that information enables them to make informed choices about their care.

Background

Assisted living may be defined as a special combination of housing, personalized supportive services, and health care. It is designed to respond to the needs of individuals who require help with activities of daily living (ADL), but who may not need the level of skilled nursing care provided in a nursing home. However, there is no uniform assisted living model, and considerable variation exists in what is labeled an ALF. For example, an ALF can be a small residential care home providing limited personal care assistance to a few residents;

it may also be a large congregate living facility providing a variety of specialized health and related services to more than 100 residents.

Assisted living is usually viewed as a specific residential care setting along the continuum between independent living and a nursing home. ALFs are similar to board and care homes in that both may provide protective oversight and assistance with some ADLs and other needs such as medication administration. According to assisted living advocates, however, what may not be evident in board and care is the assisted living philosophy that emphasizes residents' autonomy, maximum independence, and respect for individual resident preferences. Moreover, ALFs may sometimes admit or retain residents who meet the level-of-care criteria for admission to a nursing home.

According to a 1993 study, many ALFs tend to serve a frail and vulnerable population who, in some cases, are more disabled than facility managers anticipated. This study also found some ALFs that cared for residents who used catheters or oxygen, and a few who used ventilators. A 1996 industry survey described the typical resident as

- a single or widowed female,
- average age of about 84, and
- needing assistance with three ADLs such as continence and mobility.

In addition, this survey found that 48 percent of residents had some cognitive impairment, such as Alzheimer's disease or other memory disorder, and 38 percent used walkers or wheelchairs.

Most residents pay for assisted living out of pocket or through other private funding. However, public sources of funding are available to pay for some residents in ALFs. For example, some states are looking to control their rising Medicaid costs through a variety of means that include using assisted living as an alternative to more expensive nursing home care. According to a 1996 report issued by the National Academy for State Health Policy, 22 states currently make Medicaid funds available for assisted living.

States Primarily Responsible for Oversight of Assisted Living

A number of federal agencies bear some responsibility for aspects of consumer protection and quality of care in ALFs. However, even where the federal government does play a role, most oversight functions rest with the states. For example, the Social Security Administration

(SSA) and the Health Care Financing Administration (HCFA) have some authority related to assisted living. The Keys Amendment to the Social Security Act, which added section 1616(e), requires states to certify that they will establish, maintain, and enforce standards for any category of group living arrangement in which a significant number of Supplemental Security Income (SSI) recipients reside, or are likely to reside. Such settings may include board and care facilities or ALFs. HCFA requires states that have been granted a Medicaid home and community-based care waiver that includes ALF services to provide assurances that necessary safeguards have been taken to protect residents' health and safety. In both of these examples, the federal government grants broad discretion to states in carrying out their oversight responsibilities.

Few federal standards or guidelines govern assisted living, and states have the primary responsibility for oversight of care furnished to assisted living residents. In general, states' regulations tend to focus on three main areas: requirements for the living unit; admission and retention criteria; and the types and levels of services that may be provided. However, states vary widely on what they require. For example, state regulations differ in their (1) licensing standards concerning admission and discharge criteria, staffing ratios, and training requirements; (2) inspection procedures that specify frequency, notification requirements, and inspector training; and (3) the range of enforcement mechanisms that are available and used.

States also vary widely on the category or model under which they regulate these facilities. Some states regulate ALFs under existing board and care standards, some have created regulations specific to ALFs only, and others are studying how best to regulate these settings. Regarding states' regulation of board and care, our past reports and those by others have found enforcement of standards to be weak and authorized sanctions to be used infrequently. According to an AARP report, fines, even when authorized, were seldom imposed, and authority to ban admissions was limited and rarely used. But little is known about the effectiveness of board and care regulations as applied to ALFs. These reports also found the board and care home industry to have numerous quality problems, such as residents suffering from dehydration or denied adequate medical care. However, little is known about the specific quality-of-care problems ALF residents may be experiencing and whether their experiences differ from board and care residents.

Some states, including Oregon, Florida, and Connecticut, have developed specific regulations and licensing requirements for ALFs, and others are moving forward to develop them. According to consumer advocates and others, state efforts to regulate assisted living are challenged by the need to develop an approach that is flexible enough to allow for innovation in response to consumer demands and preferences yet that also protects residents who may be vulnerable due to physical or cognitive impairment. For example, Oregon has specific living unit requirements but not specific staffing requirements; for staffing, it requires that the facility's staffing is sufficient to deliver services specified in resident plans of care. Little is known about the effectiveness of these new approaches for ensuring quality of care in ALFs.

Facilities' Responsibilities Outlined in Resident Contracts

Given the variation in what is labeled assisted living and the variety of ways states regulate these settings, consumers often must rely on information supplied to them by the provider to determine whether an assisted living setting is appropriate for their needs. Although marketing materials may contain information about facility standards and services, the written contract between the facility and the resident is the key document governing care to be provided. This document generally specifies the facility's responsibility to the resident, how the facility will respond to the resident's needs and changes in health status, how quality care will be maintained, and the resident's rights and responsibilities. However, little is known about the accuracy and adequacy of information furnished to individuals and their families. As a result, consumers may be at risk if they lack the necessary information to make informed decisions about their care.

A recent limited survey of industry practices noted that contracts had no standard format, varied in detail and usefulness, and in some cases were vague and confusing. For example, none of the contracts examined mentioned how often services would be provided; a number of contracts stated only that services would be provided as the facility deemed appropriate. Furthermore, few specified what would occur if a resident's health status declined, such as what needed additional services would be provided, whether there are additional charges for those services, or whether the resident would be asked to leave because needed services could not be furnished.

According to some experts, a provision contained in some contracts that may raise consumer protection concerns is commonly referred to as the "negotiated risk agreement." When signing this agreement,

515

the resident agrees to limit the facility's potential liability for specific risks the resident assumes. For example, a mobility-impaired resident advised by the provider not to use stairs may sign an agreement accepting the risk of harm from potential falls should the resident continue this activity. Perceiving unequal bargaining power between facilities and residents, some experts have raised concerns that written agreements, such as assisted living service contracts and negotiated risk agreements, may place the resident at risk of exploitation. However, we have no indication of whether, or how often, this occurs.

Issues Needing Further Research

Many of these consumer protection and quality-of-care concerns are shared by state governments, advocates, and provider organizations, and several groups are actively engaged in developing new oversight and regulatory models specific to assisted living. For example, two national initiatives under way currently are the Quality Initiative for Assisted Living and the Assisted Living Quality Coalition. However, little is known about the extent of quality-of-care problems in ALFs, and few efforts have been made to assess the effectiveness of the various state quality assurance approaches. Furthermore, little is known about the accuracy and adequacy of information ALFs furnish to consumers and their families.

Further research is needed to determine (1) the nature and extent of problems related to consumer protection and quality of care that may be occurring in this developing market, (2) the effectiveness and adequacy of existing models of oversight and regulation and whether problems are being identified and corrected, and (3) the accuracy and adequacy of information provided to consumers and whether the information enables them to make informed choices about their care. Research into these questions should shed light on whether additional or new oversight requirements are needed to protect consumers and ensure quality of care in ALFs.

Chapter 50

When You Are Considering a Nursing Home

When You Need a Nursing Home

There are currently over 1.5 million residents of nursing homes in the United States, over two-thirds of whom are women. The nursing home population has been growing, and likely will continue to grow with the increase in numbers of older persons. While only 5 percent of the older population is in a nursing home at any one time, approximately 30 percent of all people can expect to spend some time in a nursing home setting.

Today's nursing homes are greatly improved and more accommodating to the needs of individuals than in the past. Still, most people prefer to remain in their own homes as long as possible. A number of choices are available in most communities that can help older people remain independent or to be cared for at home by their families. Community services may include homemaker/home health aide services, home-delivered meals, transportation and escort services, chore-workers, a friendly visitors program, adult day programs that provide social and health care services, respite care that provides temporary relief for caregivers, and emergency medical systems.

This chapter includes text from "When You Need a Nursing Home, *Age Page*, National Institute on Aging, 1992, "Myths and Realities of Living in a Nursing Home," ©1996 American Health Care Association (AHCA); and "How to Pay for Nursing Home Care," ©1996 AHCA; both reprinted with permission. AHCA, 1201 L Street, NW Washington, DC 20005; (202) 842-4444.

Long-Term Care Options

Although families often go to great lengths to keep older loved ones at home, they may not be able to provide the best physical and emotional care without experiencing undue stress. When home care and community services are no longer adequate, a person must decide on the best alternative arrangement for meeting personal and health care needs. The following options are available:

- Residential care facilities provide room and board and may offer social, recreational, and spiritual programs.

- Continuing care communities, a relatively new concept, ensure that all needs of the resident are met, including room and board, personal and health care, and social activities.

- Assisted living facilities include retirement homes and board and care homes. Services differ from location to location but usually include meals, recreation, security, and assistance with walking, bathing, and dressing.

- Skilled nursing facilities may be the best choice for those who require 24-hour medical care and supervision. Emphasis is on medical care with rehabilitative therapy to improve or maintain abilities.

Sometimes it is difficult to know when nursing home care is warranted. Ideally, a health care team will assess the level of care needed for the person and suggest the combination of services required. Health care teams are most likely to be found at university hospitals or community medical centers The team should include the patient's doctor, a psychiatric counselor, and a physical therapist.

Choosing a Nursing Home

Finding the right nursing home may, also be difficult. It is wise to begin the search for a suitable nursing home well in advance of seeking admission. Often the best homes will have no vacancies and long waiting lists. You can obtain the names of nursing homes in the desired area(s) from the yellow pages of your telephone directory. Good homes may be known to other families in the community or your doctor. Your area agency on aging is also a good source for assistance in locating nursing homes in your area. Other sources include the social services department of a local hospital and your local or state health department.

Begin to eliminate from consideration those homes that do not meet your needs. At the end of this section is a checklist which you can use to compare homes. Start with a telephone call to answer questions about vacancies, admission requirements, level of care provided, and participation in Medicare and Medicaid programs. (These Federal programs set certain minimum standards of care that must be met before a nursing home can be certified for participation. Nursing homes in some states can refuse to accept Medicaid patients, depending on the laws of the state.) You should also make sure that the nursing home has an up-to-date state license, and that the administrator's license is up-to-date as well. It is also a good idea to ask if the nursing home meets (or exceeds) the state fire regulations. This includes a sprinkler system, fire-resistant doors, and a plan for evacuating frail people.

Find out about access to medical and nursing services and about what arrangements exist for handling medical emergencies. You will also want to know what types of rehabilitation and social programs are offered to the residents, and you will want to evaluate the food service. Observing and talking to other residents and their families can provide you with useful information that you might not otherwise get from the staff. Look for evidence that staff members treat residents with respect and provide services tailored to the preferences and lifestyle of each individual. If you see residents restrained in any way, that nursing home will probably not be a satisfactory setting for your relative. You may want to drop in once or twice unannounced, perhaps the evening, to get an idea of staffing levels and resident activities provided in the "off" hours.

Once a selection has been made, you will want to review and be sure you thoroughly understand the nursing home's contract or financial agreement. Since this is a legal contract, it is advisable to have a lawyer review the agreement before signing.

Other Personal Needs

Better nursing homes are designed with the needs of older people in mind. Aids such as handrails, low elevator buttons, easy-to-use furniture, call buttons in bedrooms and bathrooms, and wide doorways and ramps that are accessible to wheelchairs are all indications of an environment that encourages independence in residents. Color-coded hallways and directional signs are also useful, particularly for residents with mental impairments or those with poor vision. Such aids will help residents live more independently and exercise some control over their lives.

519

Opportunities for exercise and social activity should be available to nursing home residents as well. Nursing homes can provide safe, attractive places for residents to walk or push their wheelchairs. Nonglare windows with a view to the outdoors allow those who are immobile to view outside activities and seasonal changes. Staff can also help residents remain active and alert by including them in conversations and encouraging them to participate in social activities.

Furniture placed at the center of activity—such as in the lobby or at elevators—is more likely to attract people and encourage the development of friendly relationships in the nursing home. Small dining tables and lounge areas create a home-like atmosphere and help to motivate interaction between residents.

Personal privacy, needs should be respected as much as possible. When rooms must be shared, screens or curtains can provide a measure of privacy. Places for individuals to have private conversations with friends or family members are desirable. It is also important to know that personal mail and documents are respected and that possessions are safe.

Making a Smooth Transition

Be prepared to ease the patient's transition to the nursing home. Such a change may affect the whole family and it will take some time to adjust to the new living arrangements. Some nursing homes have a social worker or nurse specialist who conducts preadmission group sessions for family members who can help the resident feel more comfortable by going with him or her on moving day and helping choose familiar items to bring along—family photos or favorite decorative items.

How often a family member visits the resident is an individual decision, but keep in mind that the presence of family members greatly helps to create a more personal atmosphere in the nursing home. Family visits offer reassurance to the resident that someone still cares. In fact, those residents whose families are involved in their care usually have higher morale and receive better care from the staff.

Resources

Persons who have problems with nursing homes may obtain assistance from the Nursing Home Ombudsman, a person in your state or local office on aging who investigates complaints and takes corrective action on behalf of nursing home residents.

Other sources of information include the following organizations:

The Nursing Home Information Service is an information and referral center for consumers of long-term care, their families, friends, and advocates. The Service provides information on nursing homes and alternative community and health services, including a free guide on how to select a nursing home. For more information, write to the National Council of Senior Citizens, Nursing Home Information Service, National Senior Citizens Education and Research Center, Inc., 1331 F Street, NW., Washington, DC 20004.

The National Citizens Coalition for Nursing Home Reform helps local organizations work for nursing home reform and improvements in the long-term care system. To learn more about the Coalition, write to the national office at 1224 M Street NW, Suite 301, Washington, DC 20005.

The American Association of Retired Persons can provide general information on long-term care for consumers. For a list of their publications, write to the AARP Health Advocacy Services, 601 E Street, NW., Washington, DC 20049. In addition, the AARP and the American Association of Homes for the Aging have information on continuing care communities. Write to the AARP/Housing Activities (at the address above) or to the AAHA at 901 E Street NW. Suite 500, Washington, DC, 20004.

For a free list of **National Institute on Aging** publications call 1-800-222-2225 or write to the National Institute on Aging Information Center, P.O. Box 8057, Gaithersburg, MD20898-8057.

Nursing Home Checklist

When you think a nursing home may be needed, plan and investigate before an emergency arises. These are some questions to guide you in making a decision:

Credentials

- Does the home have a current state license?
- Does the administrator have a current license?
- Is the home certified for Medicare and Medicaid programs?

Residents

- Do residents seem well cared for and generally content?

- Are most residents out of their beds, dressed, and, when possible, occupied?
- Are residents allowed to wear their own clothes and have some of their own furniture in their rooms?
- Is a statement of patient's rights posted?
- Is special care provided for Alzheimer's disease patients?

Facility

- Is the atmosphere warm and pleasant?
- Is the home accessible to family and friends?
- Do rooms provide privacy?
- Is there an activity room?
- Is the nursing home clean, orderly, and reasonably free of unpleasant odors?
- Are toilet and bathing facilities adequate and accessible to disabled persons?
- Are grab bars, handrails, and emergency call buttons located in rooms and halls?
- Does the building have smoke detectors, sprinkler systems, and emergency lighting?
- Does the home have a security system to prevent confused residents from wandering out of the building?
- What is the home's policy on the use of physical and chemical restraints?

Staff

- Do employees show respect to residents?
- Are enough nurses and aides on duty at all hours, including weekends?
- Is the home sensitive to cultural and minority differences?
- What is the average length of time staff have worked in the home?

Services

- Is regular and emergency medical attention assured?
- Does the home have arrangements with a hospital for transfer of patients in an emergency?
- Are pharmaceutical services available and supervised by a qualified pharmacist?
- Does the home offer physical therapy and rehabilitative services?

- Are interesting activities scheduled, including trips outside the home?
- Are arrangements made for residents to participate in religious practices?

Meals

- Is a weekly menu available?
- Are the dining room and kitchen clean?
- Are meals nutritious, appetizing, and tasty? (Eat one.)
- Does the staff assist residents who can't feed themselves?
- Are special diets available for health needs, religious or ethnic preferences?

General

- How do monthly costs compare with the cost of other homes?
- Are financial and other policies specified in a contract?
- Do the resident's assets remain in his or her control or that of the family?
- Do you feel that this facility provides the best care for its residents?

Myths and Realities of Living in a Nursing Home

Many myths exist about nursing home life. In the past decade, nursing homes, like all areas of health care, have changed dramatically in terms of staffing, policies, procedures, and general approach. Our goals as long-term care professionals are to provide both quality care and a quality way of life for our residents.

Understandably, many people fear the move from their own homes to a nursing home. People don't know what to expect and worry about relinquishing control over their lives. Long-term care providers understand these concerns, and we want residents and their families to know the difference between the myths and the realities of life in a nursing home.

Myth: A nursing home is like a hospital.

Reality: A nursing home is not a hospital. Many people enter a nursing home after a hospital stay and tend to think of the nursing home as an extension of hospital care. A nursing home is different, however. Medical, rehabilitative, and nursing care are provided as needed by qualified personnel. Yet at the same time, nursing homes try to be homes—where people can feel comfortable, find familiar faces, and build a life.

Nursing homes do not have restrictive visiting hours like hospitals. Whenever possible, residents eat in communal dining rooms rather than in their rooms. And various activities are offered each day to stimulate residents mentally, physically, and socially.

Myth: All nursing home residents are confused.

Reality: Most people slow down physically as they age. For some, this may be true of their mental processes as well. In fact, many people enter a nursing home, in part, because poor memory makes caring for themselves difficult or impossible. Often, memory problems can be reversed with adequate nutrition, exercise, social stimulation and properly controlled medication.

It is true that a large portion of nursing home residents suffers from Alzheimer's disease, an irreversible neurologic disorder that causes severe and progressive mental difficulties. In many cases, Alzheimer's residents live together in special wings where they can receive the specialized care they require.

Myth: I will have no privacy in a nursing home.

Reality: Nursing homes must strike a difficult balance between the provision of adequate supervision and much needed privacy. Common areas in nursing homes tend to be open, while resident rooms are considered private. Staff members respect resident privacy by being courteous and by knocking before entering a resident's room.

Myth: If I enter a nursing home, I will never go home.

Reality: The primary goal of the nursing home is to rehabilitate residents so that they can return to the community. In fact, many residents are discharged to home-like living arrangements. Those who cannot return to their homes permanently can make short visits, health permitting. In most states, Medicaid-certified nursing homes will hold beds for residents while they make what are termed "therapeutic home visits."

Myth: If I enter a nursing home, I will surrender my right to make decisions.

Reality: Nursing home staff strive to maximize resident independence and honor resident preferences. It is a resident's legal right to make choices about activities, schedules, health care and other aspects of facility life. Yet it is important to recognize that the facility must have some rules to secure an environment where residents can live together safely and harmoniously.

Resident councils, which are made up of residents and sometimes family members, provide an opportunity for residents to address their concerns to staff and to one another.

When it comes to treatment decisions, some residents choose to shift decision-making responsibilities to their children or other loved ones. Some residents may choose to prepare an advance directive, a legal document designed to express the resident's wishes for treatment should the resident be unable to communicate his/her desires.

Myth: Nursing homes have an unpleasant odor.

Reality: Today's nursing homes should have no lingering unpleasant odors. In fact, with the effective cleaning products available, a properly cleaned nursing home should smell pleasant. However, because many elderly nursing home residents are incontinent, an occasional odor may be noticeable. If incontinent residents are changed and cleaned promptly, there should be no lingering smell.

Myth: Nursing home residents do not receive adequate care.

Reality: Stories about inadequate care in nursing homes make news precisely because they are not typical. More common are aggressive internal quality assurance programs that constantly monitor the delivery of high quality care.

Keep in mind that inspections are made frequently by each state to ensure that government quality standards are being met. Problems are cited and plans for correcting them are put into action immediately.

Family and friends can serve as an important safety net. If you feel that proper attention or care is not being given to a specific problem, ask questions. Speak with the director of nursing and the administrator. If you are not satisfied with their responses, it may be time to find a more appropriate facility.

Myth: Husbands and wives must live apart from one another in a nursing home.

Reality: This is simply not true. Many married couples enter nursing homes together and may share rooms. In fact, the patient's bill of rights mandates that this be permitted in facilities certified to receive

Medicare and Medicaid funding. Furthermore, staff members respect the privacy of couples living in nursing homes.

Myth: Nursing home residents aren't visited regularly by family and friends.

Reality: When an elderly person needs more physical care than the family can give, professionally trained staff take over a portion of the care. However, hard as they try, the staff can never offer the same sort of social and psychological support friends and family bring to a resident. Staff members recognize this and try to encourage visits and make visitors feel welcome.

Myth: The food is terrible in nursing homes.

Reality: Good food is a matter of individual taste. Everyone has certain customary dishes and styles of preparation that no one else can duplicate. In the nursing home, some residents are placed on restrictive diets that may limit salt, fat, cholesterol, or sugar. But dietary staff make every effort to ensure that these diets are varied and appealing.

Because proper nutrition is so important to the health of residents, dietary managers should be available to discuss problems concerning food.

Myth: I will be given medications that will cause me to lose control of my thoughts and actions.

Reality: Every person has the right to know what medication he or she is taking and has the right to refuse any or all treatment. Tranquilizers, pain relieving medications, sleeping pills, and mood changers are all powerful drugs and do have a profound effect on how alert an individual remains.

Properly prescribed, these medications help rather than harm individuals. Government regulations require that residents' medications be reviewed by a consultant pharmacist and state inspectors. Staff include the residents and family in care planning. Residents and family members should ask questions about prescription medications, especially if it is felt they are being used improperly or are having a negative impact on the resident.

Myth: I will be physically restrained in the nursing home.

Reality: Nursing homes have made great strides toward reducing the use of physical restraints. Over the last few years, physical restraint use has declined significantly. As more alternatives to restraints are developed and restraint reduction programs are enhanced, restraint reduction efforts will continue to improve.

Residents and family members should know that the use of restraining devices may be used only under a physician's prescription. For example, if a person who has had a stroke has difficulty balancing while sitting, a restraint may be prescribed to facilitate sitting, positioning for eating or participation in activities or therapy. Facilities strive to give residents maximum freedom of movement while also achieving improved functions and safety.

As with prescribed medications, if you feel restraints are being used improperly, speak with a doctor, nurse, or administrator.

Myth: Nursing home care should be like hotel service.

Reality: At first glance, nursing home costs may appear high, and a newcomer might expect hotel-type accommodations. However, nursing home care is costly, not because the per day charge is high, but because many nursing home residents remain in the facility for lengthy stays. The average daily fee for a nursing home stay is $105. This daily fee covers a complete set of services, including room, board, medical care, and a full range of activity programming. Once the range of services is taken into consideration, it becomes clear that daily charges are really quite reasonable.

It's also important to note that the primary goal of nursing homes is to rehabilitate residents and to maintain good health. Staff members try to encourage residents to do for themselves as much as possible so that they can maintain a sense of independence.

Myth: Medicare or my health insurance will cover a lengthy stay in a nursing home.

Reality: Because many people mistakenly believe that Medicare or health insurance will cover their long-term care costs, they are forced to drain their savings to cover the cost of care.

Consumers should be aware that the government provides little financial assistance for nursing home care unless a resident is impoverished and qualifies for Medicaid. Under certain conditions, Medicare, the health insurance program for the elderly, covers the first 20 days of care in a skilled nursing facility. For the 21st through the 100th days, the beneficiary must share the cost of care by paying a nationally set rate of $92 a day. Medicare does not cover stays in an intermediate care facility. Most health insurance policies do not cover long-term care costs.

Long-term care insurance offers a more viable solution to paying for long-term care costs while preserving personal savings. However, due to lack of public awareness about long-term care and who pays for it, long-term care insurance currently pays only two percent of national nursing home costs.

Financing nursing home care should be approached with as much thought and preparation as any major investment. Obtain in writing what your basic charge will be and understand clearly all financial arrangements before signing a contract. For more information, see "How to Pay for Nursing Home Care," (below) and "What Consumers Need to Know about Private Long-Term Care Insurance" in AHCA's Here's Help brochure series.

How to Pay for Nursing Home Care

Long-term care is a costly proposition for which few people are prepared. Yearly costs for a nursing home stay average $38,000. Many people mistakenly believe that Medicare will cover the cost of long-term care, but Medicare only pays for approximately 9 percent of nursing home costs. Rather, Medicaid—the health insurance program for the poor—picks up almost 52 percent of the tab. Long-term care insurance accounts for a mere 2 percent of nursing home payments.

As these figures show, long-term care financing is a serious matter requiring serious planning. The following information is designed to give you a better sense of the programs and options available, as well as the benefits you can expect.

Medicare

Medicare is a federal health insurance program for people over 65 and certain disabled people under 65. It is not a long-term care program. Rather, Medicare covers only those nursing facility services rendered to help a beneficiary recover from an acute illness or injury. Medicare is administered by the federal government's Health Care Financing Administration and is divided into two parts: Hospital Insurance (Part A) and Medical Insurance (Part B). Payments are made to providers through private insurance companies with which the government contracts or through HMOs who have risk contracts with Medicare.

Eligibility. Nursing home coverage falls under Part A of Medicare and is very limited. If certain conditions are met, Medicare pays for

100 percent of the first first 20 days of care in a Skilled Nursing Facility (SNF). For the 21st through the 100th days, the patient must share the cost of care by paying a daily coinsurance rate. For 1996, the coinsurance daily amount is $92 (this amount changes annually).

Medicare pays for nursing home care only under the following conditions:

1. The nursing home is a skilled nursing facility (SNF). SNFs provide 24-hour nursing care to convalescent patients.

2. Continuous skilled nursing care or skilled rehabilitation services (as defined by the federal government) are required on a daily basis.

3. The patient has spent at least three consecutive days in a hospital and if the admission to the SNF occurs within 30 days after discharge from the hospital.

4. A physician certifies that SNF services are needed for the same or related illness for which the person was hospitalized.

Benefits. Services covered under Medicare include:

- A semi-private room;
- Meals, including special diets;
- Regular nursing services;
- Rehabilitation services;
- Drugs furnished by the facility;
- Medical supplies;

Medicare does not cover:

- Personal convenience items;
- Private duty nurses;
- Extra charges for a private room.

Medicare Part B may help pay for covered services you receive from your doctor in a SNF, if you choose to participate in the Part B medical insurance program. If you have used up your Part A coverage for a spell of illness, Part B also covers a portion of services received in a SNF, such as physical and occupational therapy. Under the Part B program, you must pay an annual premium and a deductible for all Part B services including physician services, after which Medicare pays 80 percent of the reasonable charges for covered services.

Some services that are not included under Part B:

- Routine physical examinations and tests;
- Routine foot care;
- Eye or hearing exams for prescribing or fitting eyeglasses or hearing aids;
- Immunizations, except flu and pneumonia.

How to Apply for Medicare. Contact your nearest Social Security office to find out if you are automatically covered for Part A because of credits for number of quarters worked in your lifetime. Also, if you are interested in signing up for Medicare medical insurance (Part B), the Social Security office can assist you with that process. Keep in mind, though, that you can only sign up for the insurance in the first three months of the calendar year.

Medicaid

Medicaid is a cooperative federal-state program designed to provide assistance to low-income people. It has become the major funding source for long-term care, covering nearly 52 percent of nursing home bills. Medicaid is administered by the states under broad federal guidelines. Reimbursement rates per day of care also are set by the states.

Eligibility. Medicaid will pay for nursing home care for those who meet a state-determined poverty level, provided the nursing home is "certified," meaning it meets a stringent set of government standards.

Benefits. Medicaid will pay for care in a nursing facility (NF). The amount paid is determined by each state and covers room, board and nursing care.

How to Apply for Medicaid. Contact your local Department of Welfare or Department of Health for an application. Because Medicaid is based on financial need, you will be asked for information such as residence, family composition, income, real and personal property, and medical expenses. You also will need to be sure that the nursing home which will be receiving payment is Medicaid "certified."

Risk of Impoverishment. Spouses of nursing home residents are protected from what is termed "spousal impoverishment." This refers to the required depletion of an "at-home" spouse's financial resources so that the spouse in a nursing home can qualify for Medicaid.

States are required to permit the at-home spouse to retain a "maintenance needs allowance" from the other spouse's income sufficient to bring the at-home spouse's income to 150 percent of the federal poverty level for a two-person household.

Private Long-Term Care Insurance

Because many Americans fail to plan for their long-term care needs, tens of thousands of Americans are impoverished each year by the costs of long-term care. Recently enacted health insurance legislation has helped make private long-term care insurance a more viable option to paying for long-term care costs while preserving personal savings.

The recently enacted Health Insurance Reform Act includes consumer protections for purchasers of long-term care insurance and tax clarifications for long-term care insurance which make treatment of private long-term care insurance identical to that of health insurance coverage. Starting January 1, 1997, individuals will be able to include out-of-pocket expenses for long-term care and long-term care insurance premiums with their other itemized medical expenses on their annual tax returns. Long-term care and other medical expenses are deductible, provided that they exceed the federal government's 7.5 percent threshold of adjusted gross income. Also, the insurance benefits consumers receive, for the most part, will not be taxable as income.

Long-term care insurance policy premiums are set based on several factors: age, health, length of deductible period, amount paid and duration of benefits. According to the Health Insurance Association of America, the annual premium for a low-option policy for a person at age 50 is about $400. At age 65, that same policy costs $1,100, and at age 79 or 80, about $4,300. If long-term care is required at age 85 in each of these cases, the 50-year-old person would have paid a total of $14,175 for long-term care insurance, compared to the 79-year-old person paying $26,232.

Private insurance policies are available from a variety of sources, including the American Association of Retired Persons, some employers, and an increasing number of insurance companies. More than 100 companies now offer long-term care insurance products. Contact your state insurance commissioner's office for a list of companies authorized to sell long-term care insurance in your state. As you review insurance policies, run down the following checklist to be sure the policy meets your needs:

1. How long is the deductible period? Some policies contain deductible or "elimination" periods which may bankrupt the policy holder before benefits kick in. Consumer advisors recommend a deductible period between 20 days and 100 days.

2. What pre-existing condition clauses does the policy contain? If you suffer from a particular ailment now, how long would you have to wait to receive coverage under the policy?

3. Is the policy renewable? Many policies are guaranteed renewable, others are conditionally renewable.

4. Are benefits periodically adjusted for inflation? Inflation adjustment riders are often an added expense.

5. Will premiums increase as the insured ages? If you can afford it, level premiums are preferable.

For more information on long-term care insurance, see AHCA's brochure, "What Consumers Need to Know about Private Long-Term Care Insurance."

Veteran's Programs

The Department of Veteran's Affairs (VA) provides care in its own facilities to veterans in need of skilled and intermediate nursing care. The VA also provides both skilled and intermediate care to veterans through contracts with community nursing homes. Beds are available to all veterans on a space-available basis. Contact your local VA office for more information.

A Final Note

You must be careful to find out exactly what costs are included in the quoted monthly or daily charge given by a nursing home. Does this include everything—bed; board, nursing care, medicines, laundry? Or are there extra charges? Read all papers carefully before you sign anything. Ask questions until you understand. A nursing home administrator wants you to feel confident from the beginning that the best possible care will be provided at a reasonable price.

To obtain a large print copy of this information, contact AHCA at (202) 842-1444 or send a written request to: American Health Care Association, 1201 L Street, NW, Washington, DC 20005.

Chapter 51

Palliative Medicine: Providing Care when Cure Is Not Possible

Part One: Palliative Medicine

In the United States, about 2.3 million persons die each year. More than 80% die in hospitals or other institutions, too often alone, in pain, and attached to machines. Such acute treatment, while intended to prolong life, may instead prolong and impersonalize the process of dying.

Poor communication between physicians and their seriously ill patients has been shown to be part of the problem. "We wait too long to ask the important questions: How do you want to live, and how do you want to die?" said Norman Desbiens, MD, a principal investigator for the recent SUPPORT trial of more than 9,000 seriously ill Americans.[1,2]

Palliative medicine is the active total care of patients whose disease is not responsive to curative treatment.[3] In the United States, palliation has been pioneered by the hospice movement for patients with disseminated cancer and AIDS. Yet palliative care may also be appropriate to manage suffering for patients with chronic diseases, such as congestive heart failure, emphysema, liver failure, degenerative neurologic diseases, and Alzheimer's.[4]

This roundtable discussion was organized by *Geriatrics* Editor-in-Chief Robert N. Butler, MD, to examine the role of palliative medicine in the primary care of older Americans. The panelists are affiliated with the "Project on Death in America." [For more information, contact the Project on Death in America, Open Society Institute, 888 Seventh Avenue, 29th floor, New York, NY 10106; (212) 887-1050 phone; (212) 247-3890 (fax).]

The participants in the following discussion are: Robert N. Butler, MD, moderator, is Editor-in-Chief of *Geriatrics*; professor, Department of Geriatrics and Adult Development, Mount Sinai Medical Center, New York; and director, International Longevity Center (U.S.); Robert Burt, JD, is Alexander M. Bickel professor of law, Yale University, New Haven, CT; Kathleen M. Foley, MD, is chief, Pain Service, Memorial Sloan-Kettering Cancer Center, and professor of neurology, neuroscience, and clinical pharmacology, Cornell University Medical College, New York; Jane Morris, MS, RNC, is clinical coordinator, Program on Ethics and Aging, Department of Geriatrics and Adult Development, Mount Sinai Medical Center, New York; and R. Sean Morrison, MD, is chief, Acute Care of the Elderly Unit, Department of Geriatrics and Adult Development, Mount Sinai Medical Center, New York.

Palliative Care: Definitions and Goals

Butler: Dr. Foley, would you please define palliative care?

Foley: The term palliative care has been adopted by the World Health Organization (WHO) to describe the care of patients with advanced disease. When cure is no longer possible, the goal is the achievement of the best possible quality of life for patients and their families. The WHO has recommended that governments develop palliative care programs, especially for cancer patients. Palliative medicine involves a multidisciplinary approach to treat symptoms, control pain, and address the psychological, social, and spiritual needs of the patient. It should be started during the course of a patient's illness, not just at the end of life.

Morrison: With both geriatrics and palliative medicine, the ultimate goal is to preserve a patient's quality of life and to maintain function. In both disciplines, we are not working on curing the underlying disease; we are focusing on treating the patients, preserving what's important to them, and relieving those symptoms that can be relieved.

About 1.8 million Americans are in the end stages of Alzheimer's disease—bed-bound, unable to care for themselves, unable to communicate. They are subject to numerous infections, recurrent pneumonia, and pressure sores. The tradition in medicine has been to treat those acute illnesses, rather than to focus on overall quality of life and care. Such patients would benefit from palliative care.

Burt: As a nonphysician, let me say that I am very happy that the basic enterprise of medicine is cure! But taking care of the whole patient has to go beyond cure of illness and the prolonging of life, even if it is difficult for the medical team to abandon the goal of cure. This requires a mind-set that doesn't yet seem to be instilled in medical education and the ethos of the profession.

Butler: Why can't these be integrated—cure where possible, care when cure is not possible?

Morris: I think they can. Other countries such as England, Australia, and Canada have developed board certification in palliative medicine and created it as a discipline within mainstream medical care. Palliative medicine in the United States needs to be integrated into our culture of care. In hospitals, dying patients haven't been given priority, because we don't have role models who know how to treat their symptoms. There are excellent specialists taking care of dying patients and trying to do the right thing, but there has not been an impetus to make palliative medicine academic and based on good scientific guidelines.

Butler: Perhaps every one of the 6,000 or so hospitals and 18,000 or so nursing homes should have a consultative palliative care team that would be responsible for control of pain.

Morris: That may be a good beginning. But eventually, I think every health care professional should have that knowledge incorporated into their basic education. Death is a part of the life cycle, not a clinical failure on anyone's part. In the care of patients who are dying, too often I hear, "there is nothing more we can do," as opposed to "this is what we can do to care for you during the remainder of your life."

Butler: Does the average American have access to palliative care today?

Foley: No. Medicine in the United States is structured to deliver acute care. There are several palliative care programs that have recently been created in acute care facilities, but there is a need for such programs to lead the effort in improving end-of-life care.

Butler: What stands in the way of providing palliative care?

Morris: First, health care professionals working in acute care settings are not equipped to deal with end-of-life care issues. Medical technology has made it very difficult for people to die peacefully in hospitals. And second, access and eligibility limit which individuals can be involved in a hospice program and therefore can die at home.

How and Where Americans Die

Butler: Let's look at how Americans die today. Where does death usually occur, and under what circumstances?

Foley: In the United States, about 2.3 million people die each year.[5] Between 55 and 60% die in hospitals, another 10 or 15% die in other institutions, 10 to 14% have hospice care, and another 10% die in nursing homes, separate from institutions related to acute care hospitals.[6]

Butler: Only 10 to 14% have hospice care?

Foley: The percentage has actually increased because of the Medicare hospice benefit and the expansion of that benefit to the nursing home. But it is still a small number. However, I do not want to advocate hospice as the only model of palliative care. I would like to take all of the best aspects of hospice care and make them part of standard medical care.

Butler: Hospice shouldn't be a physical place but a set of practices. Of the 2.3 million deaths, how many people die at home?

Foley: Most of the 10 to 14% who are cared for in hospice programs die at home. During the 1950s and 1960s, care for the dying moved out of the home and into the hospitals. Now, particularly with Medicare hospice legislation, there is an attempt to shift dying from the hospital back to the home with the help of hospice care.

Butler: Given a choice, most of us would probably say that our wish would be to die at home, pain-free, surrounded by family. How realistic is this today?

Morris: I don't think that's the reality. For example, a spouse or adult child may be actively involved in the care of the patient but is also in the work force and cannot leave that job to provide home care because they can't manage it financially. Also, hospice care has not traditionally been available in long-term care settings, although that's beginning to change. Some long-term care institutions have developed relationships with hospital programs, so that the full range of hospice services is available for terminally ill nursing home residents.

Foley: I think we romanticize death at home. We need to provide options that respect the individual needs of dying patients. They could die at home, if that was the appropriate place and their family can manage it. Or they could die in a hospice program, in a nursing home, or in a hospital. For some people, the best way to die may be on a respirator in an intensive care unit.

Butler: Are there differences in the way men and women die?

Burt: Many women are accustomed to the social role of caregiver, and they typically outsurvive men by a significant margin. When it comes time for these women themselves to receive care, it can be quite difficult for them.

Morris: If they are dying, there may be no husband or other family member to act as primary caregiver, and thus their options for continuing care are limited.

Butler: What do we know about the epidemiology of death for minority populations?

Foley: We know from a series of studies that Hispanics and African Americans are less well treated for their pain, both in acute situations and in the care of the dying.[7] We also have good evidence to suggest that they do not enter hospice programs. In at least one study done in New York, African Americans were reluctant to sign advance directives. They were concerned that their care would be abandoned if they were to sign do-not-resuscitate (DNR) orders.[8]

Role of the Family in Palliative Care

Butler: How attentive is medicine to the husband, the wife, or the children of the person who is dying?

Foley: Studies have demonstrated that if a patient's family can provide good care at home, there's less morbidity in bereavement than there is for those who are frustrated in obtaining good symptom control for their dying family member or cannot obtain resources to take him home, if that is what he wishes. Many patients who are very fearful of their own death report having had an experience with the death of a family member in which there was uncontrolled pain, profound psychological distress, or an inability to come to any closure in family discussions.

Morrison: As internists, we are trained to deal with the doctor/patient relationship, rather than the doctor/family relationship. But geriatrics—like pediatrics—is one of the fields where the family is important, and palliative medicine is another. We have to think about how we are going to treat the family when the patient dies.

Foley: Patients who come to our supportive care program typically tell us their physicians have told their families, "Take him home, and keep him comfortable." These are patients with significant pain, nausea and vomiting, and dyspnea. The family is at a loss about what to do or how to obtain care. There is an enormous need for physicians to learn to work with home care agencies, visiting nurse programs, and hospice programs. The physician needs to move out of the single role as primary care provider and into a multidisciplinary role that relies on the expertise of nurses and social workers and gives more control to the family.

Butler: Who coordinates getting the nurse, the social worker, the oxygen machine, the pain-killing medications into the home?

Morrison: Often it doesn't happen. It requires a knowledgeable physician to make the initial connections with a hospice program—if one is available—that can provide many of these services. There is also a myth that the primary care physician has to step back once a patient is referred to a hospice program. But most hospice programs allow the primary care physician to remain involved and to coordinate care with them.

Predicting Death and Palliative Care

Butler: The Medicare hospice benefit requires a physician to certify that the patient will die within 6 months. How can you predict that someone is going to die within 6 months?

Morrison: It is almost impossible to predict. But palliative care should not be something we start 6 months prior to death. It should be an ongoing process that starts with the diagnosis of an illness for which there is no cure.

Morris: This period is flexible. Reimbursement mechanisms are available to continue hospice services beyond the initial 6 months.

Butler: More and more Medicare beneficiaries are being enrolled in managed care organizations. What will be the impact of managed care on palliative care?

Foley: We don't know. My hope is that managed care organizations will realize that it is their mission to deliver quality care for patients at the end of life, and that the public will strongly argue for that as well. I don't think that patients should sign on with a managed care program unless it specifies what benefits they would get at the end of life.

Financial and Legal Aspects of Palliative Care

Butler: Some people would have us believe that caring for the elderly while they are dying is bankrupting the federal treasury. Is this true?

Morrison: A recent study reported in the *New England Journal of Medicine*[9] looked at where we are spending dollars for the elderly. Medicare costs are not going up because we are spending more in the last 6 months or last year of life. Rather, costs are rising because the age 65-plus population is larger now than it has ever been before.

Foley: Since Medicare was instituted, 30% of the Medicare dollar has always gone for care in the last 6 months of life.[10] And we *should* take care of people when they are the sickest.

Butler: The largest portion of Medicare money is spent on persons between the ages of 65 and 75. After that, there is a decrease in per capita spending.[11]

Foley: That's correct. Individuals who are age 85 and living in nursing homes are not coming back to hospitals for acute care. Unfortunately, there is no Diagnosis Related Group (DRG) for palliative care. If physicians were able to use "process of dying" as the diagnosis, then we would be able to provide appropriate supportive care.

Butler: Many physicians think they will be in legal trouble if they don't do everything to save the patient. They are afraid to withhold treatment when it would be justified. How can we reassure physicians?

Burt: This is a myth that the legal system somehow requires these aggressive actions. But the rules in every state are very clear: a physician is not obliged to provide aggressive treatment. Rather, a physician is obliged to provide such treatment *when that is what the patient wants or*—if the patient is not capable of speaking for him or herself—*what the family wants*.

When a physician or the medical team decides that it doesn't make sense to continue this treatment, it is time to initiate a conversation with the family and the patient about discontinuation. If the patient or his proxy or family acting for him agrees, there is no legal risk.

Over the last decade, the rules have become increasingly clear, and statutes are being considered and passed in every jurisdiction. In 1991, the Supreme Court took a useful step by proclaiming in an 8 to 1 decision that every competent patient has a right to refuse medical care, even if that refusal could lead to death. This includes nutrition and hydration, not just extraordinary care or unusual care.

Butler: Suppose that, as a physician, I decide to withhold treatment, and the decision is medically justified—that is, any peer physician in a court of law would say that this was an appropriate decision. Am I legally vulnerable?

Burt. Some recent decisions in federal court indicate that there is some legal vulnerability if a physician decides that the care is futile but the family or the patient, who is still conscious and aware, resists this decision. This underscores the importance of counseling skills and spending time with the family and patient. In 99 out of 100 cases, such conversation leads to a sensible resolution.

Learning to Cope with Dying and Death

Butler: One thing that we have learned in working with the Project on Death in America and that we have discussed today is that education about the end of life is seriously lacking, even among doctors who deal with it daily.

Burt: When you enter a profession such as medicine or law, you learn a whole new way of thinking and of being. It is only after you have mastered a set of technical skills that you can stop and recapture who you were before you started. It is my sense that a young medical student with masses of things to learn is not yet ready for death and dying issues.

Morrison: The most intense learning experience, through medical school and residency, comes when you take care of patients. But who are medical students assigned to care for in clinical rotations? It is not the patient with metastatic cancer and pneumonia who has come to the hospital to die. It is the hot appendicitis. It is the patient who is coming in with very unusual pneumonia, who is probably young because then he can talk with you. Through four years of medical school, I saw one patient die in the hospital, and that was an unexpected death.

Butler: Was anybody there to counsel you?

Morrison: Nobody. My experience involved a 29-year-old man who had had testicular cancer in the past, which everybody thought was cured. He came in with a GI bleed and ended up with emergency surgery, at which time it was found that a metastasis from his testicular cancer had created a duodenal aortic fistula. This young patient essentially died on the operating table but still had a heart beat for an hour.

I remember that the surgeon looked around and said, "There is nothing else we can do." The nurse looked at her and said, "Can't we do something?" The surgeon said, "Are you questioning my judgment?" and the nurse said, "No." The surgeon took off her gloves and walked out of the room.

A friend of the young man had brought him to the hospital in the middle of the night. The surgeon had a 2-minute conversation with the friend and left. And that was how death was dealt with at my academic medical center.

Butler: How would palliative medicine fit into a case such as that?

Morrison: In that case, it would have been difficult. But lessons about bereavement and coping with the family could have taken place right at that point.

Butler: And, as we've said, that is all part of palliative medicine.

Part Two: A Peaceful Death

In Part One [above], the panelists defined the goals of palliative care, examined how and where Americans die, and looked at the financial and legal implications of the transition from acute care to palliative care.[1b] This month, they discuss such issues as: guidelines for sedation and pain management; the principle of "double effect" with opioid analgesics; what it means when patients ask for assistance in dying; how to make the most of advance directives; and techniques physicians can use to improve communication with dying patients and their families.

Peaceful Death: Ideal vs. Reality

Butler: We have said that given a choice, most of us would probably wish to die at home, surrounded by family and friends, although this scenario is not generally the reality today. Most would probably wish for a peaceful death as well. How would you define a "peaceful death," and how attainable is it?

Morris: A particular experience that stands out in my mind involved a young married man who clearly knew he was dying and accepted it. His wishes regarding treatment and care were known by all the staff. The patient and his family had the assurance that he would have the needed support and that he would be made as comfortable as possible. As difficult as the situation was, this patient's death was "peaceful," because the patient and his family and the health care staff were working toward the same goals.

Patients and families will vary in their acceptance of death and in their expressions of sadness or confusion, but it is vital for the health care team to remain steady and focused.

Foley: I think you have to discuss with patients what *they* think is a good death.

Butler: So it's very individual?

Foley: Yes.

Butler: How do we deal with the emotional and psychological aspects of dying?

Burt: It seems to me that we have to honestly address dying as a natural conclusion of the life cycle and not be afraid of anger or depression at the end of life. Does "death with dignity" mean that everybody is supposed to go with their arms folded and smiling? That idea, it seems to me, is not only unrealistic but a harmful myth. Patients may say, "I don't feel graceful, and I don't feel happy about all of this. I am angry that I am leaving too soon." Addressing these issues is a part of satisfying dying, just as not running away from feelings is a part of satisfying living. There is much that psychiatry can do in this under-developed area.

Butler: Or, for that matter social work, psychology, or the primary care physician.

Guidelines for Sedation and Pain Management

Butler: One of the most important components of a peaceful death is adequate pain control.

Foley: Yes. One issue we often encounter while trying to control a patient's pain is whether the patient is willing to give up consciousness for pain relief. We've published data to suggest that we can provide people with adequate pain relief in about 95% of cases.[2b] There are now studies—both a study that Memorial Sloan-Kettering Cancer Center has completed[3b] and a study done in Milan[4b]—suggesting that 40% of patients in the Italian survey and 20% in our survey required sedation prior to death to ensure adequate control of their symptoms.

Our preliminary data suggest that although most patients are perceived to be comfortable, transient distress is common in the final hours of life and is related to dyspnea, agitation, and restlessness as well as pain. In most cases, distress requires treatment with symptom-specific medications, and such interventions are usually associated with an increasing level of sedation.

Butler: You don't mention anger or depression.

Foley: The studies addressed physical symptoms.

Butler: You did mention agitation.

Foley: Yes, but I am categorizing agitation as a physical symptom, usually in the case of a patient with a metabolic encephalopathy. In hospitals, both physicians and nurses are afraid to treat these symptoms and conditions with medications, because they think they will make patients addicts or kill them. This is a terrible burden to place on health care providers, for whom life is so important. That's why we need guidelines for sedation in this population of patients in hospitals, as well as guidelines for care of the dying, so that everyone feels more comfortable with the treatments.

Butler: Who is going to write these guidelines?

Foley: They already exist. They have been written by critical care societies, by individual hospitals, and by the National Hospice Organization. But I think each institution has to adopt its own guidelines because of its own organizational culture and patient population. The goal is to provide the best supportive care, and in some cases that may be sedation with intravenous opioids or barbiturates. In administering sedatives, no one should feel that he or she is killing a patient but rather doing what physicians and nurses should do—treating suffering.

Burt: In my opinion, turning these matters over to each individual hospital and each individual physician leaves much to be desired. Flexibility is great, but national regulatory interventions are really quite appropriate. There is a difference between guidelines and criminal law strictures. Guidelines are always a more sensible way to go.

Foley: At Memorial Sloan-Kettering, we have guidelines for pain management in dying patients. Pain is rated on the blood pressure and temperature charts as a fifth vital sign. The nurses have a very elaborate algorithm for treating pain, and the education level has been brought up to meet necessary standards.

When patients have questions about whether they are getting the appropriate end-of-life care or whether they should or should not be DNR, patient representatives and social workers are available to speak with them. There are also national guidelines for withholding care, weaning patients off respirators, etc. It's critical that those guidelines be incorporated into practice and become well recognized by staff.

Dr. Butler: Dr. Foley, in your experience, how do patients die?

Foley: Some well, and some not so well. In a prospective study of 100 patients at Memorial Sloan-Kettering Cancer Center, most patients were comfortable, but 28% were perceived by their nurses to be sometimes or always uncomfortable. Most patients were conscious and able to interact until the last 48 hours of life, 25% remained so until the last day of life, and about 10% until the last hour.[5b]

In the cancer population, about two-thirds of patients with advanced disease will have significant pain. Data on noncancer deaths suggest that pain is an important symptom in 75 to 80% of patients in the last year of life.[6b] So clearly, we need to address how best to treat pain in dying patients.[7b,8b]

Health care professionals also need to be adept at using various pain treatments, not only analgesic drug therapy. A primary care physician or an internist needs to know about anesthetic and neurosurgical approaches, the use of cognitive behavioral approaches, and the availability of specialized pain experts, if appropriate.

Opioid analgesics are often the mainstay of pain treatment for dying patients. However, there is enormous concern in the American population that these drugs, even in the dying, may make patients addicts. And patients will often say, "I would be a disgrace to my family if I took these drugs." So we need to educate patients and families to the fact that these are not "drugs" in that sense but medications to treat pain.[9b,10b] Society needs to know how opioids work, when and how they should be used, and when they should not be used.

The "Double Effect": Intention Is the Key

Butler: Dr. Foley, could you explain the principle of "double effect"?

Foley: In the case of the dying patient, our intent in using opioid medications is to treat pain, but a potential side effect is respiratory depression, which may secondarily shorten the patient's life. That is the "double effect."

There is enormous confusion about the principle of double effect. Physicians who don't understand it are much more willing to let patients be in extreme pain, because they fear they may hasten death if they give analgesic drugs. Treating patients with analgesics—particularly opioids, most often morphine—to control their pain in the last days of life is not a form of euthanasia. The intent is to treat suffering, not to hasten death.

Burt: There is fear among physicians of some legal adversity if a patient dies while receiving opioid medications. However, the double effect principle is well recognized in American law. A number of statutes have been passed in the last 7 or 8 years expressly indicating that the use of medication to control pain is not a punishable offense, even if it has the unintended effect of hastening death. Therefore, fear of legal response should not stop physicians from prescribing appropriate pain medication.

Morris: As Dr. Foley mentioned, many dying patients experience pain, whether or not the diagnosis is cancer. One clinical situation we see daily is the under- or mistreatment of pain in individuals who cannot verbalize pain.

Foley: Nothing would make a greater difference in our care for this population of patients than actively applying what we already know. We have a great deal of knowledge to improve pain and symptom management as well as to address their psychological needs.

Physician-Assisted Suicide: Looking for a Way Out

Butler: The public may be unaware of medicine's capabilities in the area of pain control. Perhaps the appeal of Dr. Jack Kevorkian's methods in assisting the suicides of dying patients is due to the fact that we haven't succeeded in assuring the public that they can expect reasonable alleviation of pain and other discomforts of dying.

Foley: The public has the impression that the medical establishment isn't going to take care of them when they're dying. They feel it's better to take charge themselves and make sure they have a way out. I don't want to discourage the public from taking charge, but I would like them to know what their options are: they can get better psychological care from their health care system; they can get better pain management; and they can get better symptom control.

Burt: The media success of Dr. Kevorkian is symptomatic, it seems to me, of the public's enormous fear of technology, of being "hooked up to machines." Kevorkian seems to be offering a way out. Yes, the medical profession has much to offer the American public in terms of palliative care, but many people, even those in the medical profession, still don't understand how much is available. So the first step is professional education. The second step is that the medical profession should educate patients and the public about how much genuine caring can be done at the end of life, so patients don't feel compelled to go to a Dr. Kevorkian and die in the back of a Volkswagen bus.

Morrison: I think it is very important to distinguish between the patient's (public) request for physician aid-in-dying and a true desire for a hastened death. A number of studies have now shown that a sizeable minority of physicians (particularly oncologists) receive requests for an assisted death. As Tim Quill—a strong proponent of legalization of physician aid-in-dying—has written, "a patient's request for assisted dying should be seen as a cry for help, the meaning of which can only be discovered through careful exploration."[11b]

Such requests should not be dismissed. Rather, the physician should attempt to carefully identify the reasons behind the request and explore with the patient interventions (physical, psychological, or spiritual) that could alleviate their suffering and enhance the quality of their remaining life.

Most patients who make requests for assisted deaths can have the suffering relieved with good palliative care. It is incumbent upon us as physicians to provide this care to our patients.

Communication between Physicians and Patients

Butler: When it comes to end-of-life decisions, how can we improve communication between the medical team and patients and their families?

Morris: The public looks to health care professionals for advice and leadership. If we had leadership coming from within the medical establishment about these issues, we could educate the public.

Burt: The support that Dr. Kevorkian has received shows that there is public demand for information about end-of-life issues. The health care profession should take that message very seriously.

Butler: How much candor should a physician have with patients about these issues?

Morris: It's usually best to answer specific questions a patient has at any particular time. Patients and their families often need to think about what has been said and then later to have the opportunity to clarify what they have heard and to have continuing dialogue.

If the diagnosis is made during a hospitalization, time should be scheduled to see the patient a week or two later in the community. There are studies showing that patients and families want to hear information directly from their physicians but often don't. This is not to minimize the role of nurses or other members of the medical team, but the physician needs to play an active role in educating and answering questions.

Foley: It's important to have discussions with patients and families early in the illness, in the acute diagnostic stage. That is an opportunity to talk about how they perceive their illness and their life, what kind of treatment they want, and other issues, such as: Do they want to hear bad news or only good news? What role do they want the doctor to play? Do they want the doctor to make decisions for them? Who in the family is the physician supposed to speak to (or not to speak to)?

The value of such a conversation is that it gives you insight into who the patient is and his or her decision-making capacity. Some patients want to know the statistics of their cancer, or they have looked up this information themselves. They often want to know how much time they have to get things done. Others don't want to know.

You also need to ask whether they've thought of suicide, or if anyone has agreed to aid them in death. Do they have the resources to carry out this plan? You can have this discussion with the patient in a matter-of-fact way, not as if you are making judgments for or against their decision. Show that you understand what they have thought about and what their greatest fears are.

Family members often aren't asked whether they want to be there when the patient dies. This can be quite problematic for some family members who haven't had the opportunity to make a choice.

With families, and potentially with patients, you can discuss how someone might die in the same way that you would tell them what it is like to go for an MRI, or to have an angiogram, or to have an operation. We would all—patients, families, and professionals—be much more comfortable if we took the mystery out of dying.

Butler: Why has so little been written about the experience of dying?

Foley: I don't know the answer to that, but medicine has distanced itself from death. The care of the dying is not a priority. Medical school education and residency training have very little time devoted to palliative care or hospice care. These factors then have prevented clinical research from focusing on the care of the dying.

Butler: In our work with the Project on Death in America,[1b] we have received perhaps the least response when we have requested projects on what people deal with emotionally at the end of life.

Burt: I can't believe this passage is easy for anyone. I do think, however, that end-of-life issues are easier to negotiate for a person who is profoundly religious, who has a deep sense of life's meaning beyond simply the existence we have here.

Butler: This relates to another important question. How should the medical team interact with clergy in this context?

Foley: Our hospital chaplains say that patients talk to them about dying much more than they talk to their physicians. So we need to have a way to work with the chaplains, while respecting confidentiality, of course. One focus of the Project on Death in America is to educate chaplains to serve as advocates for better palliative care and symptom control.

Morris: The medical team is still most attentive to the patient's religious beliefs when they are perceived as obstacles to care. We tend only to ask the patient what his or her religion is and put it on the chart. Often we leave to chance any discussion about what religion means to the dying patient.

Spiritual matters and formal religious practices are still a source of discomfort to many healthcare professionals. Chaplains are not routinely integrated into the care team, even when they have been asked by the patient or family to be involved.

Advance Directives: Helpful or Not?

Butler: Let's discuss the role the patient plays in making end-of-life decisions. How effective are advance directives?

Morrison: Two forms of advance directives are prevalent in this country: The *living will* is a treatment directive that lists a series of interventions that people would or would not want done in the event they were not able to make decisions themselves. The *health proxy or durable power of attorney for health care* assigns a surrogate decision-maker that the patient trusts to make decisions in the event that the patient can't make decisions for him or herself.

A lot of studies are looking at whether these are effective tools in end-of-life decision-making. I think it's too early to be making judgments about the effects of advance directives. The advance directive legislation is only about 5 years old, and we just don't know yet what its impact on medical care will be. I am optimistic; some others are not.

The most useful function of advance directives is that they open an avenue for discussion between the doctor and the patient about a difficult subject. In the primary care environment, the physician could say the following about end-of-life issues: "This is something I talk about with all my patients. Have you had any thoughts about the kind of care you would want to have?" Or, "The law provides a means for you to influence the care you receive if you are unable to speak for yourself. Have you ever had thoughts about what type of care you would and wouldn't like to receive? Are there people that you trust to make decisions for you if you are unable to do so yourself?"

Burt: We have to resist turning advance directives into simply an empty form that's sitting in the doctor's anteroom. A document with just some treatment alternatives listed and signed at the bottom is virtually useless. It is only useful if it is the basis for an exploratory conversation between patient and physician about a time when these issues will become critical. Health care professionals, and particularly physicians, should see to it that advance directives are used to initiate conversations about end-of-life decision-making.

Morris: The range of treatment choices and decisions is so complex in today's high-tech healthcare settings that it would seem vital to have the guidance of a healthcare professional in planning advance directives. For example, what are the circumstances in which one wouldn't want antibiotics or a feeding tube? In just reading the document, one might say, "Of course I would want antibiotics," or "Of course I want to be fed. I don't want to starve to death." This kind of discussion is best when it occurs within a trusting relationship between a patient and a health care professional, be it a visiting nurse or a physician.

Burt: I was struck by the way in which Richard Nixon died with an advance directive, keeping control of all of the details, letting people know beforehand what he did and didn't want. But as much as that appears to be a model to follow, I am a little cautious about it, because it reflects a mistrust of others. The idea that the individual must remain in control, dominating everything, implies that if he doesn't keep control, nobody will take care of him.

Role of "Life Review" for the Dying Patient

Butler: We may not be able to answer big questions, such as, "What is the meaning of life?" But we may know the meaning of our own life and come to terms with that life and our relationships with others.

In older persons, the "life review" is a normal developmental task of the later years characterized by the return of memories and past conflicts. In some cases, this can contribute to psychological growth, including the resolution of past conflicts, reconciliation with significant others, atonement for past wrongdoing, personality integration, and serenity.[12b]

Morrison: A life review is equally appropriate in terms of palliative care. One of the most powerful aspects of life review is that it is an opportunity to talk and to work out family relationships and some sense of inner peace.

Burt: Another aspect that I want to emphasize is the virtue of silence, of simply sitting quietly at the bedside of a dying person, without asking him or her a series of questions.

Morris: You don't need magic words. Your presence alone—being there, not doing something—has meaning for everyone involved.

References

Part One

1. The SUPPORT principal in investigators. A controlled trial to improve care for seriously ill hospitalized patients. The Study to Understand Prognoses and Preferences for Outcomes and Risks of Treatments (SUPPORT). *JAMA* 1995; 274(20):1591-8.

2. Lo B. Improving care near the end of life. Why is it so hard? *JAMA* 1995; 274(20):1634-6.

3. Cherny NI, Foley KM (eds). Pain and palliative care. Philadelphia: WB Saunders. *Hematol Oncol Clin North Am* 1996, 101(Feb).

4. Cassel CK, Omenn, GS. Dimensions of care of the dying patient. In: Cassel CK, Omenn, GS (eds). Caring for patients at the end of life. *West J Med* 1995; 163(3):225.

5. National Center for Health Statistics: Births, marriages, divorces, and death for 1994. *Monthly Vital Statistics Report* 1994, 42(12):1-23.

6. National Center for Health Statistics: *General mortality data*, 1990, table 130, section 1, 1994.

7. Cleeland CS, Gonin R, Hatfield A, et al. Pain and its treatment in outpatients with metastatic cancer. *N Engl J Med* 1994 330(9):592-602.

8. Misbin RI, O'Hare D. Discrepancy in the frequency of attempts at cardiopulmonary resuscitation and do-not-resuscitate orders in patients dying in New York hospitals (manuscript in preparation).

9. Lubito J, Beebe J, Baker C. Longevity and Medicare expenditures. *N Engl J Med* 1995; 332:999-1003.

10. Emanuel EJ, Emanuel EL. The economics of dying: The illusion of cost savings at the end of life. *N Engl J Med* 1994; 330(8):540-4.

11. Scitovsky AA. The high cost of dying revisited. *Millbank Quarterly* 1994; 72(4):561-91.

Part Two

1b. Butler RN, Burt R, Foley KM, Morris J Morrison RS. Palliative medicine. Providing care when cure is not possible. *Geriatrics* 1996; 51(May):33-44.

2b. *Cancer pain relief* (2nd ed). Geneva: World Health Organization, 1995.

3b. Ingham JM, Layman-Goldstein M, Derby S, et al. The characteristics of the dying process in cancer patients. *Proc Am Soc Clin Oncol* 1994; 13:172.

4b. Ventafridda V, Ripamonti C, DeConno F, et al. Symptom prevalence and control during cancer patients' last days of life. *J Palliat Care* 1990; 6:7-11.

5b. Cherny N, Portenoy R. Sedation in the treatment of refractory symptoms. Guidelines for evaluation and treatment. *J Palliat Care* 1994, 10:31-8.

6b. Seale C, Cartwright A. *The year before death*. Brookfield, VT: Overbury Ashgate Publishing, Ltd., 1994.

7b. *Cancer pain relief and palliative care*. Report of a World Health Organization Expert Committee. Geneva: World

Health Organization, 1990 (WHO Technical Report Series, No. 804).

8b.   Jacox A, Carr DB, Payne R, et al. *Management of cancer pain. Clinical practice guideline*. Rockville, MD: Agency for Health Care Policy and Research: March 1994. Public Health Service, U.S. Dept. of Health and Human Services publication AHCPR 94-0593.

9b.   Ward S, Goldberg E, Miller-McCauley V, et al. Patient related barriers to management of cancer pain. *Pain* 1993; 52:319-24.

10b.   Berry P, Ward S. Barriers to pain management in hospice: A study of caregivers. *Hospice Journal* 1995; 10:19-33.

11b.   Quill TE. When all else fails. *Pain Forum* 1995, 4:189-91.

12b.   Butler RN. Life review. In: Birren JE (ed). *Encyclopedia of gerontology*. San Diego: Academic Press, 1996.

Chapter 52

Anatomical Gifts

When people make plans about the final disposition after death, many choose to donate all or part of the body to medicine. It's a generous gesture. But because there are different types of anatomical gifts, it is important for people to understand more about them before they make a decision.

There are actually two kinds of anatomical gifts: body donation for medical research and organ donations for transplants. Usually a body is donated for one of these purposes, but not both.

Body Donation for Research

Thousands of bodies are needed each year for medical research, yet most institutions have little trouble obtaining them. In fact, in some urban areas, medical schools are oversupplied and will only accept bodies if prior arrangements were made for the gift. Fortunately, bodies can be stored for a limited time and transported to rural areas where they are needed.

Even if arrangements have been made, an institution will not always accept a body for donation. Some schools refuse bodies that have been autopsied or mutilated by a violent death. They may not want a body that is missing a limb or major organs. In some cases, schools

Text in this chapter is from an undated brochure produced by the National Funeral Directors Association, Inc., 11121 West Oklahoma Avenue, Milwaukee, Wisconsin 53227-4096; © NFDA Publications, Inc., reprinted with permission granted in December 1997.

also consider the weight or age of the donor at the time of death when deciding whether to accept a body.

If you plan to donate your body to medical research after death, you should first check with the institution for which your gift is intended. Ask them what their conditions are for accepting a body. And ask about transport costs. While institutions are forbidden to pay for bodies, they may reimburse the family for the cost of transporting the body. Some, however, expect the donor to provide the cost of transport. When you arrange for your gift, you should also specify whether or not the institution may send your body to another school that is under-supplied.

Organ Donations

In the past two decades, the science of organ transplantation has advanced so quickly that we almost take some operations for granted. Because of donated kidneys, thousands of kidney patients are now free of the dialysis machine. People who would otherwise be blind can see because of donated corneas. And of course, hundreds of people are happy to be alive thanks to a transplanted heart, liver, lung or pancreas. Certain bones and even skin can be transplanted—victims of severe burns may receive transplanted skin as a temporary covering until their own skin grows back.

Unlike whole bodies for research, organs for transplant are in short supply. Susan Navarro, a transplant patient services liaison at Rush Presbyterian-St. Luke's Medical Center in Chicago, says that for some organs there may be three people who need a transplant for every suitable donor. This puts doctors in the awkward position of trying to decide which patients most need the organ.

"Usually what's needed most are kidneys, livers and hearts," Navarro says. "Kidneys because so many people have kidney disease and are on dialysis for many years; livers because there's been an increase in liver disease."

Organs are in short supply partly because they can be donated only under certain conditions. "We have age limits for taking organs," Navarro explains. "We won't take a heart older than 30 in a man, or for a woman 35 to 40." Navarro explains that a younger heart is a stronger heart and more likely to remain healthy once transplanted. Younger hearts are less likely to have developed plaque in the arteries. Doctors also prefer younger donors for most other organs, although they'll take corneas, which are durable tissues, from people up to age 70.

There are restrictions other than age. As Navarro explains, once a person's heart stops beating he can only donate tissues—skin, bones and corneas—not organs.

"The potential donor is someone who comes into the emergency room still breathing but who eventually needs a ventilator," she says. If tests show that the person is "brain dead" but his organs are alive because of the ventilator, he is a good donor.

While most organs can be "banked" for a day or so, doctors prefer to transplant an organ as quickly as possible to avoid damage to the tissues. So when "brain death" occurs, medical personnel need to quickly get permission to remove the person's organs.

According to the Uniform Anatomical Gift Act, a model law created in 1968 to provide guidance to states passing their own laws, any person over age 18 may agree to donate all or any part of his body after death. Many states allow people to become organ donors simply by filling in a space on their drivers licenses. If a person has never indicated that he wants to be an organ donor, doctors can get permission from members of his family in this order of priority: spouse, adult son or daughter, parent, adult sibling, or guardian.

This can be a difficult decision for families of the donor. Because of the restrictions mentioned above, most potential donors are young victims of traumatic accidents—people struck down in their prime. Their loved ones, already in shock over an unexpected death, must then decide whether or not to give away their organs.

Navarro explains that Rush Presbyterian, like other hospitals, trains nurses to talk with families and explain the importance of organ donations. When families understand that nothing can save their loved one, but his or her organs can perhaps save someone else, most agree to donate, Navarro says.

They do occasionally refuse, however. Navarro says that people who want to be organ donors should talk about it with their families, because even if a person has signed an organ donor's card, doctors usually won't remove the organs if the family objects.

Anatomical Gifts and Funerals

Navarro says families sometimes refuse to donate a loved one's organs because they are afraid the body will be mutilated and won't be available for an open-casket viewing or funeral. This simply isn't true.

Medical personnel recognize the importance of funerals. A viewing helps confirm the reality of a death to the person's loved ones—an important step in the healing process we call grieving. A funeral brings together a community of mourners so they can share their emotions and support each other during a difficult time.

Whether the entire body or just the organs are donated, medical personnel can usually make arrangements for the body to be present for the funeral. In some instances, if the funeral director knows a body has been donated to a medical school, he will call the school and prepare the body according to their directions. The body will then be taken to the school after the funeral.

When organs are removed, the funeral director can use his restorative arts to return the body to a natural-looking state for the viewing and funeral. The body can still be buried according to the family's wishes.

In short, anyone who is inclined to donate any or all of his or her body after death should not hesitate to do so. Life is a precious gift. We can all take comfort knowing that we may offer life to someone else even when our own lives have ended.

Part Seven

Resources

Chapter 53

Who Cares: Sources of Information about Health Care Products and Services

Introduction

Every day, people face questions about health-related products and services they see in the marketplace, get in the mail, read about in the newspaper, and hear about on radio and television. Unfortunately, it can be difficult for consumers to tell the difference between facts and fiction when it comes to selecting a health care product or service.

The Federal Trade Commission and your state Attorney General, as well as other agencies and organizations, can help you see through misleading or deceptive claims and protect your consumer rights.

The FTC and your state Attorney General have written the information in this chapter to help you learn how to spot misleading or deceptive claims and where to get information—whether you're managing your own health care or that of a family member or a friend. We hope it will encourage you to ask questions and speak out if your instincts tell you that something about a health care product or service may not measure up to its promise.

Hearing Aids

"My hearing aid doesn't work too well. The dealer won't repair it to my satisfaction, even though his advertisement said the hearing aid was guaranteed. He hasn't given me a refund either. What can I do?"

An undated publication from the Federal Trade Commission and the National Association of Attorneys General.

More than 24 million Americans have some type of hearing impairment. Many people can benefit from a hearing aid, but not everyone. How will you know? The process begins with a careful fitting by a qualified audiologist or seller. Be sure to ask about a trial period when you can test the aid for free. Ask about guarantees and warranties, too. It's important to get these in writing.

Regulations that cover many important aspects of hearing aid sales for consumers are enforced by the U.S. Food and Drug Administration. One regulation requires that you are told about the need for a medical evaluation by a physician before you buy an aid; another requires that aids come with instruction books covering use, maintenance, and repair.

Who Cares:

Your State Attorney General

The Federal Trade Commission
Division of Marketing Practices
6th Street and Pennsylvania Ave., NW
Washington, D.C. 20580
(202)326-3128

The Food and Drug Administration
Consumer Affairs Information Line 1-800-532-4440 (toll-free)

American Speech-Language-Hearing Association
Consumer Hot Line 1-800-638-8255 (toll-free)

National Institute on Deafness and Other Communication Disorders Information Clearinghouse
1-800-241-1044 (toll-free/voice)

Switching Prescriptions

"I've been taking a prescription drug that really helps control a chronic problem. The pharmacist just called to say that my doctor switched me to a different drug. He says the switch will save me money because it will cost my drug-benefit plan less. But I don't know why I should switch. The new drug might not work as well. Am I giving up quality just to save the drug plan a few cents? Can I talk to my drug plan about refusing the switch?"

In the past few years, many prescription drug companies have formed business relationships with pharmacy groups and insurance companies that handle drug-benefit plans. In some cases, pharmacies and insurers receive rebates or other financial incentives when they convince a plan member to switch to a different drug made by a "partner" manufacturer. If you are uncomfortable about making a switch, call the Food and Drug Administration, your local Department of Health, or your local Board of Pharmacy. They can help you decide whether it makes sense to change your medication.

Meantime, you may want to ask your pharmacist or physician a few important questions: Will the new drug work as well for your condition? Are there different side effects or risks? Are the dosage levels the same? Is there a business connection between the pharmacist and the drug manufacturer? Will the switch save you or your benefit plan money or cost you money?

Who Cares:

Your State Attorney General

The Federal Trade Commission
Division of Service Industry Practices
6th Street and Pennsylvania Ave., NW
Washington, D.C. 20580
(202) 326-3305

The Food and Drug Administration
Consumer Affairs Information Line 1-800-532-4440 (toll-free)

National Institute on Aging
Information Center 1-800-222-2225 (toll-free/voice)
1-800-222-4225 (toll-free TTY)

Your Local Department of Health

Your Local Board of Pharmacy

American Pharmaceutical Association
Patient Information 1-800-237-2742 (toll-free)

U.S. Pharmacopeia
1-800-488-2665 (toll-free)

American Association of Retired Persons
601 E Street, NW
Washington, D.C. 20049
(202) 434-2277

Nursing Facilities

"My father is in a nursing facility. I'm really worried about him. He's losing weight. He seems disoriented. I hope he is receiving decent care. But how can I find out? Who can I talk to? What can I do?"

Every nursing home should have a complaint procedure policy. If you have concerns or complaints, ask about the policy and follow the organization's procedures. You also may want to ask the nurse in charge to review your family member's care plan. If you still are uncomfortable with the situation, speak to the director of nursing, the social worker, or the administrator or check to see if the nursing home has a family council, a group of advocates who try to improve the quality of life in the home.

Often, nursing homes operated by large corporations have toll-free telephone numbers you can use to speak to a regional supervisor.

Who Cares:

State Ombudsman

State Department of Licensing and Certification

State or Local Office on Aging

State Health or Welfare Department

Your State Attorney General

U.S. Administration on Aging
Eldercare Locater 1-800-677-1116 (toll-free)

American Association of Homes and Services for the Aging
1-800-508-9442 (toll-free)

National Citizens Coalition for Nursing Home Reform
1424 16th Street, NW, Suite 202
Washington, D.C. 20036-2211
(202) 332-2275

Alternative Medicines

"My brother has been diagnosed with cancer. He wants to find out about alternative medicine as a possible treatment. He has seen ads for a clinic that claims to have an amazing success rate using unconventional approaches to cure many forms of cancer and other serious ailments. Should he believe them?"

Many unconventional treatments for cancer and other diseases are on the market. A few have undergone rigorous scientific testing for their curative value. Many that have been tested don't show effectiveness. Still, some forms of alternative therapy are recognized as helpful in caring for patients and helping them cope with some illnesses.

Usually, a primary care physician is the best source of information about alternative medicine as a supplement to conventional treatments. If someone tries to sell you an alternative treatment by promising that it is effective, ask for a copy of the studies that prove it. Then ask your primary care physician or family doctor to review the studies to determine their credibility.

If you think you've been misled by advertisements for either alternative medicine or conventional treatments, be cautious and complain.

Who Cares:

Your State Attorney General

The Federal Trade Commission
Division of Service Industry Practices
6th Street and Pennsylvania Ave., NW
Washington, D.C. 20580
(202) 326-3305

The Food and Drug Administration
Consumer Affairs Information Line
1-800-532-4440 (toll-free)

National Cancer Institute
Cancer Information Service
1-800-422-6237 (toll-free)

American Cancer Society
1-800-227-2345 (toll-free)

Cataract Surgery

"My vision is getting worse. Things look pretty foggy. It's hard for me to drive at night because headlights really bother me. Today's newspaper had an ad about a large medical center that specializes in cataract surgery. The ad says the surgery is simple and has no risks. The center guarantees that patients will be able to see perfectly after surgery. I don't know what to do."

Cataracts are a normal part of aging; they usually develop over time and don't have to be removed immediately. You generally can wait to have the surgery until your vision begins to bother you.

If your doctor tells you that you have a cataract, ask whether you need surgery right away, what your risks are based on your general health, and what type of surgery may be appropriate for you, should you choose it.

Be suspicious of any promotion promising completely successful, risk-free cataract surgery. Cataract surgery has a very high success rate, but no surgery is free from risk. Serious complications are rare, but when they do occur, they could result in loss of vision.

Who Cares:

Your State Attorney General

The Federal Trade Commission
Division of Service Industry Practices
6th Street and Pennsylvania Ave., NW
Washington, D.C. 20580
(202) 326-3305

National Eye Institute
Bethesda, MD 20892
(301) 496-5248

National Society to Prevent Blindness
1-800-331-2020 (toll-free)

American Academy of Ophthalmology
National Eye Care Project Helpline
1-800-222-3937 (toll-free)

The National Center for Vision and Aging
1-800-334-5497 (toll-free)

Prevent Blindness America
1-800-331-2020 (toll-free)

Arthritis Cure

"I saw an ad in the paper that said, 'CURE YOUR ARTHRITIS WITHOUT DRUGS WITH THIS ALL-NATURAL, GOVERNMENT APPROVED REMEDY' The idea of a 'natural' remedy appeals to me and I'm impressed that the ad says the product is 'approved' by a government agency. But I think these so-called cures sometimes promise more than they can deliver: How can I get more information about products like this?"

The U.S. Department of Health and Human Services' National Health Information Center can help you get in touch with public and private groups that have information about traditional and alternative therapies for arthritis and other conditions. Your public library also may have a computer link to provide you with direct access to the National Health Information Center.

To check on whether a product is "government approved," to learn more about an over-the-counter drug, prescription drug, cosmetic, or medical device, or to report an adverse reaction to any of these products, call the Food and Drug Administration's Consumer Affairs Information Line. For the latest information on vitamins and nutritional supplements, call the FDA's Center for Food Safety and Applied Nutrition.

Who Cares:

Your State Attorney General

The Federal Trade Commission
Division of Advertising Practices
6th Street and Pennsylvania Ave., NW
Washington D.C. 20580
(202) 326-3131

U.S. Department of Health and Human Services
National Health Information Center
1-800-336-4797 (toll-free)

The Food and Drug Administration
Consumer Affairs Information Line
1-800-532-4440 (toll-free)

The Food and Drug Administration
Center for Food Safety and Applied Nutrition
1-800-332-4010 (toll-free)

Direct-Mail Schemes

*"Someone sent me a newspaper clipping with a product that's sup-
posed to reverse the effects of aging. On the article was a handwritten
note that said, 'Try this. It works! R.' I don't know who R is. Is this
product on the level? What should I do?"*

Some direct-mail marketers advertise their products through ads
disguised as "clippings" sent by unnamed "friends." The fact is that
R doesn't exist. The company got your name from a mailing list and
sent the note from R to you and thousands of other consumers.

Other popular tricks are to design the envelope to look like a check
or letter from a government agency, or to mimic the style of urgent
overnight mail deliveries.

If a company uses a deceptive tactic on the outside of an envelope,
be skeptical about what's inside, too. Report any questionable solici-
tation you receive in the mail to your local Postmaster or Postal Inspector. Check the phone book for the phone number.

Who Cares:

Chief Postal Inspector
United States Postal Service
Washington, D.C.
(201) 268-4298

Your State Attorney General

The Federal Trade Commission
Division of Advertising Practices
6th Street and Pennsylvania Ave., NW
Washington, D.C. 20580
(202) 326-3131

National Institute On Aging
Information Center
1-800-222-2225 (toll-free/voice)
1-800-222-4225 (toll-free/TTY)

Abusive Care Givers

"I have a home health aide who cooks for me because I live alone and I can't cook for myself anymore. Her cooking is so bad that sometimes I can't eat what she makes. She hits me. I'm afraid to tell anyone because the agency never does anything about it when my friends complain about their aides. I'm afraid no one will believe me. If I report her and she finds out, she'll hurt me more. I don't know what to do."

No one should be abused—physically or verbally—by anyone, including family members or care-givers. Everyone has the right to feel safe and secure in their own home. If you or someone you know is being abused in any way, report it. Everyone has the right to be protected.

Who Cares:

Your Local Police, Sheriff's Office, or State Attorney General

Your State Department of Aging

U.S. Administration on Aging
Eldercare Locater 1-800-677-1116 (toll-free)

For More Help

Think you've been misled or deceived by an advertisement for a health care product or service or a medical procedure? Contact your state Attorney General, or the Federal Trade Commission in Washington, DC or at one of these 10 FTC regional offices:

1718 Peachtree Street, N.W., Suite 1000
Atlanta, Georgia 30367
(404) 347-4836

101 Merrimac Street, Suite 810
Boston, Massachusetts 02114-4719
(617) 424-5960

55 East Monroe Street, Suite 1860
Chicago, Illinois 60603
(312) 353-4423

668 Euclid Avenue, Suite 520-A
Cleveland, Ohio 44114
(216) 522-4207

1999 Bryan Street, Suite 2150
Dallas, Texas 75201
(214) 979-0213

1961 Stout Street, Suite 1523
Denver, Colorado 80294
(303) 844-2271

11000 Wilshire Boulevard, Suite 13209
Los Angeles, California 90024
(310) 235-4000

150 William Street, Suite 1300
New York, New York 10038
(212) 264-1207

901 Market Street, Suite 570
San Francisco, California 94103
(415) 356-5270

2806 Federal Bldg.
915 Second Ave.
Seattle, Washington 98174
(206) 220-6363

Federal Trade Commission
6th Street & Pennsylvania Ave., NW
Room 403
Washington, D.C. 20580

World Wide Web Site at:
http://www.ftc.gov

Your State Attorney General
Office of Consumer Protection
Your State Capital

(Many Attorneys General have toll-free consumer hotlines. Check with your local directory assistance.)

Chapter 54

Health Information On-Line

Consumers are using the Internet to get information about health. How reliable is this information? That's not an easy question to answer.

It's no secret that the Internet—especially its graphics portion, the World Wide Web—is enjoying unprecedented popularity in business and professional communities, and in homes across America. A recent survey by the Times Mirror Center for the People; the Press revealed that the number of Americans subscribing to on-line services jumped from 5 million at the end of 1994 to nearly 12 million in mid-1995, while an additional 2 million people have direct connections to the Internet.

Among people with home offices, approximately one-third have access to the Internet, and, of these, about 10 percent have a home page on the Web, according to a survey conducted by the Gallup Organization and reported in the Dec. 19, 1995, issue of PC Magazine.

Another survey, by CDB Research & Consulting, indicates that consumers are showing a growing interest in obtaining information about health and beauty aids on-line as a means of supplementing traditional medical counsel. The company speculates that the discretion and convenience of the on-line environment may hold special appeal to people with disabilities and chronic illnesses.

However, easy access to virtually limitless health and medical information has pitfalls, experts caution. "My advice to consumers about information on the Internet is the same as it is for other media: You can't believe everything you see, whether it's in a newspaper, on TV,

From *FDA Consumer*, June 1996.

or on a computer screen," says Bill Rados, director of FDA's Communications Staff. Since anyone—reputable scientist or quack—who has a computer, a modem (the device that permits a computer to dial and connect to the Internet or an on-line service), and the necessary software can publish a Web page, post information to a newsgroup, or proffer advice in an on-line chat room, "you must protect yourself by carefully checking out the source of any information you obtain."

World Wide Web

By far, the most consumer-friendly part of the Internet is the World Wide Web. It is also the newest part of the Internet, having become accessible only in the past couple of years, with the wider availability of browsers such as Mosaic and Netscape Navigator. While the rest of the Internet displays text only, the Web, as it has come to be called, has the ability to display colorful graphics and multimedia (sounds, video, virtual reality) to complement text-based information. For example, sites that offer medical information on neurological diseases, such as stroke, may also contain images of the brain showing which areas are affected by disease or may have downloadable (files that can be copied from one computer to another) "movies" of actual magnetic resonance imaging (MRI) exams pinpointing blockages in blood vessels. Many legitimate providers of reliable health and medical information, including FDA and other government agencies, are taking advantage of the Web's popularity by offering brochures and in-depth information on specific topics at their Web sites. Material may be geared to consumers as well as industry and medical professionals.

But con artists have also infiltrated the Web. "A physician was browsing the Web when he came across a site that contained a fraudulent drug offering. He called us to report it," says Roma Jeanne Egli, a compliance officer in FDA's division of drug marketing. "The person who maintains the site claimed he had a cure for a very serious disease, and advised those with the disease to stop taking their prescription medication. Instead, they were told to buy the product he was selling, at a cost of several hundred dollars."

More details can't be released because FDA has a case pending against the Web site owner who, according to Egli, has a history of marketing bogus cures. She advises consumers to be skeptical when someone advocates a purported "cure" to be purchased and taken in lieu of prescribed medicine.

If you come across a suspected fraudulent offering on the Internet, alert FDA by E-mail: otcfraud@cder.fda.gov.

If con artists and scientists have equal publishing rights on the Internet, what's to keep a health-conscious consumer from getting sidetracked by an official-looking page offering unsound advice?

"This is a real concern," says Valencia Camp, of FDA's Office of Information Resources Management. "Although the Internet can be a reliable source of information, it is important to be aware that what is found there is only as good as the quality and integrity of the original information. What you find cannot be taken as gospel. It should be checked out and supported by other sources."

FDA On-Line

The FDA home page provides an excellent jumping off point for those who want to learn more about the agency and the drugs, food supplements, and medical devices it regulates. "Twenty-five cents of every dollar spent by consumers goes for something that FDA regulates," Rados notes. These products "could be used more safely and more effectively if people know more about them." Because it is expensive to print and mail materials, FDA offers many of its publications on the Internet, including the text of *FDA Consumer*.

FDA material can be downloaded to a home or office computer and then printed out. Those who don't have a personal computer can try accessing the Internet from their local library or from a community organization. If you have a computer but do not have Internet access, you can receive text from FDA's site (no graphics) by dialing by modem the agency's bulletin board service (BBS): (1-800) 222-0185; type "bbs" and select the information you want from the menu.

"Our goal is to have virtually all consumer education material available on the Internet," says Rados. "Every new piece we publish is immediately placed on our Web site. We now have more than a hundred different publications to choose from." FDA also has a "comments" button on many of its Web pages so that visitors can offer suggestions and feedback. However, questions about specific drugs, devices, or food supplements should be addressed to the agency in writing at "FDA" (HFE-88), Rockville, MD 20857, or by calling your local public affairs specialist listed under FDA in your local phonebook, Rados adds. Before beginning any particular therapy, however, consult with your doctor or pharmacist.

In addition to providing consumer education materials, the FDA site also offers technical information to help industry professionals file regulatory materials.

Exchanging Information

In Internet "newsgroups," such as Usenet groups, people post questions and read messages much as they would on regular bulletin boards. Through "mailing lists," messages are exchanged by E-mail, and all messages are sent to all group subscribers. In "chat" areas on some services and on the Internet's IRC (Internet Relay Chat) users can communicate with each other live.

Assessing the value and validity of health and medical information in news and chat groups demands at least the same—and maybe more—discrimination as for Web sites, because the information is more ephemeral and you often can't identify the source. Although these groups can provide reliable information about specific diseases and disorders, they can also perpetuate misinformation.

"Around Christmas time last year, I saw a whole bunch of messages implying that mistletoe has anti-cancer properties," recalls Serena Stockwell, editor of the medical trade publication *Oncology Times* and longtime user of various cancer-related forums and resources on one of the commercial on-line services. "I wondered where this was coming from, since it seemed a little odd."

Stockwell did some digging and discovered that in an announcement of a new drug to treat lung cancer, "one of the researchers had a slip of the tongue and said the drug was derived from mistletoe instead of periwinkle. As a result, the word soon spread to the newsgroups, where people inadvertently perpetuated the mistake."

In another instance, Stockwell saw that the herbal tea Essiac was being touted in a newsgroup as a cancer remedy. "Doctors were being questioned about it, so I assigned a reporter to cover the story," she says. As it turned out, there is no evidence to support this claim.

As with all health and medical information in cyberspace, advice in newsgroups "should not be taken by itself," Stockwell says. "As a writer and editor, I find newsgroups useful for keeping in touch with topics of conversation among patients, doctors and researchers. But to determine whether the information is trustworthy, I'd want to document it in the usual ways."

Other information services are commercial on-line services, fee-charging companies that provide vast amounts of proprietary information. They often include health and medical databases, electronic versions of popular newspapers and magazines, and their own chats and newsgroups, as well as Internet access.

The fact that information may be screened by a commercial service does not necessarily make it more reliable than other sources.

And most services do not verify what is posted in their newsgroups, nor control what is "said" in chat rooms. Health and medical material obtained through services also should be corroborated by your physician or other medical sources.

Regulatory Concerns

The fact that it is easy to publish health and medical information and reach vast audiences without having the information verified by other sources presents potential issues for FDA and other government agencies, according to Melissa Moncavage, a public health advisor in FDA's division of drug marketing, advertising, and communications. FDA has created a working group from each of its divisions to address the issues that fall within the agency's purview.

"We are working together to determine the scope and type of product information that is going directly to consumers. Product information on the Internet is unlike traditional forms of advertising and labeling. Current regulations on prescription drug advertising differ between print and broadcast media. The Internet presents additional challenges," Moncavage says.

While regulatory agencies try to devise ways of ensuring that accurate and well-balanced health and medical information is presented on the Internet, consumers "will have to use a lot more discretion in evaluating what they see," Moncavage says. "A Web page can be changed very quickly. It is easy to put up, and easy to take down. There is no guarantee that what you see one day will be there the next." So on the Internet, as elsewhere, "caveat emptor"—let the buyer beware—are watchwords for the foreseeable future.

Is This Site Reliable?

FDA staff and others familiar with Internet medical offerings suggest asking the following questions to help determine the reliability of a Web site:

- *Who maintains the site?* Government or university-run sites are among the best sources for scientifically sound health and medical information. Private practitioners or lay organizations may have marketing, social or political agendas that can influence the type of material they offer on-site and which sites they link to.

- *Is there an editorial board or another listing of the names and credentials of those responsible for preparing and reviewing the site's contents?*

- *Can these people be contacted by phone or through E-mail if visitors to the site have questions or want additional information?*

- *Does the site link to other sources of medical information?* No reputable organization will position itself as the sole source of information on a particular health topic. On the other hand, links alone are not a guarantee of reliability, notes Lorrie Harrison of FDA's Center for Biologics Evaluation and Research. Since anyone with a Web page can create links to any other site on the Internet—and the owner of the site that is "linked to" has no say over who links to it—then a person offering suspect medical advice could conceivably try to make his or her advice appear legitimate by, say, creating a link to FDA's Web site. What's more, health information produced by FDA or other government agencies is not copyrighted; therefore, someone can quote FDA information at a site and be perfectly within his or her rights. By citing a source such as FDA, experienced marketers using careful wording can make it appear as though FDA endorses their products, Harrison explains.

- *When was the site last updated?* Generally, the more current the site, the more likely it is to provide timely material. Ideally, health and medical sites should be updated weekly or monthly.

- *Are informative graphics and multimedia files such as video or audio clips available?* Such features can assist in clarifying medical conditions and procedures. For example, the University of Pennsylvania's cancer information site, called OncoLink, contains graphics of what a woman can expect during a pelvic exam. Bear in mind, however, that multimedia should be used to help explain medical information, not substitute for it. Some sites provide dazzling "bells and whistles" but little scientifically sound information.

- *Does the site charge an access fee?* Many reputable sites with health and medical information, including FDA and other government sites, offer access and materials for free. If a site does charge a fee, be sure that it offers value for the money. Use a searcher to see whether you can get the same information without paying additional fees.

If you find something of interest at a site—say, a new drug touted to relieve disease symptoms with fewer side effects—write down the name and address of the site, print out the information, and bring it to your doctor, advises Valencia Camp of FDA's Office of Information Resources Management. Your doctor can help determine whether the information is supported by legitimate research sources, such as journal articles or proceedings from a scientific meeting.

In addition, your doctor can determine if the drug is appropriate for your situation. Even if the information comes from a source that is reputed to be reliable, you should check with your doctor to make sure that it is wise for you to begin a certain treatment. Specific situations (such as taking other drugs) may make the therapy an inadvisable choice. Your doctor can decide whether the drug is suitable for you and may be able to offer more appropriate alternatives.

Sources of Internet Health Information

There are literally thousands of health-related Internet resources maintained by government agencies, universities, and nonprofit and commercial organizations. Following are the addresses of Usenet groups (newsgroups), mailing lists, and reputable sites that link to other sites with medical information. This list is by no means complete; it is offered as a jumping-off point.

Usenet Groups

Access is through the Internet provider:

- bionet.immunology (immunology research and practice)
- bionet.aging (issues related to aging theory and research)
- misc.health.diabetes (discussion of diabetes management in daily life)
- sci.med.diseases.cancer (cancer treatment and research)
- sci.med.vision (treatments for vision problems)

Mailing Lists

To subscribe, send an E-mail message to the address given; in the message area type "subscribe," followed by the name of the list and then your name.

Alzheimer's Disease
List name: ALZHEIMER
Subscribe: listserv@wubois.wustl.edu

Breast Cancer
List name: BREAST-CANCER
Subscribe: listserv@MORGAN.UCS.MUN.CA

Stroke
List name: STROKE-L
Subscribe: listserv@UKCC.UKY.EDU

Geriatrics
List name: GERINET
Subscribe: listserv@UBVM.CC.BUFFALO.EDU

(Source: *A Guide To Healthcare and Medical Resources on the Internet* by Michael S. Brown)

World Wide Web Sites

- American Cancer Society: http://charlotte.npixi.net/acs/facts.html

- American Heart Association: http://www.amhrt.org/ahawho.htm

- American Medical Association: http://www.ama-assn.org/

- Centers For Disease Control and Prevention: http://www.cdc.gov/

- Department of Health and Human Services: http://www.os.dhhs.gov/

- Food and Drug Administration: http://www.fda.gov/

- National Cancer Institute: http://www.nci.nih.gov/

- National Institutes of Health: http://www.nih.gov/

- National Institute for Allergies and Infectious Diseases: http://www.niaid.nih.gov/

- National Library of Medicine: http://www.nlm.nih.gov/

- Oncology Data Base/University of Pennsylvania (ONCOLINK): http://cancer.med.upenn.edu/about_oncolink.html

Search Programs

Because the Internet contains no central indexing system, getting the information you want quickly can be a major challenge. That's where search engines come in. These powerful tools can help narrow the field if you have a specific topic to pursue, or the name of a specific organization but no address for its site. Input a few words that describe what you're looking for, and the searcher returns a list of sites related to your query.

Be aware, however, that although a searcher can point the way, it does not evaluate the information it points to. For example, a search on the words "breast cancer" is just as likely to point to a page advertising a reconstructive surgeon or a health food store's article on the purported benefits of phytochemicals as it is to the National Cancer Institute. The reason? Scott Stephenson, production engineer and spokesman for Webcrawler, one of the popular searchers, explains. "Webcrawler scans documents and counts the number of times a particular word or expression searched for appears on a Web page. That alone determines whether the page is listed in our results, and where it appears on the list." This means that by mentioning, say, breast cancer many times in the Web page copy, a savvy marketer of bogus medicinals could draw a lot of people to his or her site. It is up to the visitor to evaluate the information the site contains. Here are a few of the many search engines:

- Alta Vista: http://www.altavista.digital.com/
- Excite: http://www.excite.com/
- Lycos: http://www.lycos.com/
- Webcrawler:http://www.webcrawler.com/
- Yahoo: http://www.yahoo.com/Health/Medicine/

—by Marilynn Larkin

Marilynn Larkin is a medical writer whose Web site links to the Web sources of health information listed in this article.

Index

Index

A

B

C

D

G

I

J

K

L

M

N

O

P

Q

R

S

U

V

VA *see* Veteran's Affairs (VA), Department of

vaccination chart *50*

Vaccine Adverse Event Reporting System (VAERS) 29, 57, 69–71, 72, 131

Vaccine Advisory Committee, National (NVAC) 58

Vaccine Injury Compensation Program, National 57

vaccines

acellular, described 53

colds 289

conjugate, described 52

costs 51

immunization rates 51, 76

influenza (flu) 290–92

see also flu shots

information sources 29

pertussis 53

requirements 51–56

whole-cell, described 71

see also immunizations

Vaccines and Related Biological Products Advisory Committee 67

VAERS *see* Vaccine Adverse Event Reporting System (VAERS)

values history, described 492

Vanquish Analgesic Caplets 310

varicella virus vaccine live (Varivax) 55–56

see also chickenpox vaccine (VZV)

varicose veins 319

Varivax (varicella virus vaccine live) 55–56

vasectomy 9

VD (venereal diseases) *see* sexually transmitted diseases (STD)

Vermont

lead-based paint information 439

radon information 455

Veteran's Affairs (VA), Department of 532

veteran's programs, long-term care 532

violence, mental health concerns 210–11

viral infections

children 303

colds and influenza 285–92

over-the-counter medications 281

Virginia

lead-based paint information 439

radon information 455

Virginia Poison Center 424

Virginia Poison Center (Richmond) 429

Vision and Aging, The National Center for 564

vision impairment screening

adults 143–46

children 20, 139–43

visiting nurses 484, 537

visualization therapy 342

vitamins

childhood safety 422

multivitamins 383–84, 425

vitamin A 363, 385

vitamin B_{15} (pangamic acid; calcium pangamate) 385

vitamin C (ascorbic acid) 292, 309, 363

vitamin D 385

vitamin E 363

see also dietary supplements

VZV *see* chickenpox vaccine (VZV)

W

waist-to-hip circumference ratio (WHR) 126–28

waiting period (insurance coverage), pre-existing conditions 36

walking 7, 390, 395, 398

Wall Street Journal 369

warfarin 279

Washington, DC *see* District of Columbia

Washington Medical Center, University of 193

Washington state, lead-based paint information 439

watchful waiting, described 186

water therapy 285

Weight Control: Losing Weight and Keeping It Off 128

Y

Z

Environmentally Induced Disorders Sourcebook

Basic Information about Diseases and Syndromes Linked to Exposure to Pollutants and Other Substances in Outdoor and Indoor Environments Such As Lead, Asbestos, Formaldehyde, Mercury, Emissions, Noise, and More

Edited by Allan R. Cook. 620 pages. 1997. 0-7808-0083-4. $75.

Fitness & Exercise Sourcebook

Basic Information on Fitness and Exercise, Including Fitness Activities for Specific Age Groups, Exercise for People with Specific Medical Conditions, How to Begin a Fitness Program in Running, Walking, Swimming, Cycling, and Other Athletic Activities, and Recent Research in Fitness and Exercise

Edited by Dan R. Harris. 663 pages. 1996. 0-7808-0186-5. $75.

Food & Animal Borne Diseases Sourcebook

Basic Information about Diseases That Can Be Spread to Humans through the Ingestion of Contaminated Food or Water or by Contact with Infected Animals and Insects, Such As Botulism, E. Coli, Hepatitis A, Trichinosis, Lyme Disease, and Rabies, along with Information Regarding Prevention and Treatment Methods, and a Special Section for International Travelers Describing Diseases Such as Cholera, Malaria, Travelers' Diarrhea, and Yellow Fever, and Offering Recommendations for Avoiding Illness

Edited by Karen Bellenir and Peter D. Dresser. 535 pages. 1995. 0-7808-0033-8. $75.

"A comprehensive collection of authoritative information." — *Emergency Medical Services, Oct '95*

"Targeting general readers and providing them with a single, comprehensive source of information on selected topics, this book continues, with the excellent caliber of its predecessors, to catalog topical information on health matters of general interest. Readable and thorough, this valuable resource is highly recommended for all libraries." — *Academic Library Book Review, Summer '96*

Gastrointestinal Diseases & Disorders Sourcebook

Basic Information about Gastroesophageal Reflux Disease (Heartburn), Ulcers, Diverticulosis, Irritable Bowel Syndrome, Crohn's Disease, Ulcerative Colitis, Diarrhea, Constipation, Lactose Intolerance, Hemorrhoids, Hepatitis, Cirrhosis and Other Digestive Problems, Featuring Statistics, Descriptions of Symptoms, and Current Treatment Methods of Interest for Persons Living with Upper and Lower Gastrointestinal Maladies

Edited by Linda M. Ross. 413 pages. 1996. 0-7808-0078-8. $75.

". . . very readable form. The successful editorial work that brought this material together into a useful and understandable reference makes accessible to all readers information that can help them more effectively understand and obtain help for digestive tract problems." — *Choice, Feb '97*

Genetic Disorders Sourcebook

Basic Information about Heritable Diseases and Disorders Such As Down Syndrome, PKU, Hemophilia, Von Willebrand Disease, Gaucher Disease, Tay-Sachs Disease, and Sickle-Cell Disease, along with Information about Genetic Screening, Gene Therapy, Home Care, and Including Source Listings for Further Help and Information on More Than 300 Disorders

Edited by Karen Bellenir. 642 pages. 1996. 0-7808-0034-6. $75.

". . . geared toward the lay public. It would be well placed in all public libraries and in those hospital and medical libraries in which access to genetic references is limited." — *Doody's Health Sciences Book Review, Oct '96*

"Provides essential medical information to both the general public and those diagnosed with a serious or fatal genetic disease or disorder." — *Choice, Jan '97*

Head Trauma Sourcebook

Basic Information for the Layperson about Open-Head and Closed-Head Injuries, Treatment Advances, Recovery, and Rehabilitation, along with Reports on Current Research Initiatives

Edited by Karen Bellenir. 414 pages. 1997. 0-7808-0208-X. $75.

Health Insurance Sourcebook

Basic Information about Managed Care Organizations, Traditional Fee-for-Service Insurance, Insurance Portability and Pre-Existing Conditions Clauses, Medicare, Medicaid, Social Security, and Military Health Care, along with Information about Insurance Fraud

Edited by Wendy Wilcox. 530 pages. 1997. 0-7808-0222-5. $75.

Continues next page

Immune System Disorders Sourcebook

Basic Information about Lupus, Multiple Sclerosis, Guillain-Barré Syndrome, Chronic Granulomatous Disease, and More, along with Statistical and Demographic Data and Reports on Current Research Initiatives

Edited by Allan R. Cook. 608 pages. 1997. 0-7808-0209-8. $75.

Kidney & Urinary Tract Diseases &Disorders Sourcebook

Basic Information about Kidney Stones, Urinary Incontinence, Bladder Disease, End-Stage Renal Disease, Dialysis, and More, along with Statistical and Demographic Data and Reports on Current Research Initiatives

Edited by Linda M. Ross. 602 pages. 1997. 0-7808-0079-6. $75.

Learning Disabilities Sourcebook

Basic Information about Disorders Such As Autism, Dyslexia, Hyperactivity, and Attention Deficit Disorder, along with Statistical and Demographic Data and Reports on Current Research Initiatives

Edited by Linda M. Ross. 600 pages. 1998. 0-7808-0210-1. $75.

Men's Health Concerns Sourcebook

Basic Information about Topics of Special Interest to Men, Including Prostate Enlargement, Impotence and Other Sexual Dysfunctions, Vasectomies, Condoms, Snoring, Sleep Apnea, Hair Loss, and More

Edited by Allan R. Cook. 600 pages. 1998. 0-7808-0212-8. $75.

Mental Health Disorders Sourcebook

Basic Information about Schizophrenia, Depression, Bipolar Disorder, Panic Disorder, Obsessive-Compulsive Disorder, Phobias and Other Anxiety Disorders, Paranoia and Other Personality Disorders, Eating Disorders, and Sleep Disorders, along with Information about Treatment and Therapies

Edited by Karen Bellenir. 548 pages. 1995. 0-7808-0040-0. $75.

"... provides information on a wide range of mental disorders, presented in nontechnical language."
— *Exceptional Child Education Resources, Spring '96*

"The text is well organized and adequately written for its target audience."
— *Choice, Jun '96*

"The great strengths of the book are its readability and its inclusion of places to find more information. Especially recommended."
— *RQ, Winter '96*

"Recommended for public and academic libraries."
— *Reference Book Review, '96*

"... useful for public and academic libraries and consumer health collections."
— *Medical Reference Services Quarterly, Spring '97*

Ophthalmic Disorders Sourcebook

Basic Information about Glaucoma, Cataracts, Macular Degeneration, Strabismus, Refractive Disorders, and More, along with Statistical and Demographic Data and Reports on Current Research Initiatives

Edited by Linda M. Ross. 631 pages. 1996. 0-7808-0081-8. $75.

Oral Health Sourcebook

Basic Information about Diseases and Conditions Affecting Oral Health, Including Cavities, Gum Disease, Dry Mouth, Oral Cancers, Fever Blisters, Canker Sores, Oral Thrush, Bad Breath, Temporomandibular Disorders, and other Craniofacial Syndromes, along with Statistical Data on the Oral Health of Americans, Oral Hygiene, Emergency First Aid, Information on Treatment Procedures and Methods of Replacing Lost Teeth

Edited by Allan R. Cook. 560 pages. 1997. 0-7808-0082-6. $75.

Pain Sourcebook

Basic Information about Specific Forms of Acute and Chronic Pain, Including Headaches, Back Pain, Muscular Pain, Neuralgia, Surgical Pain, and Cancer Pain, along with Pain Relief Options Such As Analgesics, Narcotics, Nerve Blocks, Transcutaneous Nerve Stimulation, and Alternative Forms of Pain Control, Including Biofeedback, Imaging, Behavior Modification, and Relaxation Techniques

Edited by Allan R. Cook. 608 pages. 1997. 0-7808-0213-6. $75.

Pregnancy & Birth Sourcebook

Basic Information about Planning for Pregnancy, Fetal Growth and Development, Labor and Delivery, Postpartum and Perinatal Care, Pregnancy in Mothers with Special Concerns, and Disorders of Pregnancy, Including Genetic Counseling, Nutrition and Exercise, Obstetrical Tests, Pregnancy Discomfort, Multiple Births, Cesarean Sections, Medical Testing of Newborns, Breastfeeding, Gestational Diabetes, and Ectopic Pregnancy

Edited by Heather Aldred. 752 pages. 1997. 0-7808-0216-0. $75.

For Reference

Not to be taken from this room

For Reference

Not to be taken from this room